The Experience of Motivation

The Theory of Psychological Reversals

The Experience of Motivation

The Theory of Psychological Reversals

Michael J. Apter

Department of Psychology
University College Cardiff
University of Wales, UK

1982

ACADEMIC PRESS

A Subsidiary of Harcourt Brace Javanovich, Publishers

London · New York
Paris · San Diego · San Francisco · São Paulo
Sydney · Tokyo · Toronto

ACADEMIC PRESS INC. (LONDON) LTD.
24/28 Oval Road
London NW1

United States Edition published by
ACADEMIC PRESS INC.
111 Fifth Avenue
New York, New York 10003

British Library Cataloguing in Publication Data

Apter, Michael J.
   The experience of motivation.
   1. Motivation (Psychology)
   I. Title
   153.8   BF503

   ISBN 0-12-058920-6

   LCCCN 81-66676

Phototypeset in Great Britain by Dobbie Typesetting Service
and printed by Galliard Printers Ltd.

Preface

This book is an essay in "structural phenomenology", which may be defined as the search for pattern and structure in the nature and quality of experience. More specifically, it describes a theory of motivation developed within the perspective of structural phenomenology. This theory, which is called "the theory of psychological reversals", attempts to explain the way in which the individual experiences his own motivation and the implications this has for behaviour. It should be emphasized that the level of discourse intended when referring to the structure of experience (including the structure of the experience of motivation), is to different modes of experience and the relation between them. The concern is not so much with the *content* of experience, in the sense of Gestalt psychology, but rather with the *form* of experience itself, the way in which it changes over time. In relation to motivation, the theory identifies a number of different states, characterized by different ways of experiencing motivation, and attempts to trace the way in which switches occur, often frequently, from one such state to another in the course of everyday life. Although these switches are subtle, they can nevertheless have a profound psychological significance for the individual. The theory also proposes some mechanisms to account for the patterns of switches, or "reversals", which occur.

The theory of psychological reversals had its genesis in the clinical work of Dr K. C. P. Smith, consultant child psychiatrist, and was originally devised by Dr Smith together with the present writer. Our first publication on the theory dates back to a booklet published in 1975, to mark a one-day meeting of the South West Inter-Clinic Conference in Bristol, which was devoted to a discussion of the theory (Smith and Apter, 1975). The present book is a direct outcome of collaborative work between Dr Smith and the writer, which has now extended over many years. Wherever the word 'we' is used in the text, it is intended to refer to Dr Smith and the author together.

The book is aimed primarily at psychologists and psychiatrists, but its contents should also be relevant to sociologists and anthropologists in particular. A number of topics in psychology are discussed, including motivation, emotion, personality, interpersonal relations, and psychopathology. Since it is assumed that the reader is reasonably familiar with these fields, only as much background material is referred to as is necessary to place the theory in context at the relevant points. (During the course of the book, reversal theory is also compared with one or another of the major theories in psychology; this is not intended to be presumptuous, but is simply aimed at clarifying what it is that reversal theory is saying, and how this differs from more well-established views). However, several of the chapters, notably those on synergy, are a little more discursive, since at that point the argument touches on anthropological and other types of material with which the psychologist can be assumed to be less familiar.

The aim of the first chapter is to characterize the general approach adopted in the development of reversal theory, and to try to bring out some of the distinctiveness of this approach—especially the way in which it brings together structuralism and phenomenology. (The reader may, however, prefer to skip this chapter initially and return to it later, when he is more familiar with some of the concepts used in the theory). The second chapter introduces and discusses the concepts of bistability and reversal, which play a central part in the explanations of reversal theory; it also introduces the notion of metamotivational states and systems. In Chapter 3 the telic and paratelic pair of metamotivational states are defined and their bistable relationship outlined. The next two chapters deal with the arousal-seeking and arousal-avoidance metamotivational states (which are closely associated with the telic and paratelic states), and discusses what are called parapathic emotions. These two chapters also constitute a critique of other theories of motivation, especially optimal arousal theory. In Chapters 6 and 7 the concept of synergy is introduced and illustrated; the different way in which synergies are interpreted in the telic and paratelic states becomes a central theme, as do the different types of synergy which may be experienced. In the following chapter the concepts of synergy and metamotivational state are brought to bear on the nature of humour, which in this sense becomes a test-case of the explanatory powers of the theory. In Chapter 9 a new pair of metamotivational states—the negativistic and conformist states—are added to the discussion, and their effects on experience and behaviour are considered. The perspective changes in Chapter 10 to that of individual differences, and the notion of metamotivational dominance now becomes central; other types of individual difference implied by the theory are also discussed, and intra-individual inconsistency is emphasized. This leads in the following chapter to a discussion of psychopathology in reversal theory terms; problems in family relationships are considered, as well as the classic types of individual pathology like anxiety and depression. The next chapter, which deals with the nature of religious experience and behaviour, is also, like the chapter on humour, a test-case chapter—but in this case part of the analysis makes reference to sociological and historical phenomena. In the penultimate chapter the perspective changes yet again, and questions are asked about the relationship of physiological processes to the aspects of experience dealt with by the theory, about the evolutionary significance of metamotivational systems in man, and about the possible existence of these systems in other species. Finally, the last chapter draws the main themes of the book together, restating them in summary form, and makes some concluding reflections. There is also an Appendix to the book.

We have tried to coin as few new words as possible in developing reversal theory, but the adoption of some new technical terms has been unavoidable. All of these are defined in a glossary which will be found in the Appendix. Those readers who (like the present writer) like to read the last chapter of a book first, are advised that they will need to refer to this glossary if they are to make sense of it.

The writer is particularly indebted to the following, not only for all their expert advice, and their comments on the manuscript, but also for their continuing encouragement: Mr Cyril Rushton, Senior Educational Psychologist, Wiltshire County Council (who, among other invaluable services, played a crucial role as 'midwife' in the early development of the theory); Mr Stephen Murgatroyd, Senior Counsellor, Open University in Wales; Professor Sven Svebak of the Institute of Psychology, University of Bergen in Norway; and Dr David Fontana, Senior Lecturer in the Department of Education, University College Cardiff.

Since the author has found it necessary to trespass into many fields in which he is in no way authoritative, he has had to rely on the advice of many other colleagues and friends. In this respect he wishes to record his thanks to: Professor Silverio Barriga, Professor Derek Blackman, Mr John Cleese, Dr G. Dalenoort, Professor Wilson Duff, Professor Mary LeCron Foster, Professor David Freeman, Dr Neil Frude, Professor Anthony Gale, Professor Marjorie Halpin, Dr Robert Hogenraad, Dr Paul Kline, Mr James McKenzie, Dr Susan Sara, Mr Douglas Shelley, Canon J. S. Smith, Professor Georges Thinès, Sir Michael Tippett, Dr David Williams, Dr John Wilson. He is also grateful to members of the "Psychological Reversals Study Group", including Miss S. Aris, Mr C. Blake, Mr L. Bradford, Mr D. Cowell, Mr W. Davies, Mr Arwyn Evans, Dr A. Gobell, Mrs S. Hourizi, Mrs C. Isaaks, Miss H. James, Mr R. Jones, Mrs P. Kenealy, Mr F. Koller, Dr J. Oliver, Mr T. Plotz, Mrs P. Perry, Mr R. J. Skinner, Mrs C. Taylor, Mrs J. Walters, and Mr B. Wurzburger.

He also wishes to express his gratitude to University College Cardiff for granting a year's leave of absence, during which the bulk of this book was written, to the Nuffield Foundation for awarding him a Social Science Study Fellowship to visit the University of Louvain in Belgium for three months during this period, and to the British Council for an award under their Academic Links Scheme, which has enabled the writer to maintain close contact with Professor Svebak and his colleagues at the University of Bergen in Norway.

It is also a pleasure to be able to thank those who, between them, did such a magnificent job in typing the manuscript: Mrs Margaret Boswell, Mrs Cynthia Diggins, Mrs Pauline Donovan, Mrs Joan Ryan, Mrs Sheila Spencer, and Miss Carol Thomas.

Finally, and on a more personal note, I wish to thank my wife Ivy for her continuing tolerance, both of my absence when writing and my bad temper when not. Throughout she has been my fondest antagonist and strongest support.

October 1981   Michael J. Apter

Contents

Preface   v

1. Some Characteristics of Reversal Theory   1

2. The Concept of Reversal   19

3. Telic and Paratelic States   47

4. Bistability and Arousal   80

5. Emotion: Telic and Paratelic   107

6. Reversal Synergy   136

7. Identity Synergy   154

8. Humour and Reversal Theory   177

9. Negativism and Conformity   196

10. Personality in Reversal Theory   227

11. Psychopathology and Metamotivation   246

12. Religion and Reversal Theory   276

13. The Biological Perspective   293

14. Beyond Homeostasis and Consistency   317

References   334

Appendixes A: The Meaning of an Identity   358

            B: Synergy   360

            C: The Telic Dominance Scale   361

            D: A Glossary of Terms Used in Reversal Theory   364

Index   370

To Dr K. C. P. Smith.
The true progenitor.

1 Some Characteristics of Reversal Theory

Psychology has, in the space of its short history, already become a highly specialized field of study. Some would say that this specialization is a sign of the progress of the subject as a scientific discipline, that it is an inevitable consequence of the enormous body of data which has been accumulated, the size of the literature which is related to this data and the sophistication of the techniques which continue to generate it. Others like ourselves would argue that, while specialization is doubtless necessary from many points of view, attempts at integration are also needed if psychology is to make genuine progress in understanding human activity. This means that, while careful low-level theories which are closely related to experimental data in circumscribed areas are to be welcomed, the construction of these should not preclude more general attempts at synthesis, even if the ideas involved in such attempts are necessarily more tentative, and even if they are sometimes less amenable to direct experimental testing.

The present book was written very much in this spirit of synthesis, and is intended as a contribution to the theme of integration in psychology. The book describes a developing theory which represents one attempt at integration — at finding structures and patterns which underlie an apparent diversity of phenomena in psychology, and which cut across many of the traditional boundaries within psychology and, for that matter, between psychology and such cognate disciplines as psychiatry, sociology and social anthropology. The theory is also integrative in a second way, in that it brings together two traditions in psychology, the mechanistic and the phenomenological, which are generally taken to be inimical.

The theory is general, not in the sense that it tries to explain everything in any given area, but in the sense that it has something to say about a variety of kinds of behaviour and experience which are typically regarded as being only distantly related, and which are conventionally dealt with under different headings in textbooks on psychology. It also deals with topics, like religion and humour,

1

which are rarely referred to at all in contemporary psychological texts, even though there has been a recent revival of interest in them.

We have called this theory 'a theory of psychological reversals', or 'reversal theory' for short. It has a number of general characteristics which it would be useful to state explicitly at the outset, and this is the purpose of this first chapter. Without going into extended arguments to support the assumptions underlying these characteristics, enough will be said to indicate the broad lines of the approach which has been adopted, and the reasons for doing so.

The Meaning of Behaviour

The first and most obvious characteristic of reversal theory is that *it is concerned with experience as well as with behaviour.* The theory is based on the view that behaviour cannot be completely understood without reference to the mental correlates of that behaviour, including the subjective meaning which the behaviour has for the person who performs it. Reversal theory is concerned mainly with a particular aspect of subjective meaning, namely certain ways in which the individual interprets his own motivation; but for the remainder of this section the importance of making reference to experience will be discussed at a more general level.

In emphasizing the mental concomitants of behaviour, the theory represents a return to a tradition which is, in the history of psychology, even older than the behaviourist tradition and which prefers the concept of 'action' to that of 'behaviour'. In this sense the theory may be described as a type of 'action theory'. An action may be defined as a piece of behaviour together with the mental concomitants of that behaviour, especially the meaning which the behaviour has for the person who performs it. For example, 'running' would be a piece of behaviour, but 'trying to catch the bus' an action. This use of the word 'action' goes back at least as far as Titchener who wrote: "All actions are, in part, movements; but only those movements which have conscious processes as their conditions, and other conscious processes as their concomitants, can form part of actions" (Titchener, 1902, p. 249). The term was used in a similar way in sociology by Weber (1922). In more recent years it has been taken up again by a number of philosophers and psychologists.[1]

Those who write in this vein generally conceive themselves to be anti-mechanistic, whereas reversal theory may be said from some points of view to be mechanistic. However, it is not necessarily contradictory to say that reversal theory is both an action theory and mechanistic. If action theory is anti-mechanistic, then it is only anti-mechanistic in terms of an outmoded behaviourist notion of mechanism. The more modern notion of mechanism, espoused in reversal theory, is that which derives from cybernetics. Thus to argue, as do action theorists like Harré and Secord, that a person is an active agent who initiates his own actions and monitors his own performance, does not in itself imply that he is not a machine in this more modern sense. After all, appropriately programmed computers may also be construed to initiate their own actions and monitor their own performance. No one would deny that a computer is a machine, but a computer may interact with its environment in the pursuit of certain goals without being under the immediate control of that environment: a computer may use its environment rather than be used by it.

The meaning of 'action' for writers like Harré and Secord is essentially social. For example, the movement described by 'His arm extended straight through the car window' is contrasted by them with the action 'He signalled a left turn'; both sentences have the same reference in behaviour but the second refers to an action because it has a social meaning (Harré and Secord, 1976, p.39). By contrast, in reversal theory a piece of behaviour does not necessarily have to have a social meaning for the person who engages in it, to be described as an action: its meaning may be purely personal. To give an example, going for a walk for exercise is an action in the sense that it is conceived by the person who is walking as more than a series of alternating movements; but this meaning of his action is not essentially a social meaning for the person performing the action. This is not to deny that the individual's behaviour may not be interpreted by other people who happen to observe it in essentially the same way as he himself has: that is, they observe that he is 'going for a walk' rather than just making a series of movements, and they may well guess correctly from various cues that he is walking for exercise or for enjoyment. The point is that, as far as the actor himself is concerned, his action is not necessarily intended to have a social meaning. Indeed, he may even be walking for some personal reason that nobody else could possibly guess, unless they knew him well: for instance, to avoid being expected to watch a particular television programme. In this case his walking would still be an action by our definition rather than just a movement.

One reason for this insistence on the necessity of referring to subjective states is that only in this way can sense be made of situations of 'minimal behaviour', i.e., situations in which there is little overt behaviour to observe. Such minimal behaviour may well often be rich in terms of the conscious experience which underlies it. Consider, for example, a young man and woman holding hands and looking intently into each other's eyes; an elderly lady kneeling in church; or an audience seated listening to a concert. A behavioural account of any of these situations would necessarily be inadequate, considering the significance, quality and complexity which each of these experiences is likely to have for the individuals concerned. In describing activity at a concert, the strict behaviourist would be reduced to trivia like foot taps, sneezes and shifts of position. In describing someone reading, he would be reduced to eye movements or page turning. The general point hardly needs to be laboured further:

some of the most important forms of human behaviour are minimal.

A second reason for needing to refer to conscious experience is that the *same* behaviour may have *different* phenomenological characteristics associated with it, so that one cannot hope to understand the behaviour without attempting to discriminate between different subjective meanings which the behaviour might have. Take a simple example, like the knee-jerk reflex. Part of the meaning of this reflex for the subject is that it is automatic and involuntary, and does *not* constitute a deliberate attempt to kick. In order for an observer to understand this piece of behaviour he would also need to know whether it was deliberate or a reflex response. He may be able to infer this by reference to other observable facts, such as whether the knee had just been tapped with a patellar hammer. But there are occasions on which such simple observations may, without further probing, be insufficient to determine the significance of some act to the individual. Thus, suppose that one observed a lady kneeling in church; to understand her behaviour fully one would need to know whether she saw herself as genuinely praying or was merely performing an empty ritual activity. People are constantly making judgements in everyday life about the meaning of other people's behaviour. To do this accurately, it is often essential to know whether someone sees their own behaviour as deliberate or accidental, sincere or cynical, caring or careless, playful or serious, helpful or hindering, hopeful or helpless. If one finds such distinctions necessary in the course of normal transactions with other people in everyday life, then psychological theories which purport to say something about human behaviour should do no less.[2]

There would appear to be a number of different ways in which people make inferences about other people's mental states when they perform certain actions and all these methods are in principle available to the psychologist, even if he needs to apply them more rigorously. Thus one can make such inferences on the basis of observations of antecedent events, as in the example of the knee jerk given above; or, the individual's preceding or subsequent behaviour can be taken into account; or, one may be able to make use of small cues of gestures or facial expression during the performance of the action. Most directly of all, one can ask the subject appropriate questions. These methods all have their weaknesses, but the point is that the attempt must be made to understand behaviour from the point of view of the person who is performing it, if it is to have any chance of being understood fully.

The word 'state' as used above is intended to refer to some identifiable aspect of conscious activity at a given time. Conscious experience at a given moment can therefore be characterized as a combination of a large number of such states. The use of the term 'state' in this way contrasts with its more normal usage in cybernetics.[3] Reversal theory does not look at all types of mental states, but primarily those which have to do with motivation.

The argument presented up to this point presupposes that the aim of psychology is to understand behaviour, and so far reference to conscious experience has been justified in the light of this purpose. There is, however, a far more positive reason for studying subjective experience: namely, an interest in experience in its own right. This interest can be justified by pointing out that in many situations it is really the conscious experience which is of concern to psychologists and others, rather than the behaviour;[4] but the influence of the behaviourist orthodoxy has been such as to lead to this being disguised, even if phrases like '*mental* disorder' still creep back into the literature. For example, no amount of reference to abnormal *behaviour* can disguise the fact that in clinical psychology it is really the subjective *feelings* of distress which are of concern and not 'abnormal', odd or deviant behaviour, unless that behaviour in turn causes feelings of distress of one kind or another in the person who performs it or in other people. Either way, the real criterion for deciding if the situation is a pathological one is whether distress is caused, and not how unusual the behaviour may be judged to be. Thus many kinds of unusual behaviour, e.g. that which results in original solutions to important problems, are not normally thought of as pathological.

None of this is meant to minimize the enormous methodological difficulties involved in identifying and measuring aspects of mental states. These are so well known in the psychological literature from Watson (1913, 1914, 1919) onwards that it is not necessary to rehearse them here. But the long history of the study of sensation and perception, together with the more recent development of cognitive psychology, demonstrates that it *is* perfectly possible to make testable inferences about essentially subjective processes.

The Relationship Between Mental States and Behaviour

A second characteristic of reversal theory is that *it draws attention to the complex relationship between mental states and behaviour*. It does not assume that there is a simple one-to-one correspondence between given mental states and given pieces of behaviour, such that for a given individual the same behaviour is always accompanied by the same significant mental states; or, between individuals, that similar behaviour is associated with similar significant mental states.

This point may be demonstrated particularly clearly by looking at the case of minimal behaviour as defined earlier. In human beings there is a variety of different phenomenological characteristics which might underlie a lack of gross voluntary movement. Here are a few examples. The individual may be pre-occupied with some problem, he may be praying, or he may be listening to music; in these and many other cases his concentration on his thoughts, feelings or perceptions may be sufficient to preclude action. Alternatively, he may be doing nothing because he is apathetic or fatigued or depressed; perhaps he is in a state of conflict and cannot decide which behaviour to perform in the situation with which he is confronted. Again, any movement at a given time may have an undesirable effect, e.g. when at an auction, or because he has a back injury which causes pain when he shifts position. Another possibility is that he may be obeying a command to keep still, for example he may be a soldier at attention. Or his lack of activity may be the reverse: a deliberate and negativistic refusal to act despite orders or pressure to do something; like wilful refusal to move by a child who has been ordered to bed, or refusal to catch one's eye by a waiter in a café. Perhaps he is simply waiting for something to happen: the train to reach its destination, the fish to bite, the telephone to ring, the rain to stop. He may also be in some altered state of consciousness which is associated with minimal behaviour, for example, hypnotic trance, meditation or drug intoxication. His lack of movement may be a result of some pathological condition such as occurs at times in certain states of schizophrenia, or it may be a result of head injury. He may even be asleep.

If the example of minimal behaviour seems unfair, here are some different examples. Imagine two drivers speeding on a motorway. One of them may be driving in this way because he has to reach a particular destination at a predetermined time, and he is late. It is important for him to be there on time, perhaps because his job depends on it, and he is extremely anxious about the possibility that he will not be punctual. His behaviour has a meaning for him in the context of a goal and plans to achieve that goal and he is continually evaluating his chance of achieving the goal. Now consider the second man. He may be driving his car fast simply because he enjoys doing so. He has no destination which he has to reach at a given time; he is simply doing it 'for the hell of it', because he is exhilarated by the speed and risk, or because he enjoys testing his skills as a driver. In the second case, the behaviour does not point beyond itself toward some future goal, but is its own justification in the present and, rather than feeling anxious, the driver is more likely to feel highly excited. The behaviour of these two drivers may be identical in each case, but the feelings and meanings associated with the behaviour are totally different.

Now consider two people gambling. One may be doing so because he urgently needs the money for some purpose and this is the only way he can find of getting enough money quickly. The other gambler may be gambling 'for fun', because he enjoys the risk and excitement of the gambling itself. Or consider two people arguing with each other. For one the argument is serious and concerns ideas, perhaps religious or political, which are important to him and give his life meaning. Any attack on them therefore becomes a personal threat. The other is arguing for the sake of arguing, and playfully keeps the argument going as long as he can because he enjoys the intellectual challenge. He may also enjoy antagonizing his opponent and seeing him angry and frustrated.

The reader will have noticed similarities in the last three examples and,

indeed, they are all examples which involve a pair of contrasting phenomenological states which we have labelled 'telic' and 'paratelic' respectively. This
pair of states will be discussed in detail in Chapter 3. For the moment it is
sufficient to note that these two subjective states, although typically leading to
different kinds of behaviour, may nevertheless underlie behaviour which,
superficially and for certain periods, is identical.

These kinds of considerations become particularly germane in the area of
clinical psychology, since their implication is that the same symptoms may mean
quite different things to different patients, and be evidence of quite different
phenomenological states and problems. Knowledge of the underlying mental
states is essential if the appropriate therapy is to be provided. Furthermore,
certain types of pathology which have arisen out of social interaction, especially
in the family, may have arisen because a given piece of behaviour has a different
significance to the person who performs it, e.g. a child, from that which it has for
someone who perceives it, e.g. one of the child's parents, so that the two parties
easily misunderstand each other's actions. The therapist needs to be aware of this.

In all these examples, similar behaviour may be associated with contrasting
mental states. But the opposite would also seem to be true: contrasting behaviour
may be associated with similar mental states. For example, a feeling of a need for
excitement may lead to one of a number of quite different kinds of activity,
which might include reading a novel, being rude to the neighbour, having a bet
on the horses, going to a discothèque, making love, or kicking the cat. Which one
is chosen will depend on various considerations, including time of day,
availability, habit, chance, expense and other concurrent needs. But at least
important component of the total experience, namely the feeling of a need for
excitement, will remain the same. This consideration is also important from the
clinical point of view. Thus a change of behaviour, through behaviour modification say, does not in itself necessarily imply a diminution of distress.

The implication is that behaviour is not a simple reflection of mental states,
nor are given significant mental states unvarying concomitants of given behaviours.
The analysis here implies a kind of dualism in which there are two levels of
activity. The relationship between mental states and behaviour is not unlike the
relationship between deep and surface structure in Chomskian linguistics.
Different surface structures may have the same deep structure, as in 'Sarah hit
Samantha' and 'Samantha was hit by Sarah'; alternatively, the same surface
structure may be generated from different deep structures, as in the two
meanings of 'they are flying planes', in which in one case 'flying' is a verb and in
the other an adjective.[5]

Furthermore, complex forms of behaviour which are mediated by institutions
in a society may, in fact, be associated with quite different sets of mental
concomitants in different people at a given time, or in the same people at
different times, both among those who may be identified with the institution

concerned or those whom it serves. Thus a church service, a full-dress military parade, a trade union rally, or the opening of an art exhibition, may each have a totally different meaning for different people involved, even for those performing identical roles, and serve quite different purposes for them, as indeed each may do for the same people at different times. Some institutions may well derive their strength and endurance from their potential for having a variety of different, even incompatible meanings, and from satisfying opposing needs. Institutionalized religious behaviour, which will be considered in more detail in a later chapter, provides a goods example of this in relation to the kinds of subjective meaning with which reversal theory is concerned. Incidentally, as this example attests, reversal theory can be brought to bear on topics which are normally part of the subject-matter of sociology and social anthropology; but in doing so the level of analysis remains essentially psychological.

The Principle of Inconsistency

In discussing the complex relationship between experience and motivation, the emphasis was placed mostly on the fact that, even when two people perform the same behaviour, the way they interpret what they are doing and its significance for them, may be different. It is equally the case that, when the same person performs the same behaviour at different times, its significance for him is not necessarily the same. According to reversal theory, some important aspects of the way an individual interprets his world, and what he is doing in it, fluctuate in various ways which may involve radically different interpretations being made by him at different times. Sometimes this will be disclosed in behaviour and sometimes it will not be apparent from the outside. Either way, the individual's being-in-the-world (to use Heidegger's concept) may change in significant respects. Reversal theory deals with one type of fluctuation of this kind, but the general principle illustrated by the theory is one that can be referred to as 'the principle of inconsistency'. If an individual's personality is seen from this perspective as the way in which he experiences the world, then it is possible to say that, in this respect at least, *personality is inherently inconsistent*. This type of inconsistency may also be expected to express itself on occasion as inconsistent behaviour.

Generally, however personality is defined, it is taken to be relatively stable and consistent.[6] Indeed, in certain respects it undoubtedly is, but what the 'principle of inconsistency' does is to challenge the assumption that this is true of all important aspects of personality. The argument of reversal theory is that, unless this assumption is corrected, the view of man which emerges is something of a caricature.

The nature of the fluctuations of interest to reversal theory will become clearer after the concept of metamotivational state has been introduced; meanwhile, an analogy may be helpful. It is as if the organism is a computer with a number of alternative programs for processing the same data, the selection of the operative program changing from time to time under the direction of a higher-level executive program. Just as different programs turn a general-purpose computer effectively into different special-purpose machines, so these metamotivational 'programs' effectively turn the individual into different personalities at different times. It is in this sense that personality is seen as being inherently inconsistent.

In the theory, therefore, a principle of change is emphasized, that of switching from one temporary 'mode of being' to another, which is rather different from those principles of change which are normally the centre of interest in psychology: development, adaptation, learning, and rhythmic change (e.g. diurnal cycles). The type of change to which reversal theory principally refers is not unidirectional and it is not permanent, or semi-permanent, as it is in development and learning. It does not have the regularity of such rhythms as circadian rhythms; and it is more complex than adaptive behaviour, since adaptive behaviour assumes a single optimal level of some variable. Here is an example of a change of the kind referred to in reversal theory: a child suddenly becomes disruptive in the classroom, remains disruptive for a period and then, equally suddenly, returns to normal behaviour. (For a good case study of such behaviour see Blackmore and Murgatroyd, 1980). These two switches in relation to two different modes of being of the child cannot be described in themselves as developmental, although they may occur more frequently at one developmental stage than another. Nor can they be described as forms of learning, although learning may come to influence when such switches occur; and the disruptive behaviour itself is not learned in any simple sense, since it may take a whole variety of forms and may even be novel on each occasion. The switches do not necessarily occur rhythmically and, since they work in opposite directions, they cannot both be adaptational in any simple sense, although each mode may be adaptational in its own terms once it comes into effect.

Liam Hudson (1967) has argued that there is no virtue ". . . in claiming that (an) idea is 'basically right' although obscured by the welter of people's individuality" (p.17). In a similar vein, there would be no virtue in saying that a psychological theory is basically right but obscured by the way in which people change. The way people 'differ from themselves', even over relatively short periods, must be taken into account in psychological explanation as much as the way in which people differ from each other.

The Problem of Gratuitous and Paradoxical Behaviour

A further characteristic of reversal theory is that *it treats as one of the central problems of human behaviour that of trying to understand why so much of it is apparently unrelated to biological needs.* That is, it takes as one of its key themes the question: why do human beings so often behave in ways which do *not* appear to aid the survival of either themselves or their social groups, or the species of which they are members, and which even on occasion appears to work against such survival?

As implied by putting the question in this way, such behaviour would appear, at least superficially, to fall into two classes. The first class is that of behaviour which is biologically 'gratuitous' or superfluous. That is to say, it is simply not necessary from the biological point of view, since it is apparently inessential to ensure survival. Obvious examples of such behaviour include much of that which is associated with art, religion, sport, humour and entertainment of all kinds, as well as the various types of ritual behaviour studied in "primitive" societies by anthropologists.

The second class is that of behaviour which is not only inessential, but which may even tend to militate against the survival of the individual who performs it, or others; i.e. such behaviour may actually be harmful to the individual or his social group or species. Examples include sadistic and masochistic behaviour, vandalism and hooliganism, unnecessary risk-taking as in particularly dangerous sports or in gambling, alcoholism and drug-taking, celibacy (which may endanger the species if not the individual), asceticism, violent crime, martyrdom and suicide. We shall call such self-damaging, or potentially self-damaging, behaviour 'paradoxical'. It is paradoxical because it has the opposite effect to that which, from a biological and evolutionary point of view, one would expect behaviour to have. As Menninger (1966) has said: ". . . the extraordinary propensity of the human being to join hands with external forces in an attack upon his own existence is one of the most remarkable of biological phenomena" (p.4).

Saying that an activity is *biologically* gratuitous does not mean that it has no *psychological* point. Such an activity presumably must fulfil certain psychological needs or give certain psychological satisfactions, otherwise it would not be performed at all, at least not for long. So the question is that of why humans are so constituted that psychological satisfactions are sometimes apparently unrelated to biological necessities.

The existence of gratuitous and paradoxical behaviour is peculiarly challenging to mechanistic approaches to explanation in psychology. What kind of machine, if any, would look at and appreciate paintings (see in this context the discussion by Apter, 1977), enjoy jokes, or attempt to damage itself? Or again, as Johan Huizinga has said: "Animals play, so they must be more than merely mechanical things" (Huizinga, 1949, 1970 edn. p.22). In fact, reversal theory is from one point of view a mechanistic or, as we would prefer, a cybernetic theory. Putting gratuitous and paradoxical behaviour in the centre of the picture therefore poses a direct challenge to the mechanistic assumptions of reversal theory.

There is a sense in which all such behaviour may be described as 'irrational', since it is clearly not rational to behave in a way which is inimical to one's own self-interest and even self-preservation.[7] However, it is preferable to avoid the use of the word 'irrational' or the words 'non rational', since much of such behaviour and the thinking associated with it may in itself be highly rational in the everyday sense of the word. Rationality is often a feature of the means used in such activity, if not of the goals of the activity as judged by, say, a biologist. For example, playing chess is biologically gratuitous in the sense defined here, but it is a highly rational game.

It might be objected that gratuitous and paradoxical activities are relatively trivial and that psychology has more important topics to study. Indeed, in the history of experimental psychology, topics like the psychology of religion and the psychology of humour have generally been peripheral if not actually taboo, and regarded as the domain of researchers who need not be taken too seriously. Fortunately, this attitude seems to be changing, and with excellent reason. Phenomenologically, some of those activities which have been referred to here as gratuitous, for example the activites associated with art and religion, would appear to be of the greatest importance in human experience. For at least some people, they are what gives life its meaning and significance. The dissatisfaction of many people with experimental psychology, voiced so often in the criticism that its concerns are distant from those of everyday life, surely relates as much as anything to the fact that experimental psychology has considered as unimportant and peripheral those very topics, like religion and art, which are of central importance in so many people's lives.

It is also true that some gratuitous behaviour is *not* seen as important from the point of view of the person who performs it: it is enjoyable, partly *because* it is not important. But one is left in this case with the crucial psychological and biological question of how, in the course of evolution, such behaviour came to be rewarded with feelings of pleasure. Everyday observation of human behaviour makes it immediately apparent that biologically gratuitous behaviour (both that which is seen as important, and that which is not, by the people concerned) takes up a great deal of time and energy. One suspects that if an ethologist from another planet were to observe human behaviour, then the kind of behaviours which have been listed here under the headings 'gratuitous' and 'paradoxical' would be among the most striking, and among those which most obviously called for an explanation.

Action which is psychologically essential, in the phenomenological sense that it feels important or essential to the individual, may or may not be essential in an immediate biological sense. Consider the act of painting a picture: although this may seem essential to the painter, it is presumably in itself not biologically essential. If, on the other hand, the act is that of avoiding an accident, then this is both phenomenologically and biologically essential. The converse would also appear to be the case: acts which are psychologically inessential, in the phenomenological sense that they feel inessential to the individual, may also be essential or inessential in the biological sense. Doing a crossword puzzle may seem inessential to the person doing it, and presumably *is* biologically inessential. Another act which may seem inessential, like casual sexual intercourse, may serve an essential biological purpose. If, as has been argued earlier, the relationship between mental state and behaviour is a complex one in which simple one-to-one correspondence cannot be assumed, then the implication of the present argument is that the relationship between mental state and biological need is similarly complex, and requires elucidation.

The assumption in reversal theory is that gratuitous and paradoxical behaviour must at least have their origins in processes which are biologically essential; and that behaviour which is inessential or damaging in an immediate biological sense, may often have long-term survival value for the social group or the species, if not always for the individual. Such 'inappropriate' behaviour may also be an expression of psychological predispositions which, under other conditions, would have a high survival value for the individual as well as the group. This is not to deny that, in some cases, paradoxical behaviour may be truly pathological, in the sense that it arises from 'system malfunctioning'. Rather, it is to assert that certain types of common gratuitous and paradoxical behaviour may emerge naturally, in certain circumstances, from processes which have played an important part in the evolution of man and his civilization.

Phenomenology and Cybernetics

Having so far emphasized the importance in psychology of making reference to conscious processes, the question arises as to whether reversal theory could not justifiably be described as a phenomenological theory. One problem here is that the term 'phenomenological' is itself problematic, especially in relation to psychology (see, for example, Ashworth, 1976, Letemendia, 1977). If the essence of phenomenological psychology is that it approaches the subject-matter of psychology in a manner which is free of assumptions and theoretical constructs, then reversal theory is certainly not phenomenological since the influence of cybernetic concepts and assumptions has, from the beginning of the development of the theory, been strong. Similarly, if the use of the term 'phenomenological' in 'phenomenological psychology' implies that it is derived principally from Husserl's phenomenology, then on these grounds too, reversal theory would appear not to be strictly phenomenological. In particular, treating consciousness as subject to natural laws conflicts with one of the central tenets of Husserl's philosophy.

If, on the other hand, the essence of phenomenological psychology is that it is a type of psychology which makes extensive reference to subjective experience and meaning, and in this way contrasts with behaviourist psychology which systematically avoids such reference,[8] then reversal theory is certainly phenomenological. It might be argued that this is too broad a way of defining phenomenological psychology. If so, then perhaps a preferable name for the general approach referred to would be 'experientialism', as suggested by Koch (1964, p.34). It would appear, however, that this is the way in which the term 'phenomenological psychology' has come to be understood, at least in British and North American psychology and psychiatry.[9] Defined in this way, phenomenological psychology should be closely related to 'action theory', although the two traditions have been quite distinct in their historical origins and development.

Reversal theory is also, at least equally, a mechanistic theory, in that the explanatory principles which it brings to bear are essentially mechanistic ones. The term 'mechanistic' as used here is not intended to be synonymous with 'behaviourist' or 'stimulus-response', the way in which the term is used by authors like Harré and Secord, (1972, 1976 edn., pp.30-31). Rather, the term 'mechanistic' is intended in the cybernetic sense.[10] The organism is regarded as a highly complex machine which is relatively autonomous in that it uses the environment and information from it, rather than being 'pushed around' by it. It is a machine that constructs internal models of the environment which it may use in planning ahead and guiding itself towards various goals; and a machine which solves problems heuristically as well as algorithmically. In similar vein, the nervous system is conceived as

> ". . . an organized information-processing system, governed by programs, able to store and retrieve information, and able to act on the basis of these programs and stored information in a constructive and relatively autonomous way—in other words as something like a large computer with an enormous memory store, complex input-output equipment and organized hierarchies of programs". (Apter, 1973, p.131).

So cybernetics makes it clear that machines are not necessarily simple, controlled by their environments or unintelligent. The actual design and construction of machines which are complex, autonomous, purposeful and intelligent, like the modern general-purpose digital computer appropriately programmed, demonstrates this point in the most forceful possible way. This general cybernetic view and arguments in support of it, together with various illustrations from cybernetics especially including computer simulation, have been put in more detail by the present writer in a number of previous publications (Apter, 1966, 1969, 1970, 1972a, 1973).

How does this notion of the organism as a machine tie in with some of the attitudes expressed above, with which it may at first sight appear incompatible?

In particular, can a machine be inconsistent and can it produce behaviour which is gratuitous? Both parts of this question can be answered in the affirmative. As far as inconsistency is concerned, the analogy has already been given of a computer following different programs at different times, and such programs may well have opposite effects from various points of view. As far as gratuitous behaviour is concerned, again there is no reason why such behaviour should not be produced by a machine. Consider a guided missile which misses its target: the whole of its subsequent flight may be regarded as gratuitous since it does not help the device to accomplish the aim built into it, but this does not mean that the missile is not a machine. Or, to take a rather different example, a tape punch machine quite gratuitously makes confetti. This does not mean that gratuitous behaviour in the sense described earlier is to be explained in the ways implied by these two examples, but simply to show that it is not necessary for the word 'gratuitous' to be applied only to non–machine systems.

The real difficulties would appear to arise when one comes to deal with conscious experience and subjectivity in mechanistic terms. The writer has already argued in detail elsewhere, that the idea of machine consciousness cannot be automatically dismissed out of hand (Apter, 1970, Chapter 9). As far as reversal theory is concerned it is simply submitted that, whether or not the fact of the *existence* of consciousness in human beings means that they cannot be considered as machines, some conscious processes may nevertheless be said to conform to certain cybernetic principles. At least in the case of those states considered in the theory, their occurrence is assumed to be determined lawfully according to principles which can best be described in cybernetic terms.

Characterizing reversal theory as both cybernetic and phenomenological will no doubt seem odd to many readers, since these two approaches to psychology are normally regarded as incompatible; phenomenological psychology, like action theory, is generally conceived to be anti-mechanistic and anti-deterministic, whereas cybernetics is clearly an arch-mechanistic approach to behaviour. Where phenomenology merges into existentialism, with its emphasis on free-will, cybernetics merges into engineering with its solid and necessary orientation towards predictability and control.

It was argued above that, in the light of the cybernetic definition of mechanism, there is less incompatibility than is generally supposed between action theory and cybernetics. But what of phenomenology in the broad sense defined earlier, with its orientation towards subjective experience? What reversal theory does is to show how cybernetics and phenomenology may be brought together in a complementary fashion. Instead of stopping at descriptions of subjective experience, reversal theory points to cybernetic mechanisms which may underlie the mental states, and changes in mental states, so described. Or, vice versa, instead of confining the cybernetic analysis to physiological or behavioural variables, the theory makes reference to, and indeed focuses on, mental states.[11] It should be emphasized that these mental states are in principle *defined* in terms of the individual's own subjective interpretations, not the experimenter's interpretation from outside the subject's behaviour. The definition of such mental states is therefore essentially subjective rather than objective. Accordingly, reversal theory may be seen at one and the same time as a mechanistic interpretation of subjective phenomena, and as a challenge to any approach in psychology which would overlook mental states when attempting to explain behaviour.

Structural Phenomenology

The theory of psychological reversals has been described here in a number of ways: as an action theory, as cybernetic and as, at least in a broad sense, phenomenological. There is also a sense in which the theory is structuralist, in the contemporary sense of the word as used in the social sciences.[12] Structuralist in this sense, it should be noted, is quite different from the classic psychological sense in which it is used to described the approach of such introspectionists as Wundt and Titchener; it stems rather from the linguistics work of de Saussure (1916). To Saussure, linguistic signs were not to be understood in terms of their appropriateness to that which they symbolized, which he saw as arbitrary, but in terms of their relations to each other, a given language embodying a complex structure of such relationships. These ideas were given a fresh impetus in linguistics by Noam Chomsky (1957, 1965). In a similar vein, structuralist anthropologists, following Lévi-Strauss (e.g. Lévi-Strauss, 1966), have looked on anthropological systems like myth systems, kinship systems and totemic systems, as forms of language and attempted to lay bare the structural relationships underlying the generation of these systems. In turn, this approach has also been applied in other areas like literary criticism, psychiatry and political science. Like other structuralist theories, what reversal theory attempts to do is to lay bare certain structures which underlie the phenomena of interest, and to try to understand something of the dynamics of these structures. In the case of reversal theory, the phenomena of interest are primarily those to do with the experience of motivation, and certain patterns are discerned underlying this experience. The investigation of the relationship between the level of motivational experience and the more "superficial" level of overt behaviour then follows from this.

There are many similarities between systems theory and cybernetics on the one hand, and structuralism on the other. These include the holistic approach adopted in both, their formalism, especially in terms of their fondness for binary relationships, and their attempt to delve beyond superficialities by looking for deep structures underlying surface structures. These and other similarities have been discussed by the present writer elsewhere (Apter, 1972a, 1972b). The notion that reversal theory can be regarded simultaneously as cybernetic and structuralist is therefore not problematic. Indeed, some writers like Piaget (1971), have more or less equated cybernetics and structuralism.

In contrast, the idea that the theory is both structuralist and phenomenological might be said to raise problems - the same kind of problems as the idea that it is both cybernetic and phenomenological. However, essentially the same arguments as those used above concerning cybernetics and phenomenology could be put forward to show that there is no necessary incompatibility between structuralism and phenomenology either, at least when the term 'phenomenology' is used in the rather broad sense indicated. There is no reason why, on the one hand, mental processes should not on examination disclose various structural patterns, or, on the other, why structural analysis should not be carried out on mental phenomena as well as on linguistic, behavioural or cultural phenomena. In other words, mental states may be regarded as constituting a kind of 'language' whose 'grammar' can be studied by structuralist methods.

For these reasons, it is appropriate to characterize the approach adopted in the development of reversal theory as 'structural phenomenology'. This can be defined as the study of pattern and structure in experience, where it is to be understood that it is the pattern of experience itself which is of concern, i.e. its nature and quality, rather than pattern within the content of experience in the sense of, say, Gestalt psychology. Hence, structural phenomenology focuses on the different ways in which the contents of experience are interpreted by the individual, rather than on the contents themselves, although the two are related. There are, of course, philosophical differences in distinguishing between the contents of experience and the way in which these contents are interpreted, and this is the kind of distinction that Husserl tried to make in defining 'noesis' and 'noema'. However, the general sense should be clear enough and, in any case, the rest of this book acts as an extended illustration of the approach. *One of the most salient characteristics of reversal theory therefore is that it illustrates the structural phenomenological approach.*[13]

May reversal theory be said to be functionalist as well as structuralist? In the sense of the term functional in the phrase 'structural-functional', as used in anthropology and sociology, it is certainly functional. In structural-functionalism, which is typified by the work of Radcliffe-Brown (1952), a system is examined to see how the parts relate to each other to produce a single functioning whole, so that a particular activity, e.g. a ritual, is studied in order to see how it contributes to the smooth running of the social group that utilizes it. Similarly, the mental states of interest to reversal theory are seen as constituting subsystems and systems, each subsystem contributing in its own way to the functioning of the system as a whole. There is, however, another sense of "functionalist" in anthropology and sociology; this is the attempt to explain phenomena in terms of biological needs, or of the way in which the phenomena have evolved over time.[14] This approach is epitomized by the work of Malinowski (1922). In this sense, functionalism is seen as being opposed to structuralism, since it tends to be biological, reductionist and diachronic. It would seem, therefore, that an approach could not embody this type of functionalism and remain structuralist. Nevertheless, reversal theory can be said to be functionalist in this sense too, as well as being structuralist; and so, again, it would seem that an attempt is being made to embody contradictory approaches in reversal theory. Reversal theory is functionalist since, among other things, it raises questions about the functions of gratuitous and paradoxical behaviour in human beings. And in answering these questions it makes reference to biological needs and also to the evolutionary survival value of the activities concerned. Yet, once more, as was done in reconciling structuralism and phenomenology, the argument can be made that the two approaches are not necessarily incompatible, but can be brought together in a complementary fashion. There is no reason why one should not ask about the evolution of structures, once they have been identified, or about the biological purpose which they might serve. Understanding the meaning of elements of a system in terms of their relationships to each other, the end-product of the structuralist approach, does not preclude asking other biological and evolutionary questions about parts of the system, and about the system as a whole.

Notes on Chapter 1

1. These include Macmurray (1957), Peters (1958), Melden (1961), Browning (1964), C. Taylor (1964), Hampshire (1965), Shwayder (1965), Anscombe (1966), Louch (1966), R. Taylor (1966), T. Mischel (1969), Harré and Secord (1972), Shotter (1975), Reynolds (1976), Gauld and Shotter (1977), Hornsby (1980).

2. In this respect, see the arguments of Joynson (1974).

3. For example, a typical cybernetic definition of 'state' would be as follows: "A quantity $x(t_0)$ qualifies as the state of a system at time t_0 if by giving $x(t_0)$ and the input $u(t)$ for $t \geq t_0$ the behaviour of the system is completely determined for $t \geq t_0$. (Kwakernaak, 1973, p.191).

4. It would even be possible to make out an argument that it is *always* the conscious experience which is of real interest to the psychologist, at least when dealing with human beings.

5. There is a formal resemblance here to the distinction made by phylogeneticists between analogous and homologous organs, the former being organs which have a similar function between species but different origin in development, the latter having a similar origin in development but quite possibly a different function.

6. Even when inconsistencies are recognized, as Farrell (1963) has pointed out, the attempt is made to explain them by showing hidden consistency.

7. This use of the words 'rational' and 'irrational' would be consistent with the way the words are often used in psychoanalytic, or psychoanalytic-influenced, writing. E.g. Fromm (1977) says:

"I propose to call rational any thought, feeling or act that promotes the adequate functioning and growth of the whole of which it is a part, and irrational that which tends to weaken or destroy the whole" (p.352).

8. Whereas, for methodological reasons, Husserl put the real world "in brackets", Watson may be said to have done the converse and put the world of experience "in brackets". Phenomenological psychology, as defined in this paragraph of the text, puts neither experience nor the real world, including behaviour, 'in brackets' but assumes the existence of both, and is concerned with the relationship between them.

9. Following Snygg (1941), MacLeod (1947), Krech and Crutchfield (1948), Snygg and Combs (1949), Rogers (1951), Kuenzli (1959), MacLeod (1964).

10. Wiener (1948), who coined the word, defined cybernetics as the study of control and communication in the animal and the machine. Any of the following books can be recommended as introductions to cybernetics or to 'systems theory' (which means roughly the same): Ashby (1956), Beer (1959), Pask (1961), George (1965, 1979), Buckley (1968), Bertalanffy (1968), Beishon and Peters (1972), Arbib (1972).

11. "While cybernetics can speak to some point on the objective aspects of human behaviour, it has only one thing to say on the subjective aspects, and that is—that it has nothing to say" (Ashby, 1950, p.31). This rather common view among cyberneticians is strenuously contested by the authors of reversal theory.

12. viz. Lane (1970), Ehrmann (1970), Boudon (1971), Robey (1973), Badcock (1975), Gardner (1976), Hawkes (1977).

13. As far as the author is aware, the term 'structural phenomenology' has not been used before, although the term 'phenomenological structuralism' has been applied to the work of Roman Jakobson, by Holenstein (1976).

14. It will be appreciated that in both these cases the word 'function' is being used in a way in which is different from its use in mathematics (viz. Oettinger, 1969).

2 The Concept of Reversal

Reversal theory is about reversals between metamotivational states, the factors which induce such reversals, and the implications of these reversals for experience and behaviour. In this chapter the concept of reversal will be introduced in the context of a discussion of bistability; later the term 'metamotivational state' will be defined and the nature of these states considered.

Homeostasis and Bistability

One of the most influential ideas in modern life sciences has been that of homeostasis; not that this is the word which has always been used, since other roughly synonymous words like 'stability', 'regulation' and 'equilibrium' also occur frequently in the literature. But the idea that the value of some variable can be held reasonably steady by interacting forces in a complex system has been, implicitly if not explicitly, widespread in physiology, psychology and sociology, certainly throughout much of the present century.

The word 'homeostasis' itself comes from physiology, where it was coined by Walter Cannon (1932) who used it in his description of the many bodily systems which maintain variables like body temperature, respiration rate and calcium metabolism at a constant level. But the idea in physiology goes back to at least Claude Bernard (1859) who was one of the first to emphasize the stability of a wide range of physiological variables. The concept is also deeply embedded in psychological thinking. This is particularly true in relation to the psychology of motivation, as will be illustrated in Chapter 5. Meanwhile, to give some examples from other areas of psychology: much of Pavlov's theorizing involved the notion of equilibrium, especially equilibrium between the systems of the organism and external conditions (see Ban, 1964); Jung's compensation theory of personality is essentially based on the idea of equilibrium (e.g. Jung, 1954); Kurt Lewin (1951) in social psychology wrote of 'quasi-stationary equilibria' in group

19

dynamics; and, more recently, Piaget has based much of his theorizing on the equilibrium concept in attempting to explain cognitive development. The idea runs through most of his work, but a particularly detailed discussion is given in Piaget (1957). In sociology, both Comte and Spencer used the concept of equilibrium and, indeed, it has been said of Spencer that "there is a certain likeness between (his) views . . . and those of certain modern cyberneticians" (Hearnshaw, 1964, p.110). Hobhouse not only talked about equilibrium but, as long ago as 1901, even compared the adaptability of organisms to the regulation of a steam engine by a governor, the very analogy used so often today in introducing the idea of homeostasis in popular accounts of cybernetics. In general, of course, the whole area of sociology which deals with social norms and social control is about equilibrium.[1]

The concept of homeostasis reached its apotheosis in the science of cybernetics, in which it was from the beginning one of the most central and seminal ideas, and one which epitomized the cybernetician's desire to reach a level of generality which subsumed both living and non-living, including man-made, systems.[2] Thus, homeostasis can be discerned in a variety of living systems and built into a variety of engineering systems. Furthermore, the principles by means of which homeostasis is achieved in living systems and incorporated in engineering systems, especially the principle of negative feedback, are made clear in cybernetics and stated in a general and rigorous fashion. Thus a system is described as homeostatic if it is so constructed that it tends to maintain a specified variable within two specified limits. In other words, the value of the variable tends to be stable within these limits and unstable outside them. A homeostatic system may also operate in such a way as to maintain a variable above or below a single specified limit. Negative feedback achieves stability in a system essentially through deviations in the variable itself automatically correcting these deviations: some part of the output of the system is fed back into the system in a negative way, so as to counter movement of the variable in question away from the limits specified. This represents a particular kind of equilibrium in which the variable concerned itself plays a crucial role in maintaining its own stability. In a thermostatically controlled room, the temperature of the room may itself be used to control a switch which will turn heating or refrigeration equipment on or off as required, thus maintaining the room temperature within certain limits predefined for this variable. Similarly, the variable of blood temperature is kept within certain required limits in the human body through the temperature of the blood itself which, on deviating beyond these limits, stimulates the hypothalamus to instigate physiological activity, which will counteract the deviation in temperature. To give a more complex example, a car being driven along a road is kept within limits, defined by the edge of the road and the centre of the road, by a driver who acts in such a way as to counteract deviations of this 'position on the road' variable from the required position.

Each of the above systems may be said to be homeostatic since each does indeed tend to maintain the variables in question within their specified limits, despite change in, and disturbance from, the environment, e.g. temperature change in the environment, the changing direction of the road. In each case it is the deviation of the variable itself, brought about by the disturbance, which instigates the corrective activity. Such systems may also be said to be 'adaptive' (another word widely used in cybernetics) since, through negative feedback, they adapt to change in the environment. No control system can be perfect: it is always possible that the disturbance will be too great to be counteracted successfully. But in a homeostatic negative feedback system, because of the way the system is constructed and, therefore, the way it functions, the tendency will always be for the disturbance to be opposed. Negative feedback is not the only means by which a system may achieve some measure of stability; but it is one which is found widely in biological systems, and used widely in the construction of control systems.

The ideas of homeostasis and negative feedback are extremely general, and in the examples given it has been shown how they may relate to mechanical systems (the thermostat), physiological systems (the blood temperature system), and combined man-machine systems (the car-and-driver system). Cybernetics goes well beyond this in developing the logic and mathematics of control systems: thus the speed of reaction of the feedback circuits may have to be taken into account in predicting the behaviour of a system; positive feedback circuits may become added to negative feedback circuits to increase the effectiveness of the latter; and models of the environment may be incorporated in control systems for various purposes.

Undoubtedly, the idea of homeostasis has been an important one in psychology, not least because the use of this and related concepts, like the concept of negative feedback, shows that there need be nothing mysterious about the purposefulness of living systems. Adaptiveness and action towards the future, do not necessarily imply some special teleological ability unique to biological systems, nor do they imply that such systems are excluded from the operation of the normal laws of cause and effect; on the contrary, purposefulness may be shown to be a property of even quite simple mechanical devices appropriately constructed, and to arise from systems which are governed by cybernetic principles. Nevertheless, our belief is that, although many psychological processes do indeed display homeostasis, too much emphasis on this concept has led to a limited and oversimplified view of human nature. Instead, we wish to suggest that many psychological systems are more appropriately interpreted as 'multistable' than as homeostatic, which is to say that for many psychological variables there are a number of value ranges which constitute areas of stability for the variable concerned. For each range, the principle of homeostasis applies; but much of the complexity of behaviour and experience is related to the way in which the individual switches from one to another of these value ranges, under different conditions.

The simplest form of multistability is 'bistability', where there are two areas of stability rather than the single area involved in homeostasis. It is mainly this form of multistability which will be used as an explanatory concept in the present theory because, when one looks at motivational aspects of subjective experience, the notion of bistability seems to be unavoidable. This is not to say that homeostasis cannot be recognized in certain aspects of consciousness which have to do with motivation, e.g. pain is clearly a variable with a limit beyond which one immediately feels impelled to take some kind of negative feedback action to reduce the intensity of the variable. But a number of experienced motivational variables appear to be characterized more by bistability than by homeostasis. It is also possible that, in the development of reversal theory and structural phenomenology, it will be necessary in due course to postulate more complex multistable systems in order to handle the full complexities of experience. The accepted strategy to follow, however, in trying to develop a satisfactory explanation in some area, is to start with the simplest explanation and to proceed to more complex explanations when the simplest one breaks down, or when its limitations become apparent. This is a procedure hallowed by both scientific tradition and philosophical argument. At the present stage in psychology the homeostatic concept has been used to its limits, and it is now necessary to see how much more progress can be made through use of the concept of bistability. This may in turn, however, be simply one step along the road to some form of multistability theory.

The idea of bistability, like that of homeostasis, is also found in cybernetics, but it has not been as influential as that of homeostasis across a range of disciplines such as psychology, physiology and sociology. If the values of the variables which fall within the limits of homeostasis are defined as constituting the 'preferred state' of the system or the 'preferred level' of the variable, then in the bistable system there are two such preferred states or levels, as against one in a homeostatic system. (Note that 'preferred' in this cybernetic sense merely describes value ranges of the variable which tend to be stable and makes no reference to 'value-judgements'). The difference between these two kinds of systems can be represented schematically in the way shown in the two graphs in Fig. 2.1. The hatched area in each graph represents a preferred state of the system, the left-hand graph representing a homeostatic system and the right-hand graph a bistable one. The arrows in each case show some possible changes in the value of the variable concerned, following disturbance and hence deviation in the value of the variable from that defined by the preferred state in question. In the homeostatic case the variation illustrated is around the single preferred state and in the bistable case around one of the two preferred states.

A simple example of bistability is presented by the two stable positions of any flat thin object. A playing card, for example, may be said to have two preferred states, face upwards or face downwards, and following disturbance it will tend to return to one or other of these stable states. If one edge of the card is moved through a vertical plane, while the other remains fixed, a certain point will be

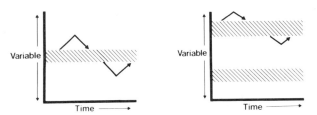

FIG. 2.1 *A graphical representation of homeostasis (graph on the left) and bistability (the graph on the right)*

reached, namely that at which the angle of the card to the horizontal is 90°, beyond which the card will fall over with its other side up. If this angle is not reached, it will fall back with the original side still uppermost. Disturbance which takes the form of changing the angle of the card with respect to the horizontal plane will cause temporary instability, following which the card will return to one or other of its two stable states.

Another simple everyday example, but this time of a system built specifically to achieve bistability, is afforded by a light switch. Light switches are usually deliberately constructed, for obvious reasons, so that the switch is either in an 'on' or an 'off' position. If the position of the switch is altered at all, it is either altered sufficiently to bring about a complete switching to the opposite position, or it is not altered enough, in which case there will be an immediate return to the original position. Only the two extreme positions of 'on' and 'off' are stable and all intermediate positions are unstable. Incidentally, the basis of digital computer technology lies in bistable switching units of one kind or another and, therefore, one of the central strands that go to make up cybernetics—the development of increasingly sophisticated computational techniques—is closed bound up with the principle of bistability.

A rather different example of bistability would be a funicular railway with its two cars, one of which goes up as the other goes down. The two stable positions are, firstly, that in which car A is at the top and car B at the bottom; secondly, that in which car B is at the top and car A at the bottom. Disturbance, which normally consists of the relative weights of the two cars being changed, causes instability and consequent movement, until the alternative preferred state is achieved.

Here is another example, this one being taken from the field of chemistry. Certain chemical reactions are reversible, which is to say that the atoms involved can constitute themselves into two different stable configurations (molecules or combinations of molecules), depending on conditions. Thus one atom of nitrogen, five atoms of hydrogen and one of oxygen can constitute themselves into either ammonia (NH_3) and water (H_2O) or ammonium hydroxide (NH_4OH). Bubbling ammonia through water sets up a reaction which produces ammonium hydroxide, whereas heating ammonium hydroxide has a catabolic effect, the produce of which is ammonia and water. Once started in either direction, the process tends to continue to completion. This is just one example of the thousands of reversible anabolic–catabolic reactions which have been identified and studied in chemistry, especially in organic chemistry.

Enough examples have now been given to demonstrate the principle of bistability and to imply how widely bistable systems occur in nature and in engineering. However, these various forms of bistability are not all of the same kind. One distinction worth making is between those bistabilities which can be referred to as 'value-determined bistabilities' and those which can be referred to as 'externally-controlled bistabilities' (Apter, 1981). In the former it is the value of the variable itself which determines which of the two possible preferred states will be the 'operative' one, i.e. the one around which control is actually taking place. In the latter, factors external to the value of the variable itself determine which of the two states is operative.[3] This distinction may be made clearer by reference to the graphs in Fig. 2.2 which contrast these two kinds of bistabilities schematically. In the upper figure, value-determined bistability is represented. Here, disturbance which causes a change in the value of the variable causes the variable to return to its original preferred level, unless the disturbance is so great that the value of the variable is driven out of what one might call one regulation range (range 'a', say, as depicted in the figure), and into the regulation range of the alternative preferred state (depicted by 'b' in the figure). In the lower figure, externally-controlled bistability is represented. Here there is only one preferred state for the whole range of values at a given time, so that even extreme deviations from a given preferred state are counteracted in the direction of that preferred state, rather than coming into the regulation range of an alternative preferred state which, temporarily at least, is non-existent. However, a change may occur so that the other preferred state becomes the viable one. The value of the variable itself does not determine which preferred state is viable; this is determined by some external controller or external disturbing force. (By 'external' here is meant 'external to the variable' not 'external to the system being considered', of which the bistable system may be a subsystem.) In this type of bistability the system as a whole may be said to have two states, each characterized by a different preferred level of the variable concerned.

Here are some examples. In the case of the playing card, the value of the variable "angle of the card" following disturbance determines which of the two stable states will be attained. Similarly, the position of the light switch determines, once the external disturbance, e.g. a finger moving the switch, is removed, which way the switch will move into stability. These are therefore both value-determined bistable systems. On the other hand, in the example of the funicular, the choice of stable state is made externally, so that movement into a new stable state is made even

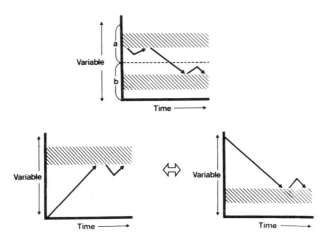

FIG. 2.2 *A graphical representation of value-determined bistability (upper graph) and externally-controlled bistability (two lower graphs).*

when, as they are initially, the two cars are jointly at the opposite extreme of stability, i.e. in the state opposite to the new stable state. This is therefore an example of an externally-controlled bistable system. Similarly, in the chemistry example, once the reverse reaction has commenced, the whole process will tend to move to the new stable configuration, even from the opposite extreme. So if one thinks of the variable in this case as being the proportion of the whole which is ammonium hydroxide (one could equally well of course identify the variable as the proportion of ammonia and water to the whole), then the value of this variable in itself does not determine which way the reaction will go.

Of course, the preferred state of the value-determined system may be chosen by an external controller, e.g. somebody switching the light switch. But in this case the control must occur *through* change in the value of the variable itself and cannot occur independently.

There is a sense in which a value-determined bistable system is static and an externally-controlled bistable system is dynamic. In the former, the system itself does not change, even if the value of the variable concerned does. Effectively, there are two subsystems which both remain active and, as the variable is driven out of the control zone, i.e. the regulation range, of one preferred state, so it becomes subject to that of the other. In the externally-controlled system, the system itself changes, the *whole* system temporarily taking one form or the other so that there is only one active preferred state at a time. The whole system therefore has two alternative 'states', each specifying a preferred level of the variable, or is composed of two *alternative* subsystems.

If one imagines a surface such as that depicted in Fig. 2.3i, and a ball which

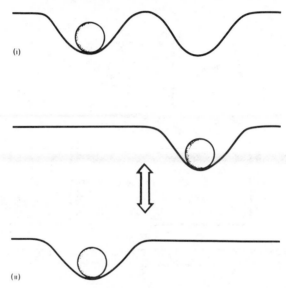

FIG. 2.3 *(i) Value-determined bistability and (ii) externally-controlled bistability, as exemplified by a ball in a 'landscape'. In (ii) the 'landscape' itself switches between two alternative forms.*

may be moved over the surface, then there are two concavities and, therefore, two positions of stability in which the ball will tend to come to rest after it has been disturbed. Should the variable be that of the position of the ball in the horizontal plane, the value of this variable immediately following disturbance determines in which of the two stable states the ball will eventually come to rest, i.e. whether it is sufficient to cause the ball to move to the other stable state or not. The system, ball plus 'landscape', is therefore a value-determined one. If, on the other hand, one imagines that the system itself changes so that there is only one concavity *or* the other at a given time, i.e. the whole 'landscape ' changes its contour as shown in figure 2.3ii, then the system is an externally-controlled one. So, another way in which these two types of bistable system can be described is to call the value-determined system a *conjunctive* system, since it consists of two subsystems both of which are in a sense active at a given time, and the externally-controlled system a *disjunctive* system, since it can only take either one form or the other at a given time. In the value-determined system, external forces only affect the system by changing the value of the variable concerned itself, i.e. disturbance can only act directly on the position of the ball and on nothing else. In the externally-controlled system, external forces may not only affect the actual value of the variable, but also determine which of the two states the system is in, i.e. the preferred level of the variable. In this case, external forces may change the contours of the 'landscape' as well as the position of the ball. Depending on what one sees as constituting the system in the externally-controlled case, these external forces can either be seen as 'disturbances', where the system consists only of the ball and the 'landscape', or as a form of 'control', where the system is seen as being part of a larger system which governs its operation. The use of the term 'control' here and in the phrase 'externally-controlled' is consistent with its use in cybernetics, where it refers to the choice of preferred level of the variable rather than to the maintenance of this level once chosen, the word 'regulation' being used for the latter (viz. Ashby, 1956). In these terms an individual choosing the setting for a thermostat would be the controller, and the thermostat itself a regulator; control of the level of heat would then be achieved through regulation.

The bistable systems which are of primary concern to reversal theory, those made up of pairs of 'metamotivational' states, are of the externally-controlled, disjunctive kind rather than the value-determined conjunctive kind. Thus, for a reversal between such states to occur, it is not necessary for the value of the variable concerned to change beforehand.

Nothing in this analysis should be taken to imply that the two preferred levels of a variable in a bistable system of either kind are necessarily operative for equal periods. For example, in a value-determined system the regulation range associated with one preferred level may be much wider than that associated with the other preferred level; other things being equal, one would in this case expect the former level to be operative for longer periods than the latter. In the externally-controlled system, one state with its associated preferred level may, for one reason or another, be operative for longer periods than the other. Wherever there is a bias in a bistable system such that the system is predisposed to spend longer periods with one preferred level operative rather than another, the system may be said to display dominance, the favoured level being the dominant one. In the externally-controlled case it is also possible to speak of a dominant *state*, this being the state associated with the dominant level. It is important to be clear about the difference between saying that a given preferred level, or state, is *operative* at a given time, and saying that it is *dominant* over time.

It should be noted that although a system may display dominance, in the sense that it is structurally predisposed to favour one preferred level rather than the other, this does not necessarily mean that the favoured level is actually operative for longer periods than the other, since environmental disturbance may induce an actual temporal inequality in the opposite direction. For example, a switch may be built with some safety factor such that the 'off' position is dominant: perhaps the switch has to be moved further in the 'on' direction than the 'off' direction before it moves automatically into the new stable state. Yet 'disturbance', in the form of the behaviour of someone who operates the switch, may mean that the switch is in fact more frequently in the 'on' position. The same considerations apply in the simpler homeostatic case, e.g. a thermostat may not actually achieve the preferred level of heat if the weather is too adverse during a particular period, but the system would still be regarded as basically homeostatic. Nevertheless, in the normal way of things one would expect the preferred level of the variable in a homeostatic system to be the most frequently attained level; and, other things being equal, i.e. with random disturbance, one would expect the dominant preferred level in a bistable system to be operative for longer periods than the less favoured level.

Dominance should also be distinguished from *lability* which, in this context, is about how frequently switching occurs. Switching may occur relatively frequently even in a system in which one of the preferred levels is highly dominant, provided that whenever a switch occurs in one direction it is quickly followed by a switch back again, but not when the switch occurs in the other direction.

It is now possible to introduce the term *'reversal'*. When two preferred levels may be interpreted as being *opposite* to each other, then switching from one of these to the other may be thought of as a reversal from one to the other. This process of reversal is one which is asserted by reversal theory to be involved in certain aspects of the dynamics of all conscious experience, and in this sense to underlie most behaviour. *It may be taken to be the central explanatory concept of the theory.*

This leads us to another level of analysis in relation to bistability. Along with the change in preferred level occasioned by a reversal may go a different *system* for regulating in terms of that preferred level, so that it is possible to talk of a reversal not only from one preferred level to another of the same variable, but also from one system to another. In this latter case one could say that there was an overall bistable system composed of two alternative and opposing subsystems. For example, suppose that the funicular railway is operated by two machines, one of which changes the weight of the car on the left-hand side, and the other which changes the weight of the car on the right-hand side. A different preferred position of the cars is associated with each of these machines and they act in opposite directions. As one machine ceases operation and the other comes into operation, one may meaningfully speak of a reversal from one system to the other.

It should be obvious that while it is possible to measure the degree to which two preferred levels are opposite, for example by measuring their respective distance from the mid-point along the dimension concerned, it is not possible to measure the degree to which two systems are opposite, except indirectly by reference to the two preferred levels which they respectively regulate in terms of, or to movement of, the variable towards these levels.

There are a number of points to be made about reversal between opposite systems. One is that such a reversal can in a sense occur without there being two different systems involved: thus, funicular railways are usually operated by a single machine which changes its direction of operation. It would be possible in this case, however, to describe the machine as changing from one kind of machine to its opposite, and in this perfectly legitimate sense there would be a reversal between opposite subsystems. Secondly, opposite systems may be involved in both value-determined and externally-controlled situations, in the former the decision about which system operates being made in terms of the value of the variable concerned. A third point to note is that terms like 'dominant' and 'operative' may be referred to systems as well as to preferred levels, and indeed the term 'operative' was initially chosen with systems in mind. Fourthly, when a reversal occurs from one system to another, it should be remembered that, although the value of the *preferred* level of the variable concerned will also reverse automatically, the *actual* value of the variable may be prevented, by some disturbance, from reversing. For example, some hitch may occur in the operation of the funicular railway such that, although the direction of operation has changed, and with it the preferred position of the cars, the cars do not in fact move to the new preferred positions. In any case, the reversal of the value of the variable will be expected to lag behind the reversal of the preferred level, because it will need to be brought across to the new preferred level by the operation of the system that underlies it; unless, of course, it is already at that level, having been held there by some disturbance at an immediately preceding time. Thus in the example of the funicular railway, the preferred position of the cars switches instantaneously, but the cars themselves need time to move to the new preferred positions. In this kind of case, which is of prime concern to reversal theory, bistability occurs in two ways. Firstly, there is bistability in relation to two preferred levels of a variable, and systems related to these two preferred levels. Secondly, there is bistability of the actual level of the variable. In the former case, reversal involves a switch between two discontinuous states/systems, in the latter it involves change along a dimension which is continuous.

A fifth point is that where there are two subsystems which operate in opposite directions, this does not in itself necessarily imply that the system which they together constitute is a bistable system. Indeed, homeostasis is often maintained, or some sort of equilibrium arrived at, through the action of systems which have opposite effects. A mechanical example of this would be the use of a heater and a refrigeration unit in a thermostatic system, each being called into action as required through negative feedback in the appropriate direction, in order to maintain a room or building at some prespecified homeostatic level. Although the heater and the refrigeration unit work in opposite directions, they may be used to counteract deviation in the service of homeostasis. A physiological example would be the way in which limb movement is controlled by opposing groups of muscles: flexors and extensors. Movement of the limb to a new position, that is to a new point of equilibrium, occurs when one group contracts and the other relaxes sufficiently to bring about the degree of movement required. The organization of the nervous system that provides for the relaxation of one group of muscles when the opposite group contracts was called "reciprocal innervation of antagonistic muscles" by Sherrington (1906). Another physiological example is provided by the reciprocal action of the two branches of the autonomic nervous system, the sympathetic and the parasympathetic, which act rather like opposing groups of muscles to bring about a certain equilibrium in the activity of the body at a given time. As one or the other branch takes effect, so a large set of physiological variables, e.g. heart rate, respiration rate, pupil size, the output of adrenaline into the blood stream, etc., are each brought to a new equilibrium level. There are various complexities in the way in which these two autonomic systems operate. For example, some innervations of the two systems may on occasion work simultaneously rather than reciprocally, and sometimes the two systems work cooperatively by alternating their actions, as when producing intestinal peristalsis. Generally, however, they appear to function in a reciprocal manner in order to produce homeostasis and, indeed, it was partly through carrying out his classic work on the effects of the autonomic nervous system that Cannon (1929) was led to the concept of 'homeostasis' in the first place. The fact that a system is made up of subsystems which operate in opposite directions, therefore, does not in itself imply bistability. Bistability only occurs where the two sub-systems are associated respectively with two different preferred levels of the variable concerned.

The pairs of opposing systems of central interest to reversal theory are those which are referred to as metamotivational. Each pair of metamotivational systems may be characterized in terms of two preferred states of a variable, or a set of pairs of preferred states of a set of variables, and may therefore be characterized as bistable. When a reversal occurs in one of these pairs from one system to its opposite, there is also therefore a concomitant reversal between preferred states, and this in turn should eventually result in a reversal in the actual value of the variable concerned, unless some disturbance is powerful enough to prevent this.

In the simplest forms of *multistability*, the different areas of stability may all be described in terms of a set of different non-adjacent ranges of values of a single variable. In principle, the set may be of any finite size. A simple example would be that of a die: since a die is six-sided, there are six distinguishable stable positions in which it may come to rest; all other positions are unstable. Compare this with the effectively two-sided playing card, which is bistable. In the most clear-cut cases of multistability, the set of discrete preferred states will be fixed and unchanging, so that a controller is limited to deciding which of the predetermined set of preferred states at a given moment is the operative one. If the value ranges of the set of preferred states can also change, it may be more difficult to tell in observing the system whether it is a multistable system or a homeostatic system with a shifting single preferred state. However, if any kind of abrupt and discontinuous switch in preferred state is observed, then it is reasonable to infer that the system is multistable to some degree or another.

In more complex forms of multistability, more than one dimension may be involved, so that the state of the multistable system as a whole must now be described in terms of vectors,[4] as must the various configurations of preferred states. Thus, if there are two dimensions a and b with two preferred states each $(a_1 \cdot a_2)$ and $(b_1 \cdot b_2)$, then there are four possible configurations of preferred states in the system as a whole: $(a_1 \cdot b_1)$ $(a_1 \cdot b_2)$ $(a_2 \cdot b_1)$ $(a_2 \cdot b_2)$. Each dimension may involve the same variable or different variables. In this way multistable systems may be built up by combining lower-level bistable or multistable subsystems. So, certain 'op art' works, which are made up by combining various components, each of which displays perceptual reversals of the Necker Cube type (see Fig. 2.5), could be said to be perceptually multistable since each such work may take up a number of different perceptual configurations. To take a more extreme example, a digital computer can be described as a multistable system, since at any given time it is in one of a large number of possible configurations of bistable preferred states. In this sense too, reversal theory may be said to be dealing with multistability rather than bistability, in that it postulates several bistable systems. At any one time, therefore, the system made up out of these bistable systems may come to rest in any one of a number of configurations of stable states.

A Simple Model of Bistability

The concepts discussed here may be clarified by thinking of a simple balance, such as that represented in Fig. 2.4i. A strip of wood has been placed across a fulcrum, and a weight attached beneath the strip towards each end, so as to bring the centre of gravity of the resulting 'cross-piece' somewhere below the pivot point of the fulcrum. Such a rudimentary system clearly displays equilibrium. If it is disturbed by an outside force, i.e. if one end of the cross-piece is pushed upwards or downwards, the cross-piece will afterwards swing up and down, and continue to oscillate in this manner until it finishes up at rest in the horizontal position once more. This horizontal position may be thought of as representing the *preferred level* of the system. (In this case the range of values of the variable 'angle of the cross-piece' which constitute the preferred level is very narrow.) The system is obviously a *homeostatic* one. It is also possible to analyse the mechanism by means of which homeostasis is maintained in this system as involving negative feedback: as the angle of the cross-piece is changed, this in

turn changes the centre of gravity of the cross-piece and causes movement under
the force of gravity of the cross-piece back to the horizontal where, once more,
the centre of gravity (marked x in Fig. 2.4ii which depicts the point around the
fulcrum in close-up) is perpendicularly beneath the centre of the cross-piece.

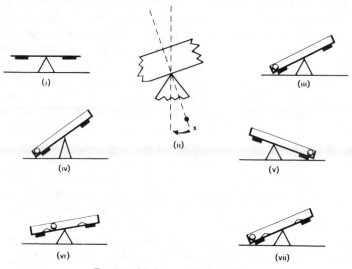

FIG. 2.4   *A balance model of bistability.*

However, the movement itself causes the cross-piece to swing beyond the
horizontal until the shift in the centre of gravity, now in the opposite direction,
causes the cross-piece to swing back again. Through a series of such swings, each
one being less than the one before, the cross-piece eventually returns to a
stationary horizontal position. The process involves negative feedback, since it is
the change in the value of the variable itself, let us say the angle which the cross-
piece makes to the vertical, which automatically initiates the corrective
movement – although the process is made more complex by the over-shooting
which also occurs, the friction which damps this down and the resulting
temporary oscillation.

Imagine now that strips of perspex are placed around the edges of the top
surface of the cross-piece, and a marble is placed in the resulting enclosure,
which is wide enough to allow the marble to run from end to end along its full
extent. Since the sides of this enclosure are perspex one can see the position of
the marble when one looks at the balance from the side, as shown in Fig. 2.4iii.
The previously homeostatic system has now been converted into a *bistable* one
since, depending on which side the marble is placed, the system will finish up in
one or other of two positions: either the left-hand end or the right-hand end of
the cross-piece will be down, and remain in that position unless there is a further

disturbance. This process of the creation of bistability is an example of what can be referred to as 'polarization'. Whichever end is down, this stable value of the variable 'angle of the cross-piece' may be defined as the *operative* one. Small disturbances of the angle of the cross-piece will be counteracted automatically by the whole system, so that the cross-piece will again come to rest in the same stable state. If, however, the variable 'angle of the cross-piece' is changed in such a way that the marble crosses from one side of the cross-piece to the other and then the cross-piece is released, the latter will come to rest with the previously uppermost end in the down position. In other words, a *reversal* will have occurred and the opposite stable state will now be operative. It will be noticed that, although bearing some superficial resemblance to oscillation, reversal is in fact quite a different process. Note also that reversals are likely to be less frequent and the system less *labile*, the more extreme the two opposite preferred levels. Thus, as the fulcrum gets higher, so the angle of the cross-piece in each stable position becomes more extreme and the system less labile, i.e. less likely to reverse following a disturbance (see Fig. 2.4iv). *Dominance* can be introduced into the system by shifting the position of the fulcrum to the left or the right, thus predisposing the cross-piece to be in one stable position rather than the other (see Fig. 2.4v).

Is the system as described here a value-determined bistable system or an externally-controlled one? As depicted so far, it is a *value-determined* one in that the angle of the cross-piece itself determines which end will come to rest in the down position after disturbance, i.e. assuming that after the angle has been changed, the marble has shifted to a new position, and then the cross-piece has been released.[5] If, however, the variable is defined as the position of the marble on the horizontal dimension rather than the angle of the cross-piece, and if the cross-piece were to be temporarily held in some way with one end down, then the system would become an *externally-controlled* one since, irrespective of where the marble was placed along the cross-piece to start with, even at the end which was uppermost, because of the slope it would always finish up at rest at the end which was fixed in the downmost position. *This externally-controlled version of the balance model comes closest to mirroring the types of reversal of most concern to reversal theory* (i.e. metamotivational reversal), especially if such a reversal is conceived to take place in three steps:

1) the angle of the cross-piece is changed so that the uppermost end becomes the downmost end;
2) the marble is placed at some point on the cross-piece;
3) the marble rolls into its new preferred position.

This also illustrates the point that the change in value of the variable, in this case the position of the marble, lags behind the change from one preferred state being operative to the other being operative.

Such a balance could be made *multistable* if a number of suitably shaped barriers were to be placed across the enclosure in the way indicated in Fig. 2.4vi; then the marble would have the possibility of coming to rest in one of a number of different positions, the actual position depending on the angle to which the cross-piece was in fact displaced. In Fig. 2.4vi the marble is shown resting against such a barrier, while in Fig. 2.4vii it is shown at rest in the more extreme position. With two barriers placed one on either side of the pivot point, therefore, there would be four stable states, defined by the position of the marble in the horizontal dimension: the system could now be said to display this degree of multistability. Multistability of a different kind could be achieved by placing a number of balances in their bistable form, i.e. each with a marble, alongside each other in parallel, and describing the state of the resulting combined system of balances as a vector of the value of the variable 'position of the marble' for each of the systems that made it up.

Finally, if two people placed themselves at either end of the balance, so that each could exert downward pressure on their respective ends, these two people would constitute *opposing systems*. If only one or the other could give the cross-piece a short downward push at a given time, the system as a whole would remain bistable, since the push at a given end would either be great enough to bring about a reversal to the opposite position of the balance, i.e. from one end being in the stable downmost position to the other end being in this position, or it would not be strong enough to do so, in which case the balance would revert to the stable position from which it started. Consider, however, what would happen if both people were simultaneously able to exert continuous downward pressure on their ends of the cross-piece. If the pressure at the two ends was unequal for a short period and then equalized again, the balance would be brought into equilibrium at some intermediate position between the two extremes, and would no longer display bistability. This illustrates the fact that the existence of two opposing systems operating on a given variable does not in itself guarantee bistability.

Reversals in Psychology

The primary aim of reversal theory is to show that various aspects of a wide range of types of experience and behaviour may be explained by reference to certain pairs of states and the reversals which occur between them. The pairs of states referred to here are those which are described in the theory as 'meta-motivational', a term which will be explained below. The status of such states is twofold. Firstly, they have explanatory status and their validity lies at this level in the degree of success which reference to such states has in throwing light on various psychological phenomena and showing unity beneath diversity. Secondly, the states are in a sense directly observable in conscious experience, once one's attention has been suitably drawn to them. In this sense they may be referred to as 'phenomenological states', i.e. states which the reader should be able to come to recognize in his own conscious experience as he gains familiarity with the theory. Although the mechanism which brings about reversal from one such phenomenological state to its opposite is not directly observable in consciousness, the phenomenological results of reversal should be discernible to anyone who is willing to observe and study the relevant features of his own mental life over a period.

It might be objected that the reversal concept as developed here is merely an artefact of the tendency of descriptive language to dichotomize. According to this argument, reversal theory has succumbed to the temptation inherent in language to describe psychological change as more discontinuous and polarized than it really is. A number of replies can be made to such an objection. Firstly, at the level of theory, the explanation of various psychological phenomena does in fact require the idea of sudden switching between opposites. The force of this argument will become clearer later, as various activities are considered in these terms. Secondly, the results of such switching may be discerned directly at the phenomenological level. Thirdly, in describing the particular pair of meta-motivational states to be discussed in the next chapter it was found necessary to coin two new words, since language did not already provide the necessary pair of antonyms. Recognition of these two states did not, therefore, have its origins in a dichotomy already enshrined in everyday language. Fourthly, there are a number of types of reversal which are already well known in psychology. These demonstrate that the reversal principle does clearly operate, at least in certain fields of psychology, and is not an effect of the exigencies of descriptive language. This makes it more reasonable *prima facie* to suppose that reversals may also operate in relation to the phenomena of primary interest to reversal theory. Let us consider some types of reversal which are already recognized in psychology. This will also help to illustrate the meaning of reversal by supplementing the examples already given.

The best known reversals in psychology are in the field of visual perception, for example the reversal associated with the so-called Necker Cube (due to the Swiss naturalist L. A. Necker in 1832). Although there are many variations on this figure, it is illustrated in Fig. 2.5 in its simplest form. Other perceptual reversals include figure-ground reversals as exemplified in Fig. 2.6, and figures like the famous "mother-in-law" picture due to E. G. Boring[6] and J. Jastrow's duck-rabbit figure.[7] In all of these there are clear switches from seeing the figure in one way to seeing it in a different way. They are all excellent examples of psychological reversals, since there can be no doubt that switching does take place when the figures are inspected: the switches are clear and even startling. Furthermore, for each figure, it is almost impossible to see the figure both ways at the same time: the different interpretations are mutually exclusive. Similarly, it is also difficult to see the figure in such a way that neither interpretation is made; the whole time one inspects the figure one is forced to see it in one way or the other. Even when the switch does take place it is rapid and it is difficult to note intermediate positions during the change from one perceptual interpretation to the other.

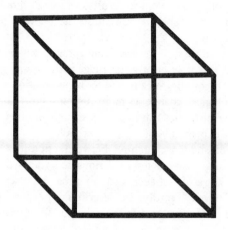

FIG. 2.5   The Necker cube.

In the field of psycholinguistics a similar situation applies in respect of ambiguous sentences. Although multistable forms may occur, most ambiguous sentences seem to have two different interpretations and in this sense are bistable. For example, consider the following four ambiguous sentences:

He was driven to work.

They are fighting men.

Here is a list of women broken down by age.

The schoolmaster never stopped swearing.

In each of these there are two mutually exclusive ways of understanding the meaning of the sentence.[8] These different interpretations are perhaps not obviously opposite in the way in which the interpretations of a Necker Cube or a figure-ground reversal figure are opposite, but a clear switching occurs from one interpretation to another as one reads and re-reads each sentence. It is difficult to read any one of these sentences without assigning it meaning, and in doing so one assigns one meaning or the other. Each meaning is a stable one which makes complete sense, and when the switch occurs from one sense to the other, it is rapid.

From the point of view of reversal theory, which deals with reversals whose immediate impact is on subjective experience, these examples are particularly germane: the phenomena concerned in the perceptual and apperceptual switches just cited are essentially subjective and need have no impact whatsoever on objectively observable behaviour. This does not mean that they cannot be disclosed by suitable experimental methods, but it does mean that they are not directly observable by the experimenter, unless he takes special steps to exteriorize them in some way.

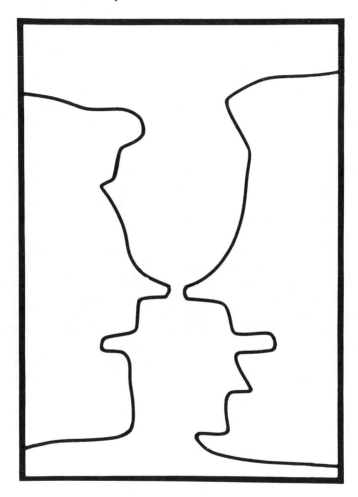

FIG. 2.6 A type of figure-ground reversal figure.

However, there is another class of reversal phenomenon: that which can be observed directly in behaviour and may even be defined in terms of behaviour in the first instance. A simple example of this is the phenomenon known as the 'reversal of reflex' effect. If one takes an unconditioned reflex of the muscle contraction type and progressively increases the strength of the stimulus, in some muscles a point is reached at which relaxation occurs instead of contraction. This type of reversal is present in many postural adjustments.[9]

Moving from unconditioned to conditioned reflexes, a type of behavioural reversal may be observed here too. Such reversals were discovered and studied by Pavlov in his classic work on conditioned reflexes. They took place when the dogs he used in his experiments were subjected to stress of one kind or another: for example, by making the intensity of the conditioned stimulus extremely strong; by increasing the delay between conditioned stimulus and reinforcement; by anomalies in the conditioning signals;[10] or by subjecting the dogs to physical stress, such as long periods of work. As a result of such conditions, the dogs produced abnormal behaviour which Pavlov found he could categorize in three ways, each representing an increasingly severe form of disturbance. The second and third involved forms of behavioural reversal. The first of the three was the so-called "equivalent" phase, in which the strength of the dog's conditioned response was the same to both strong conditioned stimuli, i.e. stimuli which previously produced a strong conditioned response, and to weak conditioned stimuli, i.e. stimuli which previously produced a weak conditioned response. The second he referred to as the 'paradoxical' phase. In this phase, strong stimuli had either no effect or only a small effect, whereas weak stimuli had a relatively strong effect: in this sense there was a reversal of the response to strong and weak stimuli. In the third phase, which he called the "ultraparadoxical" phase, the dog responded only weakly, if at all, to strong conditioned stimuli, but now responded strongly to negative, i.e. inhibitory, stimuli.[11] These experiments have become generally well known through William Sargant's attempt to generalize from Pavlov's findings in order to explain certain features of human behaviour, especially religious conversion, and to suggest therapeutic techniques for certain kinds of psychopathology (Sargant, 1957).

This serves as a reminder that the field of psychopathology also confronts the psychologist with certain kinds of behavioural reversal. The most obvious example here is that of manic–depression, in which motor function and general level of activity clearly differentiate the two opposite stable states of the patient. There are crucial experiental differences as well, but in this case it is not necessary to take special steps to exteriorize them in order to be able to discriminate the two states and observe bistability. Among other types of psychopathological switches are those which can occur between catatonic excitement and stupor. Bunney and Murphy (1973) have suggested that such changes from one clinical state to its opposite, and they cite a number of examples, should be referred to as 'behavioural switches'.

To turn to a different kind of example of behavioural reversal: in many species, including rats, rabbits, dogs and guinea pigs, reversal of sexual response patterns can be induced physiologically so that the males of the species come to act like females, and vice versa. The simplest way to achieve this is by the administration of hormones of the opposite sex, but it has also been brought about by castration followed by the transplantation of ovaries, or by the removal of ovaries and the transplantation of testes—the effect of such transplantation also, presumably, occurring through consequent hormonal changes. Since it is unlikely that the hormones themselves contain the programmes governing sexual behaviour, this evidence implies that programmes for both kinds of behaviour pattern are available to members of both sexes in the species concerned, but one of these patterns is, in the normal way of things, inhibited; i.e. the programme for female behaviour is normally inhibited in the male and vice versa. Changing the hormones changes the direction of the inhibition. The system is therefore a bistable one in which, normally, one of the two opposite states is completely dominant. However, reversal to the opposite may be induced by appropriate intervention. It is notable, incidentally, that such reversals may on occasion be induced in the natural environment, for example through dietary changes or parasitism.[12]

Metamotivational States

What are these *metamotivational* states to which reference has been made at a number of points in the preceding discussion? The answer is that they are 'frames of mind' which determine certain general phenomenological characteristics of motivation at a given time: they are about the way in which the individual interprets his own motives. Since the states are not themselves motivational states, but only determine something *about* motivation, the term *meta*motivational has been applied to them: the level of description is higher than that of the particular motives which happen to be prevailing.[13]

These states are therefore phenomenological states, or if the reader prefers, mental states, being defined in terms of interpretation by the subject of aspects of his own subjective experience. Furthermore, they do not necessarily affect the individual's behaviour, and therefore cannot always be equated unequivocally with specified kinds of behaviour, although typically they do have substantial behavioural effects. This does not mean that they cannot be studied objectively, just as subjective phenomena like sensations, perceptions or attitudes can be exteriorized in various ways for experimental and other purposes. It simply means that the states themselves, as defined, are subjective.

Another way of describing them would be to say that they are alternative modes available to the individual of assigning meaning to his actions, or lack of actions, or intended actions. In other words, they are an integral part of his interpretation to himself of his life-world and his intentions and behaviour in it. They therefore pervade and colour the whole of his mental life.[14]

As has already been indicated, these states go in pairs of opposites, each pair exhibiting bistability and reversal, one or other member of each pair being constantly operative during waking life. One of these pairs is referred to as the 'telic-paratelic' pair of states; another is composed of the states of 'negativism' and 'conformity'.

Each metamotivational state is related to a preferred level of a given variable, and to a system which regulates the variable concerned in terms of this preferred state. One may therefore refer to the telic *state*, for example, or the telic *system*, depending on which aspect is of more concern at a particular time, or which mode of reference is more convenient. This requires some clarification, especially in relation to the term 'mental state' which was defined in Chapter 1 as meaning some recognizable aspect of mental life at a given moment. Suppose the motivational variable concerned is that of felt arousal, which is in fact one of the variables involved in the telic-paratelic distinction. To say that someone is in the telic state at a given moment is to say, among other things, that there is a certain preferred level of felt arousal operative at that moment. It does *not* mean that the variable is actually in this preferred state; it may in fact, at the moment in question, have a value well outside the preferred state and may indeed even be at the opposite extreme of the dimension. The term 'state' as used here, then, is a shorthand way of saying 'having a preferred state'. If one wanted to be really precise one would have to say that 'state' in this sense meant 'being in the state of having a preferred state'.[15]

Looked at from the phenomenological point of view, this meaning of state is one type of mental state. What this implies is that the individual is aware, in some way, of having a given preferred state of the variable concerned, even if the variable is not in that state. He feels he needs a given level of felt arousal, for example, even if he does not feel arousal at that level at that moment. This feeling is one recognizable aspect of his mental life at the moment in question. The term 'preferred' can therefore be applied to the phenomenological as well as to the cybernetic aspect of motivation: the individual consciously prefers being in the 'preferred state' and derives pleasure from being in it. When the actual value of the variable concerned is outside the preferred range of values of that variable, then it is experienced as unpleasant to some degree, and a need for change will also be experienced; in other words 'tension' of some kind will be felt by the individual.

The term 'system' refers to some underlying process which operates so as to attempt to achieve the preferred level of the variable; when the individual is in the telic state this is another way of saying that the telic system is in operation at that point in time. Although it is possible to refer to mental states, it would be odd to speak of 'mental systems' in the sense of 'system' used here, especially since we assume that such systems must have a physiological basis and that much of this physiological functioning does not reach consciousness.

The term 'mood' could also have been used rather than 'state'. From the phenomenological point of view this term would be suitable on a number of grounds. Not only are moods changeable and triggered by a variety of factors, as is also the case with reversals between metamotivational states, but they colour a person's perceptions, and indeed the whole of his mental life. Moods, too, are bipolar. However, if metamotivational states are forms of mood, then they are special forms of mood in which one member of each pair is always operative throughout waking life, and in which the relationship is bistable. This may also be true of some bipolar emotions but it is clearly not true of all emotions, even bipolar ones. For example, one is not always in a state of loving or hating. Another problem is that certain states which are sometimes thought of as moods, like 'anxiety' or 'boredom', are, as will be shown, determined *by* metamotivational states. The use of the term 'mood' might therefore blur the distinction between the kinds of states normally referred to by the word 'mood' in psychology and in everyday language, and those states dealt with in reversal theory.

What factors induce reversals between opposite members of each pair of metamotivational states? There would appear to be three main classes of inducing agent. Firstly, there are events which have an immediate effect on facilitating or inhibiting reversal, and in some cases such an event will be strong enough alone to trigger a reversal. Usually these are environmental events, but there may also be certain internal events which have the same effect, e.g. the awareness of hunger, or a sudden and inexplicable pain. This category of inducing agents may be referred to as *contingent*. Secondly, it may be supposed that *frustration*, when it builds up to a certain point, will have the effect of bringing about a reversal. Thirdly, there is *satiation*: as one member of a pair remains operative over time, so some innate force for change slowly builds up. This becomes increasingly effective in facilitating a reversal, so that the reversal mechanism becomes more and more sensitive to the other reversal-inducing agencies. Eventually satiation may become powerful enough to instigate a reversal on its own account. The reversal itself is then assumed to dissipate its effects immediately. The satiation effect is one which is, in a sense, intrinsic to the reversal mechanism itself, and in this respect it differs from the other two types of effect. It lies at the heart of the inconsistency which we believe typifies much of human psychology and helps to explain something of man's restless nature, and his need for change.

Examples of these inducing agents will be given at the appropriate points in the presentation of the theory. Such agents are assumed to interact with each other in a facilitative or inhibitory way to determine whether or not a reversal will take place at a given moment.[16]

It was noted earlier that metamotivational reversals appear to be of the externally-controlled rather than the value-determined variety. In discussing the meaning of 'external control' it was pointed out that this only meant external to the variable concerned, not to the system as a whole. Thus the immediate causes of reversal, as just described, are not all environmental, and hence external to the system constituting the individual concerned, but still operate as external controllers in the sense defined earlier, in that they can change the preferred level of the variable independently of the value which that variable happens to have at the moment in question. A further point is that, not only is the question of which metamotivational system is operative independent of the actual value of the variable concerned, but it is also independent of the metamotivational systems themselves in the sense that the systems do not interact with each other to "gain ascendancy" in the manner, say, of the id and the superego in Freudian theory. Indeed, since the operation of the two members of each pair of systems is mutually exclusive, they cannot interact. Their action is not on each other, but on the common variable(s) which they regulate. In order to regulate, of course, they must also act on and through other psychological systems.

It may be helpful at this stage to summarize what has been said so far about the dynamics of metamotivational systems.

(1) Each pair of metamotivational systems regulates one or more motivational variables.

(2) Each member of each pair of metamotivational systems regulates in terms of a single preferred level of each variable concerned. The members of each pair of systems are opposite to each other in the sense that, for each variable concerned, the two preferred levels related to the two systems are at, or towards, opposite ends of the dimension concerned.

(3) The operation of the two systems is mutually exclusive, i.e. at any one time only one member of each pair of systems is operative and, therefore, only one preferred level of the variable is operative.

(4) Depending on various factors the preferred level, and the system which regulates in terms of it, may switch rapidly to its opposite, i.e. reversal may occur.

(5) Such a reversal may be brought about by various factors, singly or in combination, these factors being independent of the current value of the variable concerned, i.e. the bistability is externally controlled.

(6) As with all regulation systems, the variable may be prevented by various external disturbing forces from reaching, or resting in, the preferred level which is operative at that time.

(7) Each pair of metamotivational systems is associated with a mental state, referred to as a metamotivational state. When the variable concerned is at its preferred level for that state, pleasure is experienced; otherwise some degree of displeasure is felt, in association with 'tension'.

For completeness, one further point needs to be made about reversals between metamotivational systems. This is that, when the switch has occurred to the new preferred level of the variable in question, the particular form of this variable may have to be chosen before it can be operated on and brought into the preferred state. This is not the case in the example given above in relation to arousal, but it is the case in other instances which will be illustrated later. In such cases, reversal involves three steps:

(i)   a reversal to the opposite preferred state of the variable;
(ii) the choice of a particular exemplar of the variable;
(iii) the attempt to bring the variable, in the particular form chosen, into that preferred state.

To refer back to the balance model, this is like firstly removing the marble and changing which end of the cross-piece is in the down position; secondly, choosing a suitable marble from a set of marbles, including the one which has been removed; then, thirdly, placing the newly-chosen marble in the cross-piece enclosure so that it rolls down to the new lowest position.[17]

The Concept of Reversal in Psychoanalysis

One area of psychology in which the concept of reversal has already been used as an explanatory concept is psychoanalysis, where it is associated with the idea of the mechanism of defence known as reaction-formation. Reversal itself Freud termed one of the 'vicissitudes of instinct' (Freud, 1915), seeming to mean by this the way in which, for example, love can become converted into hate, or anger into gentleness. There are some problems, however, with the way in which the term is used within the psychoanalytic literature. Thus Freud himself uses the term 'reversal' fairly frequently in "The Interpretation of Dreams" to describe the way in which the manifest content of a dream may be the opposite of the latent content which it symbolizes (Freud, 1900). But presumably the latent content, which Freud claimed is dictated by the id, remains the same and therefore no reversal of instinct itself has taken place. Assuming that, in relation to dreams, Freud was using the term 'reversal' in a special way different from its more general use in relation to the instincts, the further problem arises as to the relationship between reversal in this latter sense[18] and reaction-formation. One way of interpreting this relationship would be to see reversal as a change within the id, and reaction-formation as the defence mechanism which makes use of this and, as a result, produces changes of behaviour. This would seem to be consistent with Anna Freud's interpretation of the relationship between the two: "In securing repressions by means of reaction formation the ego avails itself of the instinct's capacity for reversal" (Freud, A. 1937, p.175). In similar vein, Rycroft has put it that reversal is the instinctual vicissitude, while reaction-formation is the defence mechanism which exploits the possibility of reversal

(Rycroft, 1968). But inconsistencies still occur. For example, in the same work by Anna Freud she refers to reversal itself as a defence mechanism (p.40), as do other psychoanalytic writers like Glover (1949). Furthermore, in practice it is difficult to distinguish between reversal and reaction-formation since reversal, in psychoanalytic theorizing, appears to take place only in the context of reaction-formation. Indeed, it would be difficult to conceive of reversal as taking place in any other way than through reaction-formation; after all, what could it possibly mean for an instinct to be converted into its opposite except either that it feels different to the individual, or that it issues in behaviour in a different way, both of these presumably involving reaction-formation?[19]

All this makes it difficult to compare the Freudian notion of reversal in any detailed way with its use in reversal theory. However, several obvious differences do exist in the use of the concept in the two theories. Firstly, in reversal theory, the reversals themselves take place between pairs of metamotivational states, whereas in Freudian theory the reversals take place between particular needs or feelings. Secondly, reversal would appear to be seen by Freud as a fairly irreversible procedure, except in pathological ambivalence as found in obsessional neurotics. In reversal theory, reversal is normally, in contrast, a continuing process: for us, reversals remain reversible.[20]

There have been two basic aims in this chapter. One has been to emphasize the need to look beyond the concepts of homeostasis and equilibrium in psychology, especially in the area of motivation, and to combat the assumption that seems to underlie so much of psychology and sociology that central tendencies, uniformities and consistencies lie at the heart of normal behaviour. Our belief is that human psychological processes are more complex and less consistent than generally appears to be assumed in the behavioural and social sciences, and that it is possible to approach this complexity and inconsistency systematically through the use of concepts like those of reversal, bistability, multistability, opposing preferred states and dominance. The second aim of the chapter has been to explain these concepts at a general level, as a preliminary to using them in an attempt to elucidate something of the dynamics of conscious experience, and in turn to throw light on various aspects of behaviour. In this connection the concept of metamotivational states has also been introduced. It is now possible to look in more detail at one of these pairs of states.

Notes on Chapter 2

1. Russett (1966) has traced the use of the concept of equilibrium in sociology in detail in her book "The Concept of Equilibrium in American Social Thought".
2. Even here it must be recognized that cyberneticians were not the first to think of homeostasis

at a general level, what today would be called the level of general systems theory. As long ago as 1913, L. J. Henderson drew analogies between homoeostatic physiological systems, the adjustments of personality in the individual, and equilibrium in social systems.

3. The term 'value' here is, of course, being used in its mathematical rather than its philosophical or sociological sense.

4. A vector is a compound variable made up of a set of variables, the state of the vector at a given time being given by the value of each of these variables, e.g. position on a two-dimensional map is a vector made up of two variables, both of which are needed to specify any particular position.

5. Of course, if the marble is not given enough time to come to rest before releasing the cross-piece, this adds a great deal of complication to the system because there will be interactions between the acceleration of the marble and the acceleration of the movement of the cross-piece.

6. This is illustrated widely in introductory texts, e.g. Hilgard et al. (1975) p.136, McConnell (1977), p.207. The change involves such reversals as young to old, or vice versa, and beautiful to ugly, or vice versa.

7. Illustrated for example in Freeman (1948), p.393. A reversal occurs from seeing the picture in a left-to-right fashion to seeing it as right-to-left, or vice versa.

8. For a psycholinguistic discussion of ambiguity, and further examples, see Fodor et al. (1974), pp.361-367.

9. For more details, see for example Freeman (1948), pp.253-255.

10. Such as using a sequence of both positive and negative conditioned stimuli, i.e. stimuli which both signal that there *will* be reinforcement and are therefore excitatory, and which signal that there will be *no* reinforcement and are therefore inhibitory.

11. Some examples of such experiments will be found in Pavlov (1960), lecture XVI.

12. For a representative review of this whole area of reversals in sexual behaviour, see Grossman (1967).

13. This is a different use of the term 'metamotivation' from that adopted by Maslow (1973), who also uses this term in his theorizing. For Maslow a metamotive is a motive which is 'higher' than motives related to such 'basic' needs as the need for food or safety. 'Self-actualizing' people are said to be primarily motivated by metamotivations. The reversal theory use of the prefix 'meta' is strictly the more logically correct, and follows Bertrand Russell's usage in developing his theory of logical types (Russell, 1903).

14. We were tempted to refer to these states as 'metaintentional' rather than metamotivational, taking advantage of the ambiguity of the term 'intentional' so as to emphasize both the motivational aspect of the states and the way in which they influence the whole way in which the world is construed at a given time. 'Intentional' is ambiguous because it has an everyday sense, that of 'done on purpose', and a more technical phenomenological sense in which it characterizes the property of consciousness that it is always consciousness *of* something, and that it is always in this sense referential.

15. Although the term 'state' is being used here in a cybernetic sense, it is not being used in the sense sometimes used in cybernetics of meaning a characteristic of a system such that, given the environmental input to the system at that moment we can predict the resulting behaviour of the system at the next moment, together with the new state of the system at the next moment (see note 3 of Chapter 1).

16. Metamotivational systems are viewed here as being different systems, like alternative computer subroutines, so that a change from one to the other must necessarily be a discrete switch. It is therefore not the case that on some occasions the switch is discontinuous and on other occasions it is continuous to some degree or another. So, although a reversal is a form of catastrophe, it does not seem that it is in itself one to which 'catastrophe theory' (Thom, 1975) could be usefully applied, since the interest of catastrophe theory is mainly in explaining why sudden jumps sometimes occur in the value of a variable, in relation to one or more smoothly

changing control factors, and not at other times. It is of course possible that the strength of factors, like frustration and satiation, which induce reversal may show discontinuities and that catastrophe theory could throw light on these; for the time being, however, it is assumed that these factors change smoothly and act in a straightforward additive or subtractive fashion, a reversal being induced by them when some threshold is exceeded.

17. An equivalent analogy would be to see the cross-piece as much wider, with the marble able to run up and down one or another of a number of parallel grooves. Then the second step in the sequence would involve the choice of groove for the single marble.

18. This is to be distinguished from yet another use of the term 'reversal' in Freud's writing, namely 'chronological reversal', by which is meant that analysis follows a reversed course in tracing the origins of symptoms (Freud and Breuer, 1955, p.75n, p.124; originally published 1895).

19. An excellent recent discussion of Freud's concept of reversal will be found in D. Fontana's Ph.D. thesis entitled "An Investigation of Reversal and Obsessionality" (Fontana, 1978).

20. Georges Thinès has suggested that the theory should be called the 'Theory of Reversibility', which would emphasize this point (pers. comm.).

3 Telic and Paratelic States

The first pair of metamotivational states to be considered consists of the 'telic state' and the 'paratelic state'. The definition of these states, as already emphasized, is a phenomenological one since it is based on the way in which the subject himself sees his actions, not on the judgement of an external observer. These two states are characterized at some length in the first part of the chapter, the later part of the chapter dealing more with the nature and significance of reversals between them.

Characteristics of Telic and Paratelic States

The telic state is defined as a phenomenological state in which the individual is primarily oriented towards, or feels the need to be primarily oriented towards, some essential goal or goals. The paratelic state, in contrast, is defined as a state in which the individual is primarily oriented towards, or feels the need to be primarily oriented towards, some aspect of his continuing behaviour and its related sensations. The phrase 'primarily oriented towards' is meant to imply that the feature of experience concerned is 'at the focus of attention' rather than 'at the fringe of attention' i.e. it is part of the 'figure' rather than the 'ground' in the phenomenal field. Following Snygg and Combs (1949), the phenomenal field will be defined as the entire universe, including himself, as it is experienced by the individual at the instant of action.[1]

What this comes to, then, is that in the telic state the continuing activity acquires its primary meaning from the goal which the individual is attempting to attain. In the paratelic state, the ongoing activity is its own justification; if there is a goal, which is not necessarily the case, then the goal in this sense acquires its meaning from the activity rather than vice versa. Examples will be given in due course. These are the minimal definitions of the two states but, as will become apparent, they are more complex than might immediately appear from these definitions.

47

The word 'telic' has been coined from the ancient Greek word 'telos' meaning a goal or end, which is the root of the word 'teleology'.[2] The word 'paratelic' has been coined by adding the ancient Greek word 'para', meaning 'beside' or 'alongside'[3] to the word 'telic'. The two states, and the systems underlying them, are alternative ways which the individual has available to him of interpreting certain aspects of his life-world at a given moment.

Obviously those goals which are seen as being essential will change from individual to individual, and will change from time to time in the same individual. But, in general, goals which are seen to be essential fall into four classes.

1. Goals which are physiologically essential

This class is made up of goals with a physiological origin which the individual feels to be essential for himself at a given moment. From the point of view of an outside observer, e.g. a physiologist or a biologist, the individual may of course be mistaken about how crucial they are; but if he himself feels that the goal he is oriented towards is essential, then he is in the telic state. Examples of goals in this general category are the goals of avoiding danger, reducing pain, or over-coming strong hunger. Generally, these goals are ones which are necessary for biological survival in the relatively short term; if they are more long term the individual is more likely to be able to relegate them to the inessential *at the moment in question*.

2. Goals which are socially essential

Goals in this class are goals with a sociological origin which the individual feels to be essential. As before, from the point of view of an outside observer, he may be mistaken; but if he himself interprets the goal in this way, then he is in the telic state at the moment in question. These goals are seen as being essential either because they relate to some social goal which the individual believes is important for himself, like the achievement of status, power or affiliation, or because they are seen by him as essential to other members of his community, and necessary for their well-being. Examples of goals in this category might be attending church for feelings of affiliation, going to the office to earn money in order to achieve status, or working for a charity to help others who are desperately in need.

3. Goals which are essential to self-esteem

Phrased in a way which more nearly parallels the physiological case, these goals could be described as being necessary to the survival, if not of the individual's body, then of his self-esteem. This category largely overlaps the previous category, since goals like status and power are inextricably linked with self-image, as is the feeling of doing one's duty towards others. But the overlap is not necessarily complete and there may be goals which are essential to self-esteem which have not been imposed by society and which are not seen by the individual as imposed by society. For example one may do something to prove that one is capable of doing it, and no one else need know. The goal may be to put up with pain without complaining, to understand nuclear physics, or to overcome some unreasonable fear. Other examples in this general category might include the goal of passing an examination, being sexually desirable or, in some cultures, of safeguarding one's honour.

4. Goals which are essential to the well-being of the family

The goal of protecting and helping the members of one's family, or other people with whom one might have an intimate relationship, will also be felt to be essential at certain times. This category overlaps the other three, except that the focus is now on one's family, or on other people in one's community with whom one has an intimate relationship, rather than oneself. For example, there are goals which are seen as essential for one's child's physical health and safety, and, especially when the child is older, his social status, self-respect, and so on. The goals which the adult sees as essential for his or her child, e.g. the goal of acquiring social status, are not necessarily felt by the child at the time as essential, but such goals may later be learned to be felt as essential by the child from his parent's attitude. Note also that a goal chosen by a child in a paratelic state, and therefore not felt as essential by the child, e.g. to have a certain toy, may be felt as a telic goal by the child's parents, if they see it as their duty to make the child happy. Of course the converse may also occur: the youngster may see some goal, like owning a horse, as being essential, but the child's parents may fail to see this goal in the same light.

If someone is oriented towards an essential goal or goals of any of these types at a given time, then he or she may be said to be in a telic state and the resulting behaviour directed towards these goals to be telic behaviour. By contrast, in the paratelic state of mind, the goals, if there are any, are not seen as being essential. This means that they are not felt as being imposed either physiologically, or socially, in terms of the psychological necessity of maintaining or improving self-esteem, or by family needs. Here are some examples where there may be no goals at all, over and above the pleasure of the behaviour itself: throwing stones into the sea, singing in the bath, dancing at a discothèque, rowing down the river, smoking a pipe, chewing gum or walking in the rain. There is a sense, in each of these activities, in which the activity is itself the goal. Sometimes even the behaviour is minimal, and the pleasure is in the concomitant sensations, perceptions, thoughts and emotions, the continuing process here being largely unobservable from outside. Examples would include many of those listed in relation to minimal behaviour in Chapter 1, and many other examples of minimal behaviour could be added, like sitting in a café and watching the world go by. However, more usually in the paratelic state one would expect inessential goals to be experienced, obvious examples being the goals involved in most hobbies or in sports and games of all kinds.

One way of putting the distinction between these two metamotivational states is to say that in the telic state the goals pursued appear to the individual to be *imposed* on him, by the needs either of his own body, of society, of self-esteem, or of his family. In contrast, where goals are experienced in the paratelic state, they have the phenomenological quality of being *freely chosen* and the resulting activity freely entered into. In some situations, goals seem to be imposed in behaviour performed in the paratelic state, e.g. the goal of scoring points in any ball game. But if the game itself is freely entered into, then in this respect the goals of the game are also freely chosen. To put this in another way, goals in the telic state appear in the last analysis to be *unavoidable*, whereas in the paratelic state they are seen in principle to be *avoidable*. This is the basic difference between 'inessential' and 'essential' goals. In the telic state, therefore, the individual feels as if he is reacting to some need which is unavoidably imposed on him; in the paratelic state he feels as if he is acting spontaneously. This contrast can be put in its strongest form by saying that in the telic state the individual tends to feel himself to be *reactive*, in the paratelic state *proactive*.

As has been indicated, the paratelic state is not necessarily oriented towards a goal at all, but rather towards behaviour in itself, and its experiential concomitants. In these terms the two states may be contrasted as follows: the telic state is 'goal-oriented' in that it starts with goals and then looks for behaviour to achieve them, whereas the paratelic state is 'behaviour-oriented' in that it starts with behaviour, and may then look for a goal which could be achieved through such behaviour or which would be a suitable end-point for the behaviour.[4] In the paratelic case, then, the goal may be no more than an excuse to perform certain behaviour, or perform it in a certain way, e.g. to find something to collect, or to have an excuse to perform a skill, as in carpentry. This could be put rather paradoxically by saying that the end in this eventuality is used as a means, and the means becomes the end; in other words, there is a means–ends reversal.

Since the paratelic state is oriented towards immediate experience in all its aspects, of which the kinesthetic sensation of behaviour itself is only one aspect, there would be something to be said for calling it 'process-oriented' rather than 'behaviour-oriented'; in this case it could be contrasted with the 'end-oriented' nature of the telic state. The use of the word 'process' would have the advantage that it would not exclude 'thinking', and other externally unobservable processes like those involved in minimal behaviour, in the way in which the term 'behaviour' may be taken to do. This is important because the orientation of the paratelic state can be towards the enjoyment of thinking as well as behaviour, or towards some experience which is enjoyed passively with the minimum of overt behaviour. Furthermore, it would emphasize that part of the enjoyment of behaviour may be in the immediate perceptible effect which it has on the environment. Thus the enjoyment of throwing pebbles into a pond is not just the throwing behaviour, but the perception of the effect of this behaviour, i.e. the fact that it causes something interesting to happen. Similarly, when a child plays with sand, mud, paints, or clay, he is clearly intrigued with the shapes and forms which are thrown up, and with the whole process of manipulating the world. The paratelic state might therefore equally well be described as 'activity-oriented'.

One further aspect of this difference is that the tendency of the paratelic state is to *prolong* the ongoing activity, since if it is pleasant, termination will be regretted, although the regret may be offset a little by the achievement of some goal, however arbitrary or inessential. The tendency of the telic state is normally to *complete* the activity as rapidly as possible in order to accomplish the goal.[5] *In fact, a good test of whether a given person's activity is telic or not is whether the person concerned would willingly give it up in exchange for any goal which that activity might have.* If he would prefer his activity to be already successfully completed, he is likely to be the telic state; if he would prefer to be in the course of performing that activity, then he is probably in the paratelic state. This does not apply, of course, if the activity is an obviously unpleasant one. In this case someone in the paratelic state might wish to exchange the activity *for another activity*, but would still be unlikely to want to exchange it for the goal of the activity.

All the pairs of adjectives or adjectival phrases used so far to describe the phenomenological qualities of the defining aspects of these two opposing states are listed at A in Table I.

A second type of phenomenological characteristic which distinguishes the two states is that the telic state is typically 'future-oriented', since any goal which is being pursued is in the future, while the paratelic state is 'present-oriented'. In terms of Lewin's concept of life-space it could be said that someone in the telic state has a life-space with a longer time dimension than someone in the paratelic state, who tends to be relatively restricted to the present moment. In fact, in the telic state, this time-dimension may extend backwards to some extent as well as forwards, so that there may be pleasurable awareness in the telic state of a goal which *has been achieved*.

Furthermore, in the telic state, life-space may be organized in terms of a complex structure of goals and routes to goals, which may extend into the relatively distant future, whereas such goal structures as there are in the paratelic state are likely to be rather simple. In other words, in the telic state, there will be a tendency to *plan ahead*, whereas in the paratelic state of mind there will be a tendency to be more *spontaneous*, to take things as they come, to do things 'for the heck of it' and to 'live for the moment'.

TABLE I. *A listing of some of the contrasting characteristics of the telic and paratelic states.*

	TELIC	PARATELIC
A. Means–ends dimension	Essential goals	No essential goals
	Imposed goals	Freely-chosen goals
	Unavoidable goals	Avoidable goals
	Reactive	Proactive
	Goal-oriented	Behaviour-oriented
	End-oriented	Process-oriented
	Attempts to complete activity	Attempts to prolong activity
B. Time dimension	Future-oriented	Present-oriented
	'Points beyond itself'	'Sufficient unto itself'
	Planned	Spontaneous
	Pleasure of goal anticipation	Pleasure of immediate sensation
	High significance preferred	Low significance preferred
C. Intensity dimension	Low intensity preferred	High intensity preferred
	Synergies avoided	Synergies sought
	Generally realistic	Make-believe prevalent
	Low arousal preferred	High arousal preferred

For explanation of these summarizing adjectives and phrases, reference should be made to the text.

This leads us to a crucial difference between the two states. In the telic state current behaviour tends to 'point beyond itself', not only in the sense that it derives its significance from the goals concerned, but in the sense that these goals may in turn derive their significance by 'pointing beyond themselves' to yet further goals. The paratelic state, on the other hand, tends to be 'sufficient unto itself', its activities requiring no further justification beyond themselves. Another way of putting this is that the telic state tends to operate in such a way as to bring out and elaborate the significance to the actor of continuing actions in terms of wider contexts, while in the paratelic state the tendency is for each activity to be seen as far as possible as significant to itself alone, i.e. activities in this state tend to be cut off from the complex world of reality and to become phenomenologically 'encapsulated'. There may therefore be said to be a key experiential variable which differentiates between the two states, that of 'felt significance', which can be defined as the degree to which one sees the goal, and therefore behaviour towards the goal, as serving purposes beyond itself. In the telic state the preferred level of this variable is high: the individual attempts to interpret his life-world in such a way as to increase the level of this variable. In the paratelic state, on the other hand, the preferred level of the variable is low, the attempt being made by the individual to construe his life-world in such a way as to decrease the level of this variable. Since the attainment of preferred levels of experiential variables is associated with positive hedonic tone, high felt significance is experienced with pleasure in the telic state, and low felt significance with displeasure; while high felt significance is experienced with displeasure in the paratelic state, and low felt significance with pleasure.

   The definition of significance is different from the definition of 'essentialness', the latter being basically about whether or not a goal is avoidable at a given time. Whether or not a goal is seen as essential determines which state/system, telic or paratelic, is *operative*; felt significance by contrast, is a variable which is *operated on* by the telic or paratelic states/systems.[6] Although perceived essentialness may be a continuous variable, there is a threshold such that change of value across it, for whatever combination of reasons, will trigger a metamotivational reversal. Felt significance on the other hand is a continuous variable with two preferred levels, one for each metamotivational state, which may or may not be attained at a given time. A goal may therefore be experienced as sufficiently unavoidable and essential for the telic state to be induced, but the significance of the goal in the way defined may be perceived as high or low in the telic state, i.e. it may have a great deal of significance beyond itself or little; or, indeed, significance may be experienced anywhere along a 'significance dimension'. For example, the goal of getting served in a restaurant if one is hungry, may feel essential at the time, but would probably have low felt significance, whereas the goal of getting promoted at work would be likely to have high felt significance. The whole range of significance may similarly be experienced in relation to a goal in the paratelic state, if there happens to be a salient goal in that state at the time in question. Thus, the goal of winning a particular game of squash might be seen as having various further implications in terms of some club competition and therefore might be associated with high felt significance, even if, at the same time, it is not felt to be essential. The goal of hitting with pebbles a tin can floating on a pond, on the other hand, would presumably be associated in most people with low felt significance, as well as being inessential. The felt significance variable is independent of goal achievement: a goal may at a particular moment have any degree of felt significance and have been achieved or not. There must, however, be a goal to be achieved, or a goal which has just been achieved, for significance to be experienced to any extent. When there is no goal at all, which is often the case in the paratelic state, then felt significance will necessarily be minimal.

   In the telic state, therefore, the individual attempts to see every goal in a larger context. This larger context may be an individual one, for example in terms of his own career structure; or the context may be more impersonal, for example, it may be moral, political or historical. Simple goals, however urgent, e.g. to assuage hunger, are therefore felt as unsatisfactory in the telic state, unless they can be given some wider subjective meaning. In the paratelic state, wider meanings are generally eschewed and the continuing activity may even be felt to be 'prostituted' in some way if justifications for it are preferred.

Although it is possible for an activity in the paratelic state to be enjoyed for long periods through the experience of *immediate and continuing sensations*, both those which derive exteroceptively from environmental stimulation and interoceptively from the exercise of skilled activity, enjoyment in the telic state is not restricted to goal achievement. It can now be appreciated that there are a number of sources of pleasure which can be derived from continuing actions in the telic state. For one thing, as has just been indicated, pleasure may derive from the feelings of significance which attach to the pursuit of a goal, whether or not it is achieved or near to being achieved. For another, pleasure may also come from *anticipation of goal achievement*, which is enhanced if one feels that one is actually making progress towards the goal. In the telic state the individual may divide the path to the goal into many subgoals, and the attainment of each of these will then be pleasurable in itself.[7] Pleasure may also derive from a feeling of purposefulness, determination and commitment. None of this means that the achievement of a goal in the paratelic state, a realization that one is making progress towards the goal, or the experience of purposefulness, cannot add some degree of pleasure to someone in that state. Neither does any of this imply that certain kinds of sensations cannot be enjoyed in the telic state. It is rather a question of *orientation* within the phenomenal field. In one case the focus of attention within the phenomenal field is on the achievement of an essential goal, in the other it is on the enjoyment of continuing experience. So in one case the individual is particularly sensitive to one source of pleasure or displeasure, in the other case to another. In the former case, such pleasurable sensations as there are, are a bonus; in the latter case goal achievement is a bonus. (In both cases, however, as will become clear, there is equal sensitivity to the experience of arousal.)

This second type of characteristic, which is concerned with the time dimension, does not necessarily always occur along with the characteristic which defines the two states. For example, an urgent goal may need to be achieved in the near future, and may allow for little planning ahead; an important goal may, through the emotion it arouses, produce an inability to think clearly enough to plan ahead. Conversely, daydreaming about some distant future may be engaged in for its own pleasure. By and large, though, one would expect future-orientation and planning ahead to be related to telic goal-orientation. The various pairs of adjectives and phrases used in discriminating these two states in terms of the time dimension are listed at B in Table I.

A third type of phenomenological characteristic which distinguishes the telic and paratelic states is that, in the telic state there is a tendency to act in such a way as to lower the intensity of experience, while in the paratelic state there is a tendency to act in such a way as to heighten it. In particular, the whole aim of the telic state is to lower the intensity of certain aspects of experience associated with the goals being pursued, e.g. hunger, pain, fear, loneliness and inferiority, since these are unpleasant. In contrast, the aim of the paratelic state is to enjoy experience, and so the attempt is to make the experience as intense as possible. So in one case the preferred level of intensity of experience is relatively low, in the other case it is relatively high.

One way in which intensity is increased is by means of 'synergies' which may, briefly, be described as the experience of contradictory meanings in relation to a given person, place, thing or situation. These are therefore *sought* in the paratelic state, but *avoided* as far as possible in the telic state, unless they can be used towards some goal. One major type of synergy involves 'make-believe', which is therefore much more prevalent in the paratelic than the telic state, the latter generally being much more realistic. The whole topic of synergy is a complicated one to which several chapters are devoted later on.

A central feature of intensity of experience is how aroused one feels and, therefore, in the telic state 'low arousal' is preferred, while in the paratelic state there is a preference for 'high arousal'. Arousal is defined here in the phenomenological sense as 'felt arousal', rather than in a physiological sense, although the two are obviously related. So, if the defining of characteristic of the telic state is to achieve essential goals, then one might say that it is *ipso facto* to overcome the arousal which is associated with these goals before they are achieved. If the defining characteristic of the paratelic state is to enjoy the feelings associated with current behaviour, then arousal is likely to play a central part in the experience of the intensity of these feelings. Since it is assumed that the attainment of the preferred level of a metamotivational variable is pleasurable, while a lack of congruity between the preferred and the actual level of the variable is unpleasant, then low arousal will be experienced as pleasant in the telic state and unpleasant in the paratelic state, and vice versa for high arousal.

Other things being equal, the telic system will generate behaviour aimed at lowering felt arousal and the paratelic system will generate behaviour aimed at increasing felt arousal, so that the value of the felt arousal variable will tend to move in opposite directions in the two states. Thus the telic system will tend to produce behaviour designed to achieve goals, including escaping from danger, and therefore reduce arousal. The paratelic system will produce behaviour designed to bring the individual into contact with arousal-generating stimulation of one kind or another.

It is being assumed in all this that felt arousal is a phenomenological reflection of some aspect of physiological arousal, so that the arousal system is a system in its own rights on which the telic and paratelic systems operate (typically indirectly, through changing the environmental situation). They may be more or less successful in doing this, and will in any case have to overcome certain features of the arousal system which may not always work in the required direction. In particular, left to its own devices, the arousal system may be innately homeostatic rather than bistable, and the telic and paratelic systems may have to overcome a built-in tendency to intermediate levels of arousal on the part of the arousal system. Generally, they appear to be strong enough to be able to do this.

Although appropriately low arousal will always be felt as pleasant in the telic state and unpleasant in the paratelic state, and vice versa for high arousal, it is not necessarily the case that low arousal will always be pursued in the telic state and high arousal in the paratelic state. This is because there are alternative ways of achieving pleasure and avoiding displeasure in each state, and the pursuit of these may on occasion override the pursuit of the appropriate levels of arousal. Therefore, unpleasant levels of arousal may be tolerated in each state if they are compensated by other factors which contribute to the overall hedonic tone at a given time.

As already noted, high felt significance is pleasant in the telic state and unpleasant in the paratelic state, and vice versa for low felt significance, and the pursuit of the preferred level of this variable may on occasion override the pursuit of the preferred level of felt arousal. Indeed, some conflict may be experienced within each state, since high felt significance may be associated with increased arousal and low felt significance with decreased arousal. Thus, a goal which is felt to be highly significant may produce more arousal than one which is not and may be chosen to be pursued in the telic state because of its significance, despite the high arousal associated with it. (The pleasure of goal achievement may be enhanced in this case, as well.) For example, the goal which a politician might have of giving an important speech may well have meaning in terms of longer term career ambitions, and be pursued in the telic state by him even though he is more worried about the effects of failure than he would be about a less important speech. The pursuit of the goal is invested with both high significance and high arousal. The same might be true of a musician planning a concert and rehearsing for it, or a boxer arranging fighters and training for them. Conversely, in the paratelic state an individual may prefer to pursue a goal with high significance because it tends to increase the level of arousal, in this case the preferred arousal level taking precedence over the preferred significance level. Thus many sports and hobbies involve complex goal structures, so that each goal points beyond itself to some further goal, increasing the significance and arousal of each of the goals in turn. There is a danger here that such a situation will tend to induce the telic state, as indeed it may well do for most professional sportsmen, although the paratelic nature of the situation may be safeguarded if the whole goal-structure can be encapsulated in such a way that it has no significance beyond itself.

There is another respect in which the preferred level of arousal will not necessarily be the key factor at a particular time. In the paratelic state, high arousal is only one aspect of intense experience and, at a given moment, some aspect of experience other than arousal may take priority and be at the focus of the phenomenal field. For instance, in sunbathing in a paratelic state of mind, a low arousal level may be 'compensated for' by the intense sensation of heat and other pleasant sensations that often accompany sunbathing, like the sound and smell of the sea. In other words, when the individual is searching for a high intensity of experience, he may be able to choose between different aspects of experience. So, in the paratelic state he may not be seeking high arousal at the moment in question, but seeking some other intense sensation instead. For this reason, behaviour in the paratelic state can be active, as it tends to be where the search for high arousal and/or kinesthetic sensation predominates, or minimal and passive where the predominant interest is in the experience of sensations of the exteroceptive type.

One implication of the preceding discussion is that the telic and paratelic states each involve two sub-systems, one regulating in terms of felt significance and the other in terms of felt arousal, one or other of these taking precedence at a given moment. Whichever system takes precedence determines which variable is chosen for regulation if there is a conflict between them. Choice of variable in this sense, however, has no effect on the *relationship* between the level of each variable and hedonic tone, e.g. high felt arousal is still unpleasant in the telic state even if the felt significance variable is taking precedence at the moment in question; and low arousal is unpleasant in the paratelic state even if some other aspect of the experience is highly intense.

It is possible to treat each of these sub-systems as a metamotivational system in its own rights, each regulating its own metamotivational variable. Both sub-systems, that for felt arousal and that for felt significance, remain operative at all times; what alters is their success in expressing behaviour which will tend to aid the regulation of their respective variables. In turn each of these sub-systems is made up of two opposing metamotivational sub-systems. For example, in relation to felt arousal, one sub-system interprets high arousal as pleasant and the other as unpleasant, the first producing behaviour which tends to increase the level of arousal and the second producing behaviour which tends to diminish it. These two arousal-regulating systems will in fact be treated as a pair of metamotivational systems in their own rights in the next two chapters, although their telic and paratelic context is not lost sight of; and, where it is convenient to do so, the two arousal-regulating systems will continue to be referred to as telic and paratelic.

Just as at B in Table I a listing was made of the key descriptive phrases which distinguished between the telic and paratelic states in terms of the dimension of temporality, so the list at C in Table I does the same thing in terms of the dimension of intensity.

Although the telic and paratelic states may therefore be defined fairly easily, in terms of the presence of absence of goals which appear to the individual to be essential, in fact there are a number of linked sets of characteristics which tend to reverse as concomitants of the defining features, and some of these may conflict with each other. The situation is reminiscent of that obtaining between the sympathetic and parasympathetic systems, in that both these branches of the autonomic nervous system involve a set of different, but related, functions which are usually, if not always, concomitant.

Neither state, telic or paratelic, is regarded as more basic than the other. Certainly there is a sense in which one could conceive of the paratelic state as underlying a process of continuous activity, this state being replaced as and when needed by the telic state which then temporarily shapes the continuing behaviour towards some goal. But equally, one could conceive of the telic as being the basic state in which all the necessary goals are pursued, and which is replaced temporarily by the paratelic only after all these goals have been satisfied. Furthermore, there is certainly no intention to make moral judgements about the two states, to say that one is intrinsically more desirable than the other. Nor is there intended to be any implication that more pleasure is associated with one state than the other; this is something which is likely to vary from one person to another, and from time to time. However, that which is found to be pleasant (and it is legitimate to speak of pleasure here rather than reinforcement, since the domain of discourse is phenomenological rather than behavioural) will be expected to change radically. Reward is context dependent, not just in the behavioural or social sense,[8] but in the phenomenological sense described here in relation to the telic and paratelic contexts. Among other things, this has important implications for psychological research in that it may be important to identify the state of mind of the subject during the course of an experiment.

Although the two states have the same status within the theory, one of them is likely to be dominant in a given individual, i.e. the individual will have a tendency to be more often in one state than the other. The highly telic dominant individual would be one whose life tends to be centred around what he sees as essential goals and who spends much of his time in their pursuit; he is likely to plan ahead into the future, to avoid high arousal, and so on. The highly paratelic dominant individual is likely to have the opposite characteristics. It is therefore not part of the definition of a bistable system that the alternative stable states are operative for equal periods.

Two Examples

An example of an action which would normally be expected to be performed in a telic state of mind would be that of working for an examination. Here the goal of passing the examination is usually felt to be an essential one. Such a goal would normally be felt to be imposed—perhaps, in the case of a child, by parents, school or potential employers—so that the pursuit of the goal is felt in this sense to be unavoidable. Assuming that the examination is some time ahead, work may need to be planned over the period available. If the goal is seen in the perspective of an intended career, for which passing the examination is an essential preliminary, one's orientation when working towards the goal will obviously be towards the future in this respect too. This future perspective will be emphasized where there is a clear realization that passing or failing could have an enduring effect on the whole of the rest of one's life, and that the examination therefore "points beyond itself" in a significant way. The work itself is perhaps not pleasant, so one tries to finish it on each occasion as quickly as possible. But as the required books are read and essays written, great satisfaction is gained from the feeling of purposefulness, the realization of the progress that is being made, and from anticipation of attaining the goal. Difficulties, e.g. concepts not immediately understood, are not welcomed and tend to increase felt arousal which is unpleasant. If possible, one avoids such difficulties, but they usually have to be confronted and overcome; overcoming them, however, provides a real feeling of accomplishment. This feeling is a foretaste of the strong satisfaction and sense of achievement which should occur when the examination is eventually taken and passed.

In contrast, a good illustration of an action normally performed in the paratelic state of mind is afforded by the activity of swimming. Unless one happens to be a competitive swimmer in serious training, or competing, this is an activity which is not normally goal oriented at all. If there are goals, they are most unlikely to be seen as essential, or to be felt as imposed from outside. Goals like racing a friend from one side of the pool to the other, or seeing how long one can stay under water, are self-chosen and engaged in freely. One's orientation is likely to be towards the pleasure of the behaviour in itself in the present, rather than towards a goal in some distant future. What one asks is to be able to enjoy performing a particular skill or skills. Furthermore, there is the pleasure that derives from the various sensations of diving and swimming: the feeling of release as one dives, the cool shock of hitting the water, the murky other-worldliness beneath the water, the sudden burst of noise and colour as one surfaces, and the sensation of being buoyed up. Then, as one swims, one experiences the feeling of surging movement, of water streaming over one's skin, and the impression of temporary escape from gravity and freedom to move in any direction. All these may be intense experiences of exactly the kind which are relished in the paratelic state. At the same time, one attempts in a variety of ways to increase one's arousal and maintain it at a high level. Hence the challenges to races across the bath, the underwater endurance tests, the deliberately invoked danger of high diving, and all the mock fighting that appears to occur almost continuously on the fringe of swimming pools as people chase and splash each other, or throw each other into the pool, to the accompaniment of continual shouting. An ethological study of the behaviour of human beings in, and on the edge of, swimming pools would probably provide a very general insight into the variety of techniques which may be used by human beings to obtain and to maintain high arousal. The various contrasts involved may also serve to heighten the intensity of the experience: there are the alternating contrasts of being wet and dry, hot and cold, of violent activity and motionless passivity and, in diving, of being high above the surface of the water and deep beneath it in quick succession. These opposite sensations, perceptions and apperceptions are contrasted in this way as part of a deliberate attempt to increase the intensity of the experience. Additionally, 'make-believe' synergies may be involved: one may pretend humorously to be a fish or a boat, or in diving, a bird; imagine oneself rescuing someone from drowning, or being a frogman or deep-sea diver. Finally, there will normally be some reluctance to leave when the time comes to do so, and feelings of regret at being unable to prolong the activity.

Some Notes on Terminology

It must be emphasized that the word 'essential' as used in the definition of the two states does not necessarily mean 'biologically essential' or, indeed, 'essential' in any sense other than 'phenomenologically essential', by which is meant that it is seen as unavoidable and necessary by the person concerned at the moment in question. As was pointed out in discussing gratuitous and paradoxical behaviour in Chapter 1, that which is seen by an individual as being essential may or may not be essential in the biological sense. Using the terminology which has been introduced in the present chapter, this can now be restated by saying that it is true of both telic and paratelic actions that they may, or may not, be related to essential biological goals, although one would expect the relationship to such goals to be more frequent in the telic case.

It is easy to be mistaken, when observing someone else's actions, about which state of mind he or she is in: it is not necessarily possible to tell from a piece of behaviour in itself, when observed from the outside, whether it is performed in a telic or paratelic state. What is felt as being essential to one person is not necessarily felt in this way by another, or even by the same person at a different time. Watching television is normally a paratelic activity, but to the television critic it may be telic, unless he is 'off duty'. Reading poetry is normally a paratelic activity, but reading it in preparation for an examination may make it telic. Again, one person may be driven to do charity work by conscience which imposes this essential social goal on him, another because it is a hobby which he undertakes because he enjoys it. Indeed, perhaps the second person does it because he gets pleasure from the very feeling that what he is doing is more than what is required of him, and that he has therefore chosen it freely. Furthermore, the same person doing charity work may well interpret his actions in these two different ways at different times. Behaviour, which on the surface may appear to be related to a paratelic state of mind, e.g. playing a game, may in fact be performed in a telic state of mind. This is certainly likely to be the case with professional sportsmen whose very livelihood depends on their success, but it may also be true of amateurs who take their chosen sport seriously. For example, playing golf appears to be one of the most important activities in the lives of some people, and for those people their current handicap is one of the most salient components in their self-esteem. The game therefore is no longer played 'for fun', but in terms of what is seen by them as the essential goal of maintaining or improving their handicaps. To give another example, sunbathing may be undertaken either to enjoy the sensations involved or in order to acquire a suntan. In the latter case this goal would appear to be seen by some people as essential either in order to maintain a certain social status or to improve their self-image, especially in relation to sexual attractiveness, or for both of these reasons. In other words, it is undertaken in a telic frame of mind. Another example was given in the first chapter: that of driving a car at high speed. This action may be undertaken either to achieve a goal which, at the time, is seen as of overriding importance, or because the activity of driving fast is an enjoyable one.

It may have occurred to some readers that the word 'work' could be used to refer to activities performed in the telic state of mind and 'play' to those performed in the paratelic state. Although these everyday descriptive words have obvious affinities to the telic/paratelic distinction, it has been found necessary to avoid them. The main reason for this is that the words are used according to a convention which often runs counter to the phenomenological states which have been depicted here, i.e. 'work' is often paratelic and 'play' telic. This emphasizes the point made in the last paragraph. For example, playing football is something which is obviously likely to be a telic activity to a professional footballer (viz. Vinnai, 1973). The word 'work' is also sometimes equated with activity,[9] as in such phrases as "the footballer had a high work rate", used especially of English footballers, and this adds further confusion. Conversely, activities generally regarded as work may nevertheless be performed by people who, while performing them, are in a paratelic state for long periods. Scientific research would be a good example: certainly there are goals, but these are often regarded by researchers as pleasurable puzzles, like complex crosswords, and the research itself is enjoyed for its own sake. Similarly, school 'work' is not always a drudge but may be fun.

A second reason for avoiding the use of the words 'play' and 'work' to define the phenomenological states which have been labelled 'telic' and 'paratelic', is that both the words are too narrow in their range of reference to equate with telic and paratelic. For example, avoiding a car accident would undoubtedly be telic, but could hardly be called work, which usually implies an activity with some duration, and also perhaps routine repetiveness. For the same reason, having an argument with someone could hardly be called work, but might well be a telic action. Similarly, there are many activities which are usually carried out in a paratelic state of mind, but which would not normally be called 'play'. For example, having a drink in a bar, reading a newspaper, eating a good meal, watching television, swinging in a hammock, going for a walk, reading a novel and gossiping.

The basic problem is that the terms 'work' and 'play' tend to refer to behaviour rather than to states of mind, and this is generally true of the use of the word 'play' in psychology, as well as in its everyday context.[10] In contrast, the terms 'telic' and 'paratelic' are defined phenomenologically and not behaviourally, with the result that the range of human activities is categorized in a rather different way.

If the word 'work' is not appropriate, then it could still be argued that the word 'serious' might be taken as a synonym for 'telic' and 'playful' for 'paratelic'. 'Serious' would indeed be a better word for our purposes than 'work', since it is more often used to refer to an intention or a state of mind than 'work'. Unfortunately, it has other drawbacks. One is that it often means 'serious for other people' rather than for the person whose action is being described, e.g., arsony is serious in this sense, but it may not have been serious at all to the child who lit the match: it may have been an accident, or fun. Similarly, scientific research is often said to be serious, and certainly its implications for the community may be profound; but, as has just been argued, it may not be serious to the scientist himself all the time. Again, 'serious' can mean being 'determined' or 'being totally committed' as in 'He was serious about winning', whereas one can be determined to achieve a goal although recognizing it to be inessential. The word can even mean 'truthful' as in 'He meant it seriously' and this meaning of the word is even more remote from the meaning of 'telic' as defined. 'Serious' is a word, however, that does have affinities with the word 'telic' and it will therefore be used here occasionally where it seems appropriate to do so. As far as 'playful' is concerned, all the problems which relate to the word 'play' apply equally to 'playful'; but again, the word will be used here where it seems particularly appropriate in relation to 'paratelic'.

Consideration should also be given to the concept of 'alienation'. This comes originally from Marx, and refers to work which is not performed for its own sake but only as a means to an end, the end generally conceived by Marx as being subsistence or the acquisition of the necessities of life. Used in a more general sense, as it often is by sociologists, it refers to activity which is instrumental in achieving ends other than itself, rather than being expressive or carried out for its own intrinsic interest. Stated in this way it is clear that the telic state is an alienated state; indeed, the reference of the two terms, 'telic' and 'alienated', would appear to be coterminous. There are equally clear differences, however, between the way in which the term 'telic' is used in reversal theory and the way the term 'alienated' tends to be used. For one thing alienation is seen in Marxist theory and Marxist-inspired sociology, as arising from objective properties of certain patterns of social organization and therefore eliminable, rather than being an intrinsic and ubiquitous aspect of human nature as is the telic state according to reversal theory. Secondly, alienation is defined externally by the sociologist in terms of departure from some ideal conception of society and human nature which he has, and not phenomenologically by the people themselves and how they feel. For example, Holly (1971) has argued that the educational system in Britain is highly alienative because its whole orientation is instrumental, being concerned with pupils obtaining qualifications for the purpose of career advancement, rather than developing an intrinsic interest in the subjects themselves. This way of defining 'alienative' from outside does not take into account the fact that the pupils themselves, especially the intelligent and ambitious ones, may not feel themselves to be alienated by, or from, the educational system; they may identify with the system, adopt its values, and enjoy the progress they make through it. As Berry (1974) has pointed out, the would-be Oxbridge student may in the sociologist's sense be more alienated than the dull child: "The idea that alienation is greater where people are not involved is therefore quite false" (p.112). So alienation is not something which is necessarily perceived as any kind of estrangement by the people who are described by the sociologist as being alienated; rather, it is a judgement which is imposed on them by outside observers. This leads to the third difference between the term 'alienation' and 'telic state'. This is that the former term tends to be pejorative, to be used as a criticism of society and the actions of people in it, irrespective of the feelings of the people whose actions are being judged; the term 'telic state' is, in contrast, simply descriptive and neutral. Reversal theory makes no value judgements.

Returning to psychology, a distinction often made in relation to motivation is that between the two phases of 'appetitive' and 'consummatory' behaviour. The example usually cited in textbooks on learning theory is that of searching for food, which is appetitive, and then eating it, which is consummatory. Clearly, not all kinds of activities can be dichotomized in this way; for example, if an individual jumps clear of a car to avoid being run over, his avoidance behaviour can be seen as both appetitive and consummatory, since it is both an action to achieve something and its achievement. Much human activity is difficult to dichotomize clearly into appetitive and consummatory behaviour, because the goal does not obviously involve some specific form of behaviour. For example, what is the consummatory behaviour when one solves an intellectual problem, passes an examination, or gets off the train at the right station? For activities in which it is possible to identify consummatory behaviour, however, the consummatory behaviour itself is likely to be performed in a paratelic state of mind. For such activities, if the behaviour in pursuit of the goal involved was performed in the telic state, then the achievement of the goal is likely to induce a switch to the paratelic state for the enjoyment of consummatory behaviour. Take the example of eating. In this case one is not normally aware of any goal which the eating behaviour might have outside itself even if, physiologically, eating serves the goal of survival and is as essential as the appetitive behaviour which leads up to it. In eating, the taste of the food is enjoyed as well as the act of eating, but the act is also not without its satisfactions: if only the taste alone was enjoyed, one would presumably leave the food in one's mouth for as long as possible without chewing or swallowing. Eating in itself does not normally require conscious planning, although at the unconscious physiological level, co-ordination and planning is required. One's orientation to the activity is in the present, and one is sorry when it is completed. The more intense the experience, the more it is enjoyed. Indeed, in human behaviour every attempt is made to prolong and intensify consummatory behaviour, like eating, through various kinds of elaboration. (See in this respect the celebrated analysis of 'the raw and the cooked' by Lévi-Strauss, 1965). Once consummatory activity is completed, a reversal may occur once more to the telic state, in which the individual either looks back with satisfaction at the completion of the goal, or orients himself towards a new goal in the future. Alternatively, he might continue in the paratelic state by making pleasing conversation, smoking and imbibing alcohol. It should be clear, however, that while all consummatory behaviour is likely to be performed in a paratelic state of mind, the latter underlies much more than consummatory behaviour alone. An alternative formulation would be that the paratelic state automatically converts all ongoing behaviour into essentially consummatory behaviour.

The terms 'telic' and 'paratelic' need to be distinguished from several other pairs of terms which have been used by other writers:

(i) The terms 'intrinsic motivation' and 'extrinsic motivation' have been used by a number of writers in recent years of whom Deci (1975) is representative. Deci points out that there are various formulations of this distinction, but that ". . . a common element seems to be that intrinsically motivated activities are related to internally rewarding consequences which are located in the central nervous system and have no appreciable effect on non-nervous-system tissues" (p.24).

Extrinsically motivated activities, on the other hand, such as the need for food, according to this distinction do have primary effects on parts of the body other than the nervous system. Put in this way, it is obvious that the distinction between intrinsic and extrinsic motivation is, always, implicitly or explicitly, going to be a physiological or biological one, unlike the telic/paratelic distinction which is essentially phenomenological. Hence, the former distinction depends on whether or not certain bodily effects occur, the latter on whether certain types of experience do or do not occur. Thus intrinsic motivation cannot necessarily be equated with motivation in the paratelic state of mind, nor extrinsic motivation with motivation in the telic state of mind: someone may eat in the paratelic state of mind and play cards in a telic state of mind. Indeed, few particular motives can be unequivocally assigned to either the telic or paratelic state but many can be mediated by either state on different occasions. The same considerations would appear to apply to the use of the word 'autotelic' by such writers as Anderson and Moore (1960) and Klinger (1971).

(ii) Nuttin has used the terms 'means pleasure' and 'end pleasure' in a way which at first sight appears to be related to the telic/paratelic distinction. The way in which he uses the term 'means pleasure', however, discloses that he sees it in what we would describe as a telic context, i.e. the pleasure of making progress towards a goal (Nuttin, 1973, p.253-4). In the same paper, Nuttin refers to 'behavioural pleasure' and 'causality pleasure', but from the way in which he discusses these it is not entirely clear whether the pleasure is supposed to reside in the activity itself (as appears to be implied on p.245) or in its effects in attaining a goal (as appears to be implied on pp.251-2).

(iii) Csikszentmihalyi (1975) has identified and described what he refers to as 'flow experiences' in which there are no goals or rewards external to the experience itself, and the distinction between such experiences and non-flow experiences is obviously related to the telic/paratelic distinction. There are, however, forms of paratelic experience which do not correspond fully to Csikszentmihalyi's description of 'flow', e.g. one may feel bored in the paratelic state (see next chapter) but not in the 'flow' state. The paratelic and flow states are therefore not coterminous; rather, the flow experience would appear to be one form of paratelic experience.[11]

(iv) The reactive/proactive aspects of the distinction between the telic and paratelic states might seem to be related to Angyal's (1941) distinction between heteronomous events and autonomous events, the former referring to events originating outside the individual, the latter to events originating in the individual himself. Angyal's terms, however, relate to the causal attribution of events rather than to goals, and the attribution may be made by an onlooker, e.g. the psychologist, and not necessarily by the individual being observed. An autonomous event, as Angyal's defines it, *could* occur when one is in a telic state, since it could be brought about by the needs of the body.

(v) More similar to the telic/paratelic distinction is Kruglanski's distinction, in terms of attribution theory, between what he calls 'endogenous' and 'exogenous' attributions: "An action is said to be endogenously attributed when it is judged to constitute an end in itself and exogenously attributed when it is judged to serve as a means to some further end" (Kruglanski, 1975).

However, Kruglanski elaborates this distinction in a way which diverges from the conceptualization of the telic and paratelic states. In particular, he argues that an action which is endogenously attributed must be associated with positive affect ('derivation 5') and an action which is exogenously attributed must be associated with negative affect ('derivation 6'). According to reversal theory, on the contrary, an individual may find himself in the paratelic state but not enjoy the activities which he is at that moment engaged in, e.g. he may find them boring, or in the telic state and enjoy the progress he is making towards some future goal. In other words, the full range of hedonic tone may in principle be experienced in either the telic or the paratelic state in relation to any particular activity, and this is intrinsic to the nature of these states.

A final terminological point is that phrases like 'telic (or paratelic) behaviour' will occasionally be used here. There is really no such thing as a piece of telic, or paratelic, behaviour, since almost any behaviour can be performed in either state of mind. So what is really intended in these cases is 'behaviour performed at the moment in question in a telic (or paratelic) state of mind'. This type of shorthand will be used on occasion to avoid adjectival phrases which are long and clumsy. The reader must not, however, misunderstand the import of phrases in such shorthand which refer to the underlying state of mind current at the moment in question, and which are not intended to characterize any particular action or piece of behaviour in a permanent or universal way.

It might be objected that the distinction which has been made between the telic and paratelic states cannot be sustained, because it is subject to self-contradiction. In the paratelic state there are said to be no salient essential goals in the individual's phenomenal field, and yet there is, by definition, always one unavoidable goal in the paratelic state: the goal of obtaining pleasure from the continuing action or situation, and its associated sensations. This is an essential goal, according to such an argument, because it is implied in the definition of the paratelic state. This would be to miss the point, however, since the reversal theory analysis is not logical or linguistic, but phenomenological. The distinction between doing something because it is enjoyed in itself and doing it to achieve some future goal is one which, phenomenologically, is readily recognized. Rephrasing 'doing something because it is enjoyed in itself' as 'satisfying the essential goal of doing something which is enjoyed' would be to use language in such a way as to obscure a clear phenomenological difference. In any case the word 'essential' in this objection is being used in the linguistic sense of 'implied in the meaning of' rather than in the phenomenological sense of 'felt as being essential by the individual at a given moment'.[12] There is a sense in which one can *seek* to express behaviour or to achieve some kind of experience: namely, a situation in which the expression of the behaviour or the attainment of the experience is blocked in some way. For example, one can wish to ride a bicycle but discover that it has a puncture. In this case, if one sees the goal of being able to express the behaviour of cycling as essential, then one's state reverts to the telic until the puncture is mended. In general, to achieve the paratelic state at some later time can be a goal of telic activity. For instance, earning enough money to go climbing would be a telic activity if the enjoyment of the experience of climbing was felt to be something essential to be achieved at a later date; but the climbing itself might well be undertaken in a paratelic frame of mind.

To say that behaviour in the paratelic state has the ultimate goal of pleasure, whatever the means used, and in this sense is no different from behaviour in the telic state, is again to miss the phenomenological point that pleasure may come either from the movement towards, and attainment of, essential goals, as in the telic state, or from experience of some continuing action or current situation, as in the paratelic state. The pursuit of pleasure, and the avoidance of displeasure, may be said at some level of analysis or another to be reflected in all behaviour, but this trivial point does not invalidate the distinction which has been made here.

One further objection which similarly misses the point that the analysis in reversal theory is phenomenological, would be that all behaviour is reactive in some way to immediately preceding conditions, environmental or physiological, or both. Since there is no such thing as genuinely spontaneous behaviour, so this argument would run, this concept cannot be used as part of the definition of the paratelic state. Whether or not the assumption of determinism can be justified, in defining the paratelic state it is not asserted here that behaviour which occurs in this state *is* spontaneous, but only that it seems to be spontaneous and freely chosen to the person concerned, which is a different matter.

Telic/Paratelic Reversals

Reversal theory suggests that a person is in one state or the other, telic or paratelic, at all times during waking life, and that it is not possible to be in both states at the same time, since they are mutually exclusive. When reversal does occur it is rapid, and over time there is an alternation between the two states. In other words, the situation is like that relating to a perceptual reversal figure such as the Necker cube while it is being observed. An even better analogy would be to figure-ground reversals, in that there is a sense in which, as already indicated, goals in the telic state are part of the figure and means are part of the ground of the phenomenal field, the reverse being the case in the paratelic state. But unlike reversible figures, there are many different factors or circumstances which can bring about reversals between metamotivational states; these fall, as suggested previously, into three categories.

1. Contingency

The main cause of a reversal into the telic state will be the imposition on the individual of a goal which he sees as being essential. As discussed earlier, these goals are of various types. Biologically essential needs, like the need for food or drink for oneself or one's family, when they become sufficiently strong, may induce the telic state. So may various social needs, when they reach a given level of urgency and importance. Such needs might include the need for status, the need for affiliation, and the need to fulfil what is seen as being an essential and unavoidable duty of some kind. Which of these social needs are seen as essential and how urgent they have to be in order to be seen as essential will presumably depend largely on previous social learning. Finally, any kind of threat of physical danger of sufficient strength to oneself or one's family will cause a switch in the telic direction. So will any strong threat to one's self-esteem, for example the threat of appearing foolish in a social situation, or of letting someone down. Conversely, the removal of a particular threat, or the provision of a general context of security, will tend to induce the paratelic state.

As well as the imposition and achievement of goals causing reversals in one direction or the other, such reversals may also be facilitated or brought about by various social cues and contexts. Thus, hearing laughter, unless one suspects that it is directed against oneself, is likely to induce the paratelic state, whereas hearing people screaming is likely to induce the telic state. There may be various subtle cues in social situations that allow one to detect which state of mind someone else is in, and may in turn induce the same state in oneself. These would occur in what Bateson (1973) has called the 'meta-communicative level'. Similarly, social or cultural context may induce one or other of the two metamotivational states: for instance, being in a theatre, a football ground, a bingo hall, or an ice rink, will normally induce the paratelic state; being on the factory floor, in the boss's office, at the dentist's, at a police station, or in a court of law, will each be likely to induce the telic state. The effects of such contexts obviously depend on such interrelated factors as one's upbringing, previous experience and social class.

It is possible that there are other contingent factors which may induce reversals. Getting drunk, for example, appears in most people to induce a paratelic state if it is not already operative: one of the common experiences of being drunk is a feeling that nothing is essential; one's orientation while drunk is to the present moment and its enjoyment; one also often feels a strong need for high arousal, and this may give rise to any one of a large variety of behaviours, including arguing intensely, dancing, getting into fights, driving dangerously, threatening suicide, or trying to make passionate love.

While various types of contingent factors may individually act at a given moment in such a way as to increase or diminish the chance of a reversal, they presumably combine in some way so that there is an overall contingent determining effect, which depends on the strength and the direction of the effect of each. Whether a reversal actually takes place at that moment will then depend on the strength and direction of this overall effect in relation to the strength of the effect of the other two types of factors to be discussed. Sometimes, however, the strength of one factor alone, e.g. a threat of physical danger, will be sufficient to bring about a reversal by itself.

2. Frustration

Frustration in achieving an essential goal in the telic state may induce a reversal to the paratelic state, unless the needs of the telic state are too exigent. In the subsequent paratelic state one may then, for example, fantasize goal achievement, daydream, carry out some paratelic activity which is totally unrelated to the previous telic activity, or come to see the goal as, after all, unimportant. Conversely, in the paratelic state, continual frustration in the achievement of a freely-chosen and initially trivial goal may build up, until a point is reached at which the attainment of the goal is felt to be essential, and this point marks a reversal to the telic state. For example, if in trying to build a model aeroplane one keeps making a mistake which prevents its completion, the successful construction of the model may temporarily assume a desperate importance.

3. Satiation

Once one has been in one or another of the two opposing states for a prolonged period, then a switch is increasingly likely to occur to the opposite state, *even in the absence of other inducing conditions*, provided that the countervailing influences are not too strong. Thus, if one has been in the paratelic state for a while, doing nothing in particular, then one may at a certain point feel the need to behave in a solid and purposeful way in order to accomplish something worthwhile. This change implies that the underlying state has changed from paratelic to telic. Similarly, after working hard and dutifully for a period, one may feel the need to do something 'for the hell of it', and this implies that the paratelic state has replaced the telic. How long a period is needed for such satiation to occur, and which factors influence this, may depend on the nature of the activity itself. It will also be expected to vary from one individual to another, some people being more likely to satiate quickly, and therefore being more labile than others in this respect. It should be noted that satiation of some activity *within* one state or the other can also occur, e.g. in the paratelic state becoming bored with playing tennis and going for a drink. But these two levels of satiation should not be confused. Metamotivational reversal only occurs in relation to the satiation of a metamotivational state, not to satiation of some particular activity within such a state. And the satiation of a metamotivational state will have no effect on conscious experience other than through the induction of a reversal.

Reversals therefore are not necessarily induced, directly or indirectly, by external events, but may occur entirely independently: satiation is conceived here as an autonomous process. Although this is one of the concepts which helps to make reversal theory distinctive, such autonomous switching is not unique as a psychological or physiological process. An obvious example of another pair of states which satiate in this sense is that of sleep and waking. After a period, if no other factor wakes the sleeper, sleep will terminate itself; conversely, unless prevented from doing so, wakefulness eventually leads to sleep. Similarly, within sleep, switching occurs between REM and non-REM periods, and appears to do so in an innately determined way.[13] The fact that contingent factors can interfere with, and override, such processes, both in relation to metamotivational states and sleep-waking states, does not imply that the processes themselves are not basically autonomous.

Satiation of metamotivational state is what lies behind one of man's most obvious characteristics: his 'divine discontent'. No sooner does he have what he wants than he no longer wants it. It keeps him switching from one state to another, so that he has not long been in one state with, for example, one desired level of arousal, before he finds that the desired level of arousal has changed. This keeps him on the move, continually active, and never content for long.

Do reversals always occur automatically in response to factors of the kind just listed, or can they be brought under direct and voluntary control? The former would appear to be the case. An individual may *indirectly* control his own reversals, however, by deliberately bringing about changes in his environment which should themselves, other things being equal, automatically induce a reversal of state/system. For example, if he wishes to become paratelic at a given time, although he cannot do this directly, he may achieve it by going to the theatre, where the various cues in the situation, the building itself, the seating, the music, the programmes, the curtains, etc., may be sufficient to induce the state he desires. He may go to the squash courts, a bar, or settle himself comfortably in his living room in front of the television. If he wishes to induce the telic state he may achieve it by placing himself in one of his usual work settings: going to the office, sitting in front of the typewriter, or opening the shop; and the cues which result from such an action then hopefully automatically induce the telic state. This implies therefore that the individual does have some conscious control over his metamotivational states, but it is indirect. This means that the achievement of the paratelic state *can* nevertheless be a telic goal.

When a reversal is induced from one state to another, two further steps follow, making up the following three steps.

(i) A reversal from the telic to the paratelic state, or vice versa: the new state is characterized by a new orientation within the phenomenal field, together with, among other things, a new preferred level of the 'felt significance' variable.

(ii) An essential goal is identified or selected in the telic case. In the paratelic case, some activity or experience is chosen.

(iii) Activity is initiated which should have the effect of bringing the 'felt significance' variable to a high level in the telic state and reducing it to a low level in the paratelic state. So in the telic state the individual, while pursuing the goal, tends to remind himself continually of its significance and how it fits into a 'more general scheme of things'. In the paratelic state he attempts to build a conceptual frame around his activity to isolate it from implications it might otherwise have. Attaining the preferred level of this variable is pleasurable in itself, quite apart from such pleasure as that which may derive from actually attaining the goal in the telic case, or which may derive from the activity or experience itself in the paratelic case.

It may be helpful here to refer back to the balance model described in Chapter two (see Fig. 2.4). The first step above corresponds to the cross-piece of the balance being tipped from one end down to the other end down, the new position being temporarily held in place. The second step corresponds to the choice of a marble, and the third to the marble being placed on the "runway" of the cross-piece and rolling to the downmost end. Another analogy which might be helpful would be to think of two doorkeys. Choosing one key or the other would be the analogue of step one, finding a lock which the chosen key fits would be the analogue of step two, and turning the key in the lock would be the analogue of step three.

Several points about these three steps need further elaboration. The first concerns the notion that one may reverse into the telic state/system without there initially being any essential goal to pursue. This is not perhaps the most frequent form of reversal: normally some goal will present itself which will initially bring about the reversal of state/system, followed by an eventual change in the actual value of the variable, i.e. in this sense steps one and two are inverted.[14] Some forms of reversal in the telic direction will arise, however, in the absence of a particular goal. This is likely to be particularly true of the satiation form of reversal; within the category of contingent reversal-inducing agents, factors like social cues and cultural context may also induce a reversal in the absence of an obvious essential goal. In all such cases the telic state is temporarily 'content-free'; part of the operation of the telic system is then to find goals which can be felt as essential. If necessary this means taking a goal which is not normally felt as essential and then assigning a feeling of 'essentialness' to it, e.g. playing a game as if winning was of life-and-death importance, or cleaning the house from top to bottom. This is a largely unconscious process which one finds in an extreme form in obsessionality, where quite arbitrary goals are assigned an overwhelming importance and are felt to be unavoidable. A similar thing happens when a state/system reversal occurs in the opposite direction: if no obvious activity presents itself, e.g. the individual is not at the theatre, in the playground, or on a beach, he restlessly searches for some way to enjoy himself, and may even pick on an otherwise essential goal to treat in a playful paratelic way. For example, if a at a business meeting he may playfully start arguments, be disruptive, tell jokes, or set himself the sporting challenge of achieving certain results which in the telic mood he might regard as being essential to his career. So reversal into the paratelic state may occur when some activity is already continuing, but, if there is no such obvious activity, this state may also in this sense be initially content-free, and in this case the system will search for some appropriate content.

To say that a metamotivational state may at some moments be content-free is to deny that such a state necessarily has the quality of intentionality, in the technical sense in which the term is used in the phenomenological literature following Brentano and Husserl (see Chapter 2, note 14). The argument here is that the state does not necessarily have a reference, and may at moments be 'pre-intentional'. What does it mean, then, to say that the telic state is oriented to an essential goal at the first step, when the goal may still have to be selected or identified? The answer is that in this case there may be a kind of 'hole' in the centre of the phenomenal field waiting to be 'filled in', but recognized as representing an essential goal. To put it in another way, the orientation is towards the category 'essential goal', but the choice of an element within this category has yet to be made. In the terms used in Chapter 2, a particular exemplar is needed of the variable concerned. At the same time a kind of 'free-floating' purposefulness will be experienced. In the paratelic case the same considerations apply if 'step one' does indeed occur first, but this time the category from which a choice has yet to be made will be that of pleasurable activities or situations.

A further point that rises from this analysis into three steps is that although the system may change, say from the paratelic to the telic, and with it the preferred level of the 'felt significance' variable, it does not necessarily follow that the actual value of this variable will also reverse to the preferred state. The balance model of the previous chapter showed that, if the cross-piece tips so that the uppermost end becomes the downmost end, and the preferred level of the variable 'position of the marble' is therefore now at the new downmost end, the marble may be prevented from moving to the downmost end by some disturbance, e.g. a finger placed in the runway (see Fig. 2.4). Thus in terms of a paratelic-to-telic reversal, the individual may find it impossible for some reason to see much significance in the goal which he feels nevertheless impelled to pursue: perhaps for example, the goal is that of urination. Quite apart from this, a length of time may in any case be needed for the value of the variable to be brought across to the preferred level. Returning to the balance model: when the cross-piece tips so that the uppermost end becomes the downmost end, if the marble is placed on the runway at any position other than the downmost end, a short period will be needed for it to run down the slope to the downmost end, even in the absence of any interfering force. In the metamotivational example being considered here, the individual may need a little time to build up a "picture" of what he is doing in order to give it a high degree of significance. Whenever there is a discrepancy between the actual and preferred level of a metamotivational variable of this kind, the individual will experience some discomfort which is proportional to the degree of the discrepancy. As noted in the previous chapter this will be referred to as 'tension'.[15]

As suggested earlier, social context may determine whether someone is in the telic or paratelic state. In other words, whether or not some goal is seen as essential, may be determined in many cases by the social definition of the situation. The same actions, therefore, may often be converted into either telic or paratelic by suitable social definitions being accepted by the actor, provided their influence is strong enough to offset other factors. For example, one might interpret the negro slaves' fondness for singing while they worked as an attempt to try to define the situation as a form of dance, thus converting the hard physical work into paratelic activity. The attempt by fighter pilots in both world wars to turn their fighting into a kind of game with rules of its own, may be interpreted as part of an effort to make the intense experience of waiting to go into action a pleasant paratelic one; the fighting itself, one must assume, being almost invariably telic.[16] In the same vein, there is sometimes an attempt in sales departments to make the work of its salesmen more 'fun', by setting up monthly competitions with non-essential rewards like bottles of champagne for the winners, i.e. those who have sold the most during the month. Such a reward must be clearly inessential, otherwise there is the danger of merely increasing the entrenched nature of the telic state. These are all examples of the attempt to convert telic into paratelic actions, but the conversion may also occur in the opposite direction. A good example would be the way in which children's activities carried out for pleasure in themselves, e g. reading poetry or finding out how machinery works, are turned into telic actions by the school system, with its emphasis on progress, examinations and marks. Defining presence at a boring office party as a way of increasing one's chances of promotion may turn it into a telic activity, with attendant pleasurable feelings of the possibility of advancement. Conversely, learning that it is, after all, only a social occasion with no significance beyond itself may redefine it as a paratelic situation, and reduce this particular pleasure. It should be borne in mind that a paratelic activity, if it does not provide pleasure, can often be terminated and another more pleasant paratelic activity substituted, e.g. one can leave the party if it is boring and go to the cinema. Telic activity is typically less flexible than this because of the unavoidable nature of the goal as it is experienced. In both cases it is, in principle, possible to displace one's orientation: in one case from one essential goal to another, in the other from one type of activity to another.

One line of research in recent years has concerned the effect of introducing extrinsic rewards into situations which are otherwise intrinsically rewarding. For example, Deci (1972) discovered that giving a monetary reward to adult subjects who were working on a difficult but interesting puzzle, made them less likely to work on the puzzle during a non-rewarded free period than subjects who had not previously received the extrinsic reward. In a similar experiment with nursery school children, Lepper et al. (1973) found that the effect of giving a diploma as a reward to children who were led to expect such a reward for drawing with magic markers, was that these children played with the markers to a significantly less degree during a later free play period than children who had not been rewarded or who had not expected a reward for the activity, but had been unexpectedly rewarded. This general effect has now been replicated in a number of studies (viz. Kruglanski et al. 1972; Greene, 1974; Lepper and Greene, 1975). Several explanations have been put forward. One is Deci's (1975) "cognitive evaluation theory" based on Heider's (1958) attribution theory. Deci's explanation is that external rewards tend to change a person's attribution of the cause for his own behaviour from internal to external factors, and this in turn is supposed to reduce intrinsic motivation.[17] A similar explanation, based on Bem's (1972) self-perception theory, is that if a person perceives himself to be receiving an external reward, he assumes he must be extrinsically motivated and, if not, he assumes he must be intrinsically motivated. In the former case he will then only continue the behaviour if he continues to be rewarded. (See Greene and Lepper, 1975; Ross, 1976). According to reversal theory, however, the crucial factor is whether the situation is one in which the primary orientation is towards the achievement of an essential goal, whatever its source, or towards the enjoyment of the continuing activity, i.e. whether the subject is in the telic or paratelic state. In these terms, the addition of external rewards may have the effect of making an activity point beyond itself so that the individual sees the goal as primary, his behaviour being chosen to achieve it (the telic state), rather than the behaviour being primary (the paratelic state). If an activity is construed by the individual as a means to a goal, then when the goal is removed there is no point in performing the activity. In this sense the addition of an external reward can turn 'play' into 'work', and work will be discontinued when there is no point in doing it. The words 'play' and 'work' here, however, are being used not to refer to whether the goal happens to be chosen by the individual himself or by some external force, but to refer to the nature of the goal itself in the individual's phenomenal field. One must assume that in such experiments as those of Deci (1972) and Lepper et al. (1973) the goals were introduced in such a way that the subjects concerned felt during the course of the experiment that the goals were important; unlike, for example, the introduction of "fun" goals into a previously serious situation in the example of the sales office given earlier. But reversal theory would predict that it should also be possible to add extrinsic rewards in such a way that they are felt by subjects to be inessential 'frills', in which case the situation would remain a paratelic one, and the removal of the rewards would then make little or no difference to subsequent behaviour; this was a result, in fact, which occurred in three of the thirteen experiments reviewed by Deci (1975, p.155).

Although the discussion here has emphasized change *between* metamotivational states, it has also been noted in passing that change may occur *within* a metamotivational state, in respect to which particular goal is being pursued, or which particular activity is being performed. So, while remaining in the telic state, the individual may decide to work towards a new goal. Perhaps the previous goal has now been achieved or no longer seems important, or a new goal, e.g. to avoid a threat, suddenly takes priority. Similarly, in the paratelic state a new activity may be undertaken, perhaps because the old activity has lost interest or because some new opportunity for enjoyable experience unexpectedly presents itself; or there may be a change in the paratelic state from attention to arousal being the most salient feature of experience, to some other aspect of experience e.g. some sensation like taste or smell, being concentrated on. All such changes will be referred to here as 'displacements', since some salient feature in the phenomenal field is displaced by some other feature which now becomes pre-eminent in awareness.

Both of these types of change, reversal and displacement, should be distinguished from other types of change in the characteristics of a given metamotivational state. For example, in the telic state the temporal dimension of the life-space may change, in that the individual may look further ahead at some times than at others; or how much pleasure the individual derives from a given level of felt significance may vary. All such changes in the characteristics of a given operative metamotivational state, excluding displacements, will be referred to here as 'shifts'.

Patterns of Telic/Paratelic Reversal

One objection to the whole analysis of metamotivational reversals presented here would be that it is possible to be in both subjective states at the same time: it might be asserted for example, that a driver can drive his car fast both because he has an urgent appointment and because he enjoys driving fast. Our response to this would be to argue that a close examination of such cases would disclose that there is, in fact, an *alternation* between the two metamotivational states during the activity, and that this alternation might be quite rapid. If the driver is aware of the necessity of arriving on time, and this is a goal which is genuinely imposed on him and not simply chosen by him to provide an excuse for his paratelic behaviour, then his high arousal will not be felt as pleasant; barriers (such as large lorries to be passed), will produce feelings of displeasure and, in general, he will not enjoy the behaviour in itself, except so far as it is successful and allows him to anticipate the achievement of the goal, and produces a strong feeling of purposefulness. If he does enjoy the behaviour, then from this perspective it is a bonus in the same way that achievement of a goal is a bonus in the paratelic state. On the other hand, if his attention is on the sensations of the moment he may well enjoy them but, by the same token, the exigency of the goal is no longer the central phenomenological feature of his activity. He may, however, alternate from one of these perspectives to the other: as he feels that he is 'winning' and the goal loses its urgency, he may switch his attention to his driving behaviour, and begin to enjoy it. But if he falls behind his timetable, then his attention once more will become focused on the goal to be achieved and he will become more future-oriented. Furthermore, in the paratelic state he may do something deliberately dangerous, e.g. overtake when he is not sure if he has sufficient acceleration; as it becomes obvious that he has made a mistake and his life is in danger, so his mood changes to a telic one. If he escapes, however, then he may well revert almost immediately to the paratelic state, enjoy the feeling of having escaped and even convince himself that he was never really scared.

Such alternations in the course of a single action are probably common rather than exceptional. Thus, in the earlier example of action in the telic state, the person working for an examination may well pause from time to time and fantasize about what life will be like when he has passed the examination. At such times he is reversing temporarily into the paratelic state since, for a while, he forgets about the real, essential goal and instead enjoys playing with ideas which are exciting and pleasant in a make-believe way. This must be distinguished from anticipation of the goal in the telic state, which is based on a realistic view of the goal and a realistic assessment of progress towards it. Such paratelic make-believe may help him to maintain his motivation in the telic state; interactions between the *effects* of the two states, but not directly between the states themselves since they cannot be operative concurrently, are not uncommon. He may also, from time to time, find he is enjoying the work itself and becoming stimulated by some aspect of it, so that the ultimate goal recedes into the background; at these times also he would be in the paratelic state.

Over a longer period, one common pattern, as noted earlier, is for the goal in the telic state to be that of inducing the paratelic state, or of setting up conditions in which some activity in the paratelic state at a later time will be enjoyed. For example, driving to the theatre to see a play may be a telic activity, although watching the play is likely to be paratelic; earning money to go on holiday may be undertaken largely in a telic state, whereas the holiday itself should be experienced for the most part in a paratelic state.

There is also an inverse pattern: an activity is chosen and goals decided in a paratelic state, but the goals which have been chosen come to be construed later on as essential. This occurs when a freely chosen goal is imposed on oneself by oneself, so that the pursuit of it becomes telic. Here are several illustrations. One bets that one can achieve something. It is not essential to have the bet, and the whole thing is pleasantly arousing at the time. However, later on one's 'public face' and self-esteem become involved and the need to achieve the self-imposed goal takes on serious proportions. In this example, the bet is undertaken in the paratelic state, but the goal of winning the bet pursued in the telic state. A second example would be that of a researcher who commits himself to writing a chapter on his research for an edited book. At the time of the commitment it is seen as freely chosen, proactive and, since many other tasks could equally well have been undertaken, arbitrary; the whole idea is also arousing in a pleasant way. Later on, however, when contracts have been signed with the publisher and the deadline approaches, the phenomenology of the situation becomes telic. This would seem to contradict the idea that in the paratelic state the goal is always chosen to satisfy the means, since in these two examples the goals were chosen first, the means being of subsidiary importance. This is, however, only an apparent contradiction: the pleasurable *act* of choosing the goals is the behaviour which is being performed in the paratelic state in these examples, and the orientation is towards the enjoyment of this particular kind of behaviour at this moment. Subsequently, when the behaviour has to be performed to achieve the goal which has been chosen, then the state of mind does indeed become telic.

A similar way in which a reversal from paratelic to telic might occur, is when some goal is arbitrarily chosen but, when it is not achieved, builds up in importance until eventually it induces the telic state. For instance, a teenage girl might fancy the idea of owning a horse and gradually over time becomes obsessed with the idea, until it comes to be seen by her, not just as a pleasant idea, but as a central goal in life. In such ways paratelic decisions may later on become self-imposed essential goals. Conversely, a telic goal may over time come to be treated in a paratelic fashion: when someone has satisfied the telic goal of making enough money to meet what he sees as being the essential necessities of life, the goal of making money often becomes a paratelic one, engaged in for the enjoyment of the pursuit itself. This is the kind of process which Gordon Allport (1937) has discussed extensively under the heading of 'functional autonomy'.

A more specialized example of alternation of telic and paratelic states in the course of the same activity is afforded in relation to the technique of 'brainstorming', as devised by Osborn for purposes of creative problem solving (Osborn, 1963). Although the problem to be solved may be important, the idea in using this technique is to treat the problem for a period as if it were not important, to play around with related ideas and not to criticize or evaluate the ideas which have been generated. The aim is rather to turn thinking about the problem during this period into an uninhibited and unplanned activity which is enjoyable in itself, and anyone who has participated in a brainstorming session will testify that it can be highly enjoyable. In reversal theory terms, what is happening in brainstorming is that a telic activity is being turned into a paratelic one. The whole problem-solving procedure as recommended by Osborn, of which brainstorming proper is one part, involves an alternation between the two states: the problem is posed in a telic state of mind, dealt with through brainstorming in a paratelic state of mind and then, eventually, the various tentative solutions which emerge are assessed in a telic state.[18]

Alternation can occur not only in the course of the same action by an individual or a group, but also in relation to material which has a more public status. Where the results of an individual's action become public and reasonably permanent (like artefacts, writing, film, etc.), such material has the potential of being understood, acted on, used or developed in turn by others who may be in the opposite frame of mind when they do so. Thus a religious mask might be made by an African tribesman in a telic state of mind, but later on enjoyed as decoration by someone in Europe in a paratelic frame of mind. A Nazi propaganda film, a newsreel clip of some disaster, or a newspaper reporter's description of an atrocity, all presumably created in a telic state, can be enjoyed later as entertainment by people in a paratelic state. Sometimes a body of material is built up, perhaps intermittently and over a long period, by various people, some of whom are in a telic state and some in a paratelic state when they are engaged in developing it; this may, for example, be true of folklore. This is a theme which will be returned to in the later chapter on religion.

Notes on Chapter 3

1. It should be noted that this is different from the way in which the term 'phenomenal field' has been defined by Carl Rogers (1951) since, in Rogers' definition, it includes unconscious as well as conscious processes.
2. This is different from the Greek 'tele' meaning 'distant' which is as the root of such words as 'telephone', 'television' and 'telepathy'. ('Tele' is also the root of the word 'telic' as it has been used by Moreno, 1964).
3. This is used at the root of such words as 'parallel', 'paramilitary' and 'parasympathetic'.
4. This distinction between behaviour-oriented and goal-oriented behaviour is not unlike that made by the philosopher Wauchope (1948) between when he called 'living' behaviour and 'death-avoiding' behaviour.
5. An exception might be where the individual is concurrently in the negativistic state. This point will be returned to in Chapter 9.
6. In turn, it should be added, it is possible that the level of felt significance can play a part in determining whether or not a goal is perceived as 'essential'. Thus one reason why a goal may be felt to be essential is that attaining it has so many implications that it comes to be felt to be unavoidable, even if each individual implication is relatively unimportant. In this sense, high felt significance *can* help to induce or maintain the telic state, as well as being affected by the functioning of that state. In particular, there would seem to be a positive feedback relationship between the two, such that the telic state can help to raise felt significance and felt significance

can help to entrench the telic state. A similar relationship holds between felt significance and the paratelic state, except that here it is low felt significance which can help to induce and maintain the state in question (since low significance helps to 'encapsulate' any goal-oriented activity), and in turn the paratelic state tends to function so as to reduce the level of felt significance. None of this should be taken to mean that essentialness and significance are the same thing, but rather that these two aspects of the individual's motivational experience may interact.

7. An excellent discussion of this kind of structure is found in Miller, Galanter and Pribram (1960) with their T-O-T-E concept. A similar concept has been actualized in the form of a computer model by Newell and Simon (1963).

8. As proposed by Nuttin (1973, p.255).

9. See discussion by Cohen (1953).

10. See, for example, the way in which the word tends to be used in various papers in the large collection on play edited by Bruner et al. (1976).

11. Eckblad (1981) has incorporated Csikszentmihalyi's notions into an intriguing theory called 'scheme theory', which can also perhaps be conceived as a form of structural phenomenology.

12. It must be emphasized that here the word 'phenomenological' is being used in the sense of 'experiential' as discussed in Chapter 1. Ironically, in Husserl's phenomenology the term 'essence' is used in a way akin to that which has been referred to here as the linguistic sense.

13. A good physiological example of a process which alternates between two different forms is the 'nasal cycle': during the course of the day people breathe predominantly through one nostril and then predominantly through the other. Reversal from one nostril being predominant to the other being predominant occurs perhaps four or five times a day (Eccles, 1978).

14. They have been listed here in the order given earlier, for reasons of conceptual clarity. In terms of the balance model, if a marble is selected after the cross-piece has changed its position the steps are in the order given earlier, if it is selected and placed in the 'runway' before the cross-piece has changed its position, the order of steps has been inverted.

15. This analysis of tension as discrepancy between the actual level of a variable and its desired level is similar to Cabanac's (1971) analysis of sensation and hedonic tone. He uses the term alliesthesia to refer to such a discrepancy in relation to the desired and actual intensity of a sensation.

16. The various ways in which attempts are made to turn soldiering into a game have been entertainingly discussed by Giddings (1979).

17. Indeed, intrinsic motivation now becomes defined by Deci at this point in his book as motivation in which the locus of control is perceived by the individual as internal, and external motivation as that in which it is perceived as external. Such an attributional definition is clearly different from the biological definition with which he started, as discussed earlier in the chapter, and is similar to that of Kruglanski, which was also discussed earlier. This changed conception allows Deci to count rewards like praise and money as extrinsic rather than, as they would have to be by his earlier definition, intrinsic. However, he does not make explicit the fact that his definition of these different types of motivation, and their associated rewards, has changed radically.

18. There is, incidentally, evidence that brainstorming is an effective technique for solving problems in original ways (Meadow, et al., 1959; Parnes and Meadow, 1959; Parnes, 1963).

4   Bistability and Arousal

The Concept of Arousal

This is not the place to review what has now become a voluminous literature on arousal and activation, the two terms being used by many writers more or less synonymously. It may, however, be useful to remind the reader that the concept of activation dates back to the 1930s with the work of Duffy (1934, 1941), who conceived of it as the degree of energy mobilization in the organism. In studying activation, a number of physiological indices were developed, including measures of muscle tension, cardiovascular activity and the psychogalvanic reflex. However, it was not until the 1950s that the concept of arousal began to have its main impact on psychology, largely due to the impetus of the work of physiologists like Moruzzi and Magoun (1949) on the reticular activating system of the brain stem and its effects on neurophysiological arousal. At this stage the terms 'arousal' and 'activation' came to be used widely, through the influence of a number of writers (e.g. Hebb and Thompson, 1954; Hebb, 1955; Duffy, 1957; Malmo, 1958). In some areas of psychology it replaced the earlier idea of 'drive', as a way of conceptualizing motivation in terms of a unitary variable which would represent the overall intensity of motivation in an organism at a given time.[1]

Many different methods of measuring arousal have been used by different researchers, including EEG desynchronization, which is directly related to the activity of the reticular formation; various measures of autonomic reactivity, e.g. blood pressure and heart rate, psychogalvanic response, respiration rate, pupil dilation, and so on; and a number of different behavioural indices, such as measures of restlessness and body movement, sensory sensitivity, and the ease with which unconditioned reflexes may be elicited. Unfortunately, these various measures of arousal, even when they are of the same type, e.g. measures of autonomic reactivity, often fail to provide similar indications of the state of arousal of an organism at a given time, and correlations between the various measures over time are often low or even non-existent.

'Arousal' in the reversal theory sense is defined not behaviourally or physiologically, but phenomenologically. By arousal in reversal theory is meant the degree of motivational intensity which an individual experiences in consciousness at a given time: the extent to which he *feels* 'aroused' in the everyday sense of feeling 'worked up' or 'stirred up'. Strictly, this should always be referred to as 'felt arousal', but where the term 'arousal' is used here without any qualifying adjective, 'felt arousal' will be implied, unless otherwise stated. This usage is similar to the use of the term 'arousal' by other theorists, in that it assumes the existence of a single overall degree of arousal at a given moment, rather than various independent types of arousal which can co-exist. As pointed out in Chapter 3, felt arousal is one aspect of the intensity of experience, namely, that aspect which relates to motivation and emotion. This meaning of arousal is not inconsistent with the physiological and behavioural meanings; rather it focuses on arousal from a different perspective. Operationally, 'felt arousal' would have to be measured in ways different from those utilized by physiological psychologists, through rating scales, for example. One advantage of a phenomenological definition is that it allows one, at least initially, to avoid the problems which have arisen in relation to the physiological measurement of arousal. Although the physiological level has therefore temporarily been put 'in brackets', it will not be possible in discussing the theory here to avoid reference to physiological work entirely, since it will be useful at various stages to compare what reversal theory says about arousal with other more physiologically based theories. In any case, although our definition of arousal is phenomenological, it is assumed that felt arousal derives in some way or another from physiological arousal.

The dimension of felt arousal as defined here must be distinguished from several other dimensions to which the label 'arousal' has also been attached by some researchers in the area. Indeed, part of the inconsistency between different physiological measures of arousal may arise because they are measures of different types of 'arousal'. One of these other dimensions is that of drowsiness-wakefulness, the extremes of the dimension being sleep and full alertness. This is obviously different from arousal in the sense of felt motivational/emotional intensity, since it is possible to be fully awake yet with low motivation and little emotionality, and, conversely, it is possible to feel drowsy and yet emotionally 'worked up'; in fact, it is possible to be asleep and 'worked up' in this sense, as one may well be while dreaming, especially if one is having a nightmare. In physiological terms, highly aroused EEG patterns can be recorded during the so-called rapid eye-movement periods of sleep which are supposed to occur during dream periods.

The second 'arousal' dimension which must be distinguished from felt arousal in the reversal theory sense, is that of how much energy one feels oneself to have, the high end of this dimension being represented by the feeling of being energetic, lively, or invigorated; the low end of the dimension is experienced as being fatigued, enervated or 'worn out'. This is different from 'felt arousal' in our sense, in that one can clearly feel highly motivated or emotional and yet be fatigued, and one can feel energetic without necessarily feeling any strong motivation. This energy dimension may be related in a loose way with the wakefulness dimension since fatigue is typically related to drowsiness; indeed, in everyday language 'being tired' might mean either of these and, usually, if one is energetic one is wide awake. But there is no necessary relationship, and it is perfectly possible to feel drowsy without feeling fatigued or to feel fatigued without feeling drowsy.[2]

Anxiety-avoidance and Excitement-seeking

The concept of arousal has been associated closely in the literature on motivation with the idea that it has some optimal level, which is usually assumed to be intermediate in strength. According to this view the organism sometimes behaves in such a way as to increase arousal up to this optimum point when the arousal has become too low, and at other times in such a way as to decrease the arousal down to the optimum point when arousal has become too high. Influential formulations of this idea include those of Hebb (1955) who referred primarily to physiological considerations, Leuba (1955) who used the term 'optimal stimulation' with reference particularly to behavioural data, and Schultz (1965) who wrote of the process of 'sensoristasis' through which, in his view, the organism maintains an optimal level of sensory variation. All such theories are homeostatic: the organism is postulated to behave in such a way as to attempt to maintain arousal at some single preferred level.

In optimal arousal theories, the optimal position is usually conceived to be optimal not just in the sense that the behaviour of the system makes it the preferred level, but also because when this level is achieved, the organism is believed to perform better, as defined and measured in various ways, than at any other level. This idea gives rise to the well-known inverted U-curve which, it is claimed, relates arousal to performance (see, for example, Fig. 2 in Hebb, 1955[3]). Thus as arousal increases from some minimal level, so performance improves up to an optimal point; but, as arousal continues to increase, so performance deteriorates thereafter. Evidence for this curve has been adduced by numerous experimenters such as Shaw (1956), Stennet (1957), and Wood and Hokanson (1965). Fiske and Maddi (1961) suggested that the preferred level may change somewhat depending on the point of the sleeping-waking cycle in which the organism finds itself, but this is still essentially a homeostatic theory which allows for some degree of change in the locus of control. The same is true of those theories which argue that the preferred level may change for different tasks, an idea that goes back essentially to Yerkes and Dodson (1908) who formulated the celebrated Yerkes-Dodson law which relates task complexity to the optimum level of motivation. (Yerkes and Dodson did not of course write about 'arousal' which is a more modern concept).

The optimal level of arousal is also generally supposed to be the position on the arousal dimension at which the arousal is associated with the greatest degree of positive 'hedonic tone'; i.e. it is the position of most felt pleasure or, in behaviourist terms, the position which is most reinforcing. As arousal diverges from this optimal intermediate position in either direction, so the feeling associated with it becomes less pleasant and may eventually become unpleasant. This has been stated with varying degrees of explicitness by various optimal arousal theorists (e.g. Hebb, 1955; Leuba, 1955; Fiske and Maddi, 1961). In these terms, the relation of arousal to hedonic tone can be described by means of an inverted U-curve and the situation in this respect is therefore also supposed to be homeostatic. If the optimal arousal idea in relation to performance can be traced back to Yerkes and Dodson (1908), the essentials of the idea in relation to hedonic tone can be traced back even further, to Wundt (1874) who produced a form of inverted U-curve to show the relationship he believed to exist between hedonic tone and stimulus intensity. The best-known recent formulation of this kind of view must be that of Berlyne (1960, 1967, 1971).[4] It is this relationship of arousal to hedonic tone, rather than to performance, which is of interest from the point of view of reversal theory, since reversal theory is primarily concerned with the *experience* of motivation, although this may in turn have implications for performance.

In reversal theory, by contrast to optimal arousal theories, the suggestion is that there are *two* metamotivational systems with respect to arousal rather than one, and that the relationship between arousal and hedonic tone is bistable rather than homeostatic. As discussed in the previous chapter, these two different metamotivational systems can be regarded for many purposes as part of the telic and paratelic metamotivational systems respectively. As with optimal arousal theory, it is assumed that there is a stable position for the variable of arousal, in our case 'felt arousal', and that this is associated with positive hedonic tone, in experiential terms, 'pleasure'. In other words, from the point of view of these arousal-regulation systems, there is a preferred state of arousal in both the cybernetic sense, which implies a stable state, and in the phenomenological sense, which implies pleasure. The difference from optimal arousal theory is that two arousal systems are being postulated, each with its own preferred level, these preferred levels being towards opposite ends of the arousal dimension. In these terms, to describe the relationship between arousal on the one hand and hedonic tone on the other, two curves are needed rather than one: one curve showing the relationship for one system, and the other for the other system.

These two curves are shown in hypothetical form in Fig. 4.1. In one metamotivational state, the higher the level of arousal the more pleasant it is felt to be, the preferred level being high. In this state low arousal, which is felt as 'boredom', is avoided, but high arousal is sought and experienced as 'excitement'. In the other state the opposite is the case, since here the higher the level of arousal the more unpleasant it is felt to be. In this state high arousal, which is felt as 'anxiety', is avoided, but low arousal is sought and experienced as 'relaxation'.[5]

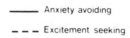

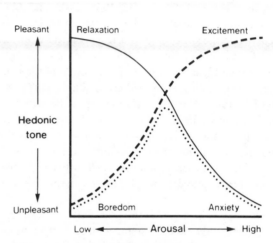

FIG. 4.1 *The hypothesized relationship between arousal and hedonic tone for the anxiety-avoidance and the excitement-seeking systems respectively.*

In terms of arousal, therefore, these two hypothetical curves represent the situation in relation to an 'excitement-seeking' (paratelic) system and an 'anxiety-avoidance' (telic) system. At this stage, then, what might be called an 'X-curve' has been substituted for the inverted U-curve of optimal arousal theory.

Inspection of the graph will disclose that the bistability of the arousal variable is an externally-controlled one, since the variable may take on a value which is at the opposite extreme to the value of the preferred state, i.e. anxiety may be felt in the anxiety-avoidance system and boredom in the excitement-seeking system. This would not be possible with a value-determined bistability.

It may be the case that arousal in itself has an innate tendency to return to some relatively intermediate resting level of its own, so that it would be homeostatic if it were not operated on at all times by one or other of the two metamotivational states under discussion. However, the present analysis implies that, even if this were the case, the operation of these two systems is generally strong enough to overcome the effects of any such tendencies, which are treated by the two systems as a form of 'external disturbance', albeit an enduring one, and acted against just like any other disturbance. This point will be returned to again in the later chapter on psychopathology.

In terms of the situation represented by the graph in Fig. 4.1, it should be clear that a given hedonic tone is brought about by a conjunction of either the excitement-seeking or the anxiety-avoidance state with a given level of arousal. One can of course interpret backwards from a knowledge of the hedonic tone and the state which is currently operative to the current level of arousal. But this should not obscure the fact that arousal is an independent variable and affective tone a dependent variable, i.e. a given level of arousal determines, for a given metamotivational state, the hedonic tone and not vice versa. This is true, however, for only that part of the dynamics of the total situation represented by the graph. In a wider sense one may suppose that hedonic tone, through some feedback loop, plays a part in increasing or decreasing the level of arousal: if it is predominantly unpleasant then the organism will be expected to take some action to change the level so as to produce a more positive tone. In other words, a negative feedback cycle is involved, only one segment of which is depicted in Fig. 4.1.

Each of the two curves represents the way in which each of the two alternative metamotivational systems functions. Since the preferred levels of arousal are towards *opposite* ends of the arousal dimension, referring to switches between these preferred levels and their related systems as 'reversals' is entirely appropriate.

The situation depicted here is bistable at two levels. At one level the metamotivational systems have a bistable relationship. Either one or the other is operative at all times, but reversal can be brought about from one to the other by a variety of circumstances. As discussed earlier, these fall under the three headings of contingency, frustration and satiation. The second level of bistability is that of the variable of 'felt arousal'. This bistability is consequent on the system bistability, in that a reversal from one system to the other entails a reversal from one preferred level of the variable to the other, and this should result in the actual level of the variable being eventually brought across to the new preferred level. If the reader is unclear, he should refer back to Chapter 2 where the distinction was made between system bistability and the bistability of a variable.

The bistability of the variable of arousal is more precarious than that of the underlying systems. For one thing, the variable is continuous rather than dichotomous, and the value of the variable normally changes relatively slowly (see Zillmann, 1971), so that the reversal is not clear-cut and discrete in the way it is between two systems. For another, many factors may disturb or impede the transition of actual arousal level from one preferred level to the other. This is evidenced by the unpleasant feelings of anxiety and boredom that it is safe to assume everyone experiences from time to time, and by the various intermediate states of arousal that one feels which fall short of the preferred levels of arousal. These disturbing forces which prevent the attainment of the preferred levels of arousal may be environmental, e.g. the environment does not provide the stimulation necessary for increasing arousal, even though this is sought; or they may be biological, e.g. feelings of sexual arousal may be more difficult to obtain immediately after orgasm.

One of the advantages of the reversal theory interpretation of arousal and affect, in comparison with the optimal arousal interpretation, is that it allows for four different arousal nouns—anxiety, excitement, boredom and relaxation—to be easily accounted for. The fact that everyday language makes a distinction between these two forms, pleasant and unpleasant, of high and low arousal respectively, encourages us to think that this is a real distinction which people recognize and which therefore should be taken into account by psychologists.

We were, however, led to the recognition of this distinction originally through phenomenological reflection, especially using a method which might be equated with Husserl's method of 'imaginative variation'.[6] The author decided, however, to exteriorize this reflective process by means of a simple experiment (Apter, 1976). Fifty varied situations were listed. Subjects, 67 psychology students, were then asked to rate each of these situations on two seven-point scales, one for the degree of arousal that they estimated they would feel in each of these situations, and one for the degree of pleasure or displeasure that they would associate with the feeling of arousal in each case. An average arousal score and an average score for hedonic tone was worked out for each item across all subjects. Briefly, the results showed that items which were found to have a low average rating on the hedonic tone scale, i.e. those in which the arousal was judged on average to be *unpleasant*, were also judged to be either particularly high or low in arousal, but not intermediate in arousal. This would be expected on the basis of both optimal arousal theory and reversal theory. On the other hand, some items which had a high average rating on hedonic tone, i.e. those in which the arousal was judged to be *pleasant*, also turned out to be just as high or low in arousal as those which had been judged to be unpleasant. This is consistent with reversal theory but inconsistent with optimal arousal theory. Some items at intermediate levels of arousal were also judged on average to be pleasant in felt arousal. This is not necessarily inconsistent with reversal theory since, if the two curves have the shape suggested in Fig. 4.1 then intermediate levels of arousal will also be expected to be pleasant. In other words, the inverted U-curve is also part of the X-curve, as indicated by a dotted line in Fig. 4.1, and reversal theory in this sense may be said to subsume optimal arousal theory.

If pleasant high arousal can be equated with excitement and unpleasant high arousal with anxiety, then these data would appear to indicate that the idea implied by some optimal arousal theorists, like Hebb (1955), that excitement is a form of *moderately* high arousal while anxiety is a form of *very high* arousal, is not well founded. On the contrary, high and low arousal would appear to have forms which are equally pleasant and unpleasant, and any attempts to reduce the distinction between excitement and anxiety to a single dimension will necessarily prove unsatisfactory in this respect. The further dimension which is required, is provided in reversal theory in terms of the anxiety-avoidance/excitement-seeking dichotomy. Although optimal arousal theory accounts for increases as well as decreases in arousal, it does not account for the need to increase up to high arousal rather than moderate arousal which appears, from the data just presented as well as common observation, to prevail under certain circumstances. Reversal theory does account for this. Furthermore, on Hebb's explanation, as arousal increases so excitement would always have to be felt before anxiety, and as it decreases excitement would always have to be felt after anxiety. This seems an unlikely supposition and one for which there is no evidence. Reversal theory makes no such assumption.

Several things need to be said about the terminology used in reversal theory, to represent the feelings of pleasant and unpleasant low and high arousal. First of all, there are obviously other words which also designate these different forms of arousal. The word 'thrill', for example is often used to describe excitement, as is 'exhilaration'; and such words as 'relief' and 'calm' describe what we have chosen to call relaxation. The words 'apprehension', 'fear', 'terror', 'worry', 'agitation' and 'panic' all describe anxiety, but do so in ways which emphasize different situations which may provoke it, or different forms of reactions with which it may be associated. Thus 'apprehension' implies a mild kind of anxiety about some ill-defined event in the near future; 'fear' is usually used to describe anxiety related to a specific object, person or event, and 'terror' to a particularly strong form of this. 'Worry' is generally used to refer to anxiety about a particular problem, and if this expresses itself in a mild way in certain kinds of behaviour it is often referred to as 'agitation'; 'panic' normally means anxiety in which some fairly immediate decision or action is required and in which, frequently, the decision or action taken is inappropriate and self-defeating. Finally, a word like 'restless' also seems to describe what we have called 'boredom', although it emphasizes behavioural concomitants of this feeling.

The second point is that not only may other words be used in different circumstances to refer to the different feelings of low and high arousal, but the four words which have now been given some special theoretical status in reversal theory — relaxation, boredom, excitement and anxiety — sometimes have meanings in everyday speech other than those intended in the theory. This problem arises since many words used in everyday speech are polysemic, i.e. have multiple meanings, and in choosing certain words and giving them a particular meaning in the theory, it has been necessary to choose one meaning at the expense of others. In doing this, however, we are not using words eccentrically, or neologizing unnecessarily, but simply 'firming up' everyday language in a useful manner.

Here are some examples of ways in which each of these four terms may be used in a sense different from that intended in the theory. First of all 'anxious' can mean 'determined' as in the sense 'anxious to win'. 'Excited' can simply mean 'elicited', as in 'passions were excited', 'interest was excited' or 'it excited fear', none of which are necessarily paratelic emotions. 'Excitement' may also simply refer to high activity which again may very well be performed in a telic state, e.g. "The prisoner became very excited" may mean simply that he showed a great deal of emotion and perhaps over-reacted to attempts to restrain him. 'Bored' would appear to be generally used in the sense in which it is used in reversal theory, but it can be used in such a way that it emphasizes the lack of anything interesting to capture the attention rather than low arousal, and although these are usually related, there may be occasions when they are not. The word 'relaxed' produces the most serious difficulties of all. The problem here is that the word would appear to have two distinct meanings, one being that of a kind of low arousal, and this is the sense in which it is being used in reversal theory, and the other referring to a state in which one feels secure rather than threatened. The latter feeling is an important determinant of the paratelic state and a feeling that tends to be maintained throughout that state since, if at any stage the individual does not feel adequately secure, he will be likely to switch to the telic state. In this other sense of 'relaxed' it is perfectly possible to be relaxed and yet simultaneously looking for, and perhaps achieving, excitement.

In trying to think of examples of the theory which might contradict experience, therefore, it is important to bear in mind the way in which the key words in the theory are being used. For example, feeling 'anxious to win' might well be a paratelic and not a telic emotion, but the sense of the word 'anxious' would in this case be that of 'determined', and so this would not constitute a contradiction of reversal theory. Another possibility is suggested by the discussion of 'parapathic emotions' in the next chapter. Similarly, it would be possible to speak of someone being simultaneously bored and anxious, i.e. with nothing to take his mind off that which is causing him the anxiety, e.g. a child waiting for a long time in a school corridor to see the headmaster. This is not strictly the sense in which the term 'bored' is being used in reversal theory, however, since in the example it refers not to a type of low arousal but to being 'fed up' with the situation and wanting to bring it to an end as soon as possible. Again, someone might say that they feel relaxed when watching an exciting programme on television; however, this would mean that they are feeling secure and unthreatened, i.e. that they are in the paratelic state, rather than that their arousal was low. So what would appear to be a contradiction, that relaxation, which has been defined as telic, and excitement, which has been defined as paratelic, can occur together, turns out not to be a contradiction: the word 'relaxation' is being used in this case in a sense which is different from that defined in the theory. Incidentally, this provides an explanation for what Schachter (1973) has designated 'Nesbitt's paradox' in relation to smoking behaviour; this is that, although nicotine is a stimulant, it is claimed by many smokers to have a 'relaxing' effect. The reversal theory explanation of this seeming paradox is that smoking tends to induce the paratelic state, perhaps by making the individual feel less threatened, and in this state the stimulation is enjoyed. The term 'relaxation' in this case applies to the fact that the paratelic state obtains, rather than to the arousal level.

It needs to be reiterated therefore that the terms 'boredom', 'relaxation', 'anxiety' and 'excitement' are being used in reversal theory in a way which is perfectly consistent with their uses in everyday speech, but in the process of making them as exact and unambiguous as possible certain other everyday meanings have had to be excluded. If this is forgotten, it may result in confusion or misunderstanding. In trying to discover what state of mind someone is in, e.g. in psychotherapy, it is of the utmost importance to establish which sense of these words a patient may be using in describing his feelings.

The difference between 'anxiety' and 'tension' as they are defined in reversal theory, should be borne in mind, especially since the two terms are often used synonymously in everyday language. Tension was defined earlier as the unpleasant feeling of discomfort which is experienced when there is a discrepancy between the preferred level of some metamotivational variable, of which felt arousal would be an example, and the actual level of that variable. Where the variable is that of felt arousal, there will be a feeling of tension as well as anxiety when arousal is high and the preferred state is low, as it is in the anxiety-avoidance state; but there will be a similar tension when the preferred state of felt arousal is high, as it is in the excitement-seeking state, and the actual level of arousal is low. In the latter case one may speak without contradiction of a state of tense boredom; indeed, by definition, boredom must always be tense in this sense. Such tension is therefore different from felt arousal. It is always a particular kind of unpleasantness or unease which goes with the awareness of a need to do something to try to change the value of a metamotivational variable. The relationship between tension and arousal is shown in Fig. 4.2 for the excitement-seeking and anxiety-avoidance states. Comparison of this figure with Fig. 4.1 brings out clearly the inverse relation between tension and the hedonic tone which arises from arousal. Presumably, the feeling of tension produces its own element of negative hedonic tone, i.e. high tension is unpleasant and low tension pleasant, and this becomes added to the overall hedonic tone the individual experiences at a given moment which, after all, comes from a variety of sources of which felt arousal is only one. It is necessary to conceive of tension and arousal as each contributing independently to hedonic tone since tension and felt arousal level would seem to be phenomenologically distinct.

The two states represented by the two curves in Fig. 4.1 can be treated as metamotivational states in their own rights in that they do not refer to specific motives like hunger, or specific goals like food, but provide ways of interpreting a general aspect of motivation, i.e. felt arousal. They are, in any case, not part of the *defining* feature of the telic and paratelic states, this being whether or not the individual is oriented towards some essential goal. But the anxiety-avoidance condition may still be regarded as part of the telic state, and the excitement-seeking condition part of the paratelic state. Thus the failure to attain an essential goal in the telic state will be accompanied by anxiety, but its achievement will normally be followed by relaxation. Since the telic state is one which is oriented to an essential goal, relaxation implies that this orientation continues for a while even after the goal has been achieved, and that relaxation is a condition in which one derives pleasure from an awareness that the goal has been achieved. In this

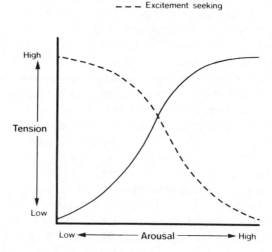

FIG. 4.2 *The hypothesized relationship between arousal and tension for the anxiety-avoidance and excitement-seeking systems respectively.*

respect the word 'relief' would be a better description of this affective state, since one can talk about relief from hunger, relief from danger, etc., and this implies that one is still aware of the hunger or danger which has now been overcome. In the paratelic state, the lack of some stimulating activity will be felt as boredom, whereas if one is enthralled by what one is doing or by something which is happening, then excitement will be felt to some degree or another.

The relationship between the telic and paratelic pair of states and the anxiety-avoidance and excitement-seeking states, however, needs further elucidation because, as indicated in the previous chapter, the telic and paratelic systems do not always generate behaviour which brings the degree of arousal to its optimal level, since some feature of the situation other than arousal may predominate. For example, in the paratelic state, low arousal may be tolerated if the focus of the phenomenal field is on some other aspect of experience; in the telic state, high arousal may be tolerated for a period, in order to achieve high felt significance, or to enjoy goal anticipation. The relationship between these two pairs of meta-motivational states can be summarized as follows.

In the telic state, the anxiety-avoidance state is at all times operative, and how pleasant or unpleasant a given level of arousal is felt to be is determined entirely by the relationship between arousal and hedonic tone which obtains in the anxiety-avoidance state. In the paratelic state, the excitement-seeking state is at all times operative and, again, the relationship between arousal and hedonic tone is that which is specified for the excitement-seeking state. In this respect, the two types of metamotivational state can be completely equated with each other, reversal into the telic state involving reversal into the anxiety-avoidance state, and reversal into the paratelic state being the same as reversal into the excitement-seeking state. When this is the perspective of the discussion, the two ways of referring to metamotivation will be treated as synonymous. The factors which induce reversal at the telic-paratelic level can also therefore be seen as identical with those which induce reversal between the one arousal-regulating system and the other. However, the telic or paratelic system may override their concomitant arousal-regulating systems, for reasons previously indicated. From the perspective of the arousal-regulating systems, therefore, the telic and paratelic systems can be regarded as possible sources of external disturbance which occasionally militate against the attainment of the preferred levels of arousal of those systems, and produce suboptimal levels of hedonic tone in relation to arousal. From this point of view the two types of metamotivational system can be regarded as independent, with one of them having the possibility of overriding the other. The word 'over-riding' is used here rather than 'control' since, in its normal cybernetic definition, 'control' means that one system can change the preferred level of a variable regulated by the system it governs; in the present case the effect is on the efficacy of the 'lower level' system in attaining the preferred level, not on the position of this preferred level on the dimension concerned. Another way of describing the relationship between these two pairs of metamotivational states/ systems would be to say that where 'preferred' is used in a psychological sense to mean 'desirable' or 'pleasant', then the two pairs of systems or states can be equated; but where it is used in a cybernetic sense, as relating to areas of stability of a regulated variable, they must be seen as having the possibility of being independent and interacting.

Many combinations of behaviour and goal may be associated with either the excitement-seeking or the anxiety-avoidance state at different times and in different people. For example, someone may be arguing with someone else on an intellectual issue. However, he may be doing this either because he is trying to avoid the anxiety presented by a threat to his deeply and sincerely held convictions, or because he enjoys the cut and thrust of the debate and the excitement of the conflict, the subject-matter of the argument being of little importance to him outside this competitive context. Either way the behaviour (arguing) may be the same and the intended goal (winning the argument) the same; but the interpretation of them is widely different. Here are several other examples. A child may have a temper tantrum either for the excitement which it provokes, or because he is anxious and wants to test how much he is loved by his parents. A thief may carry out a burglary, either because he is desperate for money and the anxiety of being without money is greater than the anxiety of being caught; or he may do it for the excitement of the crime itself, the booty being of secondary importance.

The general view being presented here on arousal is one which is to some extent consistent with the two-factor theory of emotion proposed by Schachter (1964, 1970, 1971). This claims that a given emotion is a function of level of arousal, together with some perception of the immediate environment which results in this arousal being labelled in an appropriate way. That is, there are two factors which lead to a particular emotion being experienced, the first being a given level of arousal and the second being a given cognitive interpretation of this arousal. This theory was based on the evidence from such experiments as Schachter's classic experiment with Singer (1962). When subjects were injected with epinephrine, which increased their level of physiological arousal, the emotion they reported, in the absence of accurate physiological information about the effects of the drug, was determined by environmental conditions. These conditions were artificially contrived by the experimenter and, depending on the condition, subjects interpreted their arousal either as euphoria or as anger. What reversal theory says about arousal is in one sense an elaboration of this two-factor notion, but goes beyond it by suggesting a definite structure underlying the ways in which levels of arousal are interpreted. In these terms, if environmental cues have an effect on the interpretation of arousal, it is through the induction or maintenance of one metamotivational state or its opposite. So far it has been shown how the operation of these different states may account for four, in a sense primary, types of affect, and other emotions or feelings will be related to these four in the next chapter. In reversal theory, however, the interpretation of the arousal is not determined solely by environmental cues, as it is in Schachter's theory. Thus a new interpretation, i.e. a reversal from one metamotivational system to the other, may occur not because of changing cues in the environment, but through the innate process of satiation.[7] So, although reversal theory uses the idea of arousal being interpreted in different ways, these different ways are not cognitive in Schachter's sense, since they do not necessarily depend on the processing of information from the environment at a given moment. In brief, the two factors in reversal theory in this respect are arousal and meta-motivational state, with cognitive factors entering the picture as one type of factor determining metamotivational state.

For completeness, the relationship of the two arousal-regulating metamotivational systems to learning should be given some consideration. According to reversal theory, different levels of arousal will be expected to be reinforcing at different times, depending on which system is operative, since different levels of arousal will be felt as pleasant or unpleasant in the two systems. If arousal may be equated with drive, then there is massive evidence in the field of learning theory for the reinforcing properties of low arousal. In recent years, however, a great deal of evidence has accumulated in relation to 'curiosity' and 'exploration', suggesting that activities which would appear to raise arousal may also be reinforcing. The development of optimal arousal theory was designed in part to account for this, but reversal theory provides an alternative framework for interpreting these results. One implication of reversal theory is that some pieces of behaviour, and indeed some ideas, which lead to reward in one state of mind, will lead to punishment in the opposite state, since they help to bring about opposite levels of arousal. What is learned in one state, therefore, may be totally inappropriate to the other state, and if the organism does not learn to make the correct discriminations, i.e. to use the two states as discriminative cues in learning, then maladaptive behaviour and thinking may result. Thus pathological anxiety may be due to behaviour and ideas learned in the excitement-seeking state being carried over into the anxiety-avoidance state; the same may be true of phobias.

In principle, according to this analysis, there are two different ways in which reinforcement may be obtained in relation to arousal.[8] One is to obtain a level of arousal appropriate to the state which happens to be operative at the moment in question, e.g. a level of low arousal in the anxiety-avoidance state. If the level of arousal is appropriate to the state which is not operative, however, and a reversal occurs to this state so that the level of arousal becomes automatically appropriate, i.e. its value now falls within the preferred range, then this will also be reinforcing. For example, if arousal is high, a reversal to the excitement-seeking state will result in the arousal being felt as pleasant excitement rather than as unpleasant anxiety. This raises the question of whether reversal itself may be learned, over and above the behaviour which happens to be going on at the time of the reinforcement. It was mentioned in Chapter 3 that it seemed to be difficult for someone to bring about a metamotivational reversal deliberately and voluntarily. Presumably there are good biological reasons for this: for instance, if it were easy to induce a reversal, then the individual might be able to avoid pursuing any phenomenologically essential goals, many of which may be biologically essential as well, and would then enjoy the feelings of high arousal rather than attempt to achieve such goals and reduce the arousal associated with them. There must therefore be certain factors outside the individual's conscious voluntary control which, at least in certain circumstances, outweigh his ability to invoke reversals deliberately. This does not exclude the possibility that the individual may learn to induce involuntary reversals, perhaps through some form of classical conditioning, so that certain stimuli come to have the power to induce reversal in one direction or the other. For example, an originally neutral stimulus may acquire threatening qualities and induce the telic state, and another stimulus may come to be associated with feelings of security and so be able to induce the paratelic state. The individual may then make deliberate use of such conditioned associations by presenting himself with the appropriate stimuli, if he can make them available, in order to bring about a reversal. To this extent he is therefore able to overcome, albeit indirectly, and only when the stimuli concerned are under his control, the natural barrier to deliberate reversal. A consequence of this is that biologically or psychologically maladaptive behaviour may result. This very same circumstance, however, provides a weapon for the psychotherapist, since it may be preferable in dealing with various problems to help the patient to change from one arousal-regulating system to the other rather than to change the patient's level of arousal. Thus it may be both easier and more constructive to help someone who fears social situations to define them as exciting than to teach him or her to achieve lowered arousal in such situations.

Patterns of Change

This discussion of learning leads naturally into the topic of the relationship between changes in arousal and switches between the two arousal-regulating systems. Levels of felt arousal will change over time depending on a number of factors, including whether the individual is deliberately using techniques to increase arousal (such as any of those which will be found listed in the next chapter), and whether various needs are being imposed by the body, e.g. through hunger, or by the environment, e.g. in the form of danger.

For goals which are biologically determined, there is an obvious arousal cycle in which arousal starts at a low point, builds up during an appetitive phase to some peak, at which there is a form of consummatory behaviour related to goal achievement, and afterwards sinks down relatively quickly to a low level again. This sequence would appear to be innately preprogrammed for biologically determined goals, although how long each step in the sequence takes on a particular occasion and how high arousal rises, may depend on a number of environmental circumstances. Hence, if the goal is food, then arousal will build up during an appetitive phase of behaviour until food is obtained, when the consummatory behaviour of eating will be followed by a lowering of that arousal which was due to hunger. The period of time during which the arousal builds up will depend among other things on how easily available food is in the environment. Similarly, if the goal is to escape from danger, then arousal will build up until escape occurs when it will, other things being equal, return to a low level. The length of time this takes, and the degree of arousal achieved, will depend on such factors as how great the danger is and how easily escape can be effected.

Both of these examples, obtaining food and escaping from danger, are goals which are normally felt as telic. However, there is at least one goal which, although biologically determined, is normally experienced as paratelic. This is the goal of sexual orgasm during intercourse. The same arousal cycle would appear to be followed with this as with the other goals mentioned, from the beginning of copulation through to the post-orgasmic phase. These phases have been labelled by Masters and Johnson (1966) as, in the order in which they occur, the excitement phase, the plateau phase, orgasm and the resolution phase. The first two of these are clearly appetitive, the third consummatory, and the fourth post-consummatory. Although Masters and Johnson relate each of these phases to different levels of physiological arousal, felt arousal would appear to follow essentially the same course.

In the case of a goal pursued in the telic state, the initial low arousal is felt as relaxation and then, as the need to attain the goal builds up, it is experienced increasingly as anxiety. At the point at which consummatory behaviour begins, there is normally a switch to the paratelic state, at which point the high arousal is felt as pleasant excitement.[9] The paratelic state may be maintained at this point and, as arousal diminishes again, boredom supervenes. Alternatively, at some stage during this final part of the cycle, there may be a switch back to the telic state in which case the individual feels relaxed and can look back with satisfaction at the achievement of the goal. If a new telic goal appears at this point, the cycle will start again. This is all represented by flow diagram (i) in Fig. 4.3. In the case of a goal pursued in the paratelic state, however, there are two differences. Firstly, there is not the same likelihood of switching during the cycle, as there is into the paratelic state during consummatory behaviour in the telic cycle if the consummatory behaviour is the biologically determined goal. Secondly, the arousal throughout the cycle is interpreted in a way which is opposite to the telic interpretation. So the cycle may commence with boredom, or at least at some intermediate level of arousal which will not yet be felt as excitement. As it builds up, the arousal is felt as increasingly exciting and reaches its peak during the consummatory behaviour. Following this behaviour, it falls away again until, if some way is not found of prolonging it, boredom is experienced. It is possible in some cases that a switch will now occur into the telic state in this final phase, and relaxation be felt rather than boredom. This is represented by flow diagram (ii) of Fig. 4.3.

In the telic cycle, everything is done while in the telic state, to keep the arousal low for as long as possible, and to lower it as soon as possible when it has risen too high. In the paratelic cycle, everything is done to heighten it as quickly as possible, and to keep it high for as long as it can be maintained at that level. But, in both the telic and the paratelic forms of this arousal cycle, there are likely to be stages which are enjoyed and stages which are felt to be unpleasant. In the telic cycle, arousal may reach an unpleasantly high level before it can be overcome; in the paratelic state the end point of the complete cycle, however long it may be put off, is the unpleasant one of boredom, and the only escape from this is a reversal into the telic state at the end of the cycle.

The reader may be puzzled about why sexual behaviour, which is, after all, as biologically essential as eating or drinking, is claimed to be undertaken normally in the paratelic state of mind. The reason is that the telic and paratelic states are defined phenomenologically and not biologically. In phenomenological terms, normal sexual behaviour has all the characteristics of behaviour performed in a paratelic rather than a telic state of mind. In healthy sexual behaviour, sexual arousal is felt as excitement rather than anxiety and it therefore tends to be heightened and prolonged as far as possible:[10] the behaviour and concomitant sensations are enjoyed for their own sakes rather than as achievements on the way to an essential goal; the general mood is a playful one; and the sexual situation does not, at least in non-pathological cases, appear to the participants to be imposed, but rather to be freely and joyfully chosen. It must therefore be kept in mind that the telic-paratelic distinction is not the same as a distinction between the pursuit of biologically essential and inessential goals. The fact that the sexual drive is as biologically essential to the survival of the species as the drive for food, drink and safety, does not of itself imply that phenomenologically these drives must necessarily be experienced in the same way, or mediated by the same metamotivational state.

In discussing sexual behaviour up to this point, orgasm has been regarded as consummatory and the sexual behaviour leading up to orgasm during intercourse as appetitive behaviour. But it would be possible to regard the whole of intercourse and not just that part of it constituted by orgasm, as the con-summatory behaviour; then sexual behaviour could be seen in a broader context, in which intercourse, including orgasm, would be regarded as the goal of a diversity of appetitive behaviours over a longer period. From this point of view, appetitive sexual behaviour may well, although still not necessarily, be undertaken in a telic frame of mind. In such a case the situation could be described in essentially the same terms as the situation with respect to a goal like food, with the paratelic behaviour of sexual intercourse nested in a larger telic sequence, just as the paratelic behaviour of eating may be nested in a larger telic sequence of food-seeking behaviour. In the case of both sexual intercourse and eating, the accomplishment of the act may be followed by a reversal into the telic state, and a feeling of relaxation and satisfaction at the achievement of the goal. In these terms the difference between the pursuit of sexual goals and other biologically determined goals is simply that the consummatory behaviour in the sexual case may be longer, more varied and more complex, and perhaps involve the attainment of higher levels of arousal. It is interesting, though, that human culture often appears to embody techniques, including various kinds of ritual, for making the paratelic consummatory behaviour related to such activities as eating, at least as lengthy, varied and complex as sexual intercourse can be.

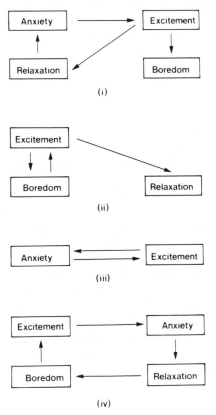

FIG. 4.3 *Some frequently occurring patterns of change between different ways of experiencing (different levels of) arousal.*

Several patterns of arousal change and reversal have now been considered which are based on what one might call an arousal cycle in relation to biologically essential goals. There is another common sequence of change which deserves to be noted, and this is represented by flow diagram (iii) of Fig. 4.3. Here some level of high arousal is given alternating metamotivational interpretations, reversals and re-reversals occurring when cues from the environment, or from the individual's train of thought which is instigated by an environmental event, trigger switches in one direction or the other. Here are some examples. In seeing a postman bringing a telegram there may be rapid fluctuations between excitement and anxiety as one passes in review the various possible messages which the telegram may contain. While sitting in an aeroplane which is taking off, one may experience alternate feelings of fear and exhilaration as one considers first one then another aspect of what might be a dangerous situation. As one sets oneself up to make a crucial putt in a game of golf, prepares to give an important lecture, or waits to be interviewed for a job, so the interpretation of the increasing arousal may fluctuate wildly between anxiety and excitement.

In a number of situations, there may be a build-up of arousal in the telic state due to some threat, followed by a switch to the paratelic state when the threat is suddenly removed or overcome, the result being that the residual arousal is felt, before it decays, as excitement. Indeed, this may be deliberately used as a way of obtaining pleasant high arousal. Hence, in many sports or other activities there may be real danger, the overcoming of which produces feeling of high excitement before the arousal subsides: mountaineering, parachuting, and pot-holing would all be examples where there is real danger. Other situations, which are not normally undertaken by amateurs, may also exemplify this, producing the same feelings in those who take part: like car-racing, bullfighting, even soldiering. Similarly, many activities which people enjoy involve, if not physical danger, at least threat of some other kind, as in gambling or, perhaps, public political debate, in which there may of course be severe threat to one's self-esteem.

Conversely, it may happen that arousal is raised initially in the paratelic state by some event which, when its significance is full realized, induces a reversal to the telic state: excitement is then converted into anxiety. For example, one must admit that one's first reaction on hearing of some calamity, or seeing an accident, is sometimes one of excitement. This is usually followed a little later by anxiety, when the full significance of the event is appreciated.

It is notable that all these examples of fluctuations between the excitement-seeking and anxiety-avoidance states involve high levels of arousal. It seems likely that reversal is less frequent at the lower end of the felt arousal dimension than the upper end, and if this is true there are a number of possible reasons. The organism may be less sensitive to stimuli which induce switches at low levels of arousal, and frustration or satiation may build up more slowly at these levels. Furthermore, most environmental events which precipitate reversals may also be ones which tend to raise the arousal level at the same time. Nevertheless, switches between boredom and relaxation do seem to occur. For example, relaxation appears to give way inevitably to boredom after a period, presumably as a result of satiation, if no other factor intervenes to induce the paratelic state on its own account. Similarly, boredom cannot be maintained for ever and, in the absence of other disturbing factors, gives way eventually to relaxation, provided the goal orientation which results from this reversal does not lead to the recognition of new goals which in turn raise the level of arousal.

The general idea that high arousal, once it has been brought about, may be felt in a different way before it subsides, would appear to be consistent with the excitation-transfer theory of Zillmann (1971). What excitation-transfer theory postulates is that an 'excitatory response', i.e. arousal, due to some stimulus situation, may decay relatively slowly, so that if a new stimulus situation is presented to the subject before it has decayed, the residual level of excitation may be misattributed by the subject to the new stimulus situation. A series of studies carried out by Zillmann and his associates have produced evidence in support of this assertion, using both physiological measures of arousal and measures of perceived, i.e. phenomenological, arousal. For example, it has been shown that arousal brought about by a standard physical exercise[11] will bring about enhanced feelings of sexual arousal in response to an erotic film, provided two conditions are satisfied. Firstly, sufficient time must have elapsed following the exercise, so that the subjects are unaware that the arousal they feel is in part due to this exercise, i.e. there must not be any obvious physiological concomitants of the exercise such as being out of breath or feeling one's heart to be pounding. Secondly, not too much time should have elapsed, otherwise the physiological arousal, as measured in this case by blood pressure, will have been entirely dissipated (Cantor, Zillmann and Bryant, 1975). In an analogous way, it was found (Cantor and Zillmann, 1973) that residual excitation, produced by watching highly arousing segments of film, intensified positive responses to music heard subsequently, provided there was an appropriate delay between the film and the music, presumably in this case to avoid subjects continuing to be preoccupied with the film rather than attending to the music. Similar transfer effects were found under appropriate circumstances from one film clip to another, i.e. a film of an unhappy encounter between two people being perceived as sadder after a high excitation film than after a low excitation film (Zillmann, Mody and Cantor, 1974). Much of the work of Zillmann's school has concerned aggression. For example, it has been shown that experimentally required aggressive behaviour may be increased if arousal has been previously heightened in some way, but only if some motivation for the aggression is provided (Zillmann, Katcher and Milavsky, 1972).

Evidence consistent with the idea that the arousal from one emotion can be converted into that of another by changing the situation, has been adduced by a number of other researchers. Jaffe et al. (1974) have shown that sexually aroused subjects are more hostile than unaroused subjects when they are subsequently given the opportunity in the experimental situation to express their hostility through aggression. Conversely, Kinsey et al. (1953) noted that anger sometimes immediately preceded sexual response, and several experiments have demonstrated how anger can enhance sexual arousal (Barclay and Harber, 1965; Barclay, 1969). It has also been shown in different ways that anxiety *can* facilitate subsequent sexual arousal (Bancroft, 1970; Dutton and Aron, 1974; Hoon, Wincze and Hoon, 1977). All these results lend weight to the idea used in reversal theory that a given level of arousal can be experienced in different ways, and that it is possible to switch from one type of experience to another at any given level of arousal.[12] Since this discussion leads away from anxiety and excitement *per se* it will not be pursued further here. The full range of emotions, including those related to aggression will, however, be discussed in the next chapter.

, Another ubiquitous pattern of arousal change and reversal, but one which is more complex than those considered so far, arises in the following way. Relaxation, through satiation and a consequent reversal to the paratelic state, leads to boredom. The individual then acts in such a way as to raise his level of arousal until it becomes experienced as excitement. At this stage, either through the behaviour having repercussions which are felt as threatening or, eventually, through satiation, a reversal to the telic state is brought about and the feeling of anxiety is experienced as a result. The individual now acts to lower his level of arousal until he achieves the feeling of relaxation. This completes the cycle, which is then ready to start again. This sequence is shown in Fig. 4.4 superimposed on the earlier graph (Fig. 4.1) of the relationship between arousal and hedonic tone. It may be more simply shown as a cycle as in flow diagram (iv) of Fig. 4.3. It will be noted that in some respects this is the converse of the pattern shown in flow diagram (i) of the same figure.

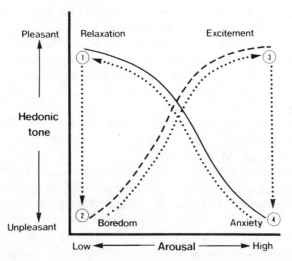

FIG. 4.4 *One commonly occurring sequence of changes between different types of experienced arousal.*

Here is an example of such a sequence. A schoolchild has just finished doing his homework in the evening and feels relaxed. This relaxation turns to boredom and so he looks around for something to do to get some excitement. Finding nothing better, he is insolent to his father and his father's angry reaction causes him some excitement. To keep the excitement up he is insolent again, but now his father's anger reaches a new pitch which makes the child anxious instead of excited. The child manages to allay his father's anger and eventually feels relaxed again.

There may well be common patterns of change other than those described in this section, but the sequences described are ones which appear to occur frequently and which, in various combinations, would seem to make up much of the complex sequence of states in relation to arousal which people experience in everyday life.

Beyond Excitement and Anxiety

A closer examination of the types of feelings which people have in relation to arousal, now requires that the picture presented so far be developed further. One reason for this is that, on consideration, it becomes clear that even in the excitement-seeking state arousal can become too high to be pleasant. Children, for example, get 'over-excited', and adults too would appear to experience a similar feeling under certain circumstances, as implied by such words as 'frenzied' and 'frantic'. This feeling is one of the components of the pathological state known as mania. Plainly, such over-excitement is still a form of excitement and is qualitatively different from anxiety, even if, like anxiety, it is unpleasant. Similarly, just as it is possible for arousal to be too high in the excitement-seeking state, so arousal can become too low to be pleasant in the anxiety-avoidance state. The word 'indifference' suggests itself here, although the word which perhaps best expresses the feeling which results is 'apathy'. This forms the 'mirror-image' of mania and may become one of the components of one type of depression. Other types of depression will be discussed in the chapter on psychopathology. Obviously apathy is qualitatively different from boredom, even if they are both forms of unpleasant low arousal. In particular, since anxiety-avoidance can be seen as an aspect of the telic state of mind, apathy, like relaxation, involves an orientation towards essential goals; but whereas the goals have already been accomplished in the state of relaxation, they may well not have been accomplished in the state of apathy. But in apathy the arousal is so low that the individual 'could not care less'. The goals, although seen as essential, produce no feeling of arousal and, therefore, the individual feels no anxiety as a result of not pursuing or achieving them.

The implication is that it is not just a question of maximizing or minimizing arousal. Rather, the preferred high and low arousal levels of the excitement-seeking and anxiety-avoidance systems, respectively, must have both upper and lower bounds, pleasure coming from the maintenance of the level of arousal *within* the appropriate range defined by these bounds. In other words, the situation is like that represented in Fig. 2.2. In these terms the relationship between arousal and hedonic tone can be represented as it is in Fig. 4.5, where the two curve of Fig. 4.1 have been extended to lower and higher levels of arousal. The result is that there are now two ditonic curves instead of the single ditonic curve of optimal arousal theory.[13] (A ditonic curve, in contrast to a monotonic curve, is one which has two regions in one of which it is increasing and in the other decreasing.) Tension, as defined earlier, will now be felt at four points of non-optimal arousal rather than two: apathy, boredom, anxiety and over-excitement.

This leads to a second unavoidable complication concerning the two hypothetical curves which relate arousal and hedonic tone. The possibility must be taken into account that the position of the peaks of these two curves in relation to hedonic tone may change, depending on various circumstances, towards higher or lower points on the arousal dimension. In the process it is possible that the maximum amount of pleasure or displeasure possible at a given time may be increased or decreased. The graph in Fig. 4.6 illustrates this by showing in dotted lines some possible variants on the anxiety-avoidance and excitement-seeking curves, in which the optimal positions, i.e. the peaks, change. This type of change is referred to as a 'shift' in reversal theory, to distinguish it from reversal on the one hand and change in the actual value of a metamotivational variable, in this case arousal, on the other. It will be recalled that a shift is defined as any change in the characteristics of a metamotivational state. In this sense a shift involves *meta*-metamotivational change.

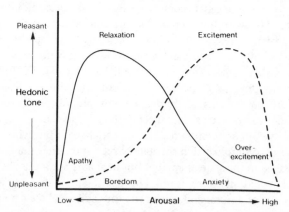

FIG. 4.5   *The relationship between arousal and hedonic tone for the arousal-avoidance system (continuous line) and for the excitement-seeking system (broken line) over the full range of felt arousal.*

Points x and y on the graph represent comparatively high states of pleasurably low and high arousal respectively. It may well be that these states of high pleasure, in extreme cases, represent certain special states of consciousness or altered awareness. In the extreme low arousal case, one thinks of certain kinds of trance, especially hypnotic trance, and of meditation. In the extreme high arousal case, one thinks of those special states of consciousness marked by ecstasy which also lead to types of trance (see Sargant, 1957).

The various factors which might bring about a shift of the optimum position for arousal on each of these curves remain to be elucidated, but certain suggestions can be made. For example, it is possible that how wide awake or tired an individual is may, at least partly, determine the optimum position.

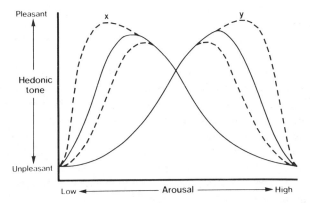

FIG. 4.6 *Some variants (broken lines) on the curves presented in Fig. 4.5, emphasizing that the peaks of these curves may shift over time.*

Various optimal arousal theorists, like Fiske and Maddi (1961) and Zuckerman (1969) have already made this suggestion, but in terms of a single optimum arousal curve. Thus, tiredness might move the optimum point of the excitement-seeking curve to a lower point on the arousal dimension, and, if the possible relationships between arousal and hedonic tone have the pattern indicated in Fig. 4.6, this would have the effect of lowering the maximum possible excitement which could be experienced under these circumstances. Being wide awake would have the opposite effect. Again, to take another variable, feelings of security might raise the optimum position of the excitement-seeking curve, allowing greater feelings of excitement to be experienced (viz. Fig. 4.6), while feelings of insecurity and vulnerability might lower it. Both of these variables, tiredness and feelings of security, might also be supposed to shift the optimum point of the anxiety-avoidance curve, tiredness increasing the extent to which it is possible to feel relaxed, i.e. pushing the peak lower down the arousal dimension, and feelings of security perhaps having the opposite effect. Both of these variables, and possibly numerous others, would presumably interact together to determine the optimum point of each of the two curves at a particular moment.[14]

By the same token, the position of the peak of these two curves would also determine how high or low arousal would have to be before apathy or over-excitement were experienced. If the peaks, representing the optimum positions, were towards the middle of the arousal dimension, then comparatively small increases or decreases in arousal would produce these feelings. Thus, if tiredness shifted the peak of the excitement-seeking curve to a lower position on the arousal dimension, this would mean that it would be easier to become over-excited; and children do indeed often seem to become easily over-excited at the end of the day. Similarly, if feelings of security shifted the peak of the anxiety-avoidance curve to a higher level of arousal, then it would be easier to feel apathetic. As the peaks of the two curves moved towards the lower and upper ends respectively of the arousal dimension, then it would become more difficult to experience either apathy or over-excitement.

Although it has been argued that the excitement-seeking and the anxiety-avoidance states are bistable, so that one is either in one or the other at a given time, nevertheless there is a sense in which a person may be said to be more, or less, excitement-seeking or anxiety-avoiding at a given time. This is because the extent of excitement-seeking or anxiety-avoidance can be represented by different positions of the peak of the curve in question. By extension one could be said to be more or less telic or paratelic at the time in question, at least in relation to the arousal variable, and also, by analogy, in relation to other variable characteristics of the two states.

Further, if the peaks are low in relation to positive hedonic tone and therefore towards the centre of the arousal dimension, then both ditonic curves approximate not only to each other but also to the single optimal arousal curve of optimal arousal theory (see Fig. 4.7). It is quite possible that for periods in everyday life these two curves are indeed fairly close to each other, for many people, so that something like a homeostatic optimal arousal situation prevails. This constitutes another way in which optimal arousal theory may be said to be subsumed by reversal theory.

One thing which is emphasised by the analysis in this chapter is the way in which stimuli may have an impact on the organism at a number of different levels at the same time. Apart from other functions which stimuli may have, e.g. eliciting responses, in terms of arousal they may have at least three different potential functions:

  (i)   they may lower or raise arousal;
  (ii) they may facilitate, or cause, a reversal from one metamotivational state to another;
  (iii) they may shift the optimum point of arousal for the two arousal systems, or indeed change other characteristics of the relationship between arousal and hedonic tone.

According to reversal theory, therefore, change may occur at a number of levels simultaneously in response to a given stimulus situation. For instance, stimuli which provide feelings of security may lower arousal, which would be a motivational effect, induce a reversal to the paratelic state, which would be a metamotivational effect, and raise the optimum point of pleasant high arousal in the paratelic state, which would be a meta-metamotivational effect. All these

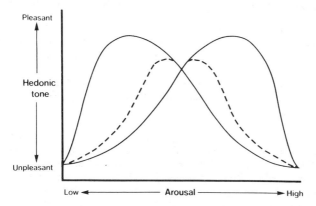

FIG. 4.7 *When the variants on the curves originally shown in Fig. 4.5 take the form shown with broken lines, the two curves taken together approximate in some respects to the single curve of optimal arousal theory.*

effects may occur simultaneously. In this case the individual would then be likely to look for stimuli which would raise arousal, without causing a reversal to the telic state or lowering the optimum point of arousal. The effects of stimuli, in the perspective of reversal theory, are therefore assumed to be considerably more complex than they are in the framework of any kind of behaviourist psychology. The situation is further complicated in reversal theory, in that changes which affect the experience of arousal may take place for reasons other than changing patterns of stimulation; thus, a reversal may be caused by satiation, or the optimum point of arousal may be shifted by tiredness.

Notes on Chapter 4

1. Eysenck's (1967) translation of his personality theory, from description in Hullian drive-reduction terms to description in terms of arousal, is symptomatic in this respect.
2. Thayer (1978), however, sees sleepiness and the feeling of being energetic as opposite ends of the *same* dimension, the dimension of energy expenditure, rather than being different dimensions, as suggested here. Interestingly, Thayer suggests that there is also a second energy expenditure dimension, one pole of which is characterized by what he calls tension and the other by placidity. This dimension may well be essentially the same dimension as that identified in reversal theory as the tension dimension.

3. This paper is, incidentally, reprinted in Fowler (1965) and Bindra and Stewart (1966).
4. Strictly the inverted U-curve can only be used in relation to what Berlyne calls 'arousal boost'. His other explanatory concept in relation to arousal and hedonic tone, that of 'arousal jag', has to be treated in a slightly different way.
5. If the term 'hedonic tone' is used to refer to the pleasant/unpleasant accompaniment to a feeling, such as that of arousal, then the four adjectives which have just been introduced may be said to represent the 'affective tone' of the feeling. This usage contrasts with that of some writers who use the term 'affective tone' to refer to what is being referred to here as 'hedonic tone'.
6. See Spiegelberg (1976), pp.680 ff.
7. Since switches between the telic and paratelic states are linked to switches between the anxiety-avoidance and excitement-seeking states, it is immaterial which of these two pairs of states is seen as being subject to satiation.
8. Many other aspects of a situation other than arousal may of course be rewarding or punishing to different degrees. It is not being claimed here that reward and punishment are *only* mediated through level of arousal.
9. If the goal is not a biologically determined one, and there is no obvious instinctive consummatory behaviour, like eating, then there is also no necessary reversal to the paratelic state at this stage and, therefore, the individual may move directly into a state of relaxation and satisfaction at achieving the goal, without the intervention of excitement.
10. If evidence is needed for this assertion, see Hite (1977) especially p.599 ff.
11. It is questionable, however, just how closely the form of arousal used in this particular experiment relates to the 'felt arousal' of reversal theory, which it will be recalled is defined as a motivational variable.
12. Rook and Hammen's (1977) paper on the cognitive factors which affect the way in which arousal is interpreted, especially arousal in sexual situations, also supports the argument here that arousal can be transferred from one emotion to another, and reviews much relevant evidence.
13. As explained earlier, the relationship between arousal and hedonic tone in the telic and paratelic systems is specified by the relationship which obtains between these two variables in the anxiety-avoidance and excitement-seeking systems which they respectively subsume, and this applies as well to the new ditonic form of the relationship being adumbrated here. Should the telic or paratelic system choose to override the regulation of the arousal variable in terms of the preferred level obtaining, suboptimal hedonic tone is likely to be experienced in relation to arousal.
14. Another factor which may be hypothesized to influence the optimum point is that of the length of time which has elapsed before the reversal. It is possible that the longer a reversal into one state or the other is delayed, the more extreme on the arousal dimension will be the peak of the curve characterizing that state following the reversal. This would be consistent, for example, with the fact that working-class people who live humdrum lives during the week, need to experience particularly high levels of arousal at weekends (Miller, 1958).

5 Emotion: Telic and Paratelic

In the previous chapter, felt arousal was discussed in relation to such emotions as excitement and anxiety. In this chapter a greater range of emotions will be considered in the light of reversal theory.

It would be possible to argue, as many like Cannon (1929) and Duffy (1962) have done, that all emotion involves high non-specific physiological arousal or activation. In a similar vein, it is suggested in reversal theory that emotion generally involves increased *felt* arousal. Of course, if boredom, relaxation and apathy are conceived of as emotions, then it might be more accurate to say that emotions involve extremes on the felt arousal dimension, at either end of the dimension. Clearly, however, most emotions involve high rather than low felt arousal, and it would be not unreasonable to argue that the low arousal 'emotions' just listed are not really emotions at all, but rather the name sometimes given to the *absence* of certain emotional qualities. In any case, most emotions involve high arousal and are therefore felt as pleasant in the excitement-seeking state and unpleasant in the anxiety-avoidance state. In this respect, therefore, the anxiety-avoidance system can be seen as a system which avoids any kind of high arousal emotion, and the excitement-seeking system as one which seeks any kind of high arousal emotion. Since there is a sense in which anxiety is only one kind of unpleasant high arousal, and excitement only one kind of pleasant high arousal, it is preferable in terms of the present discussion of emotions in general to conceive of these two systems as the 'arousal-seeking' and 'arousal-avoidance' systems. Indeed, from this point on in the book these two terms will be used rather than 'excitement-seeking' and 'anxiety-avoidance' when the intended reference is to emotions of all kinds.[1]

As pointed out in Chapter 3, these two arousal-regulating systems may be seen as subsystems of the telic and paratelic systems, and in the present chapter it will be convenient to discuss emotions in this wider metamotivational context. One reason for doing this is that emotions appear to involve an increase in the intensity of experience generally, and not of arousal alone. Another is that the

107

way in which the individual construes the nature of the goal which he is pursuing, or activity which he is undertaking, typically has some bearing on the emotion which he experiences.

Parapathic Emotions

Because of the high arousal involved, one would expect most emotions to be felt as unpleasant in the telic state.[2] It has already been asserted that this is the case with the emotion of anxiety and the related emotions of apprehensiveness, fear, terror, agitation, worry and panic. But it is true, too, of such emotions as anger, rage, hate, disgust, jealousy, guilt, grief and loathing. Of course these are all generally assumed to be unpleasant anyway, but what of emotions which are usually conceived to be pleasant: are these also unpleasant in the telic state? Excitement of course, in the way in which the term is being used here, occurs only in the paratelic state, so the question does not arise in relation to this emotion. This would also be true of ecstasy and exhilaration which are extreme forms of excitement. But what of an 'emotion' like 'love'?

The problem here is that 'love' can mean so many different things from merely liking, feeling attracted to, attached to, or protective towards, someone or something, to a strong feeling of passion, especially sexual passion. In line with the argument which has just been stated, however, one would claim that the more emotional forms of love, especially what might be called 'passionate love' are unpleasant in the telic state. It would seem that this is indeed the case, and that such love is felt in this state as a special kind of anxiety, which is even sometimes described more forcefully, especially by novelists and poets, as a form of agony. This contrasts with the excitement or even ecstasy which attend the feeling of passionate love in the paratelic state. Switches between telic and paratelic during the course of passionate love, occasion those alternations between anxiety and excitement which seem to characterize this kind of relationship. In its lower arousal forms, the feeling of love in the telic state may become associated with a complex of feelings in which security predominates so that, taken together, the feelings constitute a defence against threat, help therefore to keep arousal low, and so are felt as pleasant.

In contrast to the telic state, in the paratelic state all emotions which are associated with increased intensity of experience and increased arousal will be felt as pleasant (unless they take the arousal beyond the optimal peak, as shown to be a possibility in Fig. 4.4). This may be true of the whole range of emotions, including even those which are conventionally thought of as unpleasant: anger, disgust, guilt, and so on. The argument here is that in the telic state these *are* unpleasant, but that honest self-observation will disclose that such emotions become pleasant if they can be experienced in the paratelic state. In other words, if a high arousal emotion is felt as unpleasant, one may confidently assume that the telic state is operative. It may be the case that some emotions are almost invariably experienced in the telic state, and that these emotions are therefore typically experienced as unpleasant. Nevertheless the reversal theory thesis is that *all* high arousal emotions, however unpleasant in the telic state, can be experienced in some form in the paratelic state, and that they will always be pleasant in this state. However, to be experienced in the paratelic state without a reversal to the telic state occurring, these normally telic emotions have to undergo a type of transformation, the result of which is that they come to have in the paratelic state a special phenomenological quality which differentiates them quite clearly from the corresponding emotions in the telic state.

This special quality is one which is not difficult to recognize, but is difficult to describe. It involves a feeling of detachment, which may be only slight, as if the whole experience had a kind of paratelic 'frame' around it ('frame' being a term introduced by Bateson, 1973, and elaborated by Goffman, 1975). This frame holds back any unpleasant threatening features which the emotion might have, while allowing the associated arousal to be enjoyed. To call such emotions 'make-believe' or 'pretence' would be misleading; neither would it be accurate to call them 'pseudo-emotions' or 'quasi-emotions'. It is not that such emotions are simulated; they are genuine, but are phenomenologically marked off as different in essence from their counterparts which go by the same name. This marking off gives them a kind of 'as if' quality: the core of the emotion remains the same, but undergoes a subtle meaning shift and takes on a new significance.

Such emotions are ones that one might want to describe by putting inverted commas around them: "anger", "horror", "hate", and so on; indeed from this point on they will be placed in double inverted commas when it is intended to distinguish them simply from the original emotions from which they are derived.[3] In these terms, even anxiety may become "anxiety"; and so, although anxiety cannot, by definition, be felt in the arousal-seeking state, "anxiety" can. Hence, in watching a sport like soccer, one may be "anxious" at various times in the course of the game, e.g. while watching a penalty being taken. This feeling has much the same quality as the anxiety one might feel in waiting for the result of a medical test, which is presumably something normally associated with the telic state. But it now comes to have an enjoyable paratelic quality unless, as described earlier, the level of arousal becomes too high and goes beyond the current paratelic preferred level. It should also be remembered that it is perfectly possible, at certain stages in watching a sport like soccer, to reverse to the telic state and feel genuine and therefore unpleasant anxiety.

A special word is obviously needed to refer to such emotions. The terms 'semblant', meaning 'having a similar appearance', and 'mimetic' were considered. Both had the disadvantage that they implied that the emotion itself might not be a genuine emotion but only resemble one, whereas what we wished to depict was something about the quality of the emotion, not its existence. Ultimately we were forced to coin a new word to refer to such emotions, and decided to call them 'parapathic'. 'Para' means 'alongside' as in 'paratelic', whereas 'pathic' comes from the Greek 'pathos' which in the sense intended here, means feeling, passion or emotion. It is found in such English words as pathetic, apathy, empathy and sympathy.[4] The term 'parapathic' has a number of advantages in relation to the theory: it brings out the relationship of parapathic emotions to the paratelic state, and it does not imply that such emotions are not real, any more than the term 'paratelic' implies that no goal is being pursued.

It can be seen that emotions and their parapathic counterparts are as similar and as different as objects and the reflections of these objects in a mirror. In principle, any telic emotion may take on a parapathic form in the paratelic state. For example, one may experience a whole range of different parapathic emotions by empathizing with other people in the course of contact with them, and thus experiencing their emotions vicariously. Sometimes of course, particularly if one is genuinely sympathetic and identifies with the person concerned, the emotion may be a telic, non-parapathic one. But frequently because its origin is in someone else, the emotion, while being felt strongly, is distanced sufficiently for it to be experienced as parapathic. In general, the real world, and people's emotions in it, can be perceived as a form of theatre, and the arousal produced may then be enjoyed in the paratelic frame of mind. This serves as a reminder that the theatre itself, and the cinema, are environments which, as it were, specialise in the arousal of parapathic emotions of all kinds, providing a set of cues which help to ensure that the empathic emotions that are generated are experienced as parapathic.

A type of parapathic emotion which appears to be experienced widely and frequently is that of "fear". Presumably everybody has experienced the "fear" brought about by reading ghost stories and watching television thrillers or horror films. In general, fiction, especially of the more popular variety, makes great use of parapathic fear. Fairgrounds also make use of such "fear" by means of roundabouts, roller-coasters, and ghost trains.[5] So do many children's games like 'Murder in the Dark'. In all these cases, for the "fear" to be of the parapathic variety, it must be clear to the individual that the source of the "fear" is not really threatening; without this, the fear becomes telic and real. The source of the "fear" therefore has to be obviously unreal, as it normally is in fiction;[6] or, if there is in some sense real danger, the paratelic nature of the experience, and the fact that there is security which outweighs the danger, must be apparent. Thus real harm could come to people on a fairground roller-coaster, but the whole experience is placed in a kind of paratelic frame, by means of such devices as the special architecture of the fairground, the garish colours, the glitter, and the amplified music, all of which provide highly distinctive cues to make the situation special and set it apart from the 'real' world of everyday experience. This then allows the high arousal produced to be felt as a kind of "fear" excitement. Incidentally, it is surely the case that the level of "fear" experienced in this way can be every bit as high as real fear, or even higher; if this is true, then the contention of theorists like Hebb (1955) and Aldis (1975) that it is only *mild* fear which can be enjoyed is clearly mistaken.

In a similar way the parapathic form of emotions like guilt, grief and disgust are also enjoyed at different times. Thus "guilt" can be quite clearly enjoyable on occasion, as many must have discovered as children when smoking in secret. Similarly, some of the enjoyment of sexual behaviour comes from the "guilt" involved in breaking various taboos. The individual may therefore deliberately manipulate himself into a position of feeling guilty in order to enjoy the delicious feelings of "wickedness" which this occasions in the paratelic state. Such a feeling is, of course, a special kind of "guilt" and not real guilt. If one was really worried about breaking a sexual taboo during sexual behaviour, then this would bring about a reversal to the telic state and with it a feeling of guilt rather than "guilt".

Equally clearly, grief can also be enjoyed as parapathic grief, as it is when one 'wallows' in grief and refuses to be distracted from it. Typically, one dramatizes one's situation to oneself in such cases in order to extract as much emotion as possible. This 'self-dramatization' is a way of putting the emotion in a paratelic frame, giving it an "as if" quality and ensuring that it is felt as "grief" and not grief. What happens is that one looks at oneself and one's own emotional behaviour, as it were from outside. This may, indeed, be a healthy response to situations like bereavement, the only escape from which, however temporarily, may be to convert it to parapathic grief.[7] If one can enjoy grief in its parapathic form, the same is true of such emotions as despair and jealousy in which one can also 'wallow'. Similarly, one can enjoy such emotions as disgust, loathing, and detestation, as witnessed by people's fascination, at least on occasion, with disease, death and putrefaction. In all these cases the emotion which is enjoyed has the special phenomenological qualities which characterize it as parapathic.

A parapathic emotion which is particularly prevalent is that of "anger". The next section of this chapter will therefore be devoted to a consideration of "anger" and anger, and both forms of the emotion will be considered in the context of aggression.

There are several other points which may help to clarify the notion of parapathic emotions. The first is that, although all parapathic emotions are paratelic, not all paratelic emotions are parapathic: excitement is not parapathic and, more specifically, neither is sexual excitement. When humour is discussed in a later chapter it will become apparent that this is a paratelic "emotion" too, but it is not a parapathic one. Secondly, it must again be insisted that parapathic emotions have to be distinguished from pretence emotions: emotions which are deliberately simulated and not really felt as emotions at all. For example, in the telic state one may behave in a particular way in order to imply that one is experiencing a certain emotion, with the aim of achieving some essential end, as women or children sometimes do when they appear to be upset, for instance. Alternatively, in the paratelic state one may deliberately pretend to experience an emotion in order to produce a synergy, this being enjoyed in the paratelic state. (The notion of synergy will be discussed fully in the next two chapters). In the paratelic state one may also feign some emotion like anger in order to produce an exciting effect in the course of interaction with others. So deliberately pretended emotional behaviour in which no real emotion is felt must not be confused with parapathic emotion, the latter involving genuinely felt emotion, albeit of a special kind. Thirdly, it may be supposed that the arousal produced by parapathic emotions is sometimes so great that it goes beyond the peak of the arousal curve (Fig. 4.5) and is felt as unpleasant high arousal, even though the state remains paratelic. A final point is that, although external cues may help the individual to establish a paratelic frame within which he may experience parapathic emotions—e.g. the distinctive cues provided by a fairground, or by the literal frame of a painting, the proscenium arch in the theatre, or a television set—such cues are not always essential for this purpose. On occasion an individual will reverse into the paratelic state for some reason other than through the agency of external cues, e.g. the telic state may satiate. Once in the paratelic state the individual may then search for parapathic emotion and find it in everyday situations which do not themselves provide distinctive cues: he may for instance enjoy a family row as if it were a dramatic performance, and even engineer it for this purpose. In such a case the individual is, as it were, bringing his own paratelic frame to the situation rather than finding it already there. Alternatively, once a paratelic state is established one may, in the absence of any relevant external cues, produce parapathic emotions in oneself entirely through fantasy.

Aggression, Telic and Paratelic

The whole topic of the psychology of aggression has been widely debated in recent times, especially in relation to the question of whether or not it may be said to be instinctive.[8] The aim here is not to enter into this debate, although our discussion is relevant to it, but to argue simply that a distinction must be made when talking about aggression, between aggression which is performed in a telic state and aggression which is performed in a paratelic state, and to suggest that aggression will not be fully understood unless this distinction is recognized. By aggression will be meant behaviour in which the intention is to harm or destroy someone or something, rather than mere forcefulness of behaviour, which is the way the term is sometimes used.[9] The harm in relation to another person may of course be emotional rather than physical.

At the outset one must be careful to distinguish between aggression itself, which is a form of behaviour, 'aggressiveness' then being a propensity to behave in a certain way, and anger which is an emotion.[10] It is important to make this distinction because the feeling of anger may occur in the absence of aggression, aggressive behaviour being inhibited for some reason, and conversely aggression can occur without anger, being performed deliberately and unemotionally in order to achieve some end.[11] This is yet another example of the point made in Chapter 1, that the same behaviour may be related to quite different experiential states. In making this distinction, a distinction is also being made between related words which describe on the one hand aggressive behaviour, words like 'violence' and 'destructiveness', and words which describe feelings related to anger like 'hostility', 'hatred', 'temper', 'rage', and 'fury'.

The presence or absence of anger or aggression gives rise to four possible combinations, and each of these may occur in combination with the telic or paratelic state. The various possible combinations of these three factors is shown in Table II. Lines (1) and (2) of this table are not of interest in the context of the present discussion, but consideration will now be given to the other six combinations.

TABLE II. *Possible combinations of the presence and absence of anger and of aggression in the telic and paratelic states*

ANGER	AGGRESSION	STATE	
No	No	Telic	(1)
		Paratelic	(2)
	Yes	Telic	(3)
		Paratelic	(4)
Yes	No	Telic	(5)
		Paratelic	(6)
	Yes	Telic	(7)
		Paratelic	(8)

Let us first consider aggression which occurs in the absence of anger: lines (3) and (4) in Table II. Examples in the telic state would include much of the behaviour of soldiers and policemen in the course of their duty. Milgram's (1974) renowned experiments on obedience presumably deal in the main with exactly this kind of aggression: aggression performed in order to achieve certain imposed ends which are seen as essential. The absence of anger in such situations does not imply the absence of emotion, and it may be supposed that the purpose of the behaviour by the individual concerned is to reduce his anxiety. In this, of course, it may fail; thus a policeman may find that his aggression only increases the seriousness of his problems. The behaviour may also, because of retaliation, *lead to* a feeling of anger; but at least initially the aggression is anger-free.

In the paratelic state of mind, aggression may also occur in the absence of "anger". This aggression is of a playful kind, whether or not it is recognized as playful by others, which is performed in order to create situations which may be interesting and exciting.[12] Here are some examples: a child breaks another's toy to see the effect on the other child; a drunk in a pub looks provocatively at someone or nudges him "accidentally" in the hope that the other will react; a teenage football supporter heaves a brick through a shop window in the hope that some "aggravation" will ensue; a husband criticizes his wife's new dress in order to experience the excitement of upsetting her. In some cases the aggression may involve pretended anger and, as already emphasized, such a pretended emotion is different from a parapathic emotion. For example, a father may pretend to be angry with his son and dare him to behave in a particular way in the hope that the challenge will be responded to, and that this will lead to a family scene. Often paratelic aggression is institutionalized, as in the case of sport in which aggression and counter-aggression occur in the context of competition. Paratelic aggression may, of course, fail in producing excitement and even produce increased boredom: the drunk may be unprovoked, the wife unresponsive, the son appeasing. All this can be summarized in the two flow diagrams of Fig. 5.1, the two end-points in each case being alternatives, with the intended effect of the behaviour shown underlined.

Let us turn now to the situations represented by lines (5) to (8) in Table II. When anger is felt, this always involves arousal and may be regarded as a particular form of arousal. Sometimes such arousal will be high in the case of rages and tempers, and therefore will be felt as unpleasant in the telic state. Anger felt in the paratelic state, however, will normally be experienced as parapathic anger, and in this case the arousal associated with it will be felt as pleasant. In both states the hedonic tone will have a strength which is a function of the degree of arousal, which may be high. Examples of parapathic anger would be the empathic "anger" one might feel in listening to a friend's tale of harassment by some bureaucracy; in watching something unfair happening to the hero in a film; or in responding to the poor performance of a sports team one is supporting. Each of these cases might also, of course, involve reversal to the telic state and real anger, as occurs for example in 'flare-ups' in sport. In the paratelic state one may seek out situations which produce the arousal of "anger", whereas in the telic state one will avoid anger-producing situations as far as possible. Either way, the anger does not necessarily issue in aggressive behaviour, and aggression would certainly be most unlikely in the first two of the three examples of situations just cited which might give rise to parapathic anger.

On the other hand, both telic and paratelic anger may give rise to aggressive behaviour. It may be supposed that the expression of such behaviour in itself will, momentarily at least, bring about a lowered state of anger. Following this, however, commonsense and everyday observation tells us that there are a number of possible eventualities, depending on the response of the environment to this aggression. If the aggression is towards some inanimate object, then this may be the end of the matter. But if the aggression is towards some other person

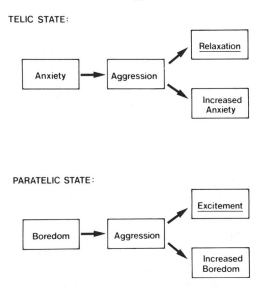

FIG. 5.1   Non-anger aggression in the telic and paratelic states, with the possible outcomes in each case.

or persons, then in the normal way of things they will react, either by retaliating, by appeasement, or by removing themselves from the situation. In the case of retaliation this may lead to renewed feelings of anger and more aggression; the whole situation may then escalate, or it may lead to a feeling of fear in the original aggressor and an attempt on his part in turn to "leave the field". In the case of appeasement or flight on the part of the victim, the feeling of anger by the aggressor will presumably eventually subside. This much is common for anger in both the telic and paratelic states, i.e. for both anger and "anger". The result of aggression in these various ways may be to increase or decrease the arousal associated with anger. The difference, of course, is that in the telic case the aim of the behaviour is to decrease the arousal, in the paratelic case to maintain or even to increase it, and in either case the behaviour may be successful or unsuccessful in attaining this end. All this is summarized in the two flow diagrams of Fig. 5.2, the three end-points in each case being alternatives; the intended effect of the aggression in the telic and paratelic states is underlined in each case. In the paratelic case, of course, "fear" would be an acceptable outcome.

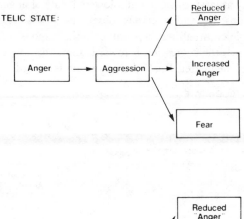

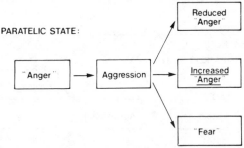

FIG. 5.2 Aggression based on anger in the telic state, or "anger" in the paratelic state, with the possible outcomes in each case.

Each of the two sequences which have been schematized in Fig. 5.2 may become a closed loop, as may the two sequences, telic and paratelic, involving non-anger aggression discussed earlier and depicted in Fig. 5.1. Thus, if boredom leads, through aggression, to increased boredom, as it may do if the individual attacked leaves the field, then this may in turn lead to increased aggression towards someone else, and so on. Similarly, increased anxiety, increased anger or reduced "anger" may all lead in the appropriate circumstances to even more aggression.

There is a further complication in all this. Aggression-without-anger (Fig. 5.1) has been dealt with here separately from aggression-with-anger (Fig. 5.2) but, clearly, the former may develop into the latter and vice versa. Thus the reduction of "anger" to a negligible level in the paratelic state (Fig. 5.2) will, in the absence of any other form of arousal, lead to the feeling of boredom; this in turn may lead to further aggression in order to obtain renewed excitement (Fig. 5.1). In the latter eventually the aggression would be occurring in the relative absence of "anger", since this has already been reduced to a low or non-existent level. Of course, the excitement achieved through such paratelic aggression may turn to "anger", and this would be the converse case: that of aggression-without-anger turning to aggression-with-anger. For example, a gang of youths may be aggressive towards some passer-by in order to achieve excitement, at this stage feeling no anger. However, a number of policemen may then arrest them so that they feel "angry" at the policemen. This leads us to yet another complication; this is that there may be a reversal from the paratelic to the telic state, or vice versa, at various points in both the with and without-anger sequences. So in the example just given, in arresting the youngsters the policemen may be so violent themselves that the youngsters reverse into the telic state and become angry, rather than "angry".

In order to understand aggression, therefore, it is necessary among other things to know whether it is associated with anger or not, and whether the intention of the aggression is to obtain excitement or avoid anxiety, to reduce anger or increase "anger". That this distinction between telic and paratelic aggression is not eccentric or unnecessary is evidenced by the fact that in everyday life one does often make exactly this distinction. To give one example, rugby players commit various kinds of violence on each other, and may do so in front of policemen standing on the touch-line; but they are not arrested. The paratelic nature of the situation is well understood. Unfortunately, in other situations the paratelic nature of the aggression may not be understood by the victim, onlookers, or by the representatives of the law, and behaviour which is no more than playful may be interpreted as serious aggression and treated accordingly. So aggression between soccer players does not reach the law courts, but aggression between the fans of each side, which research has shown is also governed by various 'rules of play' which are well understood by those taking part (Marsh, 1978 a and b, Marsh et al., 1980), may well lead to arrest and court cases.

The Pursuit of High Arousal

There are various method which the individual may use in order to bring about high arousal in the paratelic state. Some of these have been discussed in relation to parapathic emotions in general and to "anger" in particular. The attempt will now be made to give some idea of the range of different methods which are available. These methods are so many and varied that it is difficult to feel confident that any listing is exhaustive, but the techniques to be discussed here probably include all the major ones.

These methods for obtaining high arousal, including various forms of excitement, depend not just on their potential for increasing arousal, but for their doing so in a way which avoids reversal to the telic state taking place. Indeed, much of the development of human culture can be seen as the development of socially approved ways for simultaneously increasing arousal and maintaining, or reversing into, the paratelic state. In particular, this is obviously true of all types of entertainment including fiction of all kinds, art and sport. Which particular techniques an individual tends to use most frequently, however, will depend on various factors, besides availability, that determine for that individual which techniques are most arousing, and which ones generally involve the least threat and therefore the least likelihood of a reversal to the telic state.[13] Each individual must discover these for himself. Some of these techniques have already been cited by such theorists as Berlyne as ways of increasing arousal.[14] In contrast to Berlyne's various theoretical formulations, in reversal theory the assumption is that such techniques are used to obtain and maintain high, rather than intermediate, levels of arousal.[15]

1. Production of sexual excitement

Although much of human culture is concerned with raising arousal in such a way that a reversal to the telic state does not take place, at least one form of high arousal does not, under normal conditions, require the intervention of culture if the paratelic state is to be maintained: this is, as noted earlier, sexual excitement. In other words, biologically the paratelic state is the natural one for sexual behaviour, since high arousal is biologically required for orgasm. This does not mean that culturally-contrived methods for the enhancement of arousal may not be brought to bear, or that in pathological conditions reversal to the telic state during sexual behaviour may not occur in some people. But, basically, the attainment and maintenance of sexual excitement is a biological phenomenon, and forms the prototype in experience and action for all the biologically inessential forms of arousal-seeking and attainment which are so prevalent in human culture.

Stimuli which produce sexual arousal are also used *in* various cultural contexts to increase the level of excitement which would otherwise be felt, e.g. the use of erotic stimuli in advertising, and of attractive cheerleaders in American football.

2. Use of negativism

By 'negativism' in reversal theory is meant a desire or need to do the opposite of that which is required or expected in a given situation. Behaviour resulting from this can include various forms of disruption, such as arguing and causing 'situations', confrontations and conflicts, all of which can bring about pleasantly increased arousal in the paratelic state. Negativism often involves breaking taboos; but the chosen taboo has to be seen as mild by the individual, otherwise breaking it may bring about a reversal to the telic state, and consequent feelings of anxiety rather than excitement. Examples of taboos which are frequently broken in the paratelic state are swearing, getting drunk (although in some situations this may be required rather than taboo) and breaking various sexual 'taboos', like oral-genital caressing, in the course of sexual foreplay.

The behaviour which results from negativism can be arousing in itself, or can have consequences which are arousing, by making someone else retaliate, for example. The whole topic of negativism will be deferred for detailed treatment later.

3. Induction of parapathic emotions

In the paratelic state the individual often contrives to present himself with situations which produce emotions, but which do not cause reversal to the telic state. Often these emotions are those which would be unpleasant in the telic state, but which are arousing and therefore pleasant in the paratelic state while it is maintained. They have that special quality which makes them the type of emotion which has been defined as parapathic emotion. Such situations are generally either obviously make-believe, e.g. the behaviour on a stage in a theatre, or involve behaviour which is demarcated from everyday life and 'distanced' from it by means of various cues.[16] Such cues to the nature of a situation are examples of metacommunication (Bateson, 1973): they say something *about* the communication and how it is to be interpreted, rather than being part of the communication itself. Thus in a debate, factors like the physical setting and the rules of procedure, are such that a range of emotions may be felt by the debaters and the audience as parapathic: the anger, criticism and offensiveness of the debaters may then be enjoyed rather than the reverse. Of course in a situation such as this, the cues do not necessarily remain effective all the time, and temporary reversal to the telic state may occur in any of those taking part. Sometimes, however, the cues may be small and subtle, and only recognizable by people who are practiced at recognizing those particular cues in that context. Thus, members of a family may recognize when other members are behaving in a paratelic state of mind, whereas to an outsider the behaviour may seem to be genuinely insulting or hostile.

4. Use of empathy

Much parapathic emotion arises in turn out of empathy with the emotions, parapathic or otherwise, of other people. By 'empathy' here is meant the capacity to feel oneself into someone else's life world, including his or her emotions.

It does not necessarily imply sympathy with that person, but it does imply understanding him, being able to put oneself in his place and see the world through his eyes. In this sense one could empathize with someone, while still judging him to be, for example, villainous. Such empathy can also be described as vicarious emotional arousal, and it has been demonstrated by a number of researchers (e.g. Buck *et al.*, 1974).

Fiction of all kinds obviously brings about the arousal of vicarious emotions. So does conversational story-telling, including the recounting of truthful events: when people tell their stories to others, their listeners can share such emotions as surprise, anger, or disgust, and enjoy the associated arousal. For this to occur, the emotion as it is experienced by the listeners must be felt as parapathic, and empathy appears typically to be able to produce just this kind of effect by providing sufficient identification with the other person for the emotion to be felt, but sufficient distance for it to be experienced in parapathic form. There will, naturally, be exceptions to this, when empathy will produce non-parapathic emotions. Similarly, if one can observe other people's emotions in various situations, one can often enjoy these emotions in parapathic form even if they are unpleasant to those experiencing them. Television makes a great deal of use of this effect, showing close-ups of soccer players who have just scored goals, politicians who have lost elections, people whose homes have recently been destroyed in natural catastrophes, and so on. One may even enjoy eliciting emotions in other people for this very reason, whether the emotion which is provoked is an unpleasant one, e.g. jealousy (or in the extreme case of sadism, terror) or a pleasant one, e.g. excitement as someone unwraps an unexpected present.

There is an inverse effect here, too. If one can see one's own emotions through other people's eyes it is possible, as it were, to distance oneself from one's emotions, and experience them in parapathic form even when they are strongly unpleasant. It is likely that this is the effect of some forms of psychotherapy, the client coming to see his own emotions from outside, through the therapist's eyes, and coming to be able to handle them by means of this device. In the absence of a therapist, self-dramatization, in which effectively an audience is imagined, can help in a similar way. The experience of putting things in their blackest possible light when feeling miserable, in order to give oneself the pleasure of parapathic despair, is one which is surely familiar to many people. This effect was noted earlier in relation to grief.

Empathy may also be felt towards inanimate objects or patterns, and indeed it was essentially in this sense that Theodor Lipps (1903) originally introduced the term into psychology . He was particularly concerned with reactions to the spatial properties of objects, such as the way in which the perception of a vertical line can make one feel as if one is contending against gravity, or the observation of a slender shape broadening towards the top can elicit a feeling of soaring or stretching upwards. This idea can easily be extended to music so that one may experience the conflict between themes in the first movement of a symphony, or the unresolved nature of certain chords like the dominant seventh, as a form of "anxiety".[17]

5. Being in a crowd

Being in a crowd is an experience which many people find exciting in itself. This is no doubt part of the excitement of an activity like Christmas shopping, especially in one of the fashionable streets of a large city like London or New York. It is also part of the excitement of being at a party or in a night club. Frequently the attention of people in crowds, or audiences, is directed towards some common source of interest, such as a procession going past, a play, a concert, a political leader, or a game of soccer. In such cases the common emotions felt by individuals are, it seems, amplified through some kind of inter-stimulation, so that each person feels more intense about the events than he would have done had he been observing them on his own. This is presumably one aspect of what Floyd Allport called 'social facilitation' (Allport, 1924).[18] In terms of reversal theory, not only may it be the case that being in a crowd increases the level of arousal which is then felt as exciting but, at least for many types of crowd, the crowd experience itself may also provide the feelings of security which help to maintain the paratelic state in its members; it is this security which therefore allows the arousal to be felt as excitement in the first place.

6. Use of frustration

Small amounts of frustration in a given situation often, it would seem, increase feelings of arousal. A good example of the way in which such frustration is deliberately used in order to create arousal would be the flirtatious use of momentary withdrawal or refusal by one or other partner during the build-up to sexual intercourse. Strip-tease similarly creates, and plays on, frustration in order to increase arousal. So do thriller novels, where the reader is kept in suspense about the outcome; and there would be little pleasure in reading a detective novel if one knew the identity of the culprit from the outset. All games systematically rely on frustration to be exciting, since each player aims to frustrate his opponents. Arousal may also be increased by unintentional frustrations: for example, readers may have had the experience of queuing and not getting into a soccer match until after the game has started; they may recall that they experienced greater excitement at this stage, hearing the crowd noises, than they did when they eventually entered the ground and saw the game.

Indeed, in the most general sense, barriers of all kinds—difficulties, challenges, problems, etc.[19]—are often sought out, welcomed, used, and even specially constructed, in the paratelic state. This contrasts with the telic state in which barriers are avoided, since of course the aim of action in this state is generally to achieve a goal as soon as possible, and to avoid the arousal associated with its non-attainment. In rock climbing in a paratelic state of mind, a severe overhang might be a barrier to be sought out and overcome; but while carrying out a mountain rescue operation in the telic state such a barrier would be avoided at all costs. This search for, or avoidance of, barriers and frustrations is central to the whole telic/paratelic distinction.

If a frustration is sufficiently strong, of course, it may cause aggression, as Dollard (1941) and others pointed out in their frustration-aggression hypothesis. When the emotion underlying this is that of parapathic anger, then such frustration may well be acceptable in the paratelic state, especially if the aggression leads to retaliation by others and increased "anger". However, frustration is also likely, if sufficiently intense or prolonged, to induce the telic state; in this eventuality any resulting aggression will be associated with anger, and the high arousal of this anger will be felt as unpleasant. So if one is playing some game badly because one's equipment turns out to be unexpectedly faulty, or if withdrawal in a sexual encounter turns out to be genuine rather than pretence, then this frustration may well be sufficient to cause a reversal to the telic state and a feeling of genuine anger.

If it is true, as suggested by reversal theory, that frustration can cause a reversal in either direction, then there may be situations in which frustration will cause a reversal into, rather than out of, the paratelic state. It is possible that the fantasy solution to problems and other kinds of 'regressive' behaviour occur under such conditions.

7. Use of synergy

The concept of 'synergy' will be discussed extensively in the next two chapters. For the moment it can be noted that it is postulated in reversal theory that synergies raise arousal and increase the intensity of experience. They are therefore usually avoided in the telic state and sought out in the paratelic state in which the arousal associated with them is felt as pleasant.

8. Overcoming natural limitations

Overcoming the limitations of one's body would appear to raise arousal. Such limitations are so habitual that they can hardly be classified as frustrations. For example, escaping from, or overcoming the effect of, gravity plays a part in many exciting activities from children's play on swings and see-saws, to more equipment-oriented adult pursuits like flying, parachuting, hang-gliding, and mountaineering. Similarly a number of hobbies involve empathy with objects which seemingly escape from gravity: balloons, fireworks, kites, model aeroplanes, rolling hoops, spinning tops, and so on. Again, many freely undertaken activities involve overcoming the normal limitations of space so that one can affect, or be affected by, things or people at a distance beyond that which is normally possible in an unaided way. Such activities include target sports like archery, shooting and golf, and pursuits in which information is gleaned from great distances as in the use of telescopes and telecommunications of all kinds. Examples could be multiplied of pursuits which overcome one or another natural limitation, be it of strength, intelligence or bodily vulnerability. Similarly, overcoming the limits of logic, of the nature of time or of physical causality, are also exciting and part of the fascination of horoscopes, palmistry, astrology, telepathy, clairvoyance, telekinesis, black magic, seances, and the occult in general. No doubt the fun and fascination of all these different activities owes much to a variety of factors, but the common factor running through them all is the excitement which comes from escaping from physical and other natural limitations.[20]

9. Use of novelty and uncertainty

Felt arousal in response to novel or unexpected events is a common everyday experience, and it would be reasonable to suppose that, in general, the more novel or unexpected the events, the greater the arousal which is felt. Although arousal is defined in reversal theory in phenomenological rather than physio-logical terms, it is notable that much of the work on the physiology of arousal and activation can be said to have involved novel and changing stimulation. In particular, the response to unexpected and intense stimulation, like a sudden loud noise, has been studied physiologically in a number of guises, including the 'startle reaction' (Landis and Hunt, 1939), the 'startle reflex' (Sternbach, 1960), and the 'defence reaction' and 'orienting reaction' (Sokolov, 1960).

Not only do novelty and unexpectedness bring about higher arousal, but they also help to maintain it once it has been achieved; conversely, familiarity and predictability appear to lower arousal over a period. Again this is a phenomenon which will be recognized from everyday experience, but which has also been investigated physiologically. For example, Daniel (1967) showed that EEG rhythm decreased in frequency as vigilance declined in the monotonous environ-ment of a vigilance task. It has been shown (Sharpless and Jasper, 1956; Jasper, 1958) that habituation to a stimulus which is presented over and over again appears to be related to changes in reticular activating system activity.

One should therefore not be surprised to find that situations which are contrived to achieve and maintain paratelic arousal are typically characterized by uncertainty, unpredictability, unfamiliarity, unexpectedness, variety, surprise, and novelty. Provided the context is one which helps to maintain the paratelic state, and this means that the context must have opposite features like security, familiarity, and predictability, then this arousal will be felt as excitement, or in the form of a parapathic emotion like "shock", or "fear", or "anxiety". Every form of entertainment, including sport, art, fiction and humour, makes use of such properties as uncertainty, surprise and novelty within secure contexts. Thus, in the security of a modern art gallery one can enjoy the novelty of an artist's vision or technique, the uncertainty which may arise from his use of aleatory effects, or the shock of his breaking with artistic or even social conventions. At a football match the sense of security provided by the football ground, the music, the pre-match rituals of various kinds, and knowledge that the rules of the game remain constant, allows the spectator to enjoy the arousal which comes from the uncertainty of the outcome and, in a good match, the originality and variety of the play itself.

If an individual feels confident and secure enough in himself, in a paratelic mood, then he may give full rein to his curiosity, and carry out exploratory activity with the aim of making surprising, and therefore arousing, discoveries.

10. Risk-taking

People often deliberately expose themselves to quite unnecessary risks, and one must presume that one of the main reasons for doing so is to obtain excitement, or perhaps parapathic fear and parapathic anxiety. Otherwise why should people risk large sums of money as they do in gambling, or even risk their lives as they do in dangerous sports like parachuting or pot-holing? Watching other people take risks may also produce pleasant high arousal through empathy, as it does in watching such activities as bullfighting, or car-racing. In some situations there is no real risk involved, e.g. there is no physical risk to the spectator at a bullfight, but in others the enjoyment appears to come after some real danger has been mastered. What happens in such situations, as noted in the previous chapter, is that the danger brings about arousal, the removal of the danger induces the paratelic state, and the residual arousal is then felt as excitement.

11. Search for significance

In Chapter 3 it was noted that an activity which is construed as being significant is more likely to be associated with high arousal, other things being equal, than one which is not. By significance here was meant an awareness of the context of the activity and of the repercussions which the activity might have in this wider context. Significance can never be felt, except perhaps in certain mystical states, as separate from particular goals and activities, and what it does among other things is to amplify the arousal which is associated with them. For example, if the result of a game of bridge has far-ranging implications for one's future social life, then playing the game is, other things being equal, likely to be associated with higher arousal than it would be if this were not the case. Or to revert to risk taking: if the possible gains and losses of a risk are substantial and far-reaching, then the risk will presumably give rise to higher levels of arousal than it would if the risk involved negligible consequences. One can make deliberate conscious efforts to see a continuing activity in as significant a way as possible, and such an effort may enhance the level of arousal. One may also choose activities that one already associates with feelings of significance. Unfortunately, in the paratelic state the feeling of significance itself will be unpleasant, and this may more than offset the pleasure derived from the increased arousal.[21]

12. Use of stimulus properties

Many properties of stimuli appear to be physiologically arousing or, to use Berlyne's term, to have 'arousal potential'. The same properties seem also to increase felt arousal. Berlyne has discussed and studied such properties extensively, and our own examples of such properties will be listed here under the same general headings as those which he uses (Berlyne, 1971).

First of all there are psychological properties. Intense stimuli—bright colours, loud noises and so on—are more likely to be arousing than less intense, but otherwise identical, stimuli. Sheer size is also likely to be arousing, as in the perception of mountains or enormous man-made edifices such as skyscrapers or Gothic cathedrals. Repetition, too, can be used to build up arousal, as it is in music, e.g. the 'riffs' of jazz, or in other forms of entertainment, e.g. the multiplication of identically dressed people doing identical things at identical moments in a music hall chorus line or in a military tatoo. An insistent rhythm, which is another form of repetition, can also be highly arousing, and is used for this purpose in dance music of all kinds.

Secondly, there are ecological properties. These are properties which elicit responses, including an increase in arousal, because of their connection with pleasant or unpleasant conditions. Such a response may be innate, and related to particular stimuli for good biological reasons: thus the shape of the female breast may produce sexual arousal in the male, while squirming snake-like shapes seem to produce fear and revulsion. Stimuli may also acquire ecological properties for a given individual through learning: for instance, some people develop phobias for certain stimuli; others come to find that particular stimuli have sexually arousing properties which they did not have originally, and these stimuli may even become fetishes.

Thirdly, there are what Berlyne has called 'collative properties' of stimuli (Berlyne, 1960, 1971), which can be thought of as structural properties. Examples of such properties are complexity, incongruity, and ambiguity, as well as novelty. Spatial properties of the kind which Lipps described in terms of empathy, and which have already been illustrated here, may equally be counted as collative properties.

13. Use of fantasy

If all else fails, the individual may still be able to increase felt arousal, in the form of excitement or of some kind of parapathic emotion, through fantasy. This is perhaps especially true of sexual fantasy, but people fantasize about a variety of things which produce emotions of various kinds and, typically, such fantasies take the form of narrative (Singer, 1976). Such fantasizing is to be distinguished from the realistic anticipation of success by someone who is pursuing a goal in the telic state of mind, even if this anticipation takes the form of concrete images of success.

14. Use of offence mechanisms

Clearly, in psychologically healthy people, daydreaming and fantasy of the kind which has just been referred to, are undertaken quite deliberately, and with full conscious awareness of the non-realistic nature of their content. Nevertheless, some of this content may derive from unconscious material, the significance of which is not fully realized, and do so in a way which is not necessarily under complete voluntary control once the fantasizing process has started. Thus, one may not understand why one finds a particular fantasy exciting, but find it occurring regularly when one chooses to fantasize. If it is the case that the various Freudian defence mechanisms operate in the telic state in order to reduce the arousal which would arise if certain unconscious ideas and needs were recognized, the technique of bringing unconscious material into consciousness in some form or another in the paratelic state, in order to *increase* the level of arousal, might well be said to involve a type of mechanism which in this respect is the opposite of those described by Freud. In this case one would be justified in referring to such a mechanism as an *offence mechanism*. Among other things this would explain why in fantasies, dreams, myths, nursery rhymes, and so on, arousing material is often openly incorporated of a type which, from a Freudian point of view, one would expect to be heavily disguised. After all, one may actually dream about sexual intercourse, and nursery rhymes often contain material of great cruelty. It is tempting to speculate that much of psychoanalysis involves the attempt to harness this type of mechanism for therapeutic purposes.

Several points need to be made about this list of techniques used to produce high arousal. The first is to remind the reader again that, since the arousal/

hedonic-tone curves are ditonic, the use of these techniques may occasionally push arousal beyond its optimal point in the arousal-seeking state, as described in the previous chapter, so that unpleasant over-arousal will be experienced. The second point is that most of the factors listed may under certain circumstances, or if their effects are too strong, induce the telic state, and with it anxiety rather than excitement. Novelty, for example, may be so unexpected and intense that it is threatening and induces a reversal to the telic state. Negativism may provoke a reaction from someone else in a social situation which is stronger than intended, and hence this reaction becomes threatening and converts the original excitement into anxiety. Seeing some continuing activity as highly significant, and therefore serious, may be sufficient to bring about a paratelic-to-telic reversal. Becoming the focus of attention in a crowd, having to give a speech for example, is highly threatening to many people. Often, therefore, the search for excitement necessitates two steps, the first being the attainment of adequate feelings of security through setting up a safe context of one kind or another, the second being the attainment of arousal within this context;[22] hence the strict rules governing most forms of play. It is also possible, as noted previously, that the safer the context, the greater the excitement which can be felt, i.e. that the feeling of security brought about by such factors as strict rules, shifts the peak of the arousal-seeking curve further up the arousal dimension, and in the process increases the maximum potential hedonic tone, as shown in Fig. 4.6.

Another point is that there is a great deal of overlap between these separate categories, since in reality they are interlinked in a complex fashion; this is another way of saying that there is necessarily some degree of artificiality about such a listing. Thus escaping from normal limitations often involves risk-taking and novelty; negativism enters into breaking mild taboos, and into the use of small amounts of frustration, and it may produce unexpected and novel results; risk-taking also takes place in the context of uncertainty and may produce unexpected results in certain situations. In turn, novelty could have been listed as one form of stimulus property and empathy could also have been discussed, at least in part, under the heading "use of stimulus properties"; sexual arousal is initiated by the ecological properties of certain stimuli; parapathic emotions may also derive from ecological properties of stimuli and often from empathy; more generally, parapathic emotions may be a result of a number of the devices listed. Nonetheless this listing makes clear the variety of ways in which arousal-seeking may enter into behaviour.

Many situations involve the use of a number of these techniques at the same time, or in quick succession, in order to obtain and maintain arousal. To illustrate this point here are four examples.

(i) *Sexual* arousal during foreplay may be increased by breaking mild taboos, like using sexual swear words; by novelty and unexpectedness, e.g. of context, clothes, time of day, position of intercourse; by small amounts of frustration, e.g. through one partner tantalizing the other by alternately approaching and withdrawing; and by eliciting parapathic emotions, especially perhaps that of "anger". The use of such techniques for sexual purposes will be discussed further in Chapter 11.

(ii) In *sport*, the competition often involves physical risk. The rules of the game ensure, among other things, equality of opportunity for the contestants, and to this extent increase the degree of uncertainty in the result, as do certain systems of handicapping. The players competing cause each other frustration; parapathic emotions like "anger" and "anxiety" may occur among the players; and empathy on the part of the spectators is probably essential to their enjoyment of the sport.

(iii) In setting oneself a *challenge* in a paratelic state, one is doing so in the hope that the pursuit of the challenge will result in high felt arousal rather than, as in the telic state, pursuing a goal which has already been imposed in some way in order to reduce the arousal associated with it. Examples of such freely chosen challenges might range from collecting antiques, or having the best front garden in the street, to sailing the world single-handed. In general, setting challenges would appear to be a part of most hobbies and pastimes, including sport. The arousal arises in a number of ways, including the frustration which normally occurs, at least for a period, in meeting the challenge, the unpredictability of the effects of one's behaviour, the uncertainty of success, and the risk-taking which is often involved. Setting the challenge itself may involve a form of negativism[23], especially if the goal is one which is taboo, e.g. stealing underwear. It may also involve overcoming normal limitations, e.g. body-building by someone who regards himself as a weakling.

(iv) A number of the techniques described are also made use of in works of *fiction*. Uncertainty of outcome is continually necessary to maintain arousal;[24] surprise is also often used a great deal; the reader needs to feel empathy with the characters and their emotions, and as a result experiences parapathic emotions; there may be small amounts of frustration, as in the kind of teasing which occurs often in detective novels; and the whole fictional situation is inherently synergic.

A Comparison with other Theories of Motivation

It is not intended here to carry out a detailed comparison of reversal theory with other theories of motivation, but a broad indication of the way in which reversal theory differs from other theories might nevertheless be helpful.

Basically, most psychological theories of motivation are explicitly or implicitly homeostatic theories. This is clearly true of optimal arousal theory. But it is also true of other major theories of motivation which have been proposed, such as those of Freud, Lewin, Hull and Lorenz. In the work of each of these four theorists, a different term is used for the central motivational variable; but in each case the variable is supposed to have a single preferred level which is, furthermore, taken to be low, in contrast to optimal arousal theory in which the variable in question, arousal, is claimed to have an intermediate optimal value. In contrast to all these, of course, reversal theory assumes bistability rather than homeostasis.

The basis of Freud's earlier theory of motivation is the constancy, or 'stability', principle, which he took over from Fechner (1873) and restated in the following terms: "The mental apparatus endeavours to keep the quantity of excitation present in it as low as possible or at least to keep it constant". (Freud, 1920; 1955 edition p.9). This principle dates back to the beginning of Freud's psychological work, and as early as 1888 he was writing of a 'stable amount of excitation' (Freud, 1888). Whether or not the endeavour is to keep excitation as low as possible or as constant as possible, and Freud seems to vacillate between these two formulations, the principle is clearly a homeostatic one. It then forms the basis for Freud's 'pleasure principle', the idea being that 'unpleasure' is avoided if excitation, or 'tension', is kept constant or reduced to a minimum. The other principle which Freud postulated in this earlier theory is the 'reality principle', by means of which the ego inhibits the reduction of excitation if this conflicts with the need for survival.

Freud's second, later theory of motivation dates from his book "Beyond the Pleasure Principle" which was originally published in 1920. Here he adds to the pleasure principle and the reality principle, which he sees at this stage to be a modification of the pleasure principle, a new principle that is opposed to both the former principles. This he called the 'nirvana' principle which he saw as expressing a 'death instinct'. The aim of the nirvana principle is to reduce excitation not just to a low level but to zero. Clearly, this also represents a form of homeostasis. Indeed, it can now be seen that both Freud's theories are homeostatic and both are based on a principle of excitation, or 'tension', reduction.[25] Freud himself recognized that there were problems in this position since ". . . there are pleasurable tensions and unpleasurable relaxations of tension. The state of sexual excitation is the most striking example of a pleasurable increase of stimulus of this sort, but it is certainly not the only one". (Freud, 1924, 1961 edn. p.160). This was a problem which he never satisfactorily resolved within the framework of his own set of assumptions. Reversal theory suggests that it cannot be solved in terms of a single-system homeostatic theory. Freud also admitted that

"Pleasure and unpleasure, therefore, cannot be referred to an increase or decrease of a quantity . . . . It appears that they depend, not on this quantity factor, but on some characteristic of it which we can only describe as a qualitative one. If we were able to say what this qualitative characteristic is, we should be much further advanced in psychology". (Freud, 1924, 1961 edn. p.160).

Dare we claim that this qualitative factor has been identified in reversal theory in relation to different metamotivational states?

The comparatively recent motivational theory of Lorenz is fundamentally similar to Freud's. According to Lorenz (1950) 'action specific energy' builds up in an organism until it is released by some 'releaser' stimulus situation in the environment, the release taking the form of an appropriate innate behaviour pattern. The threshold of stimulation necessary to release the behaviour will become less as the action-specific energy builds up over time. In the complete absence of a releaser, a point will be reached at which the activity will finally 'go off' *in vacuo* in what has been termed a 'vacuum reaction'. This is very similar to Freud's notion of instinctive energy which has to be expressed, or of excitation which has to be held constant or lowered, or even, in the nirvana principle, totally extinguished, through some kind of mental or physical activity. The Freudian equivalent of vacuum activity would be neurotic behaviour of certain kinds. The two theories direct themselves to entirely different fields of observation: in Lorenz to the behaviour of various species of animal in their natural setting, in Freud to the behaviour of adult neurotic human beings; and there are many differences between the theories. But they are both homeostatic and postulate that when some motivational force builds up beyond a certain point, then activity is initiated to reduce the level of this force, even if the action is one which is in some sense inappropriate to the environmental situation at the moment in question. It is interesting that both theories can be described in terms of simple hydraulic models, as Lorenz himself has done for his own theory in the paper cited above, and some writers on psychoanalysis have done for Freud's (e.g. Hendrick, 1966). The point for present purposes, however, is that Lorenz's theory is only one more single-system homeostatic theory, and contrasts in this respect with bistable reversal theory.

Lewin's theory of motivation is homeostatic at several levels. The central concept is that of 'tension', which for Lewin seems to mean the kind of feeling which goes with any unsatisfied need or unattained goal or uncompleted activity. ". . . the effect of a purpose or intention is the formation of a quasi-need, that is, dynamically, of a tension system. This tension system drives toward discharge and causes activities which serve the execution of the purpose" (Lewin, 1935, p.242). Here, then, we have a statement of homeostasis which is not unlike that of Freud or Lorenz.

Homeostasis also enters at another point in Lewin's theory, in that the state of tension in a particular system is postulated to equalize itself with the amount of tension in 'surrounding' systems within the individual, so that the whole system composed of these sub-systems will tend to move into a state of stable equilibrium. This equilibrium may, however, still represent a state of tension overall, like a container of gas under pressure. It is also possible, according to Lewin, for a stable state to be reached in a system as a whole when there are still some differences in tension between the separate systems which make it up. Again, it is not necessary to go into the complexities of Lewin's theory here, but simply to note the way in which the theory assumes, and is based on the notion of, homeostasis.

From the point of view of experimental psychology, the most influential idea has been that of drive, a term which originally came from Woodworth (1918), and of drive reduction. This reached its epitome in the learning theory of Clark Hull (1943). Hull assumed that all behaviour is motivated by homeostatic drives, which may be brought about for experimental purposes through deprivation of food, water or sexual outlets, or by learned secondary drives related to them, the aim of behaviour being to reduce these drives and the physiological needs on which they are based. Hull also assumed that all reinforcement, and therefore all learning, depended ultimately on the reduction of primary homeostatic drives. In the 1950s this view came under attack for a reason which is of direct interest to reversal theory: a number of experimenters demonstrated behaviour in animals which appeared not to be based on any kind of obvious homeostatic physiological need. In one of the most notable of these many experiments, Butler (1953) demonstrated that rhesus monkeys would learn when they were reinforced by a 30-second view of the laboratory through a small window. In a later experiment (Butler, 1954), he found that the sight of other monkeys was more reinforcing than seeing moving objects.

A number of new concepts were proposed to explain the results of experiments of this kind. But the notion of homeostatic drive reduction was so deeply embedded in the minds of learning theorists, that many of these new concepts still continued to rely essentially on this notion. Thus Berlyne (1950) initially proposed that novel stimuli elicited a response which could be called 'curiosity', attention to such a stimulus resulting in the reduction of this response. Montgomery (1953) suggested that novel stimuli elicited an 'exploratory drive' which would decrease over time with exposure to the stimulus. Putting matters the other way round, Myers and Miller (1954) hypothesized that familiar stimuli evoked a 'boredom drive' that would be reduced by stimulus variety. Butler himself favoured a 'curiosity motive' and went on to demonstrate that its strength, measured with reference to visual exploration behaviour, could be increased in monkeys under conditions of deprivation, just as the strength of the hunger drive, as measured in terms of a variety of kinds of behaviour, can be increased under conditions of food deprivation (Butler, 1957). Whatever the drive postulated, whether of exploration, boredom, or curiosity, the end-product of behaviour was seen by these theorists to be the reduction of the drive to a low preferred level. Nevertheless, the idea eventually began to gain ground that an *increase* in drive in an exploratory situation could be reinforcing. Harlow proposed a 'manipulation drive' (Harlow, 1950, Harlow *et al.*, 1950) and a 'visual exploration drive' (Harlow, 1953) which he argued did not operate in a homeostatic fashion; he demonstrated, with monkeys, that reinforcement does not necessarily depend on the decrease of such drives. Montgomery (1954) showed with rats that an increase in drive could be reinforcing.

The way seemed to be open for the idea embodied in reversal theory of two different motivational systems with opposite effects. At this stage, however, the idea of arousal, and with it the idea of optimal arousal at some *intermediate* position on the arousal dimension, began to dominate the field. This idea, which in part arose out of the difficulties of drive reduction theory, appeared to solve the problem of both increase and decrease of drive being reinforcing at different times. Most of the present chapter constitutes a critique of optimal arousal theory, as does the previous chapter.

The work in the optimal arousal, or optimal 'stimulation' tradition which comes nearest to recognizing, as reversal theory does, that the individual may seek very high arousal, is the research of Zuckerman and his colleagues on what they call 'sensation-seeking'. This work had its origins in the studies on sensory deprivation pioneered at McGill University. (See Zubek, 1969, for an extensive review of work on this topic which was another factor in the development of the idea of 'arousal' and 'optimal arousal' in the 1950s). Zuckerman was interested in why some subjects were less able to cope with sensory deprivation than others, and postulated that some people had a greater need for stimulation than other people. In order to study this he developed the 'Sensation-Seeking Scale', which was a questionnaire for measuring people's need for sensation or stimulation (Zuckerman et al., 1964). The items in this inventory implied that some people may seek high stimulation. Thus one of the later versions of the scale (Zuckerman, 1971) measures four factors as well as the general factor: Thrill and Adventure Seeking, Experience Seeking, Disinhibition, and Boredom Susceptibility. Items with high loadings on Thrill and Adventure Seeking include items like: "I would like to try parachute jumping", "I would like to learn to fly an airplane", and "Sometimes I like to swim far out from the shore". These three items, and many others on the scale, would seem to involve the desire for very high levels of arousal. Zuckerman himself, however, interprets sensation-seeking entirely in the framework of optimal arousal theory and homeostasis. As he put it in an early paper "Whether due to constitution or experience, there are marked individual differences in the setting of the homeostat" (Zuckerman, 1964, quoted in Zuckerman, 1974, p.82) and the aim of the sensation-seeking scale is to find this single setting for each individual tested. He suggested in a later paper that ". . . the typical level of arousal reached when confronted with a new stimulus defines the optimal level of arousal" (Zuckerman, 1974, p.136). Although in Zuckerman's terms some individuals may seek high arousal, for example in the form of thrills of various kinds, nevertheless the optimal level of arousal for each individual is supposed to remain relatively constant. A corollary of this must be that, for many people,

sixteen different definitions of meaning. Fortunately, it will be possible to carry forward the present argument concerning cognitive synergy with a relatively general and informal notion of meaning. By 'meaning' here will be intended any phenomenologically salient characteristic which contributes to one's understanding of the nature of an identity, be the characteristic denotative or connotative.[2] It can therefore reside in a simple property or attribute, e.g. size, colour, age; an evaluation, e.g. good, ugly; a feeling-value, e.g. threatening, enjoyable; or membership of a class which may depend on other simpler properties, e.g. adult, tennis, cathedral, motor vehicle. It may also lead to the recognition of an identity as being one particular identity rather than another, e.g. the recognition of a particular person, this also depending on the presence of a set of simpler properties. In these terms, the overall meaning of an identity depends in some way on many simpler 'atomic' meaning attributes, and contra-diction between meanings can occur at either the more atomic level of attributes and properties, or the more global level of class membership and recognition of particular identity (or both at the same time). In Appendix A will be found a fuller discussion of the relationship between attributes, classes, and particular identities which is implied in this brief statement, and which underlies the discussion of synergy in this chapter and the next.

An *identity* may be an object, a person, a place, a situation, a statement, a group of people, or even oneself. The single term 'identity' will be used here to avoid the need to list all these different kinds of entity continually throughout the discussion. Sometimes what people actually perceive directly will only be *part* of the identity, the rest of the identity being inferred. For example, one normally sees only one side of a three-dimensional object at a given time, or one only sees part of a town, the existence of the rest being assumed; but both the object and the town are identities even though they are not perceived in their entireties. Identities tend to be particular rather than general, concrete rather than abstract.

Cognitive Opposites

It is widely accepted today that one of the principal ways in which experience is organized and meaning assigned to situations is in terms of 'opposition'; i.e. to understand the meaning of something, one also has to understand what it is *not*. The notion of synergy is developed on the basis of this assumption, which therefore needs to be discussed here.

The essential part which opposites play in meaning has been emphasized by a number of linguists. Thus as Benjamin Lee Whorf (1940) pointed out, in a universe in which everything is blue, the concept 'blueness' could not be developed for lack of contrasting colours. A fish could not possibly have the concept of water, since it has experienced nothing else which would contrast with it (McLuhan and Fiore, 1968, p.175). So knowing something about an identity also implies knowing something about what it is not, and these two aspects of meaning are interdependent and complementary. The presence of antonyms in language appears to point in the same direction. As Lyons (1968) has said:

> "The existence of large number of antonyms and complementary terms in the vocabulary of natural languages would seem to be related to a general human tendency to 'polarise' experience and judgement—to 'think in opposites'." (p.469)[3]

It is relevant here that, in word association experiments, if a stimulus word has an antonym, this will be the most frequent response word (viz. H. H. Clark, 1970).

Sometimes a word may have a number of different opposites, contextual clues determining which of them is most appropriate in a given instance. For example 'giving' is opposed to both 'receiving' and 'taking'; 'resistance' is opposed to both 'attack' and 'submission'; 'teaching' is opposed to both 'not teaching' and 'learning'. Similarly in the discussion of humour in a later chapter, it will be seen that the word 'man' has a number of different opposites which in different contexts reflect back different meanings onto the word 'man' itself.

Leach, among other anthropologists, has emphasized the importance of 'opposition' in relation to non-verbal communication:

> "The indices in non-verbal communication systems, like the sound elements in spoken language, do not have meaning as isolates but only as members of sets. A sign or symbol only acquires meaning when it is discriminated from some other contrary sign or symbol." (Leach, 1976 p.49)

This notion lies at the heart of structuralist linguistics and structuralist anthropology.

The idea of cognitive opposition has become a central, if much debated, notion in contemporary anthropology, particularly through the structuralist theorizing of Lévi-Strauss. To him, as to cognitive psychologists like Bruner et al. (1967), categorization is a basic and universal function of the human mind. But Lévi-Strauss further argues that the fundamental form of categorizing is binary, and that the operation of the mind is based on binary opposition. This concept is inspired largely by the work of Roman Jakobson in structural linguistics. Jakobson (Jakobson and Halle, 1956) and his colleagues of the Prague school showed that the recognizable phonemes which constitute a given language are constructed through the binary opposition of contrasting sounds. Phonemes are discriminated by means of opposing distinctive features of consonant and vowel sounds, like nasal/oral, compact/diffuse, and grave/acute. Lévi-Strauss carries this idea over into the investigation of those cultural systems which he regards as constituting 'languages', like culinary systems, totemic systems, and myth systems; and he develops highly elaborate theories based on the idea of binary opposition to account for various features of these systems (e.g. Lévi-Strauss, 1963, 1964, 1966, 1968).[4]

However much one might disagree about the details of Lévi-Strauss' analyses, he seems to have identified an important aspect of the way in which man makes sense of his world, and there is force in his argument that opposition is intrinsic to human culture and therefore to human mentality. In Lévi-Strauss' terms the binary oppositions basic to a given culture operate in a way which is largely unconscious to the members of that culture, whereas the oppositions of interest to reversal theory are oppositions *within consciousness*. If Lévi-Strauss is right, however, about the importance of binary opposition to cognitive processes, then one would expect this to have implications for conscious, as well as unconscious, processes.

While structural anthropologists like Lévi-Strauss have, as noted, been mainly concerned with the oppositions involved in such cultural 'languages' as the 'language' of costume, or of cooking, or of totem systems, they have in some cases also been concerned with the language of gesture. This is obviously more closely related to language in the normal sense than the other areas just mentioned, since its primary aim is that of communication. It is interesting in this context that Darwin, writing on the language of gesture in animals in his classic work "The Expression of the Emotions in Man and Animals" (1872, republished in 1934) postulated as one of his principles of expression the 'Principle of Antithesis'. He stated this principle as follows:

"Certain states of mind lead to certain habitual actions which are of service. Now, when a directly opposite state of mind is induced, there is a strong and involuntary tendency to the performance of movements of a directly opposite nature, though these are of no use; and such movements are in some cases highly expressive." (pp.4-5, 1934 edn.)

Darwin gives the example of a hostile dog characterized by a number of features which are naturally advantageous when the dog is about to attack an enemy: it walks upright with head raised, the hairs bristle, the pricked ears are directed forwards, the canine teeth are uncovered, the tail is held erect and rigid. When the dog approaches its master, in contrast, these features are reversed: the body sinks downwards and perhaps even crouches, the hair becomes smooth, the ears are depressed, the teeth are covered, the tail is lowered and wagged. Darwin argued that none of the latter features are of service to the animal in themselves, but have an expressive significance solely because they are the opposite of features which *are* of service. In these terms antithesis becomes an important principle in the development of expressive gesture, and is assumed to underlie the genesis of gesture in humans as well as animals.

The importance of opposition in cognitive organization is also suggested by several lines of research in psychology. In their work on "The Measurement of

Meaning" (Osgood *et al.*, 1957), Osgood and his colleagues found in using their semantic differential technique that subjects were perfectly able to place 'concepts', e.g. father, myself, abstract art, along a set of bipolar attribute scales like happy/sad, hard/soft, slow/fast, etc. This would appear to demonstrate that such oppositional dimensions do indeed underlie connotative meaning. Similarly, Kelly (1955) in using his repertory grid technique has explored the personal constructs which each individual develops to make sense of his own particular world, especially the people in it, and which consist essentially of opposite attributes like strict/lenient, kind/unkind, boring/interesting. Each construct therefore involves a contrast between two opposite poles. It is possible that only one pole of a construct is available to conscious awareness in a given individual, the other pole being said to be 'submerged'. Thus someone may describe everybody as 'kind', but this, according to Kelly, nevertheless implies the existence of the opposite pole for that person; if this were not the case, then the verbal label attached to the single pole would be meaningless. It is not entirely clear how far researchers like Osgood and Kelly are discovering the bipolar nature of cognitive organization or imposing it on their subjects by means of their investigative techniques. At the very least, though, it is significant that subjects do not appear to find any difficulty in complying with the required procedures.

It will by now have become apparent that there two kinds of opposites. First of all, there is simple mutual exclusion like 'blue' and 'not blue'. Any kind of mutual exclusion involves some feeling of opposition in the sense of the presence or absence of a certain quality. This can be thought of as constituting 'weak opposition'. Secondly there are pairs of attributes which constitute what can be thought of as 'strong opposition'. This applies to attributes which tend to be dichotomized into opposites like big/small, high/low, ugly/pretty, etc., in which the two attributes in each pair can both be identified in their own rights as involving some positive quality, rather than one of the attributes being simply a negation or absence of the other.

Opposites have also been categorized in various other ways by different writers. For example, Ogden (1967), on the basis of a detailed analysis of linguistic and psychological oppositions, has distinguished between what he calls 'opposition by cut' and 'opposition by scale'. Lyons (1968) has argued that there are different types of 'oppositeness of meaning'. His distinction is between 'complementarity', 'antonymy', and 'converseness' (p.460-470). Indeed the discussion of different types of opposites goes back to the ancient Greeks (for a detailed discussion, see Lloyd, 1966). Although it may be possible to distinguish between opposites in a variety of ways, we would argue that all types of opposites are phenomenologically similar in some respects, even 'weak' and 'strong' opposites.

This brief review suggests that 'thinking in opposites' is a fundamental feature of human experience. Meaning is assigned to an identity, at least in part, by determining which of two opposite characteristics should be assigned to it for each of a set of salient pairs of characteristics. However, what is of even greater interest here is that an identity can be simultaneously assigned *both* of a pair of opposite characteristics and therefore display contradictory meanings. Although this may not be logically possible, phenomenologically it is prevalent.

Cognitive Synergy

A chequer-board may be composed of mutually exclusive attributes, black and white squares, and in this sense therefore may be said to be both black and white. But there is no real contradiction in this case since it is the *parts* of the identity that are black and white. Situations arise, however, in which a *whole* identity may be seen to have opposite characteristics. It is this kind of situation which is referred to in reversal theory as a 'cognitive synergy'. The idea is that opposite characteristics may co-exist in the sense that one is aware of both in consciousness, in relation to a given identity, and that these opposites both contribute something to the full meaning of the identity, or contribute alternative meanings to the identity. Either way, synergies always embody some form of self-contradiction.

It might seem that the word 'ambiguity' would serve to describe such a situation, rather than 'synergy'; but we have felt it necessary for a number of reasons to use a term which is new in the present context. One reason is that although ambiguities are all forms of synergy, as will be explained later not all synergies are what would normally be called 'ambiguities'. The word 'synergy' is therefore more general than the word 'ambiguity'. Another reason is that 'ambiguity' has a negative connotation whereas it will be argued that 'synergies' can be pleasant or unpleasant depending on circumstances. Finally, the word 'synergy', deriving as it does from the Greek word 'ergon' meaning work and 'syn' meaning together, implies that two things coming together in a synergy *work together* to produce some effect which they could not have produced separately.[5] In a synergy in the reversal theory sense, two incompatible meanings when brought together appropriately will produce a special phenomenological effect which could not have been produced by either alone. In this sense the elements of a synergy, although logically antagonistic, nevertheless have a co-operative phenomenological effect. This would appear to be particularly the case where 'strong opposites' are involved.

The word 'synergy' is not completely new, but has been used for a long time in a number of disciplines to describe situations in which agents interacting together produce a greater effect, or a different effect, from that which could have been produced by the agents acting alone. (See Appendix B for a summary of these different uses). The term is therefore being used here in a particular way to refer to a particular form of synergy.

One important way in which synergies in the reversal theory sense differ from each other, is in terms of whether one level of interpretation of the identity is involved or two. In the first case, there is a change from one meaning being assigned to the identity to a mutually exclusive meaning being assigned to it. This will be referred to as a 'reversal synergy', since a reversal between opposite, or at least mutually exclusive meanings, is involved. In the second case, there are two parallel levels of interpretation, so that mutually-exclusive meanings may be assigned simultaneously to the same identity on different levels. In this case there need be no *logical* contradiction. This will be referred to as an 'identity synergy'. Identity synergies will be dealt with in the next chapter; the remainder of the present chapter will deal with reversal synergies.

For a synergy to be experienced at all, as already explained, opposite meanings must in some sense co-exist in awareness in relation to an identity. So if an identity changes its meaning in some salient respect there is not necessarily a synergy. However, if this meaning-change occurs suddenly and unexpectedly then it *is* possible for a synergy to be experienced, since part of the earlier meaning may briefly 'carry over' and for a short time continue to be experienced along with the new meaning. If one suddenly hears that a relative has died, a colleague been promoted, a bright student failed, or a friend married, there is momentarily a feeling of bewilderment while the two contradictory meanings compete, and this experience of the two different meanings is synergic. Since it is based on a change from one meaning to an opposite meaning, it is a form of reversal synergy.

The same might occur in relation to one's own self-concept, especially during periods of transition in life. A newly qualified doctor may feel a synergy between his old and new status; so may a newly married couple, or a recently imprisoned criminal. Similarly, part of the enjoyment of learning a new skill, e.g. speaking a foreign language, playing a musical instrument, or driving from the tee in golf, is that it produces a temporary synergy between one's self-image, which includes an inability to perform the act in question, and the actuality of performing it. The thrill of feeling that "It's really true, I'm married at last", or "I managed to play that piece perfectly for the first time" are at least partly due to the synergic quality of the situation.

Ambiguity and Reversal Synergy

A more complex form of reversal synergy derives from those situations which are called, in everyday language, 'ambiguities'. In ambiguity it is not possible to make a definite decision about the meaning of some identity in some respect, and so there tends to be an alternation between the different meanings, i.e. a continuing process of reversal from one to the other.

In all cases of ambiguity it is impossible for an observer to make up his mind definitively about some characteristic of an identity. At the lowest level, the ambiguity may be about some particular property, e.g. about whether a coloured shirt is red or orange. At a higher level, it may be about which class an identity belongs to: either it can be assigned to one class or to some other mutually exclusive class, e.g. whether it is a shirt or a blouse. Or it can be about whether it is one particular identity or another, e.g. which shirt a particular shirt is. In all these cases ambiguity can arise in one of three ways. Firstly, there may be a lack of information; this can be called 'incompleteness ambiguity'. Secondly, the information may have a margin of error such that it is impossible to make a decision one way or the other with confidence; this can be called a 'borderline ambiguity'. Thirdly, the information may contain contradictions; this can be called 'contradiction ambiguity'. For example, in terms of a particular property, i.e. value of a particular attribute, it may be difficult to decide whether a patch of colour is red or orange, either because it was seen extremely briefly (e.g. with a tachistoscope), because the value of the colour was on the borderline between red and orange, or because part of the patch appeared to be red and part orange.

Here are examples of these three different types of ambiguity in relation to identity, in this case the identity of a person on the telephone. Suppose someone telephones and says her name is 'Jean':

(a) Incompleteness

One may be expecting a telephone call from two different people called Jean; without further information it may not be possible to tell which one is actually telephoning.

(b) Borderline

One may not hear clearly whether she said 'Jean', or 'Joan', the sound being indistinct.

(c) Contradiction

The person on the telephone says her name is Jean Jones whereas her voice sounds like that of Jean Evans. Here ambiguity arises through conflict between different pieces of information.

As already noted, ambiguities involving class membership are of the same three types. Suppose the doorkeeper at a club to which women are not admitted has to decide whether each person who arrives at the door is a man or a woman. The decision would be difficult in a particular case if:

(a) Incompleteness

There was a lack of information: the individual was wearing a large cloak and hood, which reduced the information available about his or her sex.

(b) Borderline

The value of those attributes available for inspection were on a borderline: hair was of medium length, voice of medium pitch, trousers were being worn.

(c) Contradiction

There was conflicting information: the voice was that of a woman, but a light moustache could also be seen.

It can be seen from these examples that ambiguity of the value of an attribute can lead to ambiguity at the higher levels of class membership and the identification of a particular identity.

Earlier in the book, in discussing bistability, reference was made to ambiguous figures of the kind which have interested psychologists studying perception: such figures as the Necker cube, the duck-rabbit, and figure-ground reversals. In all these cases the ambiguity is not about the identity of the figure (one knows which particular figure in a book one is looking at), but what the figure represents. Is it a duck or a rabbit, an old woman or a young lady, a cube seen from below or from above? In all these cases there is insufficient information to allow the ambiguity to be resolved: the rest of the animal's body is missing, there is no shading on the cube, etc. And so the figure reverses as an alternation occurs from one interpretation to another, the ambiguity being of the incompleteness type.[6]

In all cases of ambiguity, there tends to be an alternation between one kind of meaning and another, between seeing the situation in one way and seeing it in a different way. In such cases, the situation is bistable and there is a reversal between the two opposite ways of seeing the identity.

Suppose, for example, that one is not sure whether someone is male or female. If the ambiguity is of the incompleteness type, then one will tend to see the person as one sex or the other and 'complete' the information accordingly, in order to make meaning out of the ambiguity, as in the Gestaltist's principle of 'closure'. If the ambiguity is of the borderline type, then the tendency will be to perceive the borderline attributes as slightly different in value so as to push one's interpretation definitely into one gender category or the other. If the ambiguity is of the contradiction type, then one will tend to see the individual as male with some female features, these being seen as exceptions to the perceived masculinity, or as female with some male features, these again being seen as exceptions. However, because there *is* ambiguity, the categorization is unstable and always likely to reverse from one 'preferred state' of interpretation to the opposite. So, although it might in principle be possible to see someone as in some sense concurrently both man and woman (hermaphrodite), or to see someone as intermediate along some notional scale of masculinity-feminity, nevertheless the situation is basically bistable: one tends in practice to assign fully one meaning or the other at a given moment.[7]

Much of this decision-making process may be automatic and unconscious, although if the situation is particularly vague or contradictory its ambiguity may force itself on the individual's attention and result in some deliberate attempt to 'solve the puzzle'. But even where the meaning-making is achieved unconsciously, the individual is still likely to become aware of the ambiguous nature of the stimulus situation through the occasional switches between meanings which are always likely to occur.

Alternative meanings in a reversal synergy may each be associated with different feelings or evaluations: is this identity to be accepted or not, encouraged or not, praiseworthy or not? So ambiguity may result in ambivalence, involving reversals between opposing feelings or eliciting opposing moods. In turn, ambiguity may lead to alternating and mutually opposed actions, and therefore underlie inconsistent behaviour.

The concern here has been mainly with perceptual rather than linguistic meanings, ambiguities and synergies, although language has been involved since classes, attributes and identities can usually be represented by verbal labels. Language itself, however, can be ambiguous: words themselves, and sentences, are also identities which may have different meanings.[8] Linguistic ambiguity may arise in various ways. The same sound may represent different words; this is known as 'homonymy'. For example 'site', 'sight' and 'cite', or 'bored' and 'board'. The same word may also have different meanings. This is known as 'polysemy'. An example would be the word 'race', meaning either running or nation. A sentence may be syntactically ambiguous in that it can be construed in different ways. It is this syntactic kind of ambiguity to which contemporary linguists, following Chomsky, have devoted so much attention. Examples were given in discussing ambiguous sentences in Chapter 2. It is possible to analyse these kinds of ambiguity in terms of class membership, as has been done here for some forms of perceptual ambiguity. Thus for homonymy it would be possible to say that bored/board is either a member of the class 'part participle' or the class 'noun.' For syntactic ambiguities, resolution could be said in Chomskian terms to involve the identification of one rather than another class of deep structure. It is not certain, however, that at the linguistic level this kind of description in terms of classes is as helpful as it is at the perceptual level.

Ambiguity: Affective Aspects

Turning now to the way in which people react to ambiguities, something of a paradox will become apparent. Most of the available evidence in psychology and social anthropology seems to show that people dislike ambiguity. Personal experience, however, and informal evidence based on everyday observations, would appear to suggest that, even if the search for meaning is intrinsic to all one's processing of information from the environment, nevertheless if it is difficult to make out the meaning, or if meaning is obtained but is unstable or contains contradictory elements, this is not necessarily unpleasant. Indeed, under certain circumstances ambiguous situations would appear to be sought out and to be enjoyed, even if the ambiguity is not resolved.

The idea that people always dislike and avoid ambiguity has been argued by a number of psychologists. Bruner *et al.* (1967) have put this particularly forcefully: "When an event cannot be . . . categorised and identified, we experience terror in the face of the uncanny" (p.12). Bartlett (1916, 1932) emphasized the abhorrence of subjects towards ambiguous stimulus situations, and suggested that 'effort after meaning' be considered as a drive. In similar vein, Tolman (1951) wrote of the existence of a 'placing need', which he saw as necessary to give objects and events definite identity. A number of researchers have provided evidence consistent with these views by reporting that subjects feel uncomfortable and dissatisfied until they have established the meanings of ambiguous stimulus configurations (viz. M. D. Vernon, 1952, p.30). Some people are likely to be subject to this need to a greater degree than others, as suggested by Frenkel-Brunswick (1949) who investigated 'intolerance of ambiguity'. People who display such intolerance are supposed to have a generalized tendency to dichotomize the world, to oversimplify, and to move only with difficulty from one interpretation of an ambiguous situation to another. Support for this concept has come, among others, from Guilford *et al.* (1959) who have, through factor analysis of personality inventory scores, identified a factor which appears to consist essentially of just such an intolerance of ambiguity.

A similar view is expressed in much of the psychological literature on attitude change. The major theories appear to have in common the idea that people detest incongruity (Osgood and Tannenbaum, 1955), imbalance (Heider, 1946), or dissonance (Festinger, 1957). This can be put at its most general by saying that according to these theorists, human beings avoid and dislike any kind of cognitive inconsistency. They therefore change their attitudes, or their behaviour, in order to remove such inconsistency when it becomes apparent. Thus Festinger, in his theory of cognitive dissonance, states that two elements of knowledge ". . . are in a dissonant relation if, considering these two alone, the obverse of one element would follow from the other" (Festinger, 1957, p.13). This is another way of describing one type of what was called here a contradiction ambiguity. Festinger continues that dissonance ". . . being psychologically uncomfortable, will motivate the person to try to reduce (it) and achieve consonance" and ". . . in addition to trying to reduce it, the person will actively avoid situations and information which would likely increase the dissonance". (p.3.)

If one examines everyday life, however, it is clear that most people at times seek out and enjoy ambiguity. As Zajonc (1960) has pointed out in discussing dissonance theory:

"Almost everybody loves a magician. And the magician only creates dissonance — you see before you an event which you know to be impossible on the basis of previous knowledge — the obverse of what you see follows from what you know.

If the art of magic is essentially the art of producing dissonance, and if human nature abhors dissonance, why is the art of magic still flourishing?"

Why indeed? And why do people continue to be fascinated not only by dissonance but by a variety of kinds of ambiguity: for example, ambiguous events which could be interpreted as flying saucers or ghosts?

In art, particularly, the use of ambiguity is so widespread that one is forced to suspect that it plays a central role in aesthetic experience. Obvious instances range from classic examples like the character of Hamlet, the enigmatic smile on the face of the Mona Lisa, and the position the arms would have taken on the Venus de Milo, to more modern examples like the use of reversal figures in 'op art', and the deliberate vagueness of plays like "Waiting for Godot". The importance of ambiguity has been emphasized by a number of writers on different art forms.

Among those who have written on the film, for instance, Raymond Durgnat has paid a great deal of attention to ambiguity. Thus in his book "Films and Feelings" (Durgnat, 1967, Chapter 19) he brings out brilliantly all the ambiguities involved in Hitchcock's masterpiece "Psycho". He concludes (p.218) that

"Like many films, *Psycho*'s aesthetic method is not that of providing enlightening information about its characters; it provides just enough to confuse us . . . Our sympathies alternate rapidly—our feelings are poured into so many moulds which are distended or smashed by contradictions, revelations, twists."

Robert Venturi has argued that ambiguity plays an essential part in good architecture, and gives a large number of examples in the course of his book on "Complexity and Contradiction in Architecture" (1966). Some of these are clearly examples of reversal synergy, as in the following quotation from his book:

"The size of Vanbrugh's fore-pavilions at Grimsthorpe in relation to the back pavilions is ambiguous from a distance: are they near or far, big or small? Bernini's pilasters on the Palazzo Propaganda Fide: are they positive pilasters or negative panel divisions? The ornamental cover in the Casino Pio V in the Vatican is perverse: is it more wall or more vault? . . . Luigi Moretti's apartments on the Via Parioli in Rome: are they one building with a split or two buildings joined?" (p.29).

Even 'pop music' appears to be pervaded by ambiguity. An excellent example is provided by the Beatles of whom Dr. Renée Fox has said:

"The wide range of the Beatles' appeal stems from their personification of many forms of duality that exist in our society. The Beatles constitute a treasure trove of such dualities. For example, they are male and yet have many female characteristics, especially their floppy hair-dos. They also play the dual role of adults and children. They appear to be good boys who nevertheless dress and pose as bad ones— London's Teddyboys". (Quoted by Braun, 1964, p.137).

Other opposite characteristics listed by Fox include the sophistication of their clothes against the homespun style of their performance; the fact that they sing and play but can hardly be heard above the din of the audience; and that they are an audience for each other in their stage act so that each is both performer and spectator.

Of all writers who have emphasized the role of ambiguity in relation to aesthetics, the best known is probably the poet William Empson. In his book "Seven Types of Ambiguity" (1930), he treated what some people had thought of as poetry's greatest deficiency, its imprecision and ambiguity, as its greatest virtue. The book has an abundance of examples, of which the following line is just one (p.47, Penguin edition): "Dust hath closed Helen's eye". In this phrase from "Summer's Last Will and Testament" by Nash, there is ambiguity about whether the dust is that which has settled on her eyelids from outside, or whether it is the dust generated by her own corruption. The ellipsis of the line results in the information given being insufficient to resolve the ambiguity. It is just this, however, which gives it its poetic strength, especially since each interpretation is related to rather different feelings about death, one seeing the dead person as beautiful and statuesque, the other as ugly and decaying. Much of Empson's work deals with more complex passages in which the multiple meanings of whole lines and even whole poems are dealt with, and in which 'meaning' is frequently used in the 'deep meaning' sense of Chomskian linguistics. The important point for present purposes is that ambiguity is argued by Empson to play a central role in aesthetic enjoyment.

In the field of anthropology, one finds the same kind of contradiction: ambiguity may be both threatening and intriguing at different times. One of the key contemporary notions in anthropology is that the ambiguities which are produced as a by-product of the conceptual systems of a given society are felt by members of that society to be threatening in some way, and so the society then treats such ambiguities in special ways. For example, Leach (1964) argues that in relation to eating, speakers of English classify animals into three types: fish (creatures that live in water), birds (two-legged creatures with wings that lay eggs) and beasts (four-legged mammals living on land). This leaves a residue of creatures which are ambiguous in terms of this category system, such as reptiles and insects. An especially anomalous creature would be a snake which is a land animal which has no legs but which lays eggs, and which therefore has a number of contradictory attributes in terms of the category system. Such ambiguous animals are treated with revulsion and perhaps fear, and people refuse to eat them. The products of the human body are also ambiguous in the sense that they are part of the body but also separate from it and therefore cannot easily be categorized as bodily or not-bodily. So faeces, urine, sweat, spittle, and semen are all seen as 'filth', treated with revulsion and generally avoided, even to the extent of being taboo in conversation.

This sort of situation can be represented by means of a Venn diagram as it is in Fig. 6.1. Logically, of course, an overlap between mutually exclusive categories is not possible, since it contradicts the 'Law of the Excluded Middle' which says that A must be either B or not-B. But many taxonomic systems may fail in the way just indicated and produce anomalies such as the snake in the example of a food system.

Similarly, Leach has argued (1964, 1976) that *boundaries* between categories inevitably give rise to ambiguity (Fig. 6.1 applies here, too). Thus a boundary in space between one man's land and another must itself actually take up space,

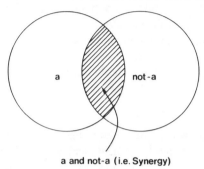

a and not-a (i.e. Synergy)

FIG. 6.1 *Synergy arises when logic 'breaks down', as depicted in this ill-formed Venn diagram.*

e.g. in the form of a fence, although it is not supposed to have any dimensions. So which side of the boundary is the boundary itself? And if it is on neither side, then what is this space which is 'out of space'? "It is the nature of such markers of boundaries that they are ambiguous in implication and a source of conflict and anxiety" (Leach, 1976, p.34). Similarly, in the course of his life an individual crosses various boundaries which mark off one kind of status from another: from child to adult, unmarried to married, sick to healthy, living to dead. The frontier in each case is ambiguous because in itself it takes up time, while belonging to neither of the times which it separates: it is therefore a kind of time which is 'out of time'.[9] According to the argument, these ambiguous frontiers threaten the category systems that give rise to them and cause feelings of anxiety. Rituals are then developed which treat the crossing of such frontiers in special ways; following van Gennep (1960) these kinds of rituals are known as 'rites de passage'. An example is the wedding ceremony, which is a transitional state marking the passage of two people across the boundary between unmarried and married.

Mary Douglas (1966) has argued in a similar vein in her analysis of the concepts of pollution and taboo. For her, ". . . dirt is essentially disorder" (p.2), or, following William James, "matter out of place" (p.164). In our society, she points out, shoes are not dirty in themselves, but only if placed on the dining room table. Food is not in itself dirty, but it is if it bespatters clothing. ". . . similarly, bathroom equipment in the drawing room; clothing lying on chairs;

out-door things in-doors; uptairs things downstairs; under-clothing appearing where over-clothing should be, and so on" (p.36). In all these cases, the object or substance is seen as polluted because it threatens to contravene a classification system. Dirt implies ambiguity in the sense of anomaly[10] and is treated as taboo, and therefore to be avoided. For the situation to be ambiguous, the object or substance which is out of place must still retain its identity: it must still be seen as hair, food or wrapping. Once the class of the identity is gone, as it will be eventually in a rubbish tip when everything has been churned up and rotted, then it can simply be classified as 'rubbish' and threatens the conceptual systems no further; at this point it is no longer ambiguous and thus loses its taboo quality.

Douglas takes this whole argument a step further by claiming that in many societies an ambiguity is felt as threatening, not just to the classification system involved, but to society as a whole, i.e. it represents some kind of generalized danger. In turn, danger implies that some kind of power is loose. So any kind of ambiguity, whether it inheres in 'dirt', in transitional states, or in certain types of anomalous activity, e.g. witchcraft, is felt to be related to the presence of a form of dangerous power. Ambiguity, danger, and power all come to be equated psychologically, and the resulting feelings of threat are reified and projected onto the forces of nature.

This being the case, a society in which such reification occurs must develop special methods to deal with the dangerous power which is believed to have been unleashed. In the course of her book, Douglas gives many examples from both 'primitive' and 'modern' societies. These fall into two major categories, one in which the attempt is made to defend against this power, and the other in which it is attempted to use the power for positive purposes. In the first case, ambiguity is avoided as far as possible. Thus a society may minimize ambiguity by over-systematizing its social structure, exaggerating the differences between different ranks, between male and female, and so on. Where ambiguity cannot be avoided it is treated as taboo, or controlled by ritual. Those who may be the repositories of evil power because of their ambiguous characteristics, i.e. witches and sorcerers, may be persecuted. In the second general case, the attempt is made to control and make beneficial use of the power, in such matters as healing, defeating the enemy, or bringing rain. Thus body dirt (spittle, sweat, skin, etc.), may be used for ritual purposes, although to which particular body margins a culture attributes power will, according to Douglas, depend on the whole social situation which the body may be said to mirror. In ritual, what happens is that some ambiguity such as that which may reside in some kind of body dirt is used in a special ritual frame. Within this frame ". . . the abomination is then handled as a source of tremendous power" (p.165). In terms of her analysis, dirt and sacredness may be intimately related in some societies in that they both represent special powers which originate from outside, and which may or may not be harnessed for the benefit of members of that society.

But there also exists anthropological material which makes one wonder whether the Leach/Douglas thesis has not been overextended and whether ambiguity might not sometimes be simply 'fun'. This may sound like naive anthropology, but it is one's irresistible impression when confronted with the exuberant ambiguity of material such as that collected together for an exhibition of thirty centuries of stone sculpture from the Indian cultures of the Pacific Northwest. All the items are illustrated and discussed by Wilson Duff (1975).[11]

For example, consider the various kinds of ambiguity exhibited by one of the stone clubs in the exhibition (listed no. 105 in Duff, 1975). As Duff pointed out, a club is inherently ambiguous, being both for life-taking and for life-preserving. In the case of this particular club, it looks like a phallus, but clearly is not; on the handle of the club is a head which could be that of either an old man or an infant; and the rest of the club could represent either a sword or a pestle. So here one is confronted with a number of different reversal synergies combined in the same object. Duff also argued that part of the fascination of the phallus itself is its ambiguity.

"A phallus is . . . a supremely ambiguous thing: equal parts life-maker and death-maker; equal parts 'pestle and dagger'; the one, in woman's hand, a life-maker; the other, in man's hand, a life waster" (p.25).

Referring to all the clubs in the collection, he put it that "These clubs seem to be in a constant state of oscillating double-reversal, faster than the snake's strike or the frog's tongue" (pp.21-22). In relation to the whole exhibition, he wrote: "Its underlying imagery, like that of the Yin and Yang of China, seems to be that of the fundamental duality of sex. Its metaphors are borrowed from animal forms and from the human body; phallic images paired with vulvic images" (pp.19-20). This is most clearly seen in the numerous exhibits which are simultaneously part vulva and part penis. But there are plenty of other synergies as well, including synergies of part and whole, outside and inside, front and back, head and body.

Unfortunately, one will never know the state of mind of the anonymous sculptors, or of those for whom they were originally creating these intriguing works. But it would seem to be at least as valid an interpretation that these objects were created joyously for their own sakes, as that they were constructed for the serious and fearful purpose of controlling some special power. While it is unsafe to assume that one's own feelings towards these objects are the same as those for whom they were originally made, they provide an enthralling spectacle for the modern observer, and in this sense at least they demonstrate the fascination which may stem from ambiguity.

To summarize, taking into account all this psychological, anthropological, and aesthetic evidence one is confronted with an apparent contradiction: that ambiguity is both liked and disliked, loved and hated, reacted to with fascination and unease. How are these opposite responses to be reconciled in a unitary theory? Clearly the only way of doing so is to assume that there are two different states of mind, each interpreting the presence of ambiguity in its own fashion, so that a given individual may experience ambiguities in each of these ways at different times and under different conditions. This idea of alternative ways of interpreting experience, in this case the experience of ambiguity, fits well with reversal theory. The fit is even closer if one assumes that these two ways can be equated with the telic and paratelic states, and are aspects of them. So, although meaning-making mechanisms may operate relatively automatically to produce some kind of meaning out of ambiguity, nevertheless when there is conscious recognition that the situation is ambiguous, e.g. there is some delay before a meaning is produced or the meaning fluctuates between alternatives, then this is felt as pleasant in one state and unpleasant in the other.

What reversal theory in fact suggests is that ambiguities, when consciously recognized, are disliked in the telic state of mind and enjoyed in the paratelic state. There are several reasons why one would expect the relationship to be in this direction. If the successful pursuit of what is seen as being an essential goal in the telic state requires information, and this information turns out to be ambiguous and to that degree unhelpful, then arousal will be increased. This will be so not only in relation to resolving the ambiguity itself, but also in relation to achieving the goal, since without resolving the ambiguity the individual will not know what to do: anxiety will be felt on both accounts. This does not mean that ambiguity may not be deliberately used in the telic state, e.g. by politicians. But the politician who makes an ambiguous statement presumably does not enjoy doing this in itself and would prefer to be clear, but merely uses such 'woolliness' as a form of defence in certain situations, e.g. where a definite decision has yet to be made by his party on some issue.

In the paratelic state of mind the ambiguity may be welcomed and enjoyed. It sets a puzzle to be solved and increased arousal may be associated with this. It may also enhance the intensity of experience through a contrast effect between the opposite meanings, especially where these are of the strong variety defined earlier. While the ambiguity remains non-threatening, the resulting heightened arousal and experience will therefore be pleasurable.

The arguments and observations in psychology and anthropology concerning ambiguity are compelling, as far as they go. People really do seem to feel anxious and uncomfortable, even threatened, by ambiguity, anomaly, and dissonance. But according to reversal theory this is only part of the total picture. Those psychologists and anthropologists who have studied ambiguity appear not to have seen beyond the telic state. Even when Mary Douglas talks about the way in which the power of ambiguity is harnessed by members of primitive societies for certain ends, the mental state of the individuals would in her account appear to remain telic, since the attempt is to use the power to attain essential goals — like rain for the crops or protection from enemies. There has therefore been a certain blindness towards something that is evident, at least from everyday observation:

this is that under the appropriate circumstances people are captivated and delighted by ambiguity, which they deliberately seek out or create for its immediate enjoyable effects. To understand the effect of ambiguity one therefore has to take into account whether the telic or paratelic state is operative at the moment in question.

Notes on Chapter 6

1. The term 'synergy' will be used to refer to both the experiences of incompatible meanings and to the mechanism which underlies this experience. The context will determine in each case which is intended.

2. It is not being implied that this exhausts all the different processes involved in meaning-making; nor is it being implied that the sense of 'meaning' used in discussing synergy is the same as that used in relation to metamotivational states.

3. Another illustration of this tendency would be the way in which in many languages nouns are divided, largely gratuitously, into two genders.

4. Lévi-Strauss is of course not alone among anthropologists in his concern with opposition; and various types of duality, polarity, symbolic inversion, structure-and-antistructure have been identified in different cultures (viz. Turner, 1969, 1974; Needham, 1973; Halliday, 1976; Babcock, 1978). It is interesting that LeCron Foster (1974) independently used the term 'reversal theory' in passing to refer to this area of study in anthropology.

5. There is a sense in which a synergy is a form of Gestalt, although it is not a form which the Gestalts themselves appear to have recognized or studied.

6. In extreme cases of incompleteness ambiguity, of course, it is possible that a host of different meanings can be easily imposed on the information. Projective tests like the Rorschach make systematic use of this type of ambiguity. Here, the meaning-making process may result in multistability rather than bistability. Apart from this, the analysis of such ambiguity remains essentially the same as that for bistable ambiguity of the type described here.

7. All this implies that, while the situation remains ambiguous, the ambiguity is resolved one way or the other through what in Chapter 2 was called 'external control', i.e. one meaning or another is *imposed*, consciously or unconsciously, on the stimulus configuration. In this case the bistability involved is of the 'externally-controlled' variety. However, if some feature of the stimulus configuration actually changes, e.g. more information becomes available, or one crucial variable changes in value, then any switch of meaning which occurs as a result would be of the value-determined type. Here we have an example of a bistable situation which would appear to be able to change from one type of bistability to another.

8. In the example of ambiguity involving 'Jean' above, the ambiguity was essentially about who was speaking rather than about the word 'Jean', although the borderline type of ambiguity illustrated in connection with 'Jean' involved word ambiguity too.

9. This would also make the transitions listed on p.142 above, forms of 'ambiguity'.

10. Strictly, as Douglas herself admits (p.37) ambiguity and anomaly are not synonymous. Anomaly implies that something is out of place whereas ambiguity implies different meanings. However, anomaly usually indicates some degree of ambiguity in the contradiction sense: the anomalous element in a situation contradicts the other elements.

11. The present writer was fortunate to have several lengthy discussions with Wilson Duff before his tragic death in 1976, and would like to place clearly on record his gratitude for the inspiration which he received from Duff's encouragement in developing reversal theory.

7 Identity Synergy

The Nature of an Identity Synergy

In the examples of reversal synergy discussed in the previous chapter, the whole of an identity is assigned one meaning in some respect, or another: a friend is married or unmarried, it is either Joan or Jean on the telephone, the Beatles are either adults or children, the piece of stone sculpture is either a vulva or a penis. Each meaning excludes the other, but during the switch from one to the other there is a momentary appreciation of both qualities; or each characteristic takes it in turn to be predominant in experience.

There is, however, another kind of synergy in which the two meanings do not logically exclude each other, even though they are contradictory and both refer to the same whole identity. What happens in this case is that there are two co-existing perspectives, or levels of meaning, in which the identity may have mutually exclusive or even strongly opposite characteristics. There is a sense therefore in which the different meanings apply to the identity simultaneously rather than successively. In other words, the identity is seen in one way *and* another, rather than one way *or* another. This type of synergy will be referred to here as an 'identity synergy'. If reversal synergy is 'either/or', then in this sense identity synergy is 'both/and': the one is disjunctive, the other conjunctive. Although there is no necessary logical contradiction in these cases, nevertheless the individual is fully aware of the meaning-contrasts involved, and there is a type of phenomenological contradiction.

While some identity synergies could perhaps be described as ambiguities, most of them would not normally be thought of in this way. Thus a toy is not normally thought of as an ambiguous object although, as will become apparent, most toys are synergic. This was part of the reason for introducing the new term 'synergy', rather than relying on the everyday word 'ambiguity'.

As with reversal synergies, reversal theory suggests that identity synergy is felt as pleasant and sought out in the paratelic state, but in the telic state is generally

154

felt to be unpleasant, and avoided. Understanding this relationship provides insight into a wide variety of types of experience and behaviour, some of which are discussed only rarely in the psychological literature.

A simple example of two parallel levels of meaning which may give rise to contradictory characteristics occurs when two time perspectives can be made to apply to the same identity, so that the identity has different characteristics in each perspective. For example, an antique object may exist in the present and be seen in the perspective of the present, but it may also be seen in the perspective of some distant past. In the first perspective it may be a personal belonging, while in the perspective of the past it may have belonged to many other people. In the present it may be rare, while at some period in the past it may have been commonplace, e.g. a candlestick, an ink pot, or a sword. In one perspective it is a rather ordinary object, in the other it is extraordinary. There is no ambiguity here in the normal sense of the word, and the qualities are not, logically, mutually exclusive, since two different meaning levels are involved. But, phenomenologically, both contrasting sets of properties may be assigned simultaneously to the same object and feelings of synergy arise. This is part of the fascination of antiques. (For a more detailed analysis of the experience of antiques, and antique collecting, see Smith and Apter, 1977).

Nostalgia would appear to involve a not unrelated form of identity synergy. On hearing a piece of music one may feel that the clock has been turned back and that one is hearing the music in the past: perhaps on the occasion one first heard it, or on some other associated occasion. Yet at the same time, one is fully aware that one is hearing it in the present. Like an antique, the music would be both of the past and of the present, although the past in this case would be more likely to be a memory of one's personal past than the recognition of some more remote historic past. This strange synergic feeling of past and present combined is an essential part of the character of the nostalgia. Homesickness is a similar feeling, but in this case the synergy relates to place rather than time.

Another way in which an identity synergy can arise is where a situation involves a context and a content, and the two have contradictory properties. As noted in Chapter 5, in a sport like soccer, for example, a feeling of security is produced by the whole context of the game: its physical surroundings, grandstand, pitch, etc., which remain the same from week to week; the standard ritual of getting into the ground; the various unvarying preliminaries to the match; and then, forming another kind of context, the strict rules of the game and the presence of a referee to ensure adherence to them by the players. Within the context of security and the expected, however, the game which unfolds, the 'content' of the situation, is full of risk and unexpectedness. The outcome is uncertain, as is the route to that outcome. Similarly, in bullfighting there is a relatively standard setting for the fight to take place, there are strict rules which determine the limits to action and, unlike in sport, which bullfighting is often mistakenly taken to be, the outcome, i.e. the death of the bull, is also pre-determined. Within this context, however, there is a large element of physical risk and the exact manner in which the inevitable outcome is achieved may vary considerably. In much of art there is a strict form, as in sonnet form in poetry and first movement form in symphonic music, but within this form great unexpectedness may occur. These secure-context/risky-content situations involve two steps. First of all the security induces the paratelic state if it is not already present. Secondly, in the paratelic state, the risk and unexpectedness has two concurrent effects. It increases arousal, which is felt as pleasant excitement in the paratelic state, and it produces a synergic quality together with the security, which is also enjoyed in the paratelic state. Clearly, the secure aspect of the situation must predominate initially, otherwise the telic state may be induced, the arousal felt as anxiety, and the synergy felt as unpleasant. The complexity of this situation arises because one of the terms of the synergy, the security, itself induces a metamotivational state which in turn determines the further effects of the synergy.

A rather different example of a context/content form of identity synergy is provided by jazz. There is a sense in which the rhythm and the melody provide a context for the musical content of improvisation. The rhythm in jazz is strong, and always remains in evidence, but at the same time the rhythm of the improvisation tends to contrast with the basic rhythm. The power of the tune is also all-pervasive, being implied by the recurring chord sequence, but the improvisation is clearly other than the standard melody. The contextual rhythm and melody, therefore, provide the listener with a feeling of inexorability and containment, while the content as provided by the soloist provides a feeling of escape. This is epitomized by Louis Armstrong's soaring phrases which appear to escape from both the rhythm and the melody, although starting and finishing within the rhythmic structure of the music, and following the chord sequence closely. Jazz therefore involves an identity synergy of restraint and freedom, both of these opposite characteristics playing a simultaneous part in one's appreciation of the music.

A different, and rather special, form of identity synergy may be experienced by religious people who believe in a supernatural dimension of existence. In fact, a large number of identity synergies are produced in most religions in the form of identities which are seen by believers as concurrently natural and supernatural. Such identities are referred to as 'sacred' (see Fig. 7.1). For example, a holy relic is a physical object in the real world which also has special supernatural qualities. In the Christian doctrine of transubstantiation, the communion wine and wafer are both natural and divine. In each case, the two mutually exclusive categories of natural and supernatural are made to overlap in experience. More examples of such synergies will be given in the later chapter on religion.

Make-believe Identity Synergies

One major type of identity synergy is worth discussing at more length. This is the kind which can be referred to as 'make-believe' synergy or 'real/imaginary' synergy. In this type, a given identity has one set of real characteristics and is then assigned another set of imaginary characteristics; it has one meaning in reality, and a different one in imagination. It should be pointed out immediately that a sacredness synergy is *not* of this type, at least for those who believe, since for them the supernatural is real and not imaginary.

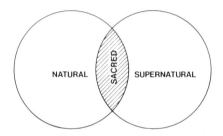

FIG. 7.1 *Sacredness as a natural/supernatural synergy.*

Suppose one picks up a sharp fragment of stone and pretends that it is a dagger. In seeing the stone in both ways at the same time one is experiencing a make-believe synergy. The object therefore has two different identities, and is a member of two mutually exclusive classes, the class 'stone' and the class 'dagger'. There is of course no logical contradiction here since the object is a stone in reality and a dagger only in imagination, these two different levels of reality and imagination referring back to and modifying the nature of the two different identities involved. This general situation is represented in Fig. 7.2. Despite the fact, however, that there is no logical contradiction, nevertheless phenomenologically, the equation of the two identities brings contradictory qualities together in awareness, so that they are experienced synergically.

The imaginary attributes of the identity must bear some resemblance to, or overlap to some degree with, its real attributes, otherwise the imaginary class membership would be difficult to sustain. But just how close the resemblance is can vary widely. In the 'dagger' example, one might have at one extreme something like a stone which vaguely resembled a dagger only in size and shape; the other extreme might be represented by a toy dagger which resembled a real one in all respects, except its lack of a sharp point or cutting edges.

Toys, of course, usually give rise to make-believe synergy, especially those which are made deliberately to suggest some type of real identity, such as dolls, dolls' houses, model cars and model aeroplanes. In these cases, many of the properties of members of the real class suggested by a given toy will be the same as those of the class of toy itself. A toy aeroplane for example will have wings, and a fuselage, like a real aeroplane. At the same time, certain crucial variables will have opposite values. For example the values of the attribute size are likely to be seen as at opposite ends of some size dimension. There is no ambiguity or confusion in this type of synergy, just a physical object with a dual meaning which is well understood.

A similar analysis could be applied to scientific models, like certain computer programs, and part of their fascination may well lie in their synergic quality. Like toys they are physical objects which are also imaginatively other physical objects, like meteorological systems or aeroplanes. An ability to handle technical concepts, however, may be necessary for this particular type of imaginative equation to be made.[1]

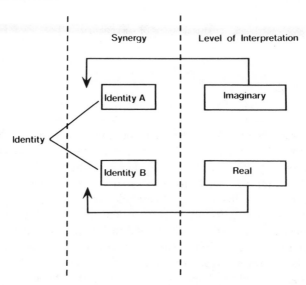

FIG. 7.2   The structure of a 'make-believe' synergy.

For an identity to become a different identity in imagination, it may be necessary to change certain attributes imaginatively, e.g. from small to large, or to imagine features of the identity which do not exist, e.g. people in a toy car; but it may also be necessary to imagine that certain features of the identity which do exist, do *not* exist. For example, one overlook the key on a clockwork car. In watching a play one disregards as far as possible the curtains and the lighting equipment. Far from reducing the impact of the real/imaginary synergy, this adds another element to it, enhancing further the contrast between the real and the imaginary. In some cases the nature of the imaginary may be entirely defined by the imagined absence of some feature of an identity that one otherwise knows to exist. In psychology itself one does not have to look far to find examples. Thus, those who adopt a behaviourist viewpoint imagine that human beings do not have consciousness, although it is reasonable to suppose that the behaviourist remains fully aware of his own consciousness. In more general terms, it could be said that behaviourism involves a make-believe synergy through the pretence that the organism is a comparatively simple object, rather than a complex living entity. This is not to comment on behaviourism as a scientific strategy, but simply to point out that in pursuing this approach behaviourists presumably experience some degree of make-believe synergy. In pure phenomenological analysis of the kind advocated by Husserl, on the other hand, one is invited to suppose that objects in the real world outside of consciousness might not exist, although again this is an imaginative act rather than a real belief. This is part of the fascination of both approaches: they both involve real/imaginary synergies of the type in which some feature of an identity, as it exists in one's phenomenal world, is imagined not to exist. There might be some point in calling them 'make-doubt' rather than 'make-believe' synergies. It must be emphasized again that no comment is being made here on the ontological status of either subjective experience or objective knowledge: the point is about the phenomenology of psychologists, for whom identities investigated may have incompatible meanings.

Turning now to representational art of all kinds, it is possible to see that the whole basis of such art is synergic, since one thing represents another and there is normally some awareness of that which is being represented, and that which is doing the representing.[2] For example, a landscape painting is an identity which is at one and the same time a real member of the class of objects which may be described as paint on canvas, i.e. 'paintings', and an imaginary member of such a class as, let us say, trees by a river, i.e. what the painting represents. As with imagining a stone to be a dagger, or imagining a toy car to be a real car, so the identity synergy involves two related levels: a combination of paint-on-canvas and of trees-by-a-river at one level, and a combination of real and imaginary perspectives at another level. At the lower level, a number of different synergies are implied in the general description paint-on-canvas and trees-by-a-river. Thus the painting is two dimensional, the scene it depicts three dimensional; the painting is motionless, the scene depicted has movement, the water flowing; the painting is an enclosed space, the scene extends freely in all directions. All these incompatibles are brought together in the same identity.

Similarly, in a descriptive poem one is aware both of that which is being described and of that which is doing the describing. One reason why the language of poetry is deliberately made difficult is in order to draw attention to itself as well as to its content and therefore bring out this synergic quality, which may otherwise be lacking in ordinary language. Difficult language becomes more 'opaque' and therefore more 'visible'. It is, as Mukarovský (1964) has put it, 'foregrounded'.

The theatre may also be said to be a form of figurative art. If the case of a role in a play is examined, the associated synergies turn out to be more complex than those involved in something like a landscape painting. This is because a role has a synergic relationship in two different directions at the same time: in one direction in relation to that which the role depicts, and in the other direction in relation to the person who acts the role.

The role is a real concrete identity, the words to be spoken together with certain actions to be performed, which is imaginately equated with another identity, e.g. Falstaff, so that one speaks of 'the role of Falstaff'. Although Falstaff is an imaginary figure and does not exist outside the role, nevertheless, having been created, the fictional character is felt by theatre-goers to have an imaginary existence outside the role in the play, which merely samples this existence. So the role both is and is not the character. The situation here is essentially the same as that of a painting, as previously discussed, especially if the painting is of an imaginary scene. A painting of a real scene would be analogous to a theatrical role depicting a real person, e.g. Julius Caesar.

If, however, the relation of the role to the actor is considered, it can be seen that the role is the middle term in a double identity synergy. Firstly, the actor, while acting, partakes of two identities: that of a real person (himself) and that of a dramatic role. One knows that the actor is not really the role which he plays, that he is not speaking the lines spontaneously, that he does not have freedom of choice, that he is not really feeling the emotion that he expresses, and so on. The real person may be, let us say, Sir Laurence Olivier, and the role he is playing that of Henry V. The audience sees him as both Sir Laurence Olivier and, at the same time, in the role of Shakespeare's Henry V. All this means that there is a synergy between the actor and his role as well as between the role and that which the role depicts.[3]

This inevitably produces a third synergy, which is a direct synergy between the actor and the character depicted: in the example just given, between Sir

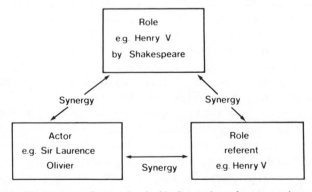

FIG. 7.3   The three types of synergy involved in the experience of an actor acting a role.

Laurence Olivier the actor and Henry V the King of England. All of this has been put in diagrammatic form in Fig. 7.3. It must be emphasized that these contrasting meanings are recognized simultaneously in conscious experience and it is this which provides the experience with the special phenomenological 'magic' which one associates with the theatre.

The theatrical situation is therefore complex in terms of synergy, and becomes more so if one realizes that imaginative identification with one or more of the characters on the stage involves yet another form of synergy. In imagination one becomes the character on stage, although of course one is fully aware at the same time that one is not that character. This can be described either by saying that the identity on stage is seen as having two identities, oneself and the character depicted, or by saying that one sees oneself as two identities concurrently. To make matters even more complicated, the same synergy can apply to the actor as well as to the character he is playing: if the actor is well known one may well identify with him personally rather than, or as well as, the person depicted by the role he is playing.

If the reader observes himself or herself carefully in make-believe situations, it will often be found that two distinct steps are involved. The first consists of recognizing that something is make-believe, or, to put it another way, of appreciating that some real identity suggests certain imaginary qualities. The second step involves entering actively into the spirit of the make-believe by imagining that the imaginary qualities are real. For example, on seeing a toy motor bike one recognizes that it is a particular physical identity and that it is so constructed as to suggest that it is a motorbike; an adult may go no further, but a child, in playing with the toy, may accept, enter into, and even develop the imaginary characteristics. Likewise, when the curtain goes up in the theatre there is a period in which one is aware of what is being depicted, and that this is different from the reality. After a period, however, one 'suspends disbelief'. One still knows that what is happening on stage is not real, otherwise one might jump on the stage and help the heroine; but in a sense one also makes the imaginary qualities part of one's own perception, accepting and internalizing them. Without this the play would remain a charade with little real interest or involvement. Both steps involve real/imaginary synergy, but the nature of 'the imaginary' changes. At the second step the imaginary is imagined to be real. To put this another way, at the first stage one says to oneself "This is pretence"; at the second stage one says "Now I shall pretend that it is not pretence". The second stage therefore involves a kind of metalevel of interpretation of the situation, and an even higher level of synergy than that of whether the identity is imaginary or real (as depicted in Fig. 7.2).

Everyday language is generally not helpful in talking about make-believe synergies, because the distinctions which need to be made between the two parties to such a synergy are often confounded in the same word. The word 'landscape' for example means both paint-on-canvas, a physical object that can be moved around, bought and sold, and also a particular kind of subject depicted, which cannot be moved around, or bought and sold. Similarly the word 'toy' means both a physical object, a piece of moulded plastic of a certain shape, and also something which has a particular imaginative meaning. The object without the imaginative meaning would not be a toy of this kind, but just a lump of plastic. Neither would the imaginative meaning without attachment to a particular physical object constitute a toy. Language does not make these distinctions because both aspects are always linked. These different aspects have to be distinguished, often by awkward verbal formulations, in order to see that there is a synergy involved. This might be taken to imply that every identity which is a member of some class involves synergy: a house is a particular object of bricks and mortar, but also something which has a meaning as a member of a certain class, e.g. type of architecture. However, the two meanings here are not in any way incompatible, whereas synergy requires that the different meanings are incompatible in some way: thus paint-on-canvas is in an obvious sense incompatible with trees-by-a-river.

Synergies Involving the Self

Many kinds of make-believe synergy involve the *self* as one of the components. The way one might identify with an actor playing a role is an example which has already been cited. To give another example: in playing a game one might pretend to be a champion playing in a championship.[4] One's perception of one's own identity is not, in normal people, altered by this, but is made part of a synergy in which the other term is an identity with characteristics which are clearly different from one's own. The 'magic' which children feel when they pretend to be teachers, engine-drivers or cowboys must derive, at least partly, from the synergy involved. Most people would probably agree that on actually becoming something that they had played at in make-believe as a child, for instance becoming a teacher, the reality turned out to be far less exciting than the make-believe. This is because make-believe is a form of synergy which disappears when one's imaginary identity becomes real, and no incompatibilities of meaning remain.

One may be helped in entering into an identity synergy involving the self by actually changing one's external appearance in some way, in order to impersonate the imagined identity: e.g. by putting on a uniform or, as in so many rituals studied by anthropologists, by wearing a mask.[5] In this way one may 'become' a soldier or a nurse, a healer or a god, while at the same time remaining oneself. The same applies to personal adornment, to cosmetics and prosthetics.

The make-believe process may on occasion work in the opposite direction, so that for some identity with imaginary properties, the properties turn out to be real. For a short period the imaginary meaning may linger on, even though one is aware of the new reality, and while this dual meaning remains one experiences a new kind of real/imaginary synergy. Although the reversal involved might seem to make this a reversal synergy, it is in fact a type of identity synergy, since *two* different levels of interpretation are involved: the real and the imaginary. The most obvious cases of this type of synergy involve the self as the identity in question. For example, one might imagine oneself in a favourite daydream as in New York. If, one day, one does actually have the opportunity to visit New York, then that which has always been firmly established as an imaginary characteristic of oneself now becomes real. On arriving in New York one can 'hardly believe it'. There is an air of unreality which is typical of this kind of synergy. In this particular example, it is as if one had been suddenly transported into the realm of a holiday brochure, or a detective film. In this form of real/imaginary identity synergy, instead of starting with a real identity and adding certain imaginary characteristics, the situation is reversed: the imaginary properties turn out not to be imaginary. This process depends on a make-believe synergy existing in the first place, but turns it into a different, inverse kind of synergy. Rather than calling it make-believe, it could perhaps be better characterized as 'make-real'. It is relevant in terms of this particular example, that when people travel they take photographs not so much of the places they visit as of themselves-in-those-places. The photographs then capture the synergy that has just been described, and which lies at the heart of tourism: that of oneself somewhere else, of fantasy made reality.

Here are some other examples of individuals in situations in which they may be expected to experience this kind of synergy, which is usually accompanied by a sense of unreality. A teenage girl attends a concert by the Beatles or some equally prestigious 'pop group'; a lover of Renaissance art visits the Sistine chapel; an archaeologist uncovers a Roman mosaic; a young woman is given an expensive diamond. For such situations to produce 'make-real' synergy, the situation must beforehand have been a fantasy situation, and the fantasy element must continue in consciousness for a period. Until the imaginative aspect dies away, then the situation has a double nature of the kind which has just been described. The examples given so far have been of pleasant, wish-fulfilment types of situation; but the same kind of synergy may also occur in situations in which something imaginary has been dreaded, and then comes true. For example, a man's wife leaves him, the defendant in court loses the case, someone returns home to find that he has been robbed. In these cases, too, part of the old meaning that relates to one's self-identity, 'I'm loved' 'I'm successful', 'The things I own are permanently mine', continues residually alongside the new identity to produce synergy.

The Relationship of Reversal and Identity Synergy

Although reversal synergies and identity synergies have, for the sake of clarity, been discussed separately up to this point, nevertheless there is a sense in which there is really only one, simultaneous type of synergy, both of them being variants on this single type.

Suppose that an identity has two mutually exclusive characteristics, A and B. It might appear at first sight that what happens in a reversal synergy is that the identity is initially assigned characteristic A, and this is suddenly replaced by characteristic B, the change-over being instantaneous. However, as already suggested, a closer examination of what happens discloses that the transformation is not as discrete as this would seem to imply, but rather that there is a short period during which both characteristics are assigned simultaneously to the identity. In other words, when characteristic B is assigned to the identity, characteristic A takes a short time to 'recede' and the synergy is experienced in its full force during this short time. So the synergy derives from a kind of 'carry-over' effect. The changing situation can be represented as follows:

$$\boxed{\text{A}} \longrightarrow \boxed{\text{A and B}} \longrightarrow \boxed{\text{B}}$$

Thus although a Necker cube is seen in two distinctive alternating ways, part of the fascination of this figure may be that whichever way it is seen at a given moment, one continues momentarily to be strongly aware of having seen it in the alternative way, so that even if there is no perceptual overlap, some form of apperceptual overlap occurs.

This point about reversal synergy has already been brought out in some measure in the examples of transitions from seeing oneself in one way to seeing oneself in another way. That is, following on a change in some characteristic of oneself, e.g. from the class unmarried to married, one sees oneself for a short period *both* as what one was and as what one is. Other people may also see one in both ways at the same time for a brief period. The actual duration of van Gennep's 'rites de passage' (see previous chapter) may well be roughly co-extensive with these feelings.

A close examination of what occurs in an identity synergy reveals that there is nothing static about such a synergy but that the two opposing components tend to become salient alternatively, thus setting up a continuing series of reversal synergies. For example, a religious believer in contemplating a Holy relic may be alternately aware of it primarily as a physical object or as a spiritual presence, and these opposing interpretations may alternate rapidly or relatively slowly. A listener to a piece of jazz may be more aware alternately of the structural context or of the improvisatory content. A spectator at a soccer match may be predominately aware at different times of the secure context of the match and the uncertainty of the content. There are, however, regular moments when the two meanings overlap, providing strong feelings of synergy. This may be represented as follows:

$$\boxed{A} \rightarrow \boxed{A \text{ and } B} \rightarrow \boxed{B} \rightarrow \boxed{B \text{ and } A} \rightarrow \boxed{A} \rightarrow \boxed{A \text{ and } B} \ldots$$

However, this does not bring out the full complexity of what happens in the identity synergy case, since there are always in such a case *two* levels of meanings, one of which predominates at a particular moment, except for those moments of overlap during transition. A slightly different way from that used above is required to represent identity synergy fully. Let us juxtapose the opposing characteristics by means of a horizontal bar dividing the space into two meaning areas, the area which is at the focus of attention being above the bar and the area which is in the background being below the bar. Then an identity synergy involving the opposition of A and B would be represented by $\boxed{\frac{A}{B}}$ at the moment when the individual is primarily aware of A, and his awareness of B is marginal. Then the alternation involved can be represented in the following kind of way:

$$\boxed{\frac{A}{B}} \rightarrow \boxed{A \text{ and } B} \rightarrow \boxed{\frac{B}{A}} \rightarrow \boxed{B \text{ and } A} \rightarrow \boxed{\frac{A}{B}} \ldots$$

In the case of identity synergy, then, synergy would appear to arise in two ways. First of all, it arises during a moment of transition in exactly the same way as it does in reversal synergy. Secondly, there is a weaker form of synergy between one property which is part of the figure in the phenomenal field, and a contrasting property of the same identity which is part of the ground.

What this analysis shows then is that, paradoxically, reversal synergies are based on simultaneous appreciation of opposite properties of an identity, and identity synergies involve a succession of changes including reversals which, again, in turn depend on simultaneity. The complexity and fluidity of meaning in the phenomenal field therefore means that reversal and identity synergies are closely and inextricably related.

Synergies of Single and Dual Identities

The difference between reversal and identity synergies turns out to be more complex than might at first have been supposed. There is, however, another type of distinction which can be made between different types of synergy which is more straightforward and cuts across the reversal/identity categories. This distinction is between synergies which are based on a single identity, and those more complex synergies which are based on two independent identities. In the first type of synergy, the same identity is shown to have different properties; in the second type, two different identities are shown to have some of the same properties.

A synergy emerges from a single identity when that identity is seen to have contradictory characteristics of some kind. For example, in the case of a reversal synergy, one learns 'out of the blue' that a bachelor friend has just got married so that there is a momentary conflict between the characteristics 'married' and 'unmarried' in relation to that particular person. Or, to cite another example already given, one is not sure whether someone is a man or a woman, this ambiguity again being based on a single identity. In the case of an identity synergy of this type, a single identity is assigned contradictory properties from different perspectives, e.g. a given antique object is seen as being both commonplace and rare.

A synergy derives from two separate identities when these identities cannot be distinguished, or are equated in some way. In the previous chapter an example was cited of a reversal synergy of this type: the experience of being unable to distinguish whether the voice on the telephone was that of Joan or Jean. In the present chapter many examples have been given of identity synergies based on two identities. Thus most make-believe synergies involve interpreting one identity, for instance a stone, as another identity, such as a dagger.

What happens in such dual identity synergies is shown in Fig. 7.4, which depicts two such synergies, a simpler one above and a more complicated one below. In each case the left-hand side of the figure shows the two identities separately, and the right-hand side shows them when they are combined into a synergy. The representation of the synergies is by means of 'ill-formed', i.e. technically illegitimate, Venn diagrams (cf. Fig. 6.1 which is similarly ill-formed). For two different identities to be combined in some way in experience they must have some similarity which 'holds them together'. This is represented in the synergy shown above in the figure, by a common property X, and it is represented by common properties X and Y in the more complex case below. Having been brought together in this way, the *dissimilar* properties of the two identities also necessarily overlap, so that the identities share not only one or more common characteristics, but also certain mutually exclusive characteristics. In the synergy shown above, properties Y and not-Y have been brought into the same 'conceptual space' in this way, while in the case below, the equation of the two identities has meant that P, Q, and R have been similarly brought together with not-P, and not-Q, and not-R respectively. In other words, the synergy of the two identities in the latter case entails a number of separate synergies of different characteristics. As has been emphasized before, although such a situation is logically impossible, because it represents a number of contradictions, phenomenologically it is perfectly possible; and the figure is intended to represent an experiential rather than a logical situation.

For example, as was noted earlier, a toy aeroplane will share certain properties with a real aeroplane: it will have wings and a fuselage, for instance, and it might even fly. On the other hand, other properties of a toy aeroplane and a real aeroplane will be mutually exclusive: thus the toy will be small and a real aeroplane large, and the toy will be unable to carry passengers while a real aeroplane may be able to do so. To turn to a different example, a painting and the scene depicted may share similar colours and shapes as seen from a given

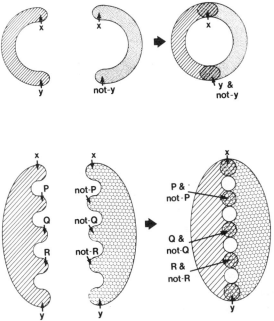

FIG. 7.4   *The structure of synergies based on two separate identities, depicted by means of ill-formed Venn diagrams. A simple case is shown above and a more complicated case below.*

standpoint, but there will also be a wealth of obvious differences, such as the fact that one is two-dimensional and the other three-dimensional. In all such cases of synergy the two identities are made to overlap conceptually through their similarities, with the result that the experience of the dissimilarities cannot be avoided. The resulting paradox of similarity and difference in the same conceptual space is what gives the two identities the special 'living' or 'dynamic' quality which is characteristic of synergies.

Each of the examples of make-believe synergy cited earlier in the chapter involved a real concrete identity, such as a toy, a painting, or an actor, being equated in imagination with some other identity, which it could be said to represent. It is, however, possible to transpose the whole synergy into some medium so that neither identity is directly perceived, both of them being represented in some way and imagined. This is essentially what happens in *metaphor*: two identities are represented in language and are equated by one being talked about as if it were the other.[6] So the state is talked about as if it were a ship, 'the ship of state'; some research topic as if it were part of physical space, 'this research area'; a woman as if she were some animal, 'a bird'. The same, of course is true of *simile*, which can be regarded as an explicit form of metaphor. In Burn's immortal line "My love is like a red, red rose" two different identities, my love and a rose, are equated through such similarities as beauty, freshness, fragility, desirability, and naturalness. In doing so, all the differences between a woman and a flower are also brought into the single 'knot of meaning' which has been created.

It should be immediately evident from the examples of metaphor just given that not all metaphors are necessarily synergic, since most everyday metaphors are 'dead metaphors' (which is itself a dead metaphor): the opposite identities and properties of these identities have been lost sight of. But a new and original metaphor, or one which is developed in some way, e.g. in a speech from a play, or a poem, becomes synergic because it entails two different identities being equated in some salient say. Since both parties to the metaphor are represented in language, more flexibility is possible than when one of them is directly perceived. In particular, both parties to the synergy may be fantastic, e.g. fairies, Martians, or unicorns, rather than only one having this potential. Also, one or both parties to the synergy may be relatively abstract, e.g. the state, illness, the weather. It might be argued that such abstractions are not identities in the way in which identities have been defined here, so that the definition of synergy should be extended to cover cases where there is no identity involved at all. However, one suspects that most people tend to experience particular concrete images in relation to such abstractions and that, if they do not, the power of the synergy is at least somewhat diminished. Indeed, the case may not be so very different from that of those metaphors and similes which do apparently incorporate concrete identities, since the identities themselves in these literary figures often consist of little more than category names. Thus in Burns' simile a rose is, strictly speaking, a class rather than an identity and the same may even be said of 'my love'. However, again, on reading the words most people presumably create reasonably concrete images which relate to particular identities.

An individual can, of course, experience a synergy of the metaphoric type without the intervention of any medium at all: he can imagine the two identities directly for himself. This may occur in daydreaming, for example, and Rothenberg (1980) has argued that creative thinkers often deliberately bring together incompatible identities in their thoughts, and that originality may be achieved in this way. What most people's daydreams more obviously do, however, is to develop the simpler form of synergy where a given identity has contradictory properties: for example in wish-fulfilment daydreams, some unobtainable goal is obtainable and the excitement derives not just from imaginary goal achievement, but from the obtainable/unobtainable synergy which is involved. In general, much of fantasy is exciting not in spite of it being only imaginary, but *because* it is imaginary and contrasts synergically with what is known to be the case.

Synergy in the Telic State

Most of the examples provided in this chapter have been of identity synergies which by their nature are typically experienced in the paratelic state. This is either because they are sought out in this state, as is the case with most kinds of make-believe synergy, or because some feature of the synergy itself tends to induce the paratelic state, e.g. security/risk synergies, when the secure aspect of the situation is initially dominant. Several identity synergies have been mentioned, however, which may be experienced in the telic state. Homesickness is an example. Indeed, it can be presumed that this is normally experienced in the telic state, because an overriding *need* to be back at home is usually felt as part of the experience; this unpleasant feeling is then accentuated by the combination of aspects of the situation which suggest the nearness of home being combined with other aspects that suggest distance. 'Make-real' synergies may also often be experienced in the telic state. When the individual discovers something unpleasant about himself or his situation, e.g. that his wife has left him, the contrast between his current unhappy state and the immediately preceding state produces a synergy which is experienced as telic. This may of course lead to self-dramatization, as discussed in Chapter 5, in which the paratelic state may be induced and the feelings of "distress" enjoyed, the synergy now becoming an aspect of the paratelic state.

A further example of identity synergy which may be experienced as telic is that which is involved in telling lies. In this case, one is making a statement whose meaning to oneself involves both truth and falsity, and this is an example of a make-believe synergy, the truth representing something 'real' about some identity, and the falsity something 'imaginary'. A child may say that a bar of chocolate was given to him by a stranger, this being imaginary to him, whereas he knows that he stole it, this being the reality. Lying also typically involves a further degree of complexity, since it involves the conceptual attempt to reverse the situation just described, to make the imaginary quality real, and the real imaginary. The result is that there is a double synergy. The lie says that x is true and implies that y is false, in relation to an identity; the child's knowledge is that x is false and y is true. So both x (it is stolen) and y (it is a gift) are each in a sense imaginary and real in different aspects of the situation. It is hardly surprising, therefore, that lying is felt to be disagreeable in the telic state. (There may well, of course, be other reasons why it should be unpleasant in the telic state too, such as a feeling of guilt.) In the paratelic state, in contrast, lying is pleasant: it is playful pretence, a kind of game involving an exciting risk. Children may 'fib' for this very reason. Pathological liars may be people who specially enjoy this particular kind of identity synergy. This is not to deny that lying may serve a practical purpose in the telic state, and be a means to an end which is felt to be important; and the attainment of this end may give pleasure. For example, one might pretend to like someone in order to get him to agree to some course of action which one believes to be essential. But the point being made here is that there is no pleasure in the synergy in itself in the telic state.

Reversal synergies as well as identity synergies can of course occur in the telic state. One particular interesting type consists of ambiguities which arise when a message can be understood at two distinct levels. One level consists of the ostensible message, for example what someone says. The other level, which (as noted earlier) Bateson (1973) has called the 'metacommunicative' level, consists of a message *about* the first level, e.g. it might consist of an expression by the speaker which indicates that the ostensible message upsets him. Where messages have such a structure, the possibility arises that the content of the metalevel may in some way contradict the message at the other level, thus producing an ambiguity. For example, someone may say something aggressive, but at the same time give metacommunicative signals that the message is not to be taken seriously, but is playful—the signals might include something obvious like a wink, or be more subtle, e.g. a slight exaggeration of some gesture, or the hint of a smile. Often such ambiguities arise from a contradiction between what is said and the tone of voice in which it is said: like apologizing in a bad-tempered voice, asking for more information in a bored voice, giving an order in a hesitant voice, calling for calm in a frightened voice, and so on. An action concurrent with the message may also contradict it: a mother might ask her child to come to her, but not make any movement to receive the child, implying that the request was not meant.

It might seem that there are two different perspectives in such cases and that, therefore, identity synergy is involved rather than reversal synergy; in fact, from the point of view of the individual who is trying to make sense of the situation, there is only one perspective, with two genuinely contradictory messages being given. So, although the two levels are different in terms of their formal relationship *with each other*, phenomenologically they both have the same type of relationship to the individual concerned, and pose a genuine logical problem. The synergy therefore is of the reversal type.

A particular class of such ambiguities has been labelled by Bateson as 'double-bind'. The double-bind situation is one in which no matter what a person does, he 'can't win'. If he behaves in accordance with the message, then he is punished; but if he behaves in accordance with the metamessage, he is also punished. One example which Bateson gives (op.cit. p.188) is of an incident which he observed when a schizophrenic patient was being visited by his mother in hospital. Because he was pleased to see her, the patient impulsively put his arm around his mother's shoulders. Her response to this was to stiffen, which caused him to withdraw his arm. She then asked "Don't you love me any more?" He blushed, and she said: "Dear, you must not be so easily embarrassed and afraid of your feelings". For the patient this situation was a double-bind because if he showed his affection to his mother he was punished for it, but he was also punished for not showing his affection. The combination of her gesture of stiffening and her reprimand for his withdrawal constituted a two level message which the patient could not respond to without 'losing'.

Bateson's main argument is that sustained subjection to double-bind, usually in the family context, can induce schizophrenia. Whether or not this is true, and it seems to be highly arguable, in terms of the reversal theory analysis double-bind is *par excellence* a form of telic synergy, with the additional feature that not only is there the cognitive discomfort of contradiction, but any action only leads to punishment. The individual is faced with two meanings in a situation in which he has to take some action to achieve an essential goal, and each meaning has negative implications for him.

Another, different type of telic reversal synergy occurs when some acceptable property of an identity is suddenly and unexpectedly replaced by an unacceptable property, so that the first meaning carries over and produces a synergy with the second. This may be called an acceptable/unacceptable synergy. If this meaning-reversal also induces, or helps to maintain, the telic state, as it will normally be expected to do, then, especially if arousal is high, displeasure will be experienced in relation to the synergy and the associated arousal. In other words, the displeasure in such a case is due not to the unacceptable property alone, but also to the synergy of acceptable and unacceptable properties. For example, one is given a watch as a present which one expects to be a particular, expensive, make; but it turns out to be a different, inexpensive type of watch. One's upset is not due to having been given a cheap watch, so much as having been given a cheap watch after having expected an expensive one.

Acceptable/unacceptable synergies can also be of the identity synergy variety. Here there are two different possible interpretations of a given situation, one of them acceptable and one unacceptable. At a given time one of these interpretations will be at the focus of attention, i.e. will predominate, while the other will be at the fringe of the phenomenal field as a currently rejected alternative. This provides a weak form of synergy. However, synergy will be felt strongly if the acceptable interpretation suddenly gives way to the unacceptable and hurtful interpretation, which takes its place at the forefront of experience. The identity remains the same, and is often the self in this synergy, but the acceptable interpretation is replaced by an unwelcome one which the individual has previously avoided facing fully. Often this occasions a concomitant reversal from the paratelic to the telic state, and the parapathic form of some otherwise unpleasant emotion, e.g. grief or disgust, is transformed into its normal unpleasant form. For example, on hearing the bad news that a relative has died, one may initially avoid facing the real truth of the information and remain in the paratelic state in which the arousal associated with the news is enjoyed as a form of excitement, or as parapathic grief. But the moment is usually not long delayed when full acceptance of the truth of the event becomes unavoidable and its significance 'sinks in'. At this point one switches into the telic state and experiences the synergy, in this case between the acceptable 'dramatic' notion of death, which is rather unreal, and the unacceptable real nature of death, in its full force. Subsequently there will be a weaker form of the synergy since the 'dramatic' interpretation will become part of the background. And as long as the unacceptable nature of death remains in the foreground, the telic state will be maintained, and the synergy be unpleasant.

If the switch from the acceptable to the unacceptable is sudden enough in either the identity or the reversal version of this synergy, and if the level of felt arousal is sufficiently elevated, crying will probably result. In fact, although sorrow may be felt for a variety of different reasons, it seems likely that, in adults at least, crying only occurs in the face of an acceptable/unacceptable synergy. And this type of synergy will tend to produce tears even if the situation giving rise to it is not one which produces grief. So, for example, tears of rage may occur if the real inexorability of some frustration is confronted and accepted to be unavoidable. Or there may be tears of guilt if the culpable aspect of one's behaviour is suddenly recognized after a period during which one has tried to 'explain it away' to oneself. However, since crying is likely to be a response to a strong version of the synergy, and since this strong version only occurs relatively briefly at the moment of reversal, when the different meanings 'overlap', it is to be expected that crying will not continue for long. In this view, crying will only be maintained over longer periods if both elements of the synergy are continually 'reactivated' in the phenomenal field. In other words, crying will be prolonged only if there is an alternation between accepting and refusing to accept some truth in the identity synergy case; or only if, in the reversal synergy case, the nature of some property continually changes in the phenomenal field between the acceptable and unacceptable forms, e.g. because of its ambiguity.

It is interesting that an acceptable/unacceptable synergy which involves a switch in the opposite direction, from the unacceptable to the acceptable, also generally seems to give rise to crying, even though this often involves a concomitant switch from the telic to the paratelic. For example, praising a mother in the clinic for the way she has brought up her 'problem' child typically induces weeping. The feeling associated with this sort of crying is often described as relief, although 'release'(from an unacceptable interpretation of the situation) might be a better description since arousal remains high for the duration of the experience. It would appear then that crying generally indicates in adults that an acceptable/unacceptable synergy is being experienced in conjunction with a reversal between the telic and paratelic states, in the presence of high arousal, and that this is the case whichever the direction of the reversal.[7]

The Mechanism of Synergy

Drawing together some of the threads of this chapter and the last, it is now possible to consider in a general way the nature of reversal and identity synergy, and to suggest some mechanisms which might underlie its phenomenological effects in the telic and paratelic states. As mentioned previously, two general effects seem to be involved, the first concerning felt arousal, and the second the intensity of experience in relation to the identity.

First of all, then, synergies appear to increase felt arousal to some degree, helping to push it towards levels which are experienced as pleasant in the excitement-seeking state and unpleasant in the anxiety-avoidance state. How is this brought about? Clearly a number of contingent factors associated with the synergy may raise arousal: the synergy may be novel and unexpected, have sexual connotations, or involve risk. But there is also an inherent property of synergy which in itself tends to heighten arousal, and this is that a synergy, especially a reversal synergy, always involves some element of puzzle or paradox. In the telic state this naturally leads to an attempt to solve the puzzle, or to overcome or avoid the paradox, and failure to do so will lead to increased arousal which will be felt as anxiety. As Mary Douglas would put it, such a situation causes a feeling of threat. The resultant insecurity further entrenches the telic state. If the synergy is seen as a form of ambiguity, and the normal automatic mechanisms for deriving meaning from ambiguity are insufficient, then the individual may deliberately impose one meaning on the situation and interpret the ambiguity in one way rather than another; but the incompatible meaning is always likely to break through and the situation therefore remains inherently threatening and unstable. All this implies that finding some way to overcome such a threat, and solve the problem bound up in it, is a telic goal in its own rights; but the synergy may also arise during the pursuit of some other essential goal and act as a barrier to its attainment. In this case the increasing anxiety may be more closely related to this than to the puzzle of the synergy in itself. Thus a financier considering an investment in a particular company would be worried about contradictory information concerning that company, not so much because of the contradiction in itself, but because he would have to resolve the ambiguity before being able to make a decision about his investment. In general, then, synergies may interfere with action towards goals by producing ambivalence, conflict, indecision, and vacillation.

In the paratelic and associated excitement-seeking state, by contrast, the puzzle of a synergy will be accepted and enjoyed simply as a puzzle, with perhaps a slight but pleasant feeling of bewilderment. Here any increased felt arousal is likely to come not so much from an attempt to resolve the paradox, although this may occur on occasion, as from a feeling of freedom from the oppressive laws of logical thinking. This is particularly the case with make-believe synergies. Far from being threatening, synergy in the paratelic state is more likely to be felt as a joyful form of release, and the associated arousal will of course be enjoyed in the paratelic state.

The second kind of phenomenological effect of synergy is that it enhances the intensity of experience, or makes the identity involved 'come to life'. The opposite meanings which enter into the synergy appear to 'play off' each other, so that each of them becomes phenomenologically enhanced, the effect being reminiscent of contrast effects in perception.

Perceptual contrast effects, both simultaneous and successive, are well established; and phenomena such as those associated with complementary colours, contrasting tastes and visual after-effects of various kinds, are part of the classical subject-matter of experimental psychology. All these phenomena are produced by the juxtaposition in space or time of opposing attributes, each enhancing the phenomenological qualities of its opposite. Thus when complementary colours like red and green are placed alongside each other, the vividness of each colour is enhanced: the green seems to be greener and the red to be redder as a result of the contrast. This could be called sensory synergy, since the two colours interacting together produce an effect which neither could have produced alone. Similarly, if the red is presented to the eye immediately after the green, then the red will seem more brilliant and vivid than it otherwise would have done. The contrast effect in the simultaneous contrast case may, in fact, be the same as in the successive case if it is assumed that the eye scans backwards and forwards between the colours. On the other hand, the successive case is the same as the simultaneous if some quality 'carries over'. Here are several other examples of contrast effects: an acid seems more sour to taste after something sweet has been tasted, and salt and sweet, if applied simultaneously to different parts of the tongue, seem more salty and more sweet than they would if tasted singly; warm water seems hotter to a hand which has previously been placed in cold water than to a hand which has been placed in hot water.[8]

Clearly, then, the intensity of qualities in experience is increased by such successive or simultaneous juxtaposition, and so one would expect contrast effects to be used in the paratelic state.[9] For example, on holiday one enjoys the contrast of the cold sea after the heat of sunbathing, or the heat of a sauna after the cold of a shower. In pornography, a woman seems more provocative if partly dressed (since there is a contrast between being dressed and undressed) than if completely naked. In art much use is made of contrast effects (e.g. see Lucio-Meyer, 1973); this was made one of the central principles of the Bauhaus movement. Itten (one of those who taught at the Bauhaus) wrote:

"The basis of my theory of composition was the general theory of contrast. The chiaroscuro (brightness-darkness) contrast, the material and texture studies, the theory of forms and colours, the rhythm and the expressive forms were discussed and demonstrated in terms of their contrast effect" (Itten, 1975, p.12).[10]

In architecture, Venturi (1966) has shown with many examples how contrast may be utilized, e.g. ". . . the juxtapositions of elements contrasting in size yet proportional in shape, like the pyramids of Gizeh, characterise a primary technique of monumentality" (p.62). Again,

". . . the Villa Palomba juxtaposes contrasts: its contradictory relationships become manifest in discordant rhythms, directions, adjacencies, and especially in what I shall call superadjacencies — the superimpositions of various elements" (p.60).

Contrasts in his descriptions of various buildings include those of texture, size, shape, direction and rhythm. (See especially Venturi, op. cit., Chapter 8).

The concern of the present chapter is with meaning rather than with simpler perceptual and sensory effects. Perceptual and conceptual contrast effects, however, merge into each other. If a tall man stands next to a short man, the tall one will seem taller and vice versa.[11] This could be regarded as a perceptual effect, or a conceptual effect in relation to membership of some class, depending on whether one attended to the attribute 'height', or the classes 'tall men' and 'short men'. If this is the case, then it is not impossible to talk about contrast effects at the conceptual level, in terms of opposite meanings, as well as at the sensory/perceptual level. However, at the conceptual level, a simple temporal or spatial juxtaposition of different identities with opposite characteristics is not likely to be as effective as it is at the sensory level. The mutual enhancement of complementary colours is more striking than that of tall or short men, as in the example just given. The reason must presumably be that, whereas essentially spatial effects, like patches of colour, can be best brought together in physical space, so conceptual effects can only be linked closely in conceptual space – which means effectively that they have to be attached to the same identity or to different identities which have been equated in some way. This must be particularly so with those meaning contrasts which do *not* depend directly on any simple kind of perceptual contrast, but depend on greater degrees of subjective interpretation, such as the contrast between good and bad, or between ugly and beautiful.

One major reason therefore why identity synergies and reversal synergies are sought out or created in the paratelic state is that they bring together opposite meanings in the closest possible way, with the result that both meanings become more vivid, and the experience of the identity as a whole is a more pleasurably intense one.

Notes on Chapter 7

1. The nature of models has been discussed in more detail by the present writer elsewhere, especially in relation to works of art (Apter, 1977).
2. As Lange (1907) put it in his theory of aesthetics, art is 'conscious self-deception'. Viz. discussion in Berlyne (1971) pp.151-2.
3. Although this is more complicated than the situation in respect of a toy car, a toy can also assume a double identity synergy if it is made out of some kit which, like the actor, can 'assume a number of forms'. In such a case there is one synergy between the kit and the toy and another synergy between the toy and what it represents. A toy car may be made out of a Meccano kit, and the car be a model of a Rolls-Royce. The first synergy is between kit and toy, the second one between toy and real car.
4. This is of course different from goal anticipation in the telic state, since the goal in the telic state is a genuine goal, and thinking forward to it does not imply fantasizing that it has already been attained.
5. As one anthropologist has written of the wearing of masks in ritual: ". . . it is essential to the meaning of a mask that there is a human being inside of it. The essence of a mask is that a man *is* what he *is not*". (Halpin, 1979, p.46). Many other examples of identity synergy will be found in this interesting paper.
6. It is also possible to have 'visual metaphors', as Aldrich (1971) and Rothenberg (1980) among others have pointed out. For completeness, it should be noted that simple single-identity synergies may also exist entirely within some medium like language. For example, a fictional character may be assigned many kinds of contradictory traits.
7. We are indebted to Professor Sven Svebak for discussions which led to this formulation of the structure of experience underlying crying.
8. In the present context it is not necessary to go into the question of the possible physiological processes which underlie different contrast effects. Numerous theories have been put forward in the history of psychology, one of the most general and impressive modern theories being Helson's adaptation-level theory (Helson, 1947, 1964).
9. This is not to say that combinations of opposites may not also have their uses in the telic state, since the joint presence of two opposites, as epitomized by the Chinese Yin-Yang symbol, may give a feeling of completeness and security, particularly if equally strong. This feeling, however, once attained is likely to induce the paratelic state, in which case the contrast effect comes to have the function discussed here.
10. Contrasts he lists include: large-small, long-short, broad-narrow, thick-thin, black-white, much-little, straight-curved, pointed-blunt, horizontal-vertical, diagonal-circular, high-low, area-line, area-body, line-body, smooth-rough, hard-soft, still-moving, light-heavy, transparent-opaque, continuous-intermittent, liquid-solid, sweet-sour, strong-weak, loud-soft, as well as the seven colour contrasts.
11. Evidence for this kind of effect has been adduced by researchers working in the framework of adaptation-level theory (e.g. viz. review in Chapter 13 of Corso, 1967).

8 Humour and Reversal Theory

Situations which are variously described as 'comic', 'humorous', or 'funny' have long resisted satisfactory explanation in psychology. Indeed, according to one widely held view, it may be unwise to generalize about humour at all.[1] However, there is no denying that, phenomenologically, something essential about the experience of humour remains identical, whatever the situation which calls it forth, and that it is therefore reasonable to suppose that some common structure or mechanism may be involved.[2] The aim of the present chapter is to show that there is indeed at least one type of structure which appears to underly all humorous situations. This structure, and the mechanism related to it, can be identified in terms of the ideas developed in the earlier chapters of this book.

Humour as Synergy

On examination it will be found that all identities which provoke feelings of humour are identity synergies, in that they involve two different levels of interpretation. One of these levels can be referred to as that of reality and the other that of appearance, so that every example of humour can be characterized as involving 'real/apparent' synergy. Real/apparent synergies are closely related to those synergies which have already been discussed at some length and referred to as real/imaginary, i.e. make-believe, synergies. But there is a fundamental difference, and it is this difference which has led to the need to characterize the synergy of humour in a rather different way. An identity which gives rise to the feelings which are associated with humour *appears*, or *purports*, to be something other than what it turns out to be. What it purports to be is indeed in some sense imaginary, but it is implied by the identity that it is real and not imaginary, whereas to the observer it is clear, or becomes clear, that it is not.

Often these two levels are appreciated by the observer at the same time, and in this case a general suffusive feeling of funniness is experienced. In other forms of

177

humour, however, there is a sudden realization of the real nature of the identity, which had been hidden up to that point, and when this happens a sudden surge of humour will be felt, which may well issue in overt laughter. In this case there is a reversal from one meaning to another, but strictly this does not constitute a reversal synergy in the sense defined previously, since the synergy is essentially between two different levels of interpretation and no real logical contradiction is involved. However, it comes close to being a reversal synergy since at the initial stage there is to the observer only one level of meaning, it only becoming apparent that there are two levels after the reversal has taken place. Using the method of representing synergies introduced in the last chapter, the reversal-of-meaning situation in humour could be represented as:

$$\boxed{\text{A}} \longrightarrow \boxed{\text{`A' and B}} \longrightarrow \boxed{\dfrac{\text{B}}{\text{`A'}}}$$

Inverted commas have been added here to show that A comes to be seen as an appearance only. In the other, more straightforward identity synergy form of humour, one meaning will typically be at the focus of attention and the other at the fringe, although as always with identity synergies the relationship between the two meanings is likely to fluctuate:

$$\boxed{\dfrac{\text{`A'}}{\text{B}}} \longrightarrow \boxed{\text{`A' and B}} \longrightarrow \boxed{\dfrac{\text{B}}{\text{`A'}}} \cdots$$

Nevertheless, in this case the individual is at all times aware, in one way or another, of both meanings. Since it will be necessary to refer to these two forms of humorous situation, and do so in a way which does not imply that one is equated with reversal synergy and the other with identity synergy, the sudden-change-of-meaning humour will be called 'transition' humour, and the other form 'non-transition' humour.

In a make-believe synergy one knows at the outset what something is, and then adds to its meaning by imagining it as some further identity or as having some different properties. To reiterate the example given earlier, the individual imagining that a stone is a dagger knows that the stone is a stone, and invents its identity as a dagger. Even with a toy, one invents the extra dimension of meaning; although in this case it is suggested by the form of the toy. In transition humour, by contrast, one thinks one knows at the outset what something is, and then discovers that it already has a different real meaning. So instead of starting with something real and adding some form of pretence, one starts with what turns out to be some form of pretence, i.e. an appearance, and discovers what the reality is that is lying behind it.[3] This reality may emerge in a number of different ways: by accident, by incompetence, by the perspective changing, and so on. Instead of adding something imaginary, something real is added and what was supposed to be real is shown to be imaginary. In short, transition humour involves discovery rather than invention. One discovers the reality behind an appearance, rather than knowing the reality and combining this with something imaginary of one's own. A toy dagger is a make-believe synergy if one knows that it is a physical object and that one is pretending it is a dagger. But suppose that one thinks some object really is a dagger and watches someone in a fury try to stab someone else with it, only to find that it has a blade which retracts into the handle – in other words that it is really a toy. Such a situation would be funny, since the reality would turn out to be different from the appearance. This situation could be represented as:

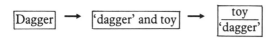

In the case of non-transition humour, one is aware throughout both of the reality and of the appearance, rather than suddenly discovering the reality. So one does not have a sudden shock of recognition of the reality of a kind which may produce laughter, but contemplates the reality throughout in relation to the appearance, and feels amusement as a consequence. Otherwise, the situation is essentially the same. Why, then, would a toy dagger not in itself produce non-transition humour? One is aware from the beginning that it is a physical object which is not a dagger, and yet it has the appearance of a dagger. The answer must be that under normal circumstances, one is also aware that one is using it to aid one's own imagination; there is no implication from outside that the appearance *is* the reality rather than merely pretence. For humour there must be a suggestion that the appearance is the reality, even if, in non-transition humour, the suggestion is one which is 'seen through' from the outset. The identity must purport to be something which it is not, or the situation in which the identity finds itself must purport this. If one sees an attack with a dagger which one already knows to be a toy dagger with a retracting blade, the situation is still a humorous one, but this time of the non-transition variety. In this case there is no shock of discovery that the dagger is not really a dagger, since one is aware of this throughout. However, the implication within the situation is that the dagger really is a dagger, otherwise the individual would not be trying to use it to attack someone else. Hence the use of the term 'appearance' rather than 'imagination', in depicting non-transition as well as transition humour. In the example just given, the dagger *appears* within the context of the situation to be real even if, in observing the situation, one knows throughout that it is not.

Although the characteristics of humour depicted so far are necessary for humour to be experienced, they are not sufficient. Something ²lse is required as well, and this is that the reality should in some way be 'less than' the appearance. This implies that some sort of evaluation enters into the situation, although the 'less than' relationship may be of various kinds: lower in status, less in monetary value, weaker, and so on. To put it another way, the difference between the appearance and the reality must be affective/evaluative as well as cognitive: one characteristic must have a positive sign, as it were, and the other a negative sign, the positive sign attaching to the 'appearance' and the negative sign to the 'reality'.[4] These signs apply to the identity, not to the effect the identity might have for the observer, which might be the reverse: a pompous man falling down acquires a negative sign, but this may be pleasant to a spectator who dislikes him and finds the situation funny. This implies that there is a special type of synergy which is always involved in humour: a synergy between 'less than' and 'more than'; i.e. between inferior, in this evaluative sense, and superior. This is not to say that certain particular characteristics are *always* evaluated as less or more than certain others, and the evaluation at a given moment may depend on contingent factors like context. But for the situation to be felt as humorous the negative sign must be attached to the 'reality' at the moment in question.[5]

This second synergic aspect of a humorous situation distinguishes humour from another type of real/apparent synergy, namely that in which the reality turns out to be 'more than' it appears. Thus in the denouement of a detective story, previous events in the story may be seen in a new light, which shows that their previous appearance was misunderstood by the reader. This is not funny, but is more likely to be astonishing or even 'breathtaking'. Similarly, at the end of a ghost story something may happen which puts previous events in a new and more awesome perspective. If a psychoanalyst apparently explains the 'real' meaning of one's behaviour in some instance, this is more likely to be felt as profound than comic. In chemistry, one learns something about the real structure of the physical world, as distinct from its apparent structure, and what is learned may be fascinating, or, to some no doubt, boring; but it is certainly not humorous.

Humorous identity synergies may be exemplified in terms of comic personalities, since these are based on incompatible characteristics which underlie all their actions through perhaps many comic episodes. Although particular actions or events which involve them may be of a transition humour type, the amusement to be derived from their unique and enduring comic personalities is that of non-transition humour. For example, the character of Don Quixote principally involves a continuing synergy between being dignified and undignified, and between chivalry and foolishness; Falstaff's character a synergy between bravery and cowardice, pomp and ignominy, craftiness and stupidity; Charlie Chaplin's 'little tramp' character, a synergy between such opposites as competent and incompetent, helpful and helpless, meticulous and shabby. In all these cases only one of the characteristics in each pair is real, the other being an appearance which is maintained more or less well-which does not preclude it being supposedly felt to be true by the character himself. Don Quixote is really undignified, although supposedly he feels himself to be dignified; Falstaff is really cowardly although he makes out that he is brave; Charlie Chaplin may try to be helpful and give the appearance of helpfulness but, through accident or clumsiness, be extremely unhelpful and even downright dangerous. In each case one of the characteristics has a positive evaluation and the other a negative one: thus bravery has a 'positive sign' and cowardice a 'negative sign'.

Turning now to transition humour, any joke will serve as an example, since all jokes are based on the same form of synergy.

Waitress: "What would you like to drink, sir?"
Customer: "Champagne, please."
Waitress: "Which year?"
Customer: "Immediately."

There are two ways of analysing this particular joke depending on whether the customer is seen as clever and cynical or whether he is seen as a fool. In the latter case, the 'punch-line' has a momentary appearance of being sensible, but a reality of being foolish. If, however, the customer is being clever and commenting on the slow service, then he is showing that a question which has one apparent meaning could be taken to have another 'real' meaning which has pejorative implications for the waitress. Either way, there are two different meanings involved, one representing an appearance and one a reality; and in each case the reality has a negative evaluation, in one case in relation to the customer, in the other in relation to the waitress.

Here is another example: Question: "How far can a dog run into a forest?" Answer: "Only half way, after that he'll be running out of the forest." Here various assumptions that one might make about the question turn out to have no foundation: the reality is only an appearance and is inferior to the appearance. One might assume that the question is difficult, even unanswerable with the inadequate information given, and yet it turns out to be easy and obvious. The question appears to be about dogs and forests, but turns out to be about no more than the use of words. In this particular case the joke is of the self-referential variety, since the whole statement which constitutes the joke turns out to say less than might have been expected. It consists of a question which is not really a question, and an answer which is not really an answer. Indeed, like all jokes which tend to produce a groan rather than a laugh, this is a joke which is not really a joke. To put it another way, the joke is a recursive one: it is a joke against itself, and the joke in part lies in the fact that it is not a joke. These various opposite interpretations are linked through the identity of the statement as a whole remaining the same whatever the interpretation which is put on it.

A simpler form of self-referential humour is any statement which a person might make in a tone of voice opposite to that implied by the content of what is said, so that the message says two opposite things at the same time. For this to be funny, one of the messages has to be seen to be real, usually that implied by the tone of voice, and the other to be apparent, the former in some sense being inferior to the latter. For example, someone might say "Don't panic" in a panicky voice[6] or "How very interesting" in a bored voice. If these additional features concerning reality and appearance are not present, so that there is a straight logical contradiction between the statement's two meanings, then the situation reverts to the type met with in the previous chapter in connection with the description of Gregory Bateson's ideas on ambiguity and double-bind, where both alternatives are equally real.

There are many different opposites which may enter into the real/apparent synergy of humour. These include such opposites as: important/trivial, intelligent/stupid, sacred/profane, poor/rich, familiar/strange, white/negro, safe/dangerous, private/public, large/small, and young/old. In general, it would appear that the more exaggerated the contrast between opposites, the more humorous the result. A big masculine man, e.g. a boxer or wrestler, dressed in a flouncy feminine dress, is likely to be funnier than a more normal sized man dressed in a woman's trouser suit.

Sometimes a given characteristic has more than one possible opposite with which it may enter into a humorous synergy at different times. This is particularly true of the class 'man' which generates a set of opposites. Together, this set seems to occur particularly widely in comedy. The set is made up of four opposites, each bringing out, through its opposition, a different particular meaning of 'man'. One is 'animal', another is 'child', a third is 'woman' and a fourth is 'machine'. So 'man' can mean 'not animal', 'not child', 'not woman', or 'not machine' in different contexts. Humour is often created by bringing one of these opposites of man into a real/apparent synergy in combination with 'man', as in the example just given of a man dressed as a woman. What this comes to is that many standard comedy situations involve a man appearing as an animal, or an animal appearing as a man, a man appearing as a child, or a child appearing as a man, and so on. Examples of each of these types of real/apparent synergy are given in Table III. 'Reality' here is to be understood within the terms of the medium in question e.g. in line 1 Mickey Mouse is neither a real animal nor a real man; but within the terms of the cartoon he is 'really' an animal, but one which behaves like a man by standing upright, wearing man's clothes, and talking.

How does this relate to the 'less than'/'more than', or inferior/superior notion? Viewing it in this way implies that 'man' on some occasions must be inferior to the opposite involved and sometimes superior. This would indeed seem to be the case. Thus looking at line 7 of the Table III, 'man' is clearly superior to a machine and the humour arises from the pretence that the machine is more than it is; but in the context of line 8 (slapstick), in which a man is treated like an

Table III. The various types of humour which derive from different kinds of man/non-man synergy.

	APPEARANCE	REALITY	EXAMPLE
1.	Man	Animal	Mickey Mouse and similar cartoon characters.
2.	Animal	Man	Pantomime horse.
3.	Man	Child	Peanuts and similar strip cartoon figures.
4.	Child	Man	Circus clown.
5.	Man	Woman	'Masculine' woman in situation comedy.
6.	Woman	Man	Pantomime dame.
7.	Man	Machine	Ventriloquist's doll.
8.	Machine	Man	Slapstick.

object, being knocked down like a ninepin, spun like a top, dropped like a sack of coal, or kicked like a football, clearly a machine (or, more generally, an object) would be superior to a man since it would not be hurt by such treatment. Similarly, although a man is generally taken to be superior to an animal (as in line 1), there are situations in which the animal is superior to a man. Thus if in a British pantomime two men together pretend to be a horse by sharing a horse costume, and then they try to do something which only a horse could do successfully, e.g. jump over a high fence, the men become inferior (line 2). On examination similar considerations will be found to apply to the other real/ apparent synergies in this table, in each case the reality being seen to be inferior to the appearance on the occasion which elicits felt humour. If the opposites are highly exaggerated this may also exaggerate the inferior/superior evaluation.

There is another more subtle way in which synergies involving 'man' as the reality component may become funny, even if 'man' is seen as superior to that which he appears to be on such occasions. This arises when the man or men in question are trying to act the appearance successfully, but fail to do so. Let us take the example again of two men in a pantomime horse. The humour in this situation may derive not from the fact that what appears to be a horse is really two men, but that the two men who act the part do so disastrously by continually letting themselves down and 'giving the game away'. The synergy here is not between the appearance of a horse and the reality of two men, but between the appearance of actors, i.e. the appearance of two-men-acting-the-part-of-a-horse, and the reality of their being non-actors rather than actors, if one can call people who fail at acting 'non-actors'. The men from this perspective are not inferior because they do not constitute a horse: they are inferior because they do not succeed in *acting* the horse successfully. This can be put in a seemingly paradoxical way by saying that if an actor is someone who succeeds with his appearances, then humour can arise if the reality is that the actor does *not* succeed with his appearances. In a similar way, if the man playing a British pantomime dame continually 'gives the game away' that he is a man, the consequence is an actor/non-actor synergy. This kind of synergy is not of course confined to situations listed in Table III but to any kind of acting situation. An actor attempting to play the part of Henry V, but with a wooden leg, would also be funny, since he would be unable to provide the necessary illusion. In all these cases, for the synergy to be of the real/apparent type, the 'actor' must at least purport to be acting successfully.

In discussing identity synergy in the previous chapter, it was noted that such synergies could involve either a single identity or two identities. Both these types of identity synergy also occur in humour. For example, seeing a man dressed up as a woman means seeing a single identity in relation to two mutually exclusive characteristics: maleness and femaleness. On the other hand, seeing a comedian impersonate a well-known politician would involve two identities, in this case two people, being brought together into the same meaning-complex (as represented by Fig. 7.4). It was also noted in the previous chapter that one of the identities in a two-identity synergy could be directly perceived, or that both elements in the synergy could be represented in some medium like language, as is the case with metaphor. The same is obviously true of humour, too, a comedian in slapstick comedy exemplifying the first type and a joke the second. Jokes involving two identities are therefore in this respect like metaphors and similes, although they are unlike them in the other ways indicated in the present chapter. A metaphor or simile can always be turned into a joke, however, by taking the property which is supposedly shared by the two identities and showing that some other, inferior, property is really intended. Thus: "My love is like a red, red rose—she's prone to get greenfly" would be a transition type of humour in which the initial implication of the simile turns out to be only apparent and a new, less complimentary implication replaces it. Likewise: "My love is like a red, red rose—her knees are as sharp as thorns" and "My love is like a red, red rose—she wilts very quickly in the heat."

There has not been the space here to interpret an extended example of humour in terms of reversal theory. A detailed analysis of part of an episode from the BBC comedy series "Fawlty Towers" has, however, been carried out, and will be found in Apter (in press, a).

The Mechanism of Humour

At this stage it is possible to ask the fundamental question: Why is it that humour is enjoyed? The reversal theory answer is that it is one form of paratelic high arousal. What a humorous situation does is twofold: firstly it increases, albeit temporarily, the level of arousal which is felt; secondly it brings about a switch to the paratelic state, or it helps to maintain this state. The key to understanding this mechanism is that the telic-to-paratelic switch is rapid, while the eventual lowering of arousal takes longer; high arousal is therefore enjoyed for a while in the paratelic state. (The synergy may also be enjoyed in the paratelic state, because, like all synergies, it increases the intensity of experience.) In the presence of the real/apparent synergy the resulting pleasure is felt in the particular form of humour.

Arousal is basically brought about by a humorous synergy in the way in which all synergies induce arousal, as discussed in the last chapter. In particular, a comic synergy is, at least initially, a puzzle and arousal follows on the attempt to make sense of puzzles. The comic situation may only be puzzling momentarily, as is the case in the synergy of transition humour, but once there has been some increment in arousal this may take a little time to dissipate, and before it does the situation is felt as pleasant. In the non-transition case there is a prevailing atmosphere of incongruity which, while not perhaps boosting arousal to the same degree, helps to maintain it at a pleasantly high level over a rather longer period. The synergies of humour also typically involve some degree of unexpectedness, and the surprise which results also raises arousal. Unexpectedness is not intrinsic to synergy but is played on in humour. This is more obviously the case with transition than with non-transition humour. In the latter case the continuing incongruity could be said to constitute an enduring form of minor surprise, and in any case in good comic situations the opposites are continually working themselves out and displaying themselves in novel ways, so that there is 'an expectation of the unexpected', which presumably helps to keep up the level of arousal. Yet other extrinsic methods of generating arousal may also be added to the intrinsic arousal-generating properties of synergy.

Initially, then, real/apparent synergy induces arousal through its puzzling quality. If the individual is already in a paratelic state this will be felt as a pleasant challenge; if he remains in a telic state it will be felt as an unpleasant threat. Either way, this stage is extremely transient, and in the transition case may endure for only a fraction of a second or so. The next step is that the paratelic state is induced if it is not already present. If threat induces the telic state, then the sudden removal of threat may induce the paratelic state. This type of synergy itself therefore plays a part in inducing the paratelic state because by its very nature the threat involved turns out to be illfounded, as the full nature of the synergy in all its aspects discloses itself. Initially the contradiction between mutually exclusive characteristics will be recognized. But it is quickly realized that the two mutually exclusive meanings do not really constitute a contradiction in the logical sense—since one of the two is only an apparent meaning, and the synergy is of the identity rather than the reversal type. To put it another way, the synergy is only a playful synergy: like a make-believe synergy it only pretends to assign opposite meanings to the same identity. At this level of analysis the whole situation turns out to be 'inferior' since what purported to be a genuine puzzle turns out to be only a pretended puzzle. There is always an element of superior/ inferior synergy in this respect, therefore, as well as in the content of the comic situation. The playfulness may also be implied if the opposites involved are highly exaggerated, especially if they are exaggerated beyond normal limits.[7] If the identity itself is threatening in some way (e.g. the boss, foreigners, terrorism, illness, a forthcoming examination or interview, an aggressive acquaintance), a further part in the removal of threat may be played by the fact that the identity is downgraded, even if only playfully, because it turns out to be less than it purported to be. In other words, the real nature of the threatening identity is seen to be less than its apparent nature. In this way too the removal of threat may help to induce the paratelic state.

Once the paratelic state is induced, the arousal will be enjoyed, and the greater the arousal the greater the humour which will be felt and the greater the enjoyment.[8] Part of the enjoyment of humour may also derive from a feeling of release from the laws of logic, and indeed this feeling of escape and freedom may help, however temporarily, to maintain the degree of arousal at a reasonably high level. However, one of the very features of real/apparent synergy which induces the paratelic state, i.e. that the feeling of release from logic is only a playful one, may to the same degree attenuate this particular effect. But there should, in any case, be enough residual arousal from the original puzzling features of the synergy to produce pleasurable feelings for a while; and various other extrinsic methods of inducing and maintaining high arousal may continue to be present throughout the process. For example, a comedy in the theatre may keep up arousal in the audience in various ways which are extrinsic to the humour: the plot may contain many twists which are surprising in ways over and above the surprise of the humour synergies, as is the case in situation comedy and bedroom farce; tension, in the everyday rather than reversal theory sense, may develop through the course of the plot, especially if it is a comedy thriller; parapathic emotions of various kinds may be generated; and the subject-matter itself may be arousing: make-believe violence and sex, in particular, seem to play a prominent part in comedies. The arousal which is generated and maintained in these ways then makes the felt humour stronger than it otherwise would have been.

It is not entirely clear just how large a part the synergic aspect of humour itself generally plays in increasing arousal and inducing a reversal to the paratelic state, and how large a part is played in each case by other factors. Thus the unexpectedness of the synergy, rather than the fact that the identity displays synergy, may often play the major part in bringing about arousal, as may various other factors of the kind which have already been mentioned. Similarly, various metacommunicative signals may serve to point up the paratelic nature of the situation involving a real/apparent synergy, especially in the case of deliberate comedy: e.g. certain facial expressions, the starting of stories with such phrases as "There was this man, see . . .", or even the direct statement that what follows is intended to be funny. It is possible that these play a much larger part in inducing the paratelic state than the synergy itself. The environmental context may also play a part. The relative importance of these different factors in different humorous situations remains to be elucidated. What is clear is that by one means or another, for an identity to be felt as humorous, there must be sufficiently high arousal, the state must be paratelic and the identity itself must give rise to a real/apparent synergy, in which the apparent nature of the identity is seen as superior to the real nature which is disclosed.

In summary, therefore, what appears to happen is that a real/apparent synergy, generally involving some degree of unexpectedness, brings about a temporary increase in arousal, and this is followed immediately by a reversal to the paratelic state, if the individual is in a telic state. The paratelic state may also be induced by an appropriate environmental context or appropriate metacommunication. The conjunction of paratelic state and high felt arousal produces a feeling of pleasure, for the length of time that the arousal remains high. The synergy itself may also be felt as pleasant in the paratelic state to the degree that it enhances the intensity of experience. In the presence of real/apparent synergy in the phenomenal field, this pleasure has that special experiential quality which is recognized as the feeling of humour. This is all represented by means of the flow diagram in Fig. 8.1. In this diagram the connecting lines which join and continue together represent conjunctive conditions, e.g. increased felt arousal and

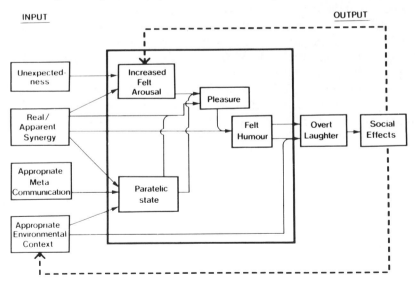

FIG. 8.1   The humour process.

the presence of the paratelic state are both required for pleasure to be felt; separate lines represent disjunctive conditions, e.g. unexpectedness or real/ apparent synergy can independently increase arousal.

In Fig. 8.1. the effects of the environmental context are also depicted, and these alone may be sufficient to induce the paratelic state. Thus being in a theatre, a public house, or at home in front of the television set, may all identify the situation, unless other factors intervene, as a non-threatening paratelic one. The social environment has also to be taken into account: if other people seem to be at ease and in a playful mood, then this may well induce the paratelic state. Obviously this is closely related to metacommunicative signals from the source of the information to which one is attending, for instance the winks and smiles of the person telling the joke. Overt laughter, provided it is not felt to be directed at oneself, would also appear to be a strong cue that the situation is paratelic and, therefore, a powerful stimulus to induce the paratelic state. This is true if the laughter comes from the source of the information – the raconteur, comedian or actor – or if it is part of the social context, i.e. comes from other people who act as the audience.

If overt laughter is considered in a social context, it becomes clear that such laughter may operate between the individuals composing the group in such a way as to increase the extent to which all of them experience humour in relation to some comic situation.[9] Suppose that there is a threshold above which the strength of felt humour issues in overt laughter. If a given individual in a social situation reaches this threshold and laughs, then this laughter becomes, for the others, part of the environmental context, and helps them to define this context as paratelic. This means that, in the presence of the real/apparent synergy, other members of the group are more likely to be in a paratelic state and interpret their feelings as humour than would otherwise be the case. Furthermore, the overt laughter may well help to increase the level of felt arousal in the others and if the degree to which humour is felt is a function of arousal, then the laughter will also be likely to increase the strength of the felt humour in other members of the group. This in turn means that other members of the group are more likely to laugh aloud and this laughter will further amplify the group effect, inducing laughter in more and more members of the group until a stage should be reached at which, other things being equal, all members of the group will be enjoying the humour and laughing. This should then continue until some other factor intervenes such as the decrease in the arousal effect of the synergy through familiarity, or the removal of the synergic aspect of the situation. Another way of putting this would be to say that there are two positive feedback loops from overt laughter, one helping to define the situation as paratelic and the other serving to increase felt arousal. These two loops are shown in Fig. 8.1 where the feedback part of the loop is drawn in a dotted line to indicate that the effect occurs through *other* members of the group, and is not an autonomous individual process.

What happens if, for some reason, the paratelic state is not induced in the presence of a real/apparent synergy? Suppose, for example, that the environmental context is inappropriate, or the metacommunicative signals are strongly of the telic variety. Arousal will still be expected to result, but now, in the telic state, this will be felt as unpleasant. In fact the word 'embarrassment' exactly depicts this feeling of unpleasant high arousal in relation to a real/apparent synergy, and embarrassment may be taken in this sense to be the converse of 'felt humour'. This is obviously the case when humour is directed at oneself, the implication being that one is 'less' than one appears to be; the threat in this case has the effect of maintaining the telic state, or even of bringing about a reversal into the telic state from the paratelic. Embarrassment may also be felt in the presence of 'bad taste', e.g. someone joking when the environmental context is inappropriate, or if one empathizes with someone who is obviously anxious about the jokes he is telling and provides involuntary metacommunicative cues to this effect. On the other hand, if the empathy produces a feeling of parapathic embarrassment, then it may be enjoyed in the paratelic state; this would appear to be part of the emotion in such situations as those mentioned earlier, in which an actor is unsuccessful in appearing to be what he purports to be-a situation which may be deliberately produced by a comedian whose discomfiture we enjoy parapathically.

One final point is that a humorous situation may simultaneously involve a number of different real/apparent synergies. Indeed, it may well be the case that the greater the number of synergies that are combined, and perhaps the more complex the structure into which they are assimilated, the more amusing the comic situation will be. Real/apparent synergies may be brought together in a variety of ways. The simplest kind of combination involves simply adding different identities which each display real/apparent synergy of different kinds. Thus the various characters in a comedy play may each predominantly represent one type of real/apparent synergy, one character showing competence and incompetence, another cowardice and bravery, and a third both love and hate of the other sex. Sometimes such identities may have a symmetrical relationship to each other, so that a real characteristic of one is an apparent characteristic of the other, and vice versa. In this way the two identities become knit into a tighter and more complex structure. For example, the British comedians Morecambe and Wise are 'mirror-images' of each other in this sense: Morecambe is a 'wise guy' pretending to be foolish. Wise (note the name) is a foolish man pretending to be clever. Each of them represents an identity synergy, but at the same time the two taken together represent a contrast of a formal kind that can be described as inversion. One might call such a relationship of two opposite synergies combined a 'co-opposition'; we believe that such relationships occur in other kinds of synergy outside the humorous context too, e.g. in art.

In the examples just given, real/apparent synergies were brought together by combining different identities each displaying some form of real/apparent synergy. However, a single identity may also have different real/apparent synergies combined within it. If the identity is a single individual, then his character may be complex enough to incorporate a number of opposites in a humorous way. The 'little tramp' character of Charlie Chaplin would be a good example. However, the different synergies may become more tightly knit, and the character of the identity made more complex, by one term of the synergy having more than one opposite. For example, Snoopy, in the American 'Peanuts' cartoon, is an animal who is acting like a man who, in turn, often pretends to be a World War I fighter pilot ace. Here Snoopy as a man has two opposites. On the one hand he is opposite to an animal. On the other hand, if one takes the character of the man whom Snoopy pretends to be as that of a normal unheroic American, then this character enters into a synergy with the heroic character of the fighter pilot—a synergy which can most simply be represented as heroic/unheroic, but which has other features as well. In the first synergy this unheroic American adult is the 'apparent' term in the synergy, in the second synergy he is the 'real' term. It is possible when synergies are combined in this sort of way, for both the two different characteristics involved to be combined twice, in the first case characteristic A being the apparent term and characteristic B the real term, with the situation being inverted in the second case. An example of this is provided in the British television comedy series "Dad's Army" which takes as its subject the activities of a contingent of the 'Home Guard' in England during the Second World War, manned by men who are too old to join the regular army and go abroad, or who are disqualified in some other way from doing so. A number of the central characters behave like children; but at the same time they are children who are pretending to be men, by being dressed up in soldiers' uniforms, carrying guns, and so on. In this case both synergies are man/child synergies, but in one case the child is the apparent term and in the other case the real term, and vice versa for men. Throughout this chapter, the word 'real' is only used in a relative way and does not imply any kind of absolute ontological status.

A comparison with Other Theories

This chapter has constituted a brief account of the reversal theory approach to the complicated topic of humour, a topic which has recently started to interest psychologists again.[10] Fortunately, for the purposes of exposition, most theories of humour can be placed within a reasonably small number of traditional categories, each category containing those theories which relate to one classic theory of humour or another; and most recent work is related to one or other of these categories. Therefore, a brief comparison of reversal theory with each of these theoretical traditions should be sufficient to indicate broadly the manner in which reversal theory is distinctive.

First of all, there is the psychoanalytic tradition, based on Freud's interpretation of wit and humour (Freud, 1905, 1928). Freud divided jokes into two kinds: those which are innocent and harmless and those which, to use the customary English translation, are 'tendentious'. In the innocent joke it is the technique of 'jokework' which makes one laugh, in the tendentious joke the purpose is to express sexual or aggressive feelings which would otherwise be repressed. From the psychoanalytic point of view, then, tendentious humour, like dreaming, makes possible the satisfaction of a sexual or aggressive instinct that would otherwise remain inhibited. With tendentious humour the pleasure comes from the expression of what is normally hidden and the release from inhibition. As far as innocent humour is concerned, it is difficult to see what the source of pleasure is in psychoanalytic terms, or how the idea of jokes being enjoyed for their own sakes as a form of intellectual activity ties in with the rest of psychoanalytic theory, despite references to 'psychic economy'.

There are clearly a number of major differences between the reversal theory and the Freudian interpretation of humour. Firstly, what Freud would have considered to be innocent humour would in reversal theory terms be humour in which the arousal comes more from the nature of the synergy itself than from such extrinsic factors as the subject-matter. Tendentious humour would be that in which more of the arousal comes from the subject-matter than from the structure of the synergy. But in both cases, which do not in any case constitute a dichotomy in reversal theory, the mechanism underlying the humour remains essentially the same, whereas to Freud the mechanism involved in tendentious humour is quite different from that involved in innocent humour. As far as tendentious humour is concerned, the individual's main aim in Freudian terms is to *lower* 'tension' or 'excitation', whereas in reversal theory terms it is to *raise* arousal. These, and other differences, in particular the reversal theory emphasis on conscious processes in humour, as against the psychoanalytic emphasis on the central part played by unconscious processes, stem from the fundamentally different psychological assumptions made in the two theories.

Many other theorists have also proposed in different ways that humour results in relief, tension reduction, or the lowering of arousal. The general category 'relief theory' is sometimes used in texts on humour. A comparatively recent example would be Berlyne's attempt to apply his version of optimal arousal theory to humour. He suggests (Berlyne, 1960, 1968, 1972) that pleasure comes from the reduction of arousal from a level higher than the optimal arousal level down to that level; in order for this to happen, the joke must first raise arousal above the optimal point and then reduce it. This is known as the 'arousal-jag hypothesis'.[11] In reversal theory, while agreeing that a joke may cause a temporary increase in arousal, it is this increase which is claimed to be felt as pleasant and not the subsequent reduction. Godkewitsch (1972, 1976), using physiological measures, has shown that felt humour is in fact related to the amount of arousal *produced* by the punch lines of jokes rather than *reduced* by them, and this evidence is strongly supportive of the reversal theory position. Rickwood (1978) has also produced evidence which points in the same direction. There is a sense in reversal theory in which jokes involve relief, but this is in relation not to arousal, but to the induction of the paratelic state, through the realization that there is no real threat in the situation. There is some similarity here to Rothbart's view (Rothbart, 1973, 1976, Rothbart and Pien, 1977) that arousal within safety is one of the necessary characteristics of felt humour.

A second group of theories have been labelled 'superiority theories'. These date back to Hobbes who in his "Human Nature" (1650), and more briefly in "Leviathan" (1651), argued that the feeling and pleasure of humour derives from a sudden increase in self-esteem as a result of a realization that one's own situation compares favourably with the misfortunes or inadequacies of others. This he described in a famous phrase as a feeling of "sudden glory". In other words, it involves a sudden feeling of superiority.[12] Obviously this idea plays a part in reversal theory, but in a modified form: it is not that the individual enjoying the humour sees himself to be superior to the identity concerned, but that the appearance of the identity is superior to its own reality; or, to put it the other way round, that the reality turns out to be inferior to the appearance. This may result in the individual feeling superior to the identity, but this personal feeling of superiority according to reversal theory is not a necessary precondition for the feeling of humour to result. In any case, in reversal theory the pleasure is not that of feeling superior, but derives indirectly from the induction of the paratelic state, which may in part be due to the change of evaluation of the threatening qualities which an identity synergy may initially appear to display.

One major theory of humour which is sometimes classified as a form of superiority theory is that of Bergson (1901). He defined humour as 'Something mechanical encrusted on the living' (p.37, 1911 English edition). With great ingenuity, and generalizing the idea of the mechanical to cover any kind of rigidity, he attempted to show that his formulation covered all kinds of humour. In reversal theory terms, however, one can see that Bergson has simply picked on one type of synergy (man/machine synergy) and attempted to generalize from this to all types. The resulting overgeneralization is not particularly convincing. If one is to generalize from man/machine synergy to humour in general, then it is surely the synergic aspect which must be generalized, not the man/machine relationship which is simply a special case of synergy.

So-called 'incongruity theories' form the largest of all categories of theories of humour. Indeed, there are so many different forms of incongruity theory that the category is not as helpful as that of relief theories, including psychoanalytic theories, or of superiority theories. Incongruity theories stress the cognitive aspects of humour, rather than the emotional and motivational. By the same token, they tend to be more concerned with the form of jokes and other humorous situations than with their content. Such theories are usually taken to date back at least to Kant's comments on laughter in his "Critique of Judgement" (1770), and to Schopenhauer's "The World as Will and Representation" (originally published in 1819). Other more modern incongruity theories include those of Maier (1932), Eastman (1921, 1936), and Koestler (1949, 1964). Incongruity is generally seen by such theorists to involve contradiction between what is expected in a given situation and what does actually happen, or turn out to be the case.

One influential form of incongruity theory is that humour derives from the 'resolution of incongruity' (Suls, 1972; Shultz, 1976). Rothbart and Pien (1977) illustrate this idea in terms of the question and answer cited earlier in this chapter, and chosen as an example here for this very reason: Question: "How far can a dog run into a forest?" Answer: "Only half way, after that he'll be running out of the forest". They argue that "The initial incongruity of the question and the punchline is made entirely meaningful by recognising that the unexpected answer is definitionally correct" (op. cit. p.37). Certainly in this case there is a sense in which an incongruity is resolved: an incongruity between the expectation based on the question and the actuality of the answer provided. But resolving an incongruity in itself is not normally funny. For example, understanding a difficult line of poetry, or making sense of a balance sheet which seems to contain contradictions, does not normally have a comic effect. So something more must be involved. This 'something more' according to reversal theory is the *recognition* of contradiction or incongruity, of a particular kind. For, in resolving the incongruity between the question and answer in the example just given, a number of other incongruities are displayed, all of them of the real/apparent type. As indicated earlier, the punch line adds a new characteristic to the interpretation of the question, this being opposite to that previously supposed. Where the question appeared to be difficult, it is now seen to be easy; and where it appeared to be about dogs and forests, it is now seen to be about the meaning of the word 'into'. Furthermore, the answer, which turns out to be logically appropriate, is nevertheless also seen as inappropriate to the meaning of the question as it was originally understood. As a result of all this, the whole question and answer sequence which appeared to say something, in reality says practically nothing; and there is a sense in which the joke is not a joke, or at least not a very good one, and that is, paradoxically, why it *is* a joke. The 'resolution' of the incongruity by the punch line therefore *demonstrates* a new set of incongruities in the form of real/apparent synergies, and in each of these cases the reality turns out to be different from the appearance, and the identity involved is downgraded. The resolution is therefore not the defining quality of the joke, but the *means for setting up* new incongruities, and it is these incongruities which are enjoyed as humour rather than the resolution.

This view of humour is supported by the fact that many comic situations involve incongruity without resolution. For example the phrase "Don't panic" spoken in a frightened voice is an incongruity, or in reversal theory terms a real/ apparent identity synergy, which is amusing without there being any resolution involved. While resolution of incongruity may therefore play a part in some forms of humour, especially jokes, it is not the defining feature–this residing in the nature of the incongruities themselves.

In part, reversal theory is itself an incongruity theory, since it attempts to identify a particular kind of formal cognitive structure common to all humorous situations. The types of incongruity which it places at the centre of the picture, however, are those of incongruity between mutually exclusive meanings, between inferior/superior evaluations and between the apparent and the real — rather than between the expected and the unexpected as in most other incongruity theories, although unexpectedness also plays a part in reversal theory in terms of its arousal potential. Furthermore, reversal theory differs from most other incongruity theories in that it is equally concerned with motivational and emotional considerations, metamotivational mediation between cognitive structure and the feeling of humour being an essential feature of the analysis. Any incongruity theory must at some stage meet the challenge of explaining why some forms of incongruity are felt as unpleasant, even frightening, and others are felt as pleasant, and specifically as humorous. Reversal theory, unlike most incongruity theories, does respond to this challenge.

Notes on Chapter 8

1. E.g. See Chapman and Foot (1976b), p.4.
2. This does not of course apply to the overt act of laughing which may relate to a variety of different types of experience, as Giles and Oxford (1970) among others have pointed out.
3. It was something like this aspect of humour that was particularly remarked on by Gordon Allport in his discussion of humour (Allport, 1937, p.223).
4. Often in make-believe synergy, too, a negative sign will attach to the real and a positive sign to the imaginary, e.g. a dagger would normally be more valuable, useful, etc. than a stone. But the other differences between make-believe and humorous synergies remain.
5. It is well known that a young child will smile at the image of a face, however schematic. This seems to happen first at about the age of 10 weeks (Spitz and Wolf, 1946), and is usually interpreted as meaning that the face is a stimulus that automatically releases the smile response. However, it may well be the case that this is the first situation in which a child recognizes a real/apparent identity synergy in which the reality is inferior: the image is not the same as, and inferior to, a real face; but at the same time it is recognizably a face of sorts.
6. British readers will know that this was one of the catch phrases of the character Corporal Jones in the BBC comedy series "Dad's Army".
7. Consistent with this is evidence that extreme insult is judged to be less insulting than mild insult, La Fave et al. (1977).
8. Evidence in support of such a relation between arousal and perceived funniness has been found by a number of researchers including Schachter and Wheeler (1962), Levi (1963),

Lamb (1968), Shurcliff (1968), Averill (1969), Langevin and Day (1972) and Chapman (1976).

9. Viz. Foot and Chapman (1976) on the social effects of laughter.

10. As witness the collections of papers edited by Goldstein and McGhee (1972), and Chapman and Foot (1976a, 1977). A good recent survey of work on the psychology of humour will be found in Wilson (1979).

11. Berlyne also suggested an "arousal boost" hypothesis, which is simply that a joke raises arousal to a pleasant level. This would be consistent with the reversal theory interpretation, except that Berlyne interpreted his hypothesis in the light of an optimal arousal model, so that his assumption was that the boost involved a moderate increment in arousal to some single intermediate arousal level.

12. A review of the experimental literature on superiority theory will be found in La Fave et al. (1976).

9 Negativism and Conformity

Up until this point the discussion of metamotivation has been dominated, in one way or another, by attention to the telic and paratelic states, and by the two arousal-regulating states which are associated with them. In the present chapter, however, a new and independent pair of metamotivational states, and their corresponding systems, will be introduced and discussed. These are the 'negativistic state' and the 'conformist state'.

The Concept of Negativism

Although negativism has never been a central concept in psychology, the term has nevertheless been used from time to time in several branches of the subject. In particular, 'negativism' has been used in child psychology to refer to behaviour which can otherwise be characterized by such adjectives as 'awkward', 'cussed', 'contrary', 'perverse', 'obstinate', 'rebellious', 'defiant', or just plain 'naughty'. It is then contrasted with behaviour which can be described as 'obedient', 'polite', 'compliant', 'well-behaved', and 'good'. Examples of negativistic behaviour would be refusal to eat or to sleep, defiance of orders by a parent, and the deliberate performance of a forbidden act like scribbling on the wall, or climbing over furniture.

It is generally agreed by writers on child psychology and psychiatry that there is a period which reaches its peak somewhere between one-and-a-half and three-and-a-half years old, in which the child is particularly negativistic; this has often been called the 'negativistic period' or 'period of resistance'. At times during this period the child will systematically respond with "No" to every suggestion by parents or other adults and may not just refuse to obey, but deliberately do the opposite of whatever has been suggested. Many psychologists first became aware of it through the difficulties encountered in testing children at about the age of three, difficulties mentioned early in the history of testing by Binet and Simon

196

(1905). Levy and Tulchin (1923, 1925) who observed 983 children during testing, found that resistance to testing was particularly pronounced between 18 and 23 months in girls and 30 to 35 months in boys. Goodenough (1929), studying 380 children during intelligence testing, found the peak for negativism for girls to be 18 months, and for boys to be 30 months. Reynolds (1928), who studied negativism in experimental situations similar to mental testing conditions, using 229 children between the ages of two and five-and-a-half, found the peak of negativism to be at two years of age; resistance was invoked more by expecting the child to imitate than by any other demand. Studies of children in the home and nursery school also began to disclose that negativistic behaviour was generally characteristic of children at the ages of two to three (e.g. Bridges, 1931; Goodenough, 1931). Although studies of negativism appear to have gone out of fashion, having reached their peak in the nineteen-twenties and thirties, the phenomenon of negativism appears to be well established, together with the idea of a negativistic period during early development.

A second area in which the term 'negativism' has been used is that of clinical psychology and psychiatry, especially to refer to one of the symptoms of some types of schizophrenia. It is also known as 'resistance', or even 'contra-suggestibility' or 'contrariety'. Bleuler, in his great pioneering work on schizophrenia, was particularly concerned with schizophrenic negativism, about which he wrote a monograph (Bleuler, 1912). Negativism is said to be passive when the patient does not do the things he should, e.g. when he does not get out of bed in the morning, and active when he does the opposite of what he is asked to do. In schizophrenia, negativism of the active or passive kind may take an extreme form in which the negative reaction occurs automatically and immediately in reaction to any request or suggestion. Thus, when told to step forward, such a patient will do nothing in the passive case or automatically step backward in the active case. There is also an opposite extreme, *conformism*, in which all suggestions are automatically obeyed as if the patient had no will of his own. *Ambivalence* in schizophrenia is also sometimes said to involve negativism. Thus, when the patient decides on an action, it seems that this automatically suggests the opposite action, and produces ambivalent feelings. This may result in alternating contradictory behaviour: for example, getting up, then sitting down, then getting up again, in a continuing sequence.[1]

Negativism in children, or in psychiatric patients, is usually defined behaviourally, although intentions on the part of the child or the patient, and hence phenomenological states underlying the behaviour concerned, are often implied. In reversal theory, by contrast, negativism will be treated phenomenologically from the outset, with the negativistic and conformist states being defined in terms of what the individual sees himself to be doing rather than in terms of his behaviour as such.

The feeling state that is being referred to here as the 'negativistic state' is one which can be described in many ways in everyday language. Feeling 'bloody-minded', 'bolshie', 'awkward', or 'obstinate'; 'looking for trouble', 'digging one's heels in', 'being difficult': these would all be ways of describing it. Sometimes action in response to the feeling will be inhibited, at other times expressed as, perhaps, in swearing, walking on the grass despite a notice saying one should not, refusing to accept bad service in a restaurant, or parking on a yellow line.

When high arousal is associated with the negativistic state in the telic mode, then the emotion experienced is likely to be that of *anger*. *Indeed, it would appear that it is the operation of the negativistic state which transforms anxiety into anger.* Anything which increases the arousal at such a time, e.g. frustration, will also increase the intensity of the anger experience. If an act of aggression results from anger, then the feeling of anger appears to reach a temporary peak during the act, presumably because arousal is highest at this time. In the paratelic state, by contrast, the conjunction of the negativistic state with high felt arousal will be experienced as parapathic anger: a kind of excited defiance.

Negativism in an individual always involves three related components in his or her phenomenal field. The first consists of some other individual, or some social group or situation, which is perceived as exerting some pressure on him or her. This can be called the 'source'. The second component consists of some perceived expectation, norm, convention, suggestion, request, requirement, rule, law, command, order, injunction, prohibition, threat or dictate, deriving from the source. For convenience, one term will be used to represent this range of words with different shades of meaning. The word 'requirement' has been chosen, since this word is stronger than those like suggestion or request, but weaker than such words as injunction or dictate. A requirement may be some permanent general feature of a situation, like a rule or a convention, or it can be specific and temporary like a command or an order, and therefore the word can be used to cover either type of felt pressure. The third component is a feeling on the part of the individual who perceives the requirement and the source, of a desire or need to reject such a requirement, and therefore also to act against the source of the requirement. It is this third component which is the essence of the negativistic state, but it acquires meaning through reference to the first two components. Put at its simplest, then, *the feeling of being in a negativistic state can be defined as 'wanting, or feeling compelled, to do something contrary to that required by some external agency'.* The conformist state can be defined most simply as the absence of this feeling.[2]

The negativistic state must be distinguished from what will be called 'felt negativism'. This can be defined as the degree to which one actually perceives oneself to be acting against some salient requirement. It should be clear that one can be in a negativistic state and yet unable to perform any kind of negativistic behaviour, and therefore experiencing low felt negativism. For this reason one cannot equate felt negativism and the negativistic state. In fact 'felt negativism' can be seen as the key variable on which the negativistic and conformist states act, in rather the same way as 'felt arousal' is the key variable for the excitement-seeking and anxiety-avoidance states. In these terms the preferred level of felt negativism is high in the negativistic state and low in the conformist state, and hedonic tone may therefore be expected to be high when felt negativism is high in the negativistic state and low when it is high in the conformist state. The variable could equally well have been called 'felt conformity', in which case its relationship to the negativistic and conformist states would have been the inverse of that just described.

There are a number of points which need to be emphasized or amplified at the outset:

(i) Negativism and conformity defined in this way are both essentially *relational*, in the sense that they require reference to some source, or potential source, of requirements with which a person has, or can have, some kind of interactional relationship. Typically this source is social and consists either of an individual giving an order or creating expectations of some kind, or of a group which acts as a reference group in relation to norms and conventions. So the source in the individual's phenomenal field gives rise to requirements which the individual responds to in either a negativistic or conformist manner, the response to the requirement being at the same time a response to the source. The situation can be represented by a simple hierarchy:

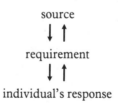

Felt negativism involves seeing oneself to be acting against some external force, which is typically felt to be more powerful than oneself in some way. In fact, one's reaction in this respect may itself be determined, or strongly influenced, albeit indirectly, by external forces, e.g. by one's parents through the mediation of conscience. This is not, however, the way it is felt by the individual at the moment in question, who perceives himself to be making his own decisions.

(ii) Consistent with the phenomenological approach of reversal theory, the negativistic and conformist states and felt negativism are, as already noted, defined in phenomenological terms. Just as the term 'arousal' which is already widely used in a physiological sense is given a phenomenological meaning in reversal theory as 'felt arousal', so negativism, which is usually defined by reference to overt behaviour, is also given a phenomenological meaning in the theory. Reversal theory, however, distinguishes between two aspects of negativism in relation to experience: firstly, the feeling of a desire to behave negativistically and secondly, the extent to which one sees oneself to be behaving in this way, i.e. as the degree to which one sees oneself to be doing what one should not do.

There is a sense in which other people, including external observers, can play a part in the second aspect of negativism, by providing feedback which helps the individual to assess how negativistic his behaviour is. This can therefore help to determine the strength of his felt negativism. But felt negativism does not necessarily depend on this: negativism can be expressed in a subtle way so that if there is a 'victim' of the behaviour, this 'victim', and indeed others who may happen to observe the behaviour, are unaware of its true significance, although the instigator of the behaviour is fully aware of what he is doing. In any case, even where the behaviour of other people affects a person's degree of felt negativism, this is still defined in terms of *his or her* own interpretation of what is happening and *his or her* own experience of the situation.

(iii) Following the requirements of some source, e.g. traffic regulations, may become so automatic that one no longer notices that there is an external source, but rather feels the requirements to be internal in origin. Felt negativism cannot then normally arise in relation to such requirements because they are *felt* to come from inside rather than from an external agency; although, as will be seen later, this can be complicated by self-negativism.

(iv) A requirement can be about some goal which should, or should not be achieved, e.g. 'Finish your homework!' or 'Do not pick the apples!' It can also be about the route to some goal: 'Finish your homework quickly!' or 'Do not pick the apples in that way!' Negativistic behaviour can therefore either be towards some goal or some way of achieving the goal.

(v) There are two ways in which one can decide to express one's negativistic state: by refusing to do that which is required, and by doing the *opposite* of that which is required. These two ways correspond to the active and passive negativism of schizophrenia (see above). Which way is chosen may depend on a number of factors, one being that some requirements have clear opposites while others do not, so that active negativism requires more decision-making in some cases than passive negativism. Thus the opposite to 'Close your mouth!' is obviously 'Open your mouth!' But what is the opposite of 'Eat!'? Is it to refuse to put food in one's mouth, to put food in one's mouth and have it there without masticating, to swallow it without masticating, to spit it out, or to defecate?

(vi) The requirement may be about some belief which one is required to adopt, rather than about behaviour. Felt negativism would then be most likely to arise from publicly denying the truth of this belief or idea, or publicly espousing an opposite belief.[3] For example, in response to Christianity, the first course might be represented by declarations of agnosticism and the second by atheism or by conversion to some other religion. The belief may of course involve evaluation of some kind, aesthetic or moral, and this may, in the negativistic state, result in an evaluation being made which is opposite to that required: if every one says that a given film is outstanding one may be deliberately dismissive and even avoid seeing the film.

(vii) In the negativistic state there is always some awareness of a requirement, or at least the need for a requirement, in the foreground in the phenomenal field. By contrast, in the conformist state, a requirement, or the need for a requirement, is not necessarily so predominant in awareness. Often of course in the conformist state one *is* centrally aware of some requirement, and in this state one may feel a strong positive need or desire to conform to it. But more frequently in the conformist state there may be no special awareness of any requirement at all. This does not mean that there are times when requirements do not have psychological effects: throughout one's working life thoughts and actions are, of course, determined by large numbers of implicit requirements determining what is and is not permissible. What it does mean is that frequently one is not aware of them at the focus of attention, but responds automatically to requirements of which one is only dimly aware, if at all. In such cases, one may nevertheless be said to be in the conformist state of mind.

(viii) A special case of negativism, but one which is of fundamental importance, is that in which the reaction is against a source which is seen by the individual to be reducing his freedom of action; in other words by exerting pressure which he feels limits, or threatens to limit, his range of possible behaviours. Brehm (1966, 1974) who refers to this form of response as 'reactance' has discussed the phenomenon extensively and given many examples.

Negativism and Deviance

It must be emphasized again that the definition of the negativistic and conformist states given here is phenomenological. It refers to a feeling which may, or may not, result in some overt action. The source, particularly where this is a reference group, is that which is accepted as such by the individual himself, who may have a number of alternative reference groups available. Where the requirements consist of norms, expectations, etc., these must be recognized and understood as such by the individual: the concern of reversal theory is with the way in which he sees what he is required to do by some external source, rather than the way this is intended by the external source itself, whether an individual or a group. Negativism and conformity are therefore defined in terms of the judgements of the individual, not those of some external potential controller, or even of some outside observer or experimenter, be he a psychologist, psychiatrist, priest, policeman, or politician. This is not to deny that the individual's choices and judgements in all these respects may not be influenced, or even determined, by external social influences, especially education and upbringing. Nor is it to deny that a given requirement may not force itself unwanted upon the individual's attention. Nevertheless, the definitions are in terms of the way the individual himself sees things at the moment in question.

Behaviour which is defined as negativistic by some external observer, may well fail to correspond with behaviour performed in the negativistic state of mind as defined here. Thus, an external observer may see some act of hooliganism or vandalism as negativistic, but the individual who commits it as a member of a gang, might see his actions as conforming to the gang's expectations. Conversely, an action which appears externally to be conformist, might be carried out in a negativistic state of mind. Going to the pub in the evening might appear to be a conformist act in the British culture, but the individual himself might see it as a negativistic act towards the strictures of his wife, and deliberately carry it out for this very reason. The source of the requirement may be different from that supposed by the observer and so may be the individual's feelings of negativism or conformity towards that source.

To an external observer, it might seem that any kind of act which is damaging or hurtful must be negativistic. But a moment's consideration will show that this is not necessarily the case. Wanting to hurt, harm, or destroy can under some circumstances be conformist, in the sense that it is felt to be required, in the situation prevailing, by some salient source. Parents smacking their children, demolition men destroying a building, or soldiers fighting, may all be performing their actions in a conformist state of mind if, at the moment in question, they see themselves as complying with the requirements of their chosen reference group. Although negativism is frequently expressed through violence or aggression, it cannot be *defined* in these terms.

Furthermore, competition between people, as occurs in sport, does not normally in itself imply a negativistic state of mind. The players in a game conform to the rules of the game and the expectations of their own and opposition team-mates. The fact that the expectation is that they will play *against* their opponents does not necessarily make them negativistic: they are doing what they should be doing. The manner in which they do it may, however, derive from a negativistic state of mind on occasion: thus, a given player may deliberately do something unexpected, particularly if he is an original and creative player; or he may decide to break the rules.

How does all this relate to the sociological concept of deviance, and to sociological explanations of deviant behaviour? As far as the concept of deviance is concerned one would certainly expect from the reversal theory perspective that behaviours classified by sociologists as deviant, e.g. stealing, vandalism, drug-taking, may often be performed by individuals in a negativistic state of mind. There are, of course, a number of different sociological theories of deviance, but none of them appear to claim as reversal theory does that deviance may be enjoyable in itself, i.e. when it gives rise in the negativistic state of mind to high felt negativism, and that deviant behaviour may on occasion be performed at least partly for this very reason.

One set of sociological theories of deviance sees it as socially defined. What happens to be labelled deviant in one society may not be a deviant in another: moderate drinking in a public place would not be deviant in Britain, but would be in a Moslem country like Saudi Arabia. What is deviant in one 'subculture' may not be in another: going to church would not be deviant in a middle-class American suburb, but might be in a hippie commune in California. The implication of this widespread sociological view would appear to be that people are never deliberately deviant, but rather act in certain ways which society, or a dominant group in society, happens to label as deviant.[4] "Deviance is thus not inherent in any particular action, but is socially defined" (Berry, 1974, p.116). This is clearly quite different from the reversal theory view that people *do* on occasion act in a deliberately deviant way, that having identified some injunction or another of society in general, or some representative reference group, they deliberately flout it. For such people on such occasions, the deviance *is* inherent in the action, and fully intended to be.

Another set of sociological theories of deviance recognizes that the deviant individual may himself be aware that his actions are deviant, and he may even share the feeling of other members of his society that these actions are disreputable. Such theories then attempt to explain why the individual nevertheless persists in his deviant actions, the common core of the theories appearing to be the rather obvious notion that the deviant behaviour enables the individual to obtain things which would otherwise remain unobtainable. For example, stealing might enable him to obtain large sums of money. One theory of this type adds that the individual may need to be able to rationalize what he is doing in order to overcome feelings of guilt. Another type of theory emphasizes individual differences in the degree to which people feel constrained by the requirements of society.[5] While agreeing that a variety of goals and satisfactions may be obtained through deviant behaviour, reversal theory argues that these are often secondary to the satisfaction that derives from the deviance in itself. The attainment of otherwise unobtainable goals is not always a reason, nor is it necessarily the only reason, for the performance of deviant acts.

It should be clear from this brief discussion, that the reversal theory interpretation of deviance differs fundamentally from that of the general run of sociological theories. Although the emphasis here has been on the part played by negativism in deviance, it must be re-emphasized that behaviour which appears from the outside to be negativistic, and is classified as deviant, may well be performed in a conformist state of mind. Teenage vandals, or student 'drop-outs', may well feel themselves to be conforming to norms, these being derived from subcultures different from the subcultures of those people who define the behaviour as deviant, and they may even be unaware that they are acting against certain requirements. Reversal theory argues nevertheless that deviant behaviour *may* be chosen as a deliberate rejection of society's requirements, and suggests that often, if not always, deviant behaviour *does* have such negativistic origins. This may seem like a return to an older and unfashionable view of deviance, but we feel that an examination of the feelings underlying one's own actions discloses on occasion the negativistic state described here; it is reasonable to suppose that the state may, in some individuals at least, result in deviant behaviour.

The reversal theory explanation of deviant behaviour differs not only from sociological explanations, but also from the sort of explanations that learning theorists like to give, that deviant behaviour is merely another form of learned behaviour. It might, for example, be acquired through operant conditioning.[6] In reversal theory terms, people who are behaving in a negativistic state may well find the expression of negativistic behaviour to be reinforcing; indeed, in reversal theory, high felt negativism in this state should produce positive hedonic tone. One would therefore expect various types of negativistic behaviour to be learned under these conditions. But the point is that the individual, and not some external controlling agency, has effectively specified what will be reinforcing at a given moment. In learning theory, especially of the Skinnerian type, there would be nothing inherently rebellious or negativistic about deviant behaviour. As Rollo May is reported to have said: "I have never found any place in Skinner's system for the rebel".[7] In reversal theory, by contrast, deviant behaviour *is* claimed to be related frequently to an innate spirit of negativism and defiance.

Negativism-Conformity Bistability

It will by now be appreciated why the negativistic and conformist states as defined here constitute another pair of metamotivational states, like the telic and paratelic states and the excitement-seeking and anxiety-avoidance states. They are metamotivational in that they are about the way in which the individual interprets his own motives: they are *about* motivation, and the level of description is higher than that of particular motives. Thus, a given motive may be felt as either negativistic or conformist, depending on which state one is in and which source is at the centre of attention. Trying to complete a book on time may be seen by the writer as conforming to the publisher's requirements or defying the expectations of colleagues who do not believe it possible, and an alternation may occur between these two interpretations by the writer of his actions.

This does not imply that as a reversal takes place one completely loses sight of the alternative interpretation; rather, it drops into the background. Indeed, where the same motive is seen in alternating ways, the effect is not unlike that of figure-ground reversals: if one part of the diagram is seen as figure this in itself defines what is seen as ground, and vice versa. The member of a teenage gang may conform to the orders of the leader, even if these orders mean that he must disobey the requirements imposed by his parents, such as not to wear certain clothes, go to certain places, or behave in certain ways. Logically, conformity to one set of requirements implies negativism to another, but phenomenologically one of these may be primary in the sense that it is at the focus of awareness, while the other is secondary, being relatively marginal: i.e. one set of requirements is part of the figure and the other of the ground in the phenomenal field. Phenomenologically, therefore, there is a difference between on the one hand conforming to a group whose actions happen to contradict the requirements of others, and on the other hand contradicting the requirements of others, but doing so within a group of people who have expectations to which one conforms. For example, in the first case someone might enjoy belonging to a nudist group because he enjoys lying in the sun without a bathing costume, even though this happens to shock other people and contradict more normal requirements. In the second case, someone may enjoy shocking other people by sunbathing without wearing a swimming costume, and happen to do this by belonging to a group of nudists. The focus of the individual's phenomenal field may change from one source of requirements to the other, so that there is an alternation which may continue over a length of time between high and low felt negativism, even though the continuing action remains the same. To develop the nudist example: a person sunbathing in the nude may alternate between seeing what he or she is doing as conforming to the nudist group, or as being negativistic to other non-nudists in the area or to the requirements of society as a whole.

There is a further feature of the negativistic and conformist states which implies that they are metamotivational: each may occur, at least momentarily, in the absence of any specific negativistic or conformist goal, i.e. in the absence of any particular requirement to act with or against. Thus a reversal into the negativistic state may be brought about by satiation of the conformist state, with the result that a search is then instigated for some requirement which can be brought into the focus of the phenomenal field and acted against. Following a reversal, the negativistic state may therefore on occasion be initially free of any particular requirement. The same may be true of a reversal in the conformist direction: the individual may temporarily experience a strong need to conform to some requirement without having identified an acceptable requirement and brought it to the focus of the phenomenal field. (In fact, in the conformist state there may be no need for a requirement to be experienced at all at the centre of attention, the state being defined by absence of negativistic attention to a requirement.) Like the telic and paratelic states, it would therefore be possible to say that the negativistic and conformist states may at certain times be 'non-intentional', using the word 'intentional' in the strict phenomenological sense meaning 'having a reference'.

Like the telic-paratelic pair of metamotivational states, the negativism-conformity pair exhibits bistability. This means that at any given moment a person will feel himself to be in either the conformist or negativistic state, but reversal is always possible from one to the other and occurs in everybody from time to time for various reasons. In this particular pair, the conformist state is clearly dominant in most people; so the situation in this respect is unlike that which prevails with the telic-paratelic pair, since in the latter pair there is generally a fair degree of parity between the two states in most people. But even though the conformist state is strongly dominant in the majority of people, this does not mean that everyone is in this state *all* the time: everyone is presumably in the negativistic state from time to time as well. In a few people, indeed, the negativistic state may even be dominant.

Attainment of the preferred level of the variable 'felt negativism' is pleasant, and failure to obtain it unpleasant. Thus, high felt negativism is pleasant if one is in the negativistic state, and low felt negativism pleasant if one is in the conformist state. The feeling of negativism in the negativistic state seems to be experienced as a kind of power, independence, or release; the feeling of low felt negativism, i.e. of felt conformity, in the conformist state is felt as a kind of security. It would probably be true to say, however, that the pleasure of low felt negativism in the conformist state is less than that of high felt negativism in the negativistic state. It may seem odd to claim that people can enjoy doing what they should not do more than they enjoy conforming, but this assertion is at the heart of the argument.

Figure 9.1 represents the points just made in graphical form. The similarity to Fig. 4.1, concerning felt arousal, will be immediately evident. Four adjectives have been added to the figure, which indicate at least some aspect of the feelings which are experienced in each extreme combination of hedonic tone and felt negativism; although this is not a complete characterization, it is an indication of one component of the feeling in each case.

As in telic-paratelic bistability, this bistability would appear to be of the externally-controlled variety. Reversal of the *preferred* level of the variable concerned, in this case 'felt negativism', occurs first, irrespective of the *actual* level of the variable at the moment in question, and only then will the system attempt to guide the value of the variable towards the preferred level.

So what occurs during a reversal, say in the negativistic direction, can be described in three steps:

(i) There is a switch to the negativistic preferred level of the 'felt negativism' variable.

(ii) There is a search, which is perhaps unconscious, for some requirement towards which negativistic action can be taken; the end of this step is marked by the conscious identification of such a requirement.

(iii) Action is taken against the identified requirement, with the result that the level of felt negativism is likely to be increased towards the preferred high level.

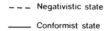

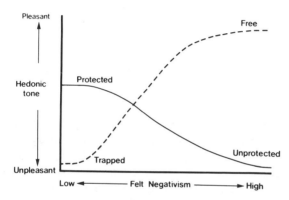

FIG. 9.1 *The hypothesized relationship between felt negativism and hedonic tone for the negativistic and conformist states.*

The reversal between metamotivational states occurs at the first step. At the second step there may already be some requirement towards which negativistic action can be taken, and this requirement may be a salient part of the situation which has induced the reversal to negativism in the first place. If not, then a search will ensue, and tension be felt until some requirement is found, or brought into existence, towards which negativistic action can be taken. (It will be recalled that it was postulated in Chapter 3 that tension will be felt if there is a discrepancy between the preferred value and the actual value of a variable.) The second step is generally not difficult to accomplish since there is always a large number of implied requirements in any situation which, even if they are not initially salient, can easily be made so, e.g. that one should not steal, or that one should work hard. Action is then undertaken against the chosen requirement, unless it is not physically possible to do so, or unless it is felt to be unwise in the light of possible consequences. In such a case a new search may be instigated for a different requirement towards which it might be possible to act negativistically.

When it is found, the negativism may be thought of as having been *displaced* from one requirement onto another. Conformity can be similarly displaced. For example, a child may not be able to act against certain parental requirements and so displaces his need to behave negativistically onto other parental requirements; or he may displace his negativism onto the requirements of another source, e.g. of an elder brother. A teenager in a gang may find that, perhaps for reasons of physical inability, he cannot conform to the orders of the leader, and so searches for some other group with a leader who sets more amenable tasks to which he *can* conform, in this way displacing his conformity.

It should not be forgotten that actions, whether intended to be negativistic or conformist, may have rewarding or punishing consequences quite apart from the pleasure or displeasure which results from their giving rise to low or high felt negativism.

Reversals between the negativistic and conformist states are brought about by the same three general classes of factors as those which induce telic-paratelic reversals.

1. Contingency

This is the major category and covers both environmental events, like an order from someone, and psychological events, like the involuntary occurrence of certain memories or ideas which suggest actions which should, or should not, be taken.

The induction of the negativistic or conformist state may be the result of a largely rational process. A given salient requirement may seem to be necessary or unnecessary, feasible or unfeasible, useful or useless, helpful or harmful, moral or immoral. Here the nature and meaning of the requirement itself, as it is interpreted by the individual, leads automatically to the negativistic or conformist state of mind. In other words, steps (i) and (ii) above are coalesced, the switch to the negativistic state, say, being part of the response to the requirement rather than preceding it. Similarly, the extent to which one recognizes the authority of the source of the requirement may play a part. In this case the induction of the conformist or negativistic state would precede a particular requirement issuing from the source in question, and therefore step (i) would indeed precede step (ii); but in the induction of the negativistic or conformist state would still be a result of rational processes of assessment. Rational processes may also lead the individual to decide whether or not he will act in accordance with his negativistic or conformist feelings: thus the sanctions available to a source of a requirement may make it unwise to act against a requirement from that source, even though one might wish to do so.

Other less rational and more emotional factors may play a large, and even determining, part in inducing a reversal. Again, the reaction may be to a specific requirement in itself and only secondarily to the source, or it may be to the source before any particular requirement is made by the source. In the former case, for example, emotional connotations which the wording of an order happens to elicit may induce the negativistic or conformist states. In the latter case, factors such as whether one likes or dislikes the source, and one's feelings of commitment to the source, may be involved. Environmental context is likely to play a part in inducing or maintaining one state or the other, largely through assigning or removing authority from the source of requirements, or increasing or decreasing suggestibility. Being a member of a large crowd, e.g. at a political meeting, or of a highly disciplined group of people, e.g. soldiers on parade, is likely to induce and maintain for a period the conformist state, whereas being an isolated individual, or a member of a disorganized 'rabble', may well help to induce the negativistic state. Emotional factors in relation to a requirement or its source, or the environmental context, may also help to determine whether actions intended to be negativistic or conformist will actually be undertaken, or whether they will remain unexpressed.

There are many other events, or aspects of situations, which may tend to induce one state or the other. To give one more example, if the source of require-ments makes claims to be strong, but at the same time can be seen to be weak (in other words constitutes a type of real/apparent synergy), then this would appear to induce negativism towards the requirements. A car park attendant who is officious, but has no power to do anything about infractions of the rules in the car park, seems to invite negativistic behaviour towards his orders. Similarly, a school teacher who apparently wears the stamp of authority and continually makes strong threats, but fails to carry them out, is more likely to have discipline problems than the teacher who makes no threats at all.

One other major factor needs to be mentioned: that of whether the individual is concurrently in the telic or paratelic state. One can be either conformist or negativistic in either the telic or the paratelic state, but negativism or conformity may be induced and utilized for different ends in the telic and paratelic states, as will be seen later.

2.   Frustration

If the attempt to act in a way consistent with the negativistic or conformist state is frustrated, this frustration may induce a reversal to the opposite state. Suppose, for example, that one feels negative towards one's immediate superior at work, but has to inhibit any action against his requirements; a point may be reached at which one reverses to feel conformist towards these requirements and their source. Con-versely, suppose one feels sympathy towards some source of requirements, but is unable to conform to them; in this case one may in the end come to feel negativistic towards the source and its requirements. Thus, if one cannot succeed in obeying instructions in a piano lesson one may eventually reject the whole situation.

This constitutes a general explanation for the way in which people's feelings eventually come into line with their actions when there is dissonance between the two, the agent of change being the frustration involved. This provides an alternative explanation for this phenomenon to that of Festinger (1957) who, in his cognitive dissonance theory, suggests that it is the dissonance itself which induces change in such situations.

The reader may feel perplexed at this stage by the variety of functions which, at different points in the book, frustration has been said to perform. Not only has it been said to be able to induce reversals in either direction between pairs of metamotivational states, such as the states of negativism and conformity, but it has also been described as one factor which can increase arousal and therefore be used to obtain excitement in the paratelic state; the part it can play in bringing about aggression has also been noted. Furthermore, although the term 'frustration' was not used a few paragraphs ago in discussing the displacement of negativism or conformity, it is clear that such displacement is another potential effect of frustration. One thing which a consideration of the topic of frustration does is to bring out yet again one of the main themes of reversal theory, which is that a given situation may have a number of concurrent psychological effects at a number of levels: thus frustration can both increase the level of felt arousal, and simultaneously play a part in changing the way in which the arousal is interpreted. However, it should also be clear that some of the effects of frustration listed here are alternatives rather than supplements. For example, displacement of negativism would be an alternative effect to the induction of a reversal to conformity. Something therefore needs to be said about which effects occur under which conditions.

To understand this it must be recognized that there are two types of frustration. The first is frustration in achieving a goal. The second is frustration in the attempt to bring a metamotivational variable, i.e. felt significance, felt arousal, felt negativism, into its preferred level. This type of frustration could also be referred to as prolonged tension. These two types of frustration are not the same since, for example, it is possible to see an essential goal as highly significant in the telic state while being frustrated in its attainment; to have pleasant high arousal in the paratelic state while attempting to overcome some mild and frustrating barrier; and to feel oneself to be acting negativistically towards a source without thereby being able to achieve some goal which remains out of reach, for instance, arguing vehemently with someone who nevertheless always finds better counter-arguments. In all these cases there is goal-frustration without frustration in relation to a metamotivational variable. But conversely, it is possible for there to be metamotivational frustration without goal-frustration. For example, a goal can be achieved, but be felt to be insignificant; or it can be achieved too easily, so that there is little chance for felt arousal to build up. It can also be achieved too easily for an adequately high level of felt negativism to be experienced. For example, having identified a difference of opinion with someone, one might start an argument with him, only to find that he gives way immediately on each point and that the goal of winning the argument is achieved without the opposition necessary to generate high felt negativism.

Frustration in achieving some goal typically gives rise to increased arousal and, if the negativistic state is operative, to anger in the telic state and parapathic anger in the paratelic state. Frustration in achieving the preferred level of a metamotivational variable, on the other hand, typically leads to displacement, e.g. to the search for a new requirement against which one can act negativistically, or a new goal which one can pursue. So in these respects the effects of the two types of frustration tend to be rather different. Both types, however, would appear to be similar in that they can each independently play a part in inducing a reversal between metamotivational states. Generally, the effects just mentioned seem to occur first, a reversal being brought about when the frustration is more prolonged. (But a reversal *can* be triggered immediately when frustration is combined with other reversal-inducing factors.) For example, frustration in achieving a goal in the telic state may initially produce increased arousal in the form of anxiety or anger before a reversal to the paratelic state occurs, when the goal is achieved in fantasy (or the arousal is enjoyed as excitement or parapathic anger). Frustration in expressing negativism, and therefore of experiencing negativism in the negativistic state, may have to build up over a period, and through a number of attempted displacements, before the conformist state is induced.[8]

There is a particular way in which frustration in achieving a goal can induce reversal between the negativistic and conformist states, which is especially worth noting since the mechanism would appear to underlie many types of experience and behaviour. If some frustration is experienced in the pursuit of a goal, telic or paratelic, one comes to focus on the barrier which stands in the way of its achievement, and in doing so comes to see the barrier as an *external pressure to conform*, i.e. as a type of source with its own requirements. If, nevertheless, one chooses to continue to pursue the goal rather than give up, then at this stage one becomes *negativistic to the barrier*, and to the perceived requirement to give up the pursuit of the goal; as a result one redoubles one's efforts.[9] Although this negativism is logically implicit in any purposeful pursuit of a goal, phenomenologically it only becomes a salient part of experience if there is sufficient frustration, and if the source of the frustration is something on which it is possible to focus.[10] One now attempts to achieve the goal primarily in order to overcome the barrier, which has become the focus of attention; hence overcoming the barrier itself becomes the goal, and one which is essentially negativistic. Of course the behaviour concerned might continue in a way which is ostensibly unchanged, despite the phenomenological change, although often there will be signs that the negativistic state has been induced, e.g. displays of irritation or annoyance, or obvious increased effort.

A typical frustration sequence illustrating these different effects of frustration might be as follows. One starts by pursuing some goal in the conformist and paratelic states, and the initially mild frustrations are felt as pleasurable excitement. However, in the face of increasing frustration in achieving the goal, attention is focused more and more on the barrier, which is seen as something to act against; i.e. the negativistic state is induced. Some "anger" may be felt at this stage. As the frustration builds up, so overcoming the barrier is seen as increasingly important and becomes an essential goal in its own right, which means that the telic state is induced. Arousal still mounts and, in conjunction with the telic and negativistic states, is felt as anger. This anger, which is unpleasant, may lead to aggression. If it is not possible to aggress against the barrier/source, i.e. there is frustration of felt negativism, the negativism will be displaced and perhaps lead to aggression towards some other source. If frustration of the expression of negativism, and therefore of overcoming the barrier and achieving the goal, continues, sooner or later there will be a reversal to the conformist state, i.e. submission to the pressure to give up, and/or to the paratelic state, i.e. the goal is no longer felt to be essential, or it is achieved in fantasy. How soon this point comes will largely depend on personality characteristics, but may also be a function of the individual's previous history of success or failure in pursuing the type of goal in question.

Here is a concrete illustration of this progression. Suppose one is playing a game of tennis which one starts to lose. Initially, in a paratelic state, the frustration of not winning raises the level of arousal, which is felt as excitement. However, suppose one continues to lose points. If there is some reason for this which can be focused on, one starts to feel negativistic towards this source, typically the opponent, but it may also be something else, e.g. a faulty racket. Overcoming this barrier becomes increasingly essential and important, so that there is a switch to the telic state, at which point the combination of the negativistic state and high arousal is felt as anger. Sooner or later this anger boils over into aggression, e.g. one insults one's opponent or throws one's racket to the court; this aggression may be towards the original source or may be a displacement, especially if one cannot for reasons of courtesy behave negativistically to the real source. As frustration continues, so one gives up trying to win and 'goes through the motions', perhaps fantasizing about what it would be like to win, or downgrading the felt significance of the game.

3. Satiation

Being in one state of mind or the other for a prolonged period may in itself, in the absence of other factors, induce a reversal. So an outbreak of bad behaviour in a class may be a function of satiation of the conformist state among the members of the class; a soldier may become 'conformist satiated' with prolonged over-restriction and suddenly decide to spend a night out of camp without leave; a driver may after many long hours of careful driving start deliberately speeding, or breaking other rules of the road.[11] In all these cases the negativistic state may also satiate and lead at some stage to a return to the conformist state and to conforming behaviour,[12] although it is likely that other factors will intervene to induce a reversal *from* the negativistic state long before satiation of this state can occur. How long this satiation effect takes to build up to a reversal may be largely a personality factor, although it is possible that it is influenced in one direction or the other by a variety of further factors such as tiredness, menstruation in women, or taking certain drugs. Getting drunk, for example, seems to induce the negativistic state in many people, and in this case the negativism is often expressed in violence.

Various factors from the above three categories may be expected to work with or against each other in some way in inducing reversals between the two states. (It is being assumed, as it was for telic-paratelic reversals, that the reversals are involuntary and not under deliberate conscious control—except indirectly through a manipulation of environmental, including social, events which may induce one state or the other.) Typically, some aspect of the environment will play a part in inducing a reversal, but occasionally it may happen that a reversal takes place where the environment plays little direct part, i.e. where the reversal is effectively induced through satiation. In such a case, the mental state occurs first and initiates a search for something towards which it can direct itself. If it is the negativistic state which is induced, one feels the need to be negativistic 'without any good reason' and seeks something to be negativistic towards.[13] At such moments, as explained above, it could be said that the state, temporarily, has no intentionality in the strict phenomenological sense. Consciousness *of* the state is of course intentional, but the state itself, for the period in question, has no further reference. Whatever identity is being focused on in the phenomenal field at the time of the reversal will be an obvious candidate to be the source of requirements to be rejected, but the individual may nevertheless search further afield. The reader will no doubt be able to recall from his own experience examples of reversals into the negativistic state which preceded recognition of some source of requirement towards which he or she could act negatively.

Once the first step of a negativism-conformity reversal has taken place, there appear to be two ways in which the second step, the identification of a requirement, may be accomplished. Firstly, it may involve changing one's feelings in a negativistic or conformist direction towards some source, or the requirements of that source. The source may already be the centre of attention, as it typically is when the reversal occurs for some contingent reason; or the centre of attention may move on to it, especially if the reversal is induced through satiation. Secondly, if the situation is one in which conformity to one requirement *implies* negativism to another, or vice versa, the reversal may simply involve a change in which *aspect* of the situation becomes the focal aspect. That is, if the 'ground' is opposite to the 'figure' in terms of negativism and conformity, then there may be a form of 'figure-ground' reversal in the phenomenal field. Thus, in terms of the example given earlier, as a writer reverses into conformism, he may simply continue writing in order to try to comply with the publisher's deadline rather than writing in order to defy the expectations of colleagues. These two types of reversal need to be distinguished, but they both involve conformity-negativism reversal in one direction or the other. In the former case, the individual's actions may take a radically different course; in the latter, the action may remain identical but be seen by him from a different perspective. This is yet one more illustration of the complex relationship between experience and behaviour which is highlighted by reversal theory.

It may be helpful to represent these two different forms of reversal schematically. If '+' represents conformity to requirements, and '-' negativism to requirements, and arrows represent reversals, then these two different forms in which the second step of reversal can occur may be represented as follows:

(i) Source A$^-$ $\rightleftarrows$ Source A$^+$
e.g. a child's feelings underlying alternate defiance and conformity towards parents.

(ii) Source A$^+$ $\rightleftarrows$ Source B$^-$
Here A implies not-B, and vice versa. In this case the source changes along with the reversal, as when the writer alternately sees publishers and colleagues as sources of requirements, towards which he is conformist and negativistic respectively. Each source can be regarded as a ground to the other's figure.

Both of these contrast with displacement of negativism which can be represented as:

(iii) Source A$^-$ $\rightleftarrows$ Source B$^-$

Often the situation is more complicated than this. To take a dramatic example, consider an isolated soldier who is not sure whether to shoot at an enemy soldier in the distance whom he knows to be wounded, or whether to go and help him. If the source of requirements which is at the focus of his phenomenal field is the army, then he may feel that this source requires him to shoot the enemy; if a religious group to which he belongs is the focal source he may feel that this requires him to go and help the enemy. Either act, shooting or helping, could be undertaken in either a negativistic or conformist state of mind. Helping the enemy would mean acting negativistically towards the requirements of the army, but conforming to those of his religious reference group; shooting at the enemy would involve acting in a way which conformed to the requirements of the army but was negative to those of the religious group. So, if he is in a negativistic state of mind, his action will depend on which source is the 'figure' in his phenomenal field and which the 'ground', and the same will be true, but with opposite effect, if he is in the conformist state of mind. If source A is the army and source B the religious group, then the structure of the whole situation can be represented as in Fig. 9.2, where each arrow represents a potential reversal. Should a reversal occur between the negativistic and conformist state while he is considering the situation, then this could have one of two alternative effects: either the same

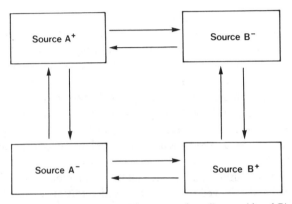

FIG. 9.2 *Possible ways of experiencing two opposite sources of requirements (A and B), and the transformations which can occur between them.*

source would remain the salient one, the change being in the vertical direction in the diagram above; or the salient source would change, the change being in the horizontal direction in this diagram. The first case would be the same as that described in (i) above and the second the same as that depicted in (ii) above. In the event of a change in both ways successively, in either order, then the effect would be a displacement of negativism or conformity, the result of this being the same as that represented in (iii) above.

Relationship to the Telic and Paratelic States

Negativism-conformity constitutes an entirely different dimension from the telic-paratelic dimension, so that either the negativistic or conformist state can occur in conjunction with either the telic or the paratelic state at a given time. The way in which the negativistic and conformist states function, however, is typically different in the two cases, as will become apparent by examining each combination of the two pairs of metamotivational states in turn. There is a sense in which either the negativistic or conformist state may be 'called up' by the telic or paratelic states to serve their purposes, and in this sense they are subservient to the telic and paratelic states. However, reversals between the negativistic and conformist states can no more be induced voluntarily than reversals between the telic and paratelic states, and therefore they have to be 'called up' by indirect means, i.e. by making deliberate environmental changes which, in turn, invoke a reversal of the 'contingency' type, or also, possibly, of the frustration type, between the states of negativism and conformity.

1. Telic conformity

If the conformist state occurs in combination with the telic state, this implies that the individual is conforming, or trying to conform, to all salient requirements during the pursuit of a goal which he sees as being essential. Achievement of the goal may itself of course be the most salient requirement of all, if the individual sees himself to be conforming to some external pressure to reach it. But other requirements, especially about the means which can be followed in pursuing the goal, may also be salient. These requirements may include rules to be followed, or at least conventions or expectations about which behaviours are appropriate in pursuit of the goal.

Examples are ubiquitous, and include all those situations in which an essential goal is pursued and achieved through perceived conformity to the requirements of some external force. For example, workers on an assembly line may be assumed to be in this combined telic-conformist state for most of the time they are at work, although this does not preclude occasional reversals into the paratelic and negativistic states. The same may be true of nurses on the ward, soldiers on parade, or schoolchildren taking examinations.

Sometimes such telic conformity requires the individual to be negativistic to the requirements of some other source. A soldier in battle, in conforming to the requirements of his commander, works against the requirements of the enemy. The subjects in Milgram's celebrated experiments on "Obedience to Authority", in obeying the experimenter, were acting negatively towards the needs of what they took to be experimental subjects, in an experiment in which they thought they were acting as assistants, by administering supposedly painful electric shocks (Milgram, 1974). (In fact, the 'subjects' were really stooges of the experimenter, and only simulated pain.) Nonetheless, both these cases, that of soldiers in battle and that of Milgram's subjects, are cases which most people would agree are examples of conformity rather than negativism. What the individuals in these cases presumably see as the most salient source of requirements is in each case the source to which they conform, the source towards which they act negatively being seen as secondary and in a sense part of the 'ground' rather than the 'figure' in that part of the phenomenal field which has to do with requirements. In short, they feel themselves to be doing what they are required to do.

2. Paratelic conformity

The conformist state may perform several functions in the context of the paratelic state. Firstly, by believing that he conforms to some group the individual may come to feel that he truly belongs to it, and this feeling of group membership may in turn provide a sense of security, thus helping to maintain the paratelic state, especially in the face of certain kinds of threat.[14] Secondly, conformist behaviour may play a part in the generation of an increased intensity of experience and heightened arousal, both of which are of course enjoyed in the paratelic state. This seems to occur when people can feel themselves to be members of large and powerful groups with which they can identify, especially when one of the aims of the group is to produce emotional reactions of some kind. Prime examples would be soccer crowds and civic parades. The same may also be true, if to a lesser extent, of protest marches, political rallies, and demonstrations by paramilitary groups. Both the feeling of belonging, and the generation of excitement, may be aided by such means as dressing identically and acting in unison, e.g. chanting, or marching in time. In these examples the groups are primary ones, but similar effects may occur with secondary groups: a teenager may feel that he 'belongs' and experience excitement through following the latest teenage fashion in clothing or dancing style.

   In all these cases, for the conformist state to be operative in conjunction with the paratelic state, any goal being pursued must be felt to be inessential. This is of course not always the case with membership of such groups as those involved in protest marches, although even here one suspects that many of those taking part lose sight of the importance of the goal for substantial periods, and experience the emotions involved, such as anger, in a parapathic form.

3. Telic negativism

If the conformist state may serve a purpose in both the telic and paratelic states, the same is also true of the state of negativism. When the negativistic state is operative in the telic context, the individual typically experiences himself as attempting to move towards some goal which is felt as essential *despite* salient requirements to the contrary from outside. That is, the individual sees himself primarily to be acting against the requirements of some external source, in order to reach a goal which he sees as essential.

   For example, if it is felt by a student that it is essential to pass an examination, then this may require acting negatively against other requirements, like paying social calls, which would prevent studying. The student would then feel himself to be acting negatively towards the source of requirements which would conflict with his telic goal. As has already been discussed, *any* type of barrier which frustrates the achievement of a goal may, if the frustration involved is sufficiently strong, induce the negativistic state in which the barrier becomes the focus of the negativism. The 'conformity to the goal' then becomes part of the background.

This is not to say that high felt negativism in the telic state is always achieved in the way suggested by this example. It is also possible to act against some source which is seen not as imposing a barrier to a goal, but as imposing a goal itself. For example, a child may decide to defy his parents by refusing to stay on at school and take more examinations, even though he has no other goal in prospect.

Here are other examples of situations in which someone in a telic state may feel himself to be acting negativistically. A worker in a factory may decide to go on strike for more pay, even though the pressures not to do so are felt by him to be enormous. A psychiatric patient may decide to try not to get better, despite the recognition that the psychiatrist is having a beneficial influence. A politician may refuse to do something which he regards as immoral, despite the sanctions which may be taken against him by his own party colleagues or by some powerful pressure group. An extreme example of telic felt negativism might be the experience of someone refusing to give way under torture, and remaining defiant.

There are a number of satisfactions that may be gained by being negativistic in the telic state. One of these is that one may thereby achieve some goal which one feels to be essential, even if there are various costs on the way. But over and above this, felt negativism itself is pleasant in the negativistic state, and this remains true in both the telic and paratelic states. Part of this pleasure may come from feeling independent and strong, which is the opposite way of experiencing security from that involved in paratelic conformity, where one feels 'part of' something else which is strong. Someone who is independent recognizes that he makes his own decisions about goals, and keeps to them, irrespective of the requirements of other sources, however powerful they might be. Indeed, the need for independence and freedom may be felt as a strong, telic, need in itself, as Brehm (op. cit.) emphasized with his notion of reactance.

In the telic state, unlike the paratelic, a negativistic action is inevitably concomitant with certain unpleasant feelings, and the result is always an unavoidable mixture of pleasant and unpleasant hedonic effects. The unpleasant effects arise because there is a dissonance between the action taken and certain of the requirements in the situation. In the telic state this dissonance is experienced as a form of conflict, which is to say as a form of synergy. For the reasons discussed in Chapter 7, synergy of any kind is felt as unpleasant in the telic state.

4. Paratelic negativism

The function of negativistic behaviour in the paratelic state is to be instrumental in the production of increased intensity of experience, including especially an increased level of excitement. The resulting felt negativism is also enjoyed in itself, without any of the unpleasant features of the telic state; after all, in the paratelic state, dissonance between actions and requirements, or between two different sets of requirements, will be felt as a form of synergy, and this will be pleasant. It is interesting in this respect that part of the pleasure both of synergies and of high felt negativism is the feeling of release: in one case from the laws of logic, in the other from the rules of man. Furthermore, if the negativistic behaviour is provocative enough to produce retaliation, then this should increase the pleasure still further, since it will increase the dissonance between the actions and the requirements of the source which is retaliating, and will also be expected to heighten felt arousal by making the situation a more generally emotional one. On the other hand, it must always be borne in mind that if the retaliation is too strong, the telic state may be induced.

Examples of paratelic negativism have been referred to earlier in Chapter 5, such as the feelings underlying what is known in Britain as 'aggro': the gratuitously aggressive behaviour of some soccer supporters. Examples abound, from writing graffiti to 'streaking', from reading banned pornography to fellatio, from crossing the pedestrian crossing against the red light to speeding in a built-up zone.[15] The reader should be able to find examples from his own experience without much difficulty. Who, after all, has not on occasion enjoyed teasing others, being deliberately provocative or risqué at a party, or committing minor infractions of the law while driving? Indeed, it is one of the underlying themes of this chapter that the negativistic state, and pleasurable felt negativism, are within the range of everyone's experience, rather than being intrinsically pathological or deviant. In all these cases, the negativistic actions are undertaken not *despite* the restrictive external requirements, but *because* of them.

It may be the case that a healthy culture is one which, among other things, produces a number of arbitrary conventions towards which people can act negativistically without damaging the society. Indeed, *most* people may act negativistically towards some of these conventions, which are really convenient myths rather than genuine requirements, and are created *in order to be* flouted. For example, oral-genital carressing may be supposedly prohibited, and yet it is indulged in by the majority of married couples (e.g. viz. Hunt, 1974): so the 'convention' about this type of sexual behaviour is what one might term a 'functional fiction'.[16]

Self-negativism

The term 'self' has acquired various meanings in psychology[17] and a number of distinctions have been made in relation to the concept. For present purposes it is useful to distinguish, as William James did in his seminal chapter on 'The Consciousness of Self' in 'Principles of Psychology' (1890), between the 'I', or subject of awareness, and the 'me' or object of awareness.[18] When one looks at oneself, introspects, or carries out phenomenological reflection, there is 'something' which does the looking, and 'something' which is looked at. This is a distinction which George Herbert Mead (1934) took up again later and made a cornerstone of his theory. By 'me' Mead intended to refer particularly to a social self: 'me' as one understands oneself to be seen by other people, especially in a social context. In this sense there may be a number of different 'me's or social selves, depending on different contexts. But as William James and other theorists have pointed out (e.g. Sarbin, 1952) there are other aspects of the self as object. These include one's body, and one's psychological proclivities, as one experiences them.

If the self polarizes into the 'I' and the 'me', then it is possible for the 'I' to see the 'me' as external to it in some way, and to see its requirements as coming 'from outside'.[19] Therefore under these conditions the 'I' can, when the negativistic state is operative, act negatively against the 'me'. This will be referred to here as 'self-negativism'. Much of what was called 'paradoxical behaviour' in the first chapter of this book, i.e. behaviour which militates against the survival of the individual who performs it, or his group, can be attributed to self-negativism of this kind.

There are a number of ways in which self-negativism may arise.[20] One of these is through what has been referred to earlier as displacement: when one cannot for one reason or another express one's negativism towards certain requirements, then one's response to this frustration may be to displace the negativism onto other requirements, possibly from a completely different source. If negativism towards all the external sources which are salient and significant to the individual are blocked off and frustrated, he may then treat himself as if he were an external source and work against his own felt requirements. In other words, his negativism, which in these terms is a propensity of the 'I', is displaced against the 'me'. This would then be one type of what Gestalt therapists have called 'retroflection' (Perls et al., 1973), by which is meant that a person substitutes himself for his environment, and acts against himself as he would have done against other persons or objects.[21] This may underlie a number of kinds of paradoxical behaviour, including masochism and asceticism, which relate to the needs of 'me' as a body; to acting in an opposite way to one's own impulses, which relate to the psychological 'me'; or to public self-denigration and humiliation, which would relate to the social 'me'. Although these are all punishing to different degrees, the displeasure may be offset in the negativistic state by the pleasure of the resulting high felt negativism.

Self-negativism in the sense of negativism by the 'I' against the 'me', may also arise where the aim of the 'I' is to make itself feel *independent* of the 'me'. Just as the individual may come to feel independent of others by acting negatively against them, so the individual's 'I' may come to feel independent of his 'me' by acting in a similarly negative way against it. This striving for independence through negativism may have biological/developmental origins, if the negativistic stage of childhood has the effect, not only of producing feelings of independence in the child, but also of actually producing some degree of real independence in the social setting of the family. This theme will be discussed further in the chapter on 'The Biological Perspective'. For the moment the point is that the 'I' may carry over this strategy of gaining feelings of independence through negativism, by directing its negativism towards the 'me'.

Why should the 'I' wish to feel independent of the 'me'? There are several possible reasons. The first occurs when the 'I' does not esteem the 'me': it may rate its psychological capacities, e.g. intelligence, to be inferior, or perhaps it is not proud of its body, or it estimates its social status to be low. In such cases there is low self-esteem which is expressed through the 'I' having a poor opinion of the 'me', and wishing therefore to distance itself from the 'me' as body, the 'me' as psychological system, or the social 'me'. It does this by acting negatively against the 'me'. Thus the 'I' deliberately denigrates the social 'me', or acts against the requirements of the body, by not taking exercise, overeating, and so on, or against perceived psychological requirements, e.g. by refusing to learn. The paradoxical result is that low self-esteem becomes even lower, and in turn induces even more self-negativism, so that a vicious circle ensues.

A second reason why the 'I' should wish to feel independent of the 'me' is the recognition that the 'me' is limited and mortal, and the belief that the 'I' is immortal, or may be immortal if only it can be disassociated from the 'me'. This takes us into the realm of the various devices used in different religions to help to bring about such disassociation. These include asceticism and the various techniques of yoga, which help to disassociate the 'I' from the somatic and psychological 'me'; and the humbling of the social self through such devices as poverty and simplicity of dress, which help to disassociate the 'I' from the social 'me'. All this reaches its culmination in those religions which practise ritual suicide, the ultimate form of self-negativism.

There is one other type of act which may be regarded as embodying self-negativism. This is the so-called 'gratuitous act', or *acte gratuit*, a term introduced by the French novelist André Gide. By this is meant an act which has no rational foundation, no motive or purpose, an act which someone performs to demonstrate to himself precisely that he has freedom of choice, and is not just a machine. It is not intended here to enter into a philosophical discussion about whether such an act is possible, but simply to note that people may on occasion perform what they see to be such acts for the *feeling* of freedom which they entail. Gratuitous acts represent a thoroughgoing attempt to be completely independent, not only from external sources of pressure, but also from the requirements of the 'me', whether these requirements are social, psychological, or somatic. In this sense such acts are self-negativistic as well as negativistic. All this relates to the Sartre's notion of 'bad faith' or *mauvaise foi*, by which is meant acting in such a way as to avoid confronting one's own freedom of choice and action. In Sartre's terms the gratuitous act could be seen as one way of overcoming bad faith, although it should be noted that Sartre himself does not see the matter in this light because it does not, as he sees it, accord with the responsibility of freedom, but is mere caprice (Sartre, 1946, p.74). If pursued, this question would take us into some of the central issues of existentialism. For present purposes, it is sufficient to notice that the deliberate performance of a gratuitous act would, in terms of reversal theory, constitute a form of self-negativism which, if the individual were to see himself as having genuinely achieved it, would provide him with feelings of independence and freedom.

If one can be negative towards oneself, then the possibility arises that one can be negative toward one's own negativism. That is, if one's negativism is seen by the 'I' as a feature of the 'me', then the 'I' can act against this feature as it can against any other. The result is that the negation is negated and there is a return to behavioural conformity, which is in fact associated, at least initially, with high felt negativism.[22] However, in such cases the conformity often gives away its origins in double-negativism by the behaviour which results being over-strict, since now both 'external' and 'internal' forces are directed towards what is seen from the outside as high conformity. Typically, the resulting supposedly conforming behaviour is exaggerated, being over-meticulous, over-ostentatious, or over-rigid.[23] For example, a mother may reject her own child because it is handicapped or deformed, and then reject her own rejection, becoming over-protective as a consequence. A sergeant-major may feel negative towards his superior officers, but then feel negatively towards this negativism; the result is that he is over-conformist and officious, stamps his foot too vigorously while coming to attention, and salutes in an exaggerated way. An individual might come to deny certain beliefs, but then deny his own denials. This double-rejection produces an unshakeable belief which is defended against attack with great fervour. This might be called the 'St. Paul syndrome', since St. Paul rejected his own rejection of Christianity.

The situation may become even more complicated in the case of schizophrenia. As Arieti and others have reported, schizophrenics sometimes go through "... a series of alternated opposite movements, rather like a cogwheel movement ..." (Arieti, 1959, p.484). Thus a patient may start a movement, stop it, start it again, and so on. Arieti interprets this in terms of the patient's fear of his own volition, the volition not to do something producing as much fear as the volition to do something. An alternative explanation, in line with reversal theory, would be that this represents an extreme form of self-negativism, in which the patient rejects his decision, then rejects the rejection, then rejects the rejection of the rejection, and so on in a recursive sequence. In other words, it is being suggested that the schizophrenic's 'ambivalence', which leads to a cycle of alternating decisions, derives from each act of the 'I' being immediately seen as an attribute of the 'me' and acted against negativistically by the 'I'.

All the situations looked at so far have to be distinguished from situations in which self-negativism is a by-product of conformity to the requirements of some external source. In other words, the external source and its requirements may be at the focus of the phenomenal field, the implied negativism towards the self being part of the ground. The soldier may have to expose himself to danger: this would not normally be self-negativism but conformity to an external power. A priest may have to be celibate, or even practise certain kinds of asceticism, but will most likely feel these acts essentially to be ones which conform to the requirements of his church rather than performing them because they act against the requirements of his own body. Even self-mutilation may be carried out in a conformist rather than negativistic state of mind, e.g. in conformity to perceived religious requirements.[24] The situations previously discussed also have to be distinguished from cases in which the self-negativism is accidental, i.e. in which an individual damages himself in order to achieve some end which is not in itself negativistic, either towards an external source or the self. Drinking, smoking, and gambling may all come into this category for most people, although for some there may well be an element of self-negativism.

This brief discussion of self-negativism shows how analysis in terms of reversal theory can remove some of the mystery from paradoxical behaviour. This is achieved basically by showing how maladaptive behaviour may result from the conjunction of the self-concept, in the sense of the 'me', and the metamotivational state of negativism. Again, one important feature of the reversal theory analysis is that behaviour which is ostensibly the same may be arrived at in different ways: thus asceticism may result from a displacement of negativism against some external source into negativism against the self; it may be part of an attempt to make the 'I' independent of the body; it may even be a result of negativism against the negativism of self-indulgence.

A Sting in the Tail

One final point on negativism: it may turn out to be a difficult topic to research, because if the experimental subject is in a negativistic state this may express itself against the requirements of the experimenter and the experiment. If the subject is compliant to the experimenter's needs, as he sees them, this seems likely to be because he is *not* in a negativistic state at the time in question, in which case his negativism cannot be studied. On the other hand, if he *is* in a negativistic state then, by the same token, he may not agree to take part in the experiment at all. If the experiment is continuing and the negativistic state is induced, he may not agree to carry on with it, or he may fail to co-operate and do what is required of him for the experiment to be successful. There are no doubt ways around this, e.g. by disguising what the experimenter really wants, or finding ways of displacing the subject's negativism, if and when it occurs, in a manner which can be studied without disrupting the experiment. But clearly, in the nature of the phenomenon, negativism presents peculiar difficulties for systematic study, especially under laboratory conditions.

One suspects that it is for this very reason that negativism has not been properly recognized within experimental psychology, or explored in any depth by experimental psychologists. If a subject is unco-operative, then it is easiest to exclude him from the experiment and replace him with another subject.[25] Such subjects, to use Goffman's terminology, could be said to be playing 'discrepant roles' (Goffman, 1969). As Harré and Secord (1972) have put it:

"Many experimenters have encountered participants in their studies who play discrepant roles. They foul up their performance by not following instructions, they engage in clowning if there is an audience composed of other participants, they perform the task in a lackadaisical and bored way. Typically, such participants are eliminated from the data analysis". (p.220)

Examples of negativism on the part of experimental subjects have been given by Masling (1966, pp.95-6) who refers to the phenomenon as 'The Screw You Effect'. To avoid this effect, experimental psychologists tend to study only subjects who are in a conformist state of mind. Thus, experimental psychology could be called the psychology of the conforming subject.

Applied psychologists, and psychiatrists, on the other hand have been unable to avoid negativism, at least in its behavioural aspects, and therefore have continued to be aware of it. They cannot normally reject the client or the patient and take another one instead, therefore they have to confront the problems of negativism and cope with them as best they can.[26] The problem of negativism in an applied setting was noted at the outset of this chapter in relation to the testing of children by educational and clinical psychologists.[27] Psychiatrists meet with negativism too, not only in the form of negativistic symptoms as described earlier, but also in the form of resistance to therapy in neurotics. Freud (1923) called this the 'negative therapeutic reaction', although he explained it entirely in terms of a need for suffering to appease a harsh conscience and overcome feelings of guilt. It has also been discussed widely in the psychoanalytic context, notably by Rivière (1936) and by Karen Horney (1936), who both put rather different interpretations on it. Some psychoanalytic writers have extended the term to describe what they see to be a character feature of contrariness, which becomes manifest in the clinical setting,[28] and this interpretation is closer to that of reversal theory.

Notes on Chapter 9

1. Negativism appears as a symptom in certain other syndromes, too, such as the comparatively rare Ganser syndrome in which the patient automatically gives incorrect answers to questions, each answer nevertheless implying that he knows the correct answer. Thus if one asks "What is twice twelve?" the patient might answer "23"; or if asked "What are three sevens?" his answer might be "20", consistently producing the correct answer minus one.
2. It will be noticed that since the conformist state, like the negativistic state, is being defined phenomenologically and not behaviourally, it cannot be equated with 'compliance' in the sense in which this term is usually used in social psychology, nor even with the term 'conformity' as it tends to be used by social psychologists.
3. Negativism could also be expressed by making fun of the belief or, more subtly, by behaving in an extreme way in conformity with the belief so as to make it seem absurd.
4. An excellent brief review of sociological theories of this type will be found in Hagan (1977), Chapter IV.
5. A survey of theories of the general type referred to in this paragraph will be found in Hagan (op. cit.) Chapter III.
6. In this view the deviant behaviour may also be 'treated' through operant conditioning, typical examples of this being given by Ayllon (1963), Burchard and Tyler (1965) and Wetzel (1966).
7. *Time*, Sept. 20th, 1971, p.52.
8. A further potential effect of both types of frustration, if sufficiently prolonged, or encountered sufficiently frequently, is to induce depression. This will be discussed further in Chapter 11.
9. This concept is obviously related to Murray's notion of 'counteraction' (Murray, 1938).
10. In the absence of any concrete identity which can be taken to be the source of the requirement, however, people often manage to give it a form of identity as 'fate', or the 'bad luck' which continues to 'dog them', or even as occult or supernatural forces.
11. In Freudian terms these would all be instances of 'acting out of impulses'. The explanation given here is an alternative to Freud's suggestion that such behaviour occurs when repression breaks down.
12. The possibility of the satiation of the negativistic state is a matter which should be of interest to the police and others concerned with the handling of such situations as negotiations with terrorists who have taken hostages.
13. The same is true of the type of conformism in which there is a definite search for something to which to conform. However, as already noted, the conformist state may be characterized on occasion simply by the absence of the need for a negative requirement, in which case there may be no search of the kind described here.
14. At the same time there is of course always the possibility, if one is a member of a large crowd, that one will experience a feeling of losing control, resulting in anxiety, and even panic. In other words, the crowd itself may be experienced as threatening. Hence, being part of a large primary group does not always *necessarily* produce feelings of security, although in most people it may do so for most of the time.

15. Some of these seem to involve synergies as well: graffiti and 'streaking' both involve a synergy of private and public; 'illicit' sexual behaviour involves a synergy of disgusting and beautiful.

16. The distinction made by functionalists in anthropology between 'norms' and 'normal behaviour', between the rules in a society which its members are supposed to follow and what they actually do, is obviously related to this. For an illustration of this distinction, see Leach (1977) p.11.

17. Hall and Lindzey in their standard text on personality discuss the theories of self and ego due to William James, Symonds, Snygg and Combs, Lundholm, Sherif and Cantril, Sarbin, Bertocci, Hilgard, Stephenson, Chein, Mead, Koffka, Freud, Jung, Adler, Sullivan, Allport, Murphy, Angyal, Cattell, Murray, and, in particular, Carl Rogers (Hall and Lindzey, 1957, especially Chapter 12). This reminds us how many different theorists have made use of the concept of self and of the variety of meanings which it has been given.

18. This distinction is not unproblematic (viz. Mischel, 1977) but it is still a helpful one in the present context.

19. This is the opposite to identification, in which something or someone else is felt to be part of the self. In one case part of the self is externalized, in the other, something outside the self is internalized.

20. Self-negativism as described here is clearly different from self-punishment in accordance with instructions from someone else, e.g. an experimenter or therapist, since such self-punishment usually occurs in the conformist state. For a review of self-punishment studies see Thoresen and Mahoney, 1974, Chapter 5.

21. Psychoanalysts have also talked of the displacement of aggression against the self when other outlets are effectively unavailable. Particular use of this concept has been made by Flugel (1955), who refers to the process as 'nemesism', and by Rochlin (1973). Freud himself, however, preferred to see self-aggression as a form of self-punishment intended to overcome feelings of guilt, especially guilt deriving from the Oedipal situation.

22. It is quite possible, however, that in many cases the individual eventually comes to accept the external interpretation, losing sight of the negativistic origins of his behaviour and viewing it instead as highly conformist.

23. The situation in such cases is therefore not unlike reaction-formation as described by Freud, in that the behaviour which results from reaction-formation is said to be exaggerated, showy, and compulsive.

24. For a discussion of religious self-mutilation, see Kushner (1967).

25. The same may well be true of recalcitrant animals in animal experiments. This point will be returned to in Chapter 13.

26. In this context see Smith (1971), Greenberg (1973), Cade and Southgate (1979).

27. In fact, some testing methods have been developed in the attempt to detect and measure degrees of negativism in testees. (See Fox and Blatt, 1969).

28. For a good review, see Sandler et al. (1970).

10 Personality in Reversal Theory

Introduction

So far in this book, psychological processes have been discussed in a way which has tended to play down reference to individual differences. In the present chapter, which deals with some of the implications of reversal theory for the study of personality, the question of individual differences will at last become the focus of attention. Because of the complexities involved, however, this chapter will necessarily be somewhat more schematic than the others.

The reversal theory approach to personality is characterized in particular by two features. First of all, its starting point is *the individual's experience rather than his behaviour,* so that the initial concern is with differences of experience between individuals rather than differences in behaviour. This is not to deny that experience and behaviour are intimately linked, but the relationship, as has been argued in previous chapters, is a complicated one. To put this point at its simplest in terms of individual differences, two individuals *may* perform similar behaviour with different underlying experiential states, or different behaviour with essentially similar underlying experiential states.

The second feature of the reversal theory approach to personality is *its emphasis on inconsistency rather than consistency.* Historically, the field of personality has been as dominated by the idea of consistency, as the field of motivation has been by the idea of homeostasis. In emphasizing inconsistency, therefore, reversal theory constitutes as much of a break with theorizing in the field of personality as its emphasis on multistability constitutes a break with the general run of theorizing in the field of motivation. The reversal theory view of personality could be put at its strongest by saying that everyone is considered in some degree to be a multiple personality.

In 1931, Franke wrote:

". . . the unity of a person can be traced in each instant of his life. There is nothing in character which contradicts itself. If a person who is known to us seems to be incongruous with himself that is only an indication of the inadequacy and super-ficiality of our previous observations". (Quoted in Zajonc, 1960).

It would be hard to imagine a statement which contrasts more starkly with the reversal theory view. Although few theorists, since these lines were written, would take quite such an extreme view, nevertheless the search for consistencies, and the assumption that these alone are the key to understanding personality, has tended to dominate thinking in the field.[1] This is typified by the widespread use of the notion of a 'trait'. This concept had its origins, at least for the English-speaking world, in the writings of Gordon Allport, who saw traits as being "bona fide mental structures in each personality that account for the consistency of its behaviour" (1937, p.289). Since then there has been much debate about the content of traits and the structure of trait systems, but the essence of the notion of a trait in the theorizing of such notable researchers as R. B. Cattell, Guilford, and Eysenck, has been that it represents some form of regularity or stability in the personality. This does not mean that such theorists fail to recognize fluctua-tions and changes of various kinds in traits; but their general approach, being based largely on factor analysis, has emphasized the search for consistencies, while change and inconsistency have tended to be relegated to the background.

It might be thought that those theorists who have argued for *specificity* rather than *generality* in relation to behavioural dispositions, have taken a line which places more emphasis on the possibility of inconsistency, and that therefore the reversal theory view in relation to inconsistency is not unusual. By 'specificity' in this respect is meant that a person's actions are supposed to be learned in specific situations, or in response to specific stimuli, and do not combine in such a way as to allow one to postulate anything like general dispositions or traits. If different actions are learned in relation to different stimulus situations, then some of these different actions may well be inconsistent with each other: an individual may learn to behave honestly in some specific situations and dishonestly in others, or aggressively in some situations but not in others. The view of what may be called the specificity school contrasts with that of the generality school, the latter positing that different actions combine in such a way as to give rise to, or disclose, general overriding dispositions or traits.[2]

Many learning theorists from Thorndike (1913) onwards, and including especially various social behaviour theorists (see W. Mischel, 1968, 1969) have argued for an essentially specifist point of view, as have some adaptation-level theorists including Helson (Helson, 1964, Chapter 9). Action theorists like Harré and Secord (1972) for whom different social contexts provide different sets of socially prescribed rules to be followed, are also in this sense specifist. While it is true that within the specificity viewpoint an individual may be inconsistent with himself under different conditions, this inconsistency is dependent on these conditions; but the same conditions are supposed to call forth the same responses. In other words, there is still consistency, but now in relation to the individual in a given situation rather than to the individual across situations. In Ruth Benedict's analysis of Japanese social behaviour (Benedict, 1946), as pointed out by Harré and Secord (1972), a Japanese man may play a number of different roles, e.g. in relation to his parents or to his nation, and appear highly inconsistent to Western eyes; but it is the roles which are inconsistent, not the people, and the same social requirements consistently call forth the same role. Similarly, according to social behaviour theorists, a Western child might learn to be aggressive in playing football, but not to be aggressive towards his parents, or when playing with his pet animals. All this is very different from the kind of inconsistency postulated in reversal theory, however, where the individual is expected to respond in different, indeed opposite, ways on occasion, in the face of the *same* conditions. In such cases, not only is someone inconsistent with himself under different conditions, he is also inconsistent with himself *under the same conditions*. It should be clear that this is a rather different and much stronger sense of inconsistency from that implied by specificity. According to specificity theory, change has extrinsic origins, depending largely on environmental stimuli and contexts; according to reversal theory, on the other hand, change may have intrinsic origins, depending on such internal processes as that of satiation in relation to metamotivational states.[3]

There is another way in which the notion of consistency enters into research on personality. Not only is it widely assumed in personality theory that people are fundamentally consistent in their traits, but it is also widely believed that they struggle for consistency when they become aware of inconsistencies in their behaviour or cognitions. This idea certainly underlies most of the theorizing in the field of attitude change. Yet as Zajonc (1960) has pointed out: "Some people who spend a good portion of their earnings on insurance also gamble. The first action presumably is intended to protect them from risks, the other to expose them to risks". This kind of inconsistency, which appears to be prevalent in everyday life, is difficult to explain in terms of theories which exclusively emphasize the struggle for consistency; but it provides no problems for reversal theory since, according to reversal theory, the individual will be expected to display opposite psychological characteristics, including attitude to risk, at various times.

It is not being argued here that general behavioural dispositions or traits do not exist, nor that context-dependent inconsistencies do not occur; indeed, reversals themselves may take place through the action of extrinsic stimuli or context changes. What is being argued is that there is a further class of change which is equally fundamental and which must also be taken into account: that of reversal for purely intrinsic reasons between opposite metamotivational states, with the possible consequence of inconsistent actions being undertaken. Because of the innate propensity to reversal, particularly through the satiation mechanism, certain ways of experiencing the world (especially in relation to motivation) change dramatically, and often affect behaviour. Observing people from outside, such behaviour changes which occur as a consequence will seem mysterious, unless a mechanism of the type posited in reversal theory is taken into account.

One final point which should be made here is that the assumption of consistency in personality has implications throughout the whole of experimental psychology, and is not confined to the field of personality alone. As Harré and Secord (1972, p.142) have pointed out, it is commonly assumed that a person's character or personality is an invariant and may be treated as such in an experiment. Thus, many experiments involve matching different individuals in terms of personality, and in others an individual's performance is compared with itself at different stages of an experiment, the individual acting as his own control. If it is the case therefore, as reversal theory suggests, that personality is *not* invariant, and may change in certain respects over relatively short periods, then this raises problems for experimental psychology by suggesting that such experimental design techniques may not be well founded.

Metamotivational Dominance

Because it is assumed in reversal theory that the individual switches between opposite metamotivational states, spending lengths of time in each, this does not mean that there are not enduring tendencies underlying this form of inconsistency. In particular, an individual may be predisposed to spend more time in one, rather than the other, of a given pair of states. One could think of such a predisposition as a trait, but the term 'trait' here would be a little misleading for the reasons outlined in the introduction to this chapter. 'Dominance' or 'bias' would therefore be better terms, neither of them implying consistency of experience or behaviour, although the bias or dominance itself may remain reasonably stable. In fact, the word 'dominance' has been chosen to be used here rather than 'bias', since it more obviously implies the existence of opposing systems.[4]

For a given person therefore, one member of each pair of metamotivational states may be said to be dominant, and the person may be thought of as displaying the dominance concerned as a personality characteristic. So an individual would be said to be 'telic dominant' if he was predisposed to spend more time in the telic than the paratelic state, and 'paratelic dominant' in the reverse case. Similarly, he would be said to be 'conformist dominant' if he was predisposed, as most people appear to be, towards the conformist state of mind, and 'negativistic dominant' in the opposite case.

The reader is reminded at this stage of the distinction, originally drawn in Chapter 2, between an operative and a dominant characteristic of a system. 'Operative' implies that some characteristic, which can be described in terms of the preferred level of some variable, is applicable to the system at a given moment; 'dominant' implies that a system is constituted in such a way that it is predisposed to display this characteristic more often than the opposite characteristic.

Dominance itself can change over time. Thus most young people appear to be paratelic dominant, but in the course of maturation this paratelic dominance would seem to be generally diminished, so that many of them become telic dominant at some stage on the way to adulthood.

One thing that it is important to be clear about is that the term 'dominance' applies to a predisposition, but this predisposition is not necessarily translated into actuality. Someone may be paratelic dominant but, because of the environment in which he finds himself, spend more of his time in the telic state. However paratelic dominant a person is, he would be unlikely to spend much time in a paratelic state in, to give an extreme example, a concentration camp; similarly, some biological factor, for instance chronic pain from some severe physiological malfunction, may push a paratelic dominant individual into a more-or-less continual telic state. As noted in Chapter 2, a homeostatic system may never actually achieve the preferred level of the variable concerned: a thermostatically-controlled house in the Tropics may never actually achieve the level of temperature which constitutes its preferred level. But the control structure of the system is such that temperature will always *tend* towards the preferred level. So dominance refers to a predisposition, not to whether the predisposition is actualized; in the general range of circumstances, however, one would expect telic dominant people to be in the telic state for longer durations than in the paratelic, and vice versa for paratelic dominant people. In trying to determine someone's dominance, therefore, one is concerned with his or her predisposition to be in one state or the other over time, rather than to the amount of time actually spent in one state or the other, although in normal circumstances the latter may give a good indication of the former.

A further complication here is that even if someone is in the telic state on a given occasion, it is possible that he will for one reason or another be unable to translate this into a suitably telic way of interacting with the world. That is, he may not at the moment in question be able to find goals which he can construe as essential, or be able to act towards their attainment if he finds them. In general, just as an observation of which state predominates in a given person over time does not in itself unequivocally indicate his dominance, so an observation of his behaviour at a given time does not in itself unequivocally indicate which state he is in at that time. These observations serve to emphasize yet again the complex relationship between mental states and behaviour.

Dominance must depend on intrinsic rather than extrinsic factors. So, if there are three classes of factors which can induce a reversal—contingency, frustration and satiation—then dominance obviously depends on the latter two. If an individual becomes frustrated more quickly in the paratelic state than the telic state, he is likely to spend longer periods in the telic state, other things being equal. Similarly, if the individual satiates much more rapidly in the paratelic than the telic state of mind then, again other things being equal, he will be likely to spend longer periods in the telic state; in fact, speed of satiation would seem to be a more crucial factor in determining dominance than frustration is since, as discussed in Chapter 9, frustration may have effects other than that of instigating reversals. In terms of the balance model of Chapter 2, the effect of a tendency for satiation or frustration to build up quickly is to move the fulcrum towards the downmost end of the balance, so making the balance increasingly susceptible to external disturbance tending to reversal and eventually, as the process continues, bringing about reversal even in the absence of external disturbing factors (see Fig. 2.4v).

Strictly, dominance is determined by factors intrinsic to the reversal mechanism itself, such as differences in speed of satiation and frustration in opposing metamotivational states. Other psychological and biological factors, such as chronic pain or feelings of inferiority may, of course, in conjunction with other factors, determine which state is more enduring over a period, but they do not in themselves determine dominance any more than factors in the physical and social environment do. Contingent factors of all kinds, therefore, may in some cases override dominance in determining the duration of opposing states over time, but they do not affect dominance itself.

Contingent factors are not entirely independent of metamotivational states, since an individual's state itself typically plays a part in determining contingent factors. Thus if an individual is in the telic state he will tend to enter into a situation which provides a continuing source of goals; if an individual is in a negativistic state he will tend to provoke contingent forces which he can act against. Now it often happens that the actions which an individual undertakes in a particular metamotivational state will have repercussions on contingent events over a long period into the future. So, although some of these events at a much later date may appear to be independent of metamotivational state, nevertheless in the longer view they could be seen as deriving from actions which arose out of one metamotivational state rather than another at an earlier time. For instance, in a telic state one may commit oneself irrevocably to some career in which telic-inducing events and circumstances are likely to predominate. Or in a negativistic state one may perform some deviant action which will have the effect of placing one in conflict with authority over a long period ahead.

In terms of the telic-paratelic pair, an asymmetry would appear to arise here. Since it is one of the features of the telic state that the individual *plans ahead*, it is much more likely that in this state he will set into action series of contingent events which influence future states than would occur if he were in the paratelic state. Now these future events may be one which, when they eventually occur, induce either the telic or the paratelic state: he may for example plan a holiday at some stage in the future (paratelic) or plan to take an examination (telic). However, it is reasonable to assume that in the telic state, the future events planned are more likely to be telic than paratelic. The effect of this should be for time to be spent increasingly in the telic state, whatever the underlying dominance. This would, however, seem to be counteracted by an opposing tendency which was noted in Chapter 3: that in the paratelic state, by its very nature, one attempts to prolong any experience which is enjoyable in itself, and will therefore *at the time* of such an experience be likely to provide oneself with a continuing series of events which will help to maintain the paratelic activity. Since these opposing effects seem largely to 'cancel each other out', this no doubt contributes to the fact that in most people the amount of time spent in each state is not inordinately disproportionate. The telic and paratelic states are mutually exclusive in that a person can only be in one or the other at a given time, and this means that direct conflict between them is not possible in the way that, for example, the id and superego are thought in Freudian theory to conflict with each other. Nevertheless, they can conflict *indirectly*, in the way which has just been indicated, by having opposing influences which come into effect at different times.

Although the degree to which the telic state is dominant over the paratelic, or vice versa, is, for the reasons outlined, not a trait in the conventional sense, it should still be possible to measure it as a personality characteristic. Whilst it is not obvious that a conventional personality inventory constitutes the best approach to measuring dominance of this kind, nevertheless it is one technique which initially suggests itself. Consequently, such a scale has now been developed and is called the 'Telic Dominance Scale' (Murgatroyd, Rushton, Apter and Ray, 1978). It could equally well of course have been called the 'Paratelic Dominance Scale', and scored in the opposite direction.

The scale consists of three subscales of 14 items each, making 42 items in all. Each item requires the respondent to make a choice between two alternatives which represent telic and paratelic choices respectively. A 'not sure' response is also available for each item. The respondent is asked to make the choice in terms of which alternative he would usually prefer in each case. The items are scored in a telic direction, one point being given for each telic response; 'not sure' responses are scored as a half, this being an accepted practice in such inventories (e.g. Eysenck and Wilson, 1975). A score is obtained for each subscale and the subscale totals summed to obtain a total telic dominance score.

The three subscales correspond to the three general dimensions which characterize the telic-paratelic dimension as described in Chapter 3: a means-ends dimension, which is the defining dimension, a time dimension, and an intensity dimension. The first of these dimensions gives rise to a subscale which is labelled 'serious-mindedness'; this can be described as the degree to which an individual is likely to be oriented towards goals which he himself sees as essential or important to himself (or others with whom he identifies), rather than goals which he sees as being arbitrary or inessential. The second dimension is measured by means of a subscale labelled 'planning orientation', which is defined as the degree to which an individual is likely to plan ahead and organize himself in pursuit of goals, rather than to take things as they come. In other words, it is the degree to which a person is usually oriented towards the future rather than the present, and the frequency with which he gains pleasure from the achievement of goals, or the anticipation of goal achievement, rather than from immediate behaviour or sensations. The third subscale relates to the intensity dimension, but concentrates on arousal. It is labelled 'arousal avoidance', and is defined as the degree to which an individual is likely to avoid situations which generate high arousal and seek situations in which induced arousal levels tend to be low.

An example of a serious-mindedness subscale item would be: 'Eating special things because they are good for your health' or 'Eating special things because you enjoy them'. An example of a planning-orientation subscale item would be: 'Planning a holiday' or 'Being on holiday'. An example of an arousal-avoidance subscale item would be: 'Steady routine in life', or 'continual unexpectedness or surprise'. The complete scale will be found in Appendix C, together with information about which items fall on which subscales and the telic choice within each item.

The full details of the way in which the scale was constructed, and the various studies concerning its validity and reliability, will be found in Murgatroyd et al. (1978). But one result which is of particular interest in the present context, concerns the inter-correlations between the subscales on the first version of the test, before any selection had taken place by means of item analysis. These correlations were all positive and significant at the 1% level. This supports the hypothesis that the three features of the telic state, although logically distinct, nevertheless tend to go together.[5] It was also found that the correlations involving the arousal–avoidance subscale were lower than those of the other two scales, although still significant. This is consistent with the argument in Chapter 3 than the arousal-regulating systems are essentially subsystems of the telic and paratelic states which may on occasion be overridden, suboptimal levels of arousal being compensated by other features of the overall situation at the time in question. The significance of the fact that these findings derived from the original set of items, chosen and put into the three subscales by a panel of five judges in terms of face validity criteria, is that the result could not have been an artefact of the item analysis by means of which the final scale was chosen. (Among other criteria used in the item-analysis for selecting and rejecting items was that of item:subscale and item:total-scale correlations, and this would itself have brought about higher correlations between the subscales in the final version of the test).

An objection to the development of the Telic Dominance Scale might be that psychometric scales already exist to measure what appear to be the same characteristics as the Telic Dominance subscales. Planning-orientation, for example, might be said to be already measured as part of the Eysenck's Impulsiveness Scale (Eysenck and Eysenck, 1977) and arousal-avoidance, inversely, by Zuckerman's Sensation-Seeking Scale (Zuckerman *et al.*, 1964; Zuckerman and Link, 1968; Zuckerman, 1971, 1974). While it may turn out that what such scales measure is related to what the subscales of the Telic Dominance Scale measure, it must be remembered that the *raison d'être* of conventional personality tests, and this seems to be accepted by such researchers as Eysenck and Zuckerman, is to predict *behaviour*. In contrast, the primary interest of reversal theory in relation to personality, and hence the primary interest in the development of methods of measuring telic dominance, is to characterize subjects' predispositions to *experience* the world, to perceive, structure and interpret it, in certain ways. Although this has implications for behaviour, experience is not reflected in behaviour in any simple way. Furthermore, the rationale behind the Telic Dominance Scale, being based as it is on the notion of reversals between opposing states, is very different from that underlying such scales as the Impulsiveness Scale or the Sensation-Seeking Scale. These differences are unfortunately obscured by the requirements of the questionnaire technique used; but they should become clearer when projective and other techniques are eventually developed for the measurement of telic dominance.

There are other problems which also arise with the Telic Dominance Scale in relation to reversal theory, quite apart from the usual range of problems which beset personality inventories. One is that of the extent to which the preferences expressed reflect the underlying dominance of one system or the other, and how far they reflect reactions to the environment in which the individual typically finds himself—although, as noted above, these are usually likely to be related. A second problem is that of how far an individual is able to judge what his usual preferences are rather than his current preferences. However, the high test–retest reliability correlations for periods of up to a year (reported in Murgatroyd *et al.*) imply that the test is measuring some reasonably enduring personality characteristic rather than a current state and, by the same token, that people *can* make such general judgements of the kind required by the test. Perhaps the most fundamental problem is one which the theory itself highlights: a given choice of an action does not *necessarily* of itself imply one state or another, and certainly cannot be equated unequivocally with one state. This problem relates more to those items which specify choices between particular actions than it does to those which require the respondent to choose between general statements like 'Taking life seriously' as against 'Treating life light-heartedly'. To take an example: one item requires the respondent to choose between 'Improving a sporting skill by playing a game' and 'Improving it through systematic practice', the telic choice being taken to be the latter. It is not inconceivable, however, that someone might practise in a paratelic state of mind, enjoying the performance of the skill in itself, and play the game in a telic state of mind in which the improvement of the skill is open to comparison with the improvement of playing partners and therefore open to threats to self-esteem. Despite these problems, the Telic Dominance Scale represents a good start in measuring the characteristic concerned, as implied particularly by the satisfactory results of the validation studies. But it may be necessary eventually to evolve rather different and more appropriate techniques. One approach is to use the items as the basis of a structured interview, in which an attempt is made to elicit from the subject the way he interprets each item and *why* he made the choice he did in each case.[6] Another possible approach would be to allow the subject himself to determine which statements relate to which metamotivational state for him, and only then, as a second step, have the subject indicate in some way his preferences in relation to all the statements.

The whole question of metamotivational dominance, and the measurement of such dominance, also arises in relation to the negativism/conformity pair. Although it seems safe to assume that conformity is the dominant state in most adults, the extent to which it is dominant is presumed to vary from person to person, and in some cases it is possible that negativism may even be dominant. Negativism dominance would certainly appear to be a frequent characteristic among children aged between one-and-a-half and three-and-a-half, the 'negativistic period' as discussed in Chapter 9, but it may well occur in certain adolescents and adults as well. A psychometric instrument to measure dominance in relation to this meta-motivational pair is in the process of being devised.[7]

Individual Differences in Relation to Reversals

Individuals differ in a variety of ways in relation to metamotivational states, quite apart from differences in dominance. Let us look at these differences systematically in terms of the three steps involved when a reversal occurs. It will be recalled that these are: (A) reversal of metamotivational state; (B) the acquisition of a content for the new state; and (C) action in terms of this content.

1. Step one

(i) Lability

Individuals may differ in respect of how easily, and therefore, other things being equal, how often, they reverse between metamotivational states. This may be a general characteristic across metamotivational states or specific to each pair.

Either way, lability will be expected to depend on such factors as those indicated by the following questions:

(a) How quickly does satiation build up and reach a threshold beyond which a reversal is instigated? The question here is not that of the difference *between* members of a pair of metamotivational states in this respect-this would relate more to dominance-but of the average of *both* members of a pair taken together.

(b) How quickly does frustration build up? Again, the question here is not that of the difference between members of a pair, which would relate in the first instance to dominance, but of the average of both members of a given meta-motivational pair. It is not just a matter here of how fast frustration builds up but also of how low the threshold is for a reversal to be triggered in response to frustration.

(c) How sensitive, and vulnerable, to contingent effects *in general* is the individual? In other words, is he or she in general highly responsive to changes in context, to subtle social cues, or to other more obvious stimuli of the type which bring about a reversal?

(d) Towards which *particular* contingent effects is the individual most sensitive and vulnerable? Differences between individuals may greatly depend on such sensitivities, which may in turn have their genesis in either innate factors or previous learning history. So the question is: which particular events are, for a given person at different times, highly likely to occasion a reversal, and which are unlikely to do so? Thus a particular person may be sensitive to a whole range of possible stimuli which, for instance, are felt as threatening during sexual intercourse, and the occurrence of any of these may be sufficient to induce the telic state, and consequent dysfunction, under these conditions. Another person may be almost entirely insensitive to any but sexual stimuli once intercourse has commenced. Again, a given person may become highly sensitive to the possibility of insult in a state of drunkenness and therefore prone to reverse to the negativistic state, whereas another person may become relatively immune to insult when drunk. Matters are further complicated by the fact that a number of stimuli may occur contemporaneously and add to, or detract from, each other's power to induce a reversal in one direction or the other. Reversal may also be a function of context and of immediately antecedent conditions; for example a loud noise may be felt as more threatening and therefore be more likely to precipitate a reversal to the telic state in a dark lane on a quiet night, than in a noisy bar at lunch time.

(e) An individual may indirectly bring about a reversal in himself by providing himself with the necessary cues, e.g. he may induce the paratelic state by arranging to meet someone who usually provides him with the social cues he needs, or by entering a cinema or a public house. So it is possible to ask, in relation to this process, how far an individual is capable of providing himself with the cues that he needs, and whether on the whole he is inclined to control his own metamotivational states in this way rather than letting reversal occur freely. If an individual is willing and able to control his own metamotivational states in this way, he can use this either in the service of lability or of stability; he can also use it to bring about the greater duration of operation of one member of a pair of metamotivational states than the other.

There may of course be interactional effects between these five factors, or between these factors and other variables. For instance, both the absolute and relative influence of each of these factors may depend on such physical effects as tiredness, or illness. The relative importance of these different factors, not to mention the interactional effects, may also vary from individual to individual. Clearly, it would be useful to develop psychometric tests of individual differences in lability and of the importance of different factors in inducing change in different people.

(ii) Characteristics of the states themselves

To discuss the characteristics of the metamotivational states themselves it will be necessary to look at each pair of states individually, and for these purposes it is convenient to treat the anxiety-avoidance/excitement-seeking pair as a pair of states in its own right.

(a) *Telic/paratelic.* These two states may differ between individuals in a number of respects, as suggested by the variety of questions which might be asked about the way in which each of these states is expressed in the phenomenology of a given individual. Concerning the telic state, one might ask such questions as the following. To what extent does the individual normally feel 'trapped' in relation to a goal which he takes to be essential, or to what extent does he generally feel threatened by such goals? Once a goal has been interpreted as essential, how far does the individual tend to look and to plan ahead to attain it? What kind of significance does he tend to assign to it? How far, if at all, does felt arousal take precedence over felt significance? To what extent do his plans typically involve elaborate hierarchies of conscious subgoals? How rigid or flexible are his plans, and to what extent does he generally envisage difficulties and make contingency plans? Do his levels of aspiration tend to be high or low? How far does his time perspective refer backwards as well as forwards; in particular, is he continually judging his present situation in terms of previous aspirations and expectancies? At what perceived distance from the goal does he start to feel the pleasure of anticipation of success? How optimistic or pessimistic does he tend to be? Similarly, in relation to the paratelic state, there are a number of questions which suggest themselves. What in general is the relative importance to the individual in this state of high felt arousal or low felt significance? To what extent does the individual have a tendency to feel 'free', or to have a feeling of 'release' in the paratelic state? How narrow or broad does his focus of attention tend to be in terms of all the sensations he is experiencing at a given moment?

What time interval, other things being equal, constitutes 'the present moment' for the individual? How far does the individual consciously judge, or categorize or structure his sensations and experiences even in the paratelic state? Clearly the answer to any of these questions in relation to either the telic or the paratelic states will depend to some extent on particular circumstances and the nature of the goal or sensations: but one might expect there to be underlying tendencies within individuals, and it is to these that such questions are directed.

(b) *Anxiety-avoidance/excitement-seeking.* It was argued in Chapter 4 that certain aspects of the two curves relating arousal and hedonic tone may vary, i.e. 'shift', in a given individual over time, depending on various factors, such as tiredness. But the curves may also differ between individuals in the sense that for different individuals the typical curves may have different shapes and positions.

For instance, the maxima of the curves may differ as shown in Fig. 10.1, or the minima, as in Fig. 10.2 , as may the positions of the maxima and minima on the arousal dimension as shown in Fig. 10.3. The shape of the curves may also vary,

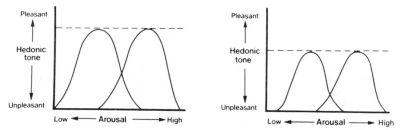

Fig. 10.1 Possible variations in the maxima of the curves representing the two arousal-regulating systems.

as is exemplified for the excitement-seeking curve in Fig. 10.4; in this particular example the right-hand graph effectively shows a threshold which must be exceeded on the arousal dimension for the individual to feel pleasure at all, whereas the change is a more gradual one in the left-hand figure. It should also be remembered that the situation may not be symmetrical and that the anxiety-avoidance and excitement-seeking curves may differ from each other in terms of maxima, minima, and shape. One implication of all this is that if, as might be expected, moderate amounts of felt arousal are easier to obtain, but more extreme levels of felt arousal, high or low, are more difficult to achieve, then individuals in whom the maxima of the two curves are typically near the centre of the arousal dimension will be expected to experience pleasure in relation to arousal more easily than those in whom the maxima are towards the extremes, especially if the curves are of the type shown on the right in Fig. 10.4.[8]

There is therefore a variety of respects in which individuals may differ from each other, in terms of typical arousal/hedonic-tone curves. The degree and

manner in which the curves change within an individual under different
conditions may also be different from individual to individual: the curves may
shift a great deal in some individuals and little in others, the factors which bring
about shifting may differ between individuals, and there may be limits beyond

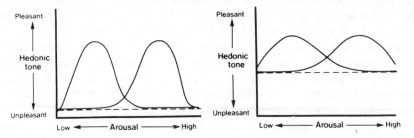

FIG. 10.2   Possible variations in the minima of the curves representing the two arousal-regulating
systems.

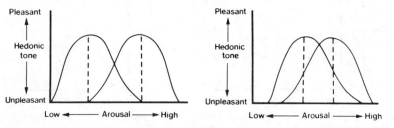

FIG. 10.3   Possible variations on the positions on the arousal dimension of the maxima of the curves
representing the two arousal-regulating systems.

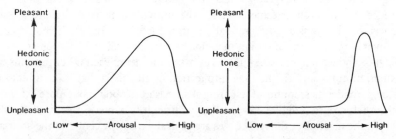

FIG. 10.4   Possible variations in the shape of the excitement-seeking curve.

which shifts cannot be wrought, e.g. the maximum pleasure which can ever
under any conditions be felt in relation to arousal, may be different in different
individuals.

(c) *Negativism/conformity.* The typical curves for felt negativism in the negativistic and conformist states may vary from individual to individual. Just as with the arousal/hedonic-tone curves, so with the felt-negativism/hedonic-tone curves, the maxima and minima of the two curves may be different, as illustrated in Fig. 10.5 and 10.6, and so may the shapes of the curves. Unlike the curves for felt arousal, however, it is assumed at present that the maxima of the felt negativism curves are at the extremes of the felt negativism dimension and are therefore not ditonic.

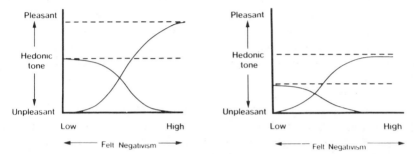

FIG. 10.5 *Possible variations in the maxima of the curves representing the negativistic and conformist systems.*

The relation between the two curves representing each of the two metamotivational states will also be expected to vary from individual to individual. It would seem to be a safe assumption that the peak of the felt negativism curve is higher for the metamotivational state of negativism than it is for the state of conformity; i.e. more intense pleasure *may* be felt from it. But how much more pleasure can be experienced in relation to negativism, rather than conformity, may vary from individual to individual, and it is conceivable that, in some cases, the pleasure of low felt negativism in the state of conformity may be higher than the pleasure of high felt negativism in the state of negativism.

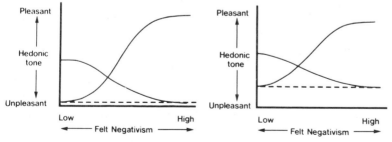

FIG. 10.6 *Possible variations in the minima of the curves representing the negativistic and conformist systems.*

It may also be assumed, as it was for the arousal/hedonic-tone curves, that for a given individual the position and shapes of these curves will shift at different times and under different circumstances. But the manner in which they shift, how easily they shift, the particular conditions which bring about shift, and so on, constitute yet another type of individual difference variable.

2. Step two

The second step, when a reversal occurs, is for the new metamotivational state to acquire a suitable content. For example, in the telic state a particular goal must be adopted. This step is closely related to step one, in that the conditions which have brought about the reversal, if they are contingent, tend to specify the content. So, if some external danger initiates the telic state, then this danger automatically becomes, or one should say remains, the focus of attention in that state, at least initially. If the state is induced by some physiological need, like hunger, then this will specify the essential goal for the individual at that time. Similarly, step three is closely related to step two in that the content determined at step two will tend largely to specify the sort of *action* which is taken at step three, e.g. to escape from danger, or find food.

Despite the influence of contingent conditions on content, systematic individual differences in relation to content do nevertheless affect the process at step two. For one thing, the contingent conditions which arise may themselves derive from earlier actions which the individual has taken, and therefore be related to such characteristics as the individual's dominance in terms of each metamotivational state, the extent to which he deliberately puts himself in positions in which events are likely to occur that will initiate reversals, which sort of events he tends to choose for this purpose, which events apart from this are particularly powerful in his case in inducing reversal, and his preferred spheres of action — intellectual, physical, or social — which will influence whether the content is likely primarily to involve ideas, objects, or people. Even more to the point, when reversal is brought about by satiation, rather than contingent conditions or frustration, there may initially be no obvious content at all, so that the individual's preferences, predilections, or cognitive associations will be likely to play a particularly large part in determining the content immediately following such a reversal.

All this means that it is possible to ask various questions about the individual's tendencies in relation to content in each metamotivational state. Thus, in relation to the telic state, one might ask what types of goal the individual tends to see as essential, other things being equal. Are they usually personal, or does he identify easily with the needs of others, including especially, of course, members of his family, and adopt the satisfaction of their needs as essential goals of his own? Are they goals which he sees himself to be independently choosing and imposing on himself, or are they more likely to be goals which he sees as being imposed by forces outside himself? Are certain kinds of goals more likely to be seen as essential than others; e.g. goals involving the satisfaction of immediate physiological needs, the attainment of social status, the acquisition of material possessions, or the overcoming of intellectual puzzlement? In relation to the paratelic state it is relevant to ask whether the individual has a preference for one kind of paratelic pleasure rather than another. Does he tend, other things being equal, to concentrate on the pleasures of immediate sensations, e.g. as in sunbathing, or wine-tasting; on the pleasures associated with emotions, as in enjoying a play or a film; or the pleasures that arise from the performance of a skill, as in hitting a golf ball correctly, or dancing? In other words, what particular kind of intensity of experience does he focus on and attempt to amplify? If, in the paratelic state, the focus is on the emotions, then does the individual have strong preferences between the various parapathic emotions? Or is he, perhaps, obsessed by sexual excitement (which is not a parapathic emotion)? In other words, in the paratelic state the preferences for different kinds of content may be linked to the preferences which the individual has in relation to the different possible techniques (as listed in Chapter 5) for gaining arousal. Similar kinds of questions arise in relation to the negativistic and conformist states. Does the individual tend to be negativistic or conformist towards people, objects, or ideas, to the extent that these can be distinguished in particular situations? In the negativistic state, how far is he prone to focus his negativism on himself?

The question of flexibility also arises here. How easy is it to dislodge the individual from one content to another? Obviously this depends for a given person at a given time on the conditions prevailing: thus it will be easier in the telic state to displace the content away from the goal of escaping from some threat to a different goal, if the threat is mild rather than strong. Similarly, it will be easier to displace negativism from one requirement to another if the source of the initial requirement is relatively passive and ineffectual. At the same time, though, one would expect individual differences also to play a part: other things being equal some people will be more flexible than others, and movement from one kind of content (goal, requirement, type of intensity of experience, etc.) to another will for them occur relatively readily during the time a given metamotivational state prevails. How rapidly interest in a particular content satiates for a given individual is also relevant here, and is different, it should be noted, from satiation of a metamotivational state.

3. Step three

At step three the individual carries out, or attempts to carry out, actions, in terms of the content acquired at step two. Accordingly, if he is in the telic state and an essential goal is identified, then he will normally attempt to pursue the goal. He will also attempt to assign as much phenomenological significance to this goal as he can, and this deliberate cognitive attempt to make the goal as significant as possible can be seen as an action which occurs at the third step. Similarly, if he is in the negativistic state, he will be likely to act negativistically towards the requirements of some source which he identifies.

One obvious individual difference which arises here is that of how intensely tension is felt by the individual, if there is a failure to bring the metamotivational variable concerned—felt significance, felt arousal, felt negativism—into the preferred level for the operative metamotivational state. It will be recalled that tension is defined in reversal theory as the feeling which arises when the defining variable of the metamotivational state that is operative does not reach its preferred level. It is assumed that its strength is a function of distance from the optimal level of the salient variable; the precise nature of this function may of course differ from one variable to another, and from one individual to another. Thus, if an individual is in the telic state but cannot attach significance to the goal he is pursuing, or is in the negativistic state but cannot for some reason act against some identified requirement, then he will experience tension to some degree or another. It will be appreciated that this kind of failure is different from failure to achieve a goal in the telic state or actually to cause some damage or harm in the negativistic state. It is rather a failure to see oneself to be acting in a way which involves a significant goal in the former case, or to be acting negatively towards a requirement in the latter case, irrespective of the success of the action. In other words, as noted before, tension is the same as that type of frustration which relates to the preferred level of metamotivational variables rather than to goal achievement. Tension may of course have its origins in step two rather than step three, in that if no suitable content, e.g. no salient requirement, can be found, then a suitable action cannot be undertaken. People may well be expected, then, to vary in relation to how prone they are to develop feelings of tension. In these terms, action could be initiated because a critical value is reached either of the salient variable, e.g. arousal, or of tension, or of both together.

Finally, of course, within each metamotivational state the individual will have a number of characteristics which influence the nature of his actions in that state. Most of these stem directly from factors which have already been discussed in terms of steps one and two. For example, if he reverses easily his actions *may* be comparatively erratic. If, in the excitement-seeking state, he generally has difficulty in achieving the preferred level of arousal because of the shape and position of the curve involved, then his actions may be more frantic or extreme than those of others. If in the telic state he tends to see intellectual goals as more essential than physical goals, then his actions are more likely, other things being equal, to involve thinking rather than overt behaviour. Nevertheless, the individual may have certain innate behavioural predispositions and learned skills, which cause him to express the different metamotivational states in different ways quite apart from these influences from earlier steps. In the telic state he may have learned that he can achieve a particular essential goal better by one means than another. In the excitement-seeking state he may find that he can achieve excitement better in one way, e.g. the use of synergies, negativism, risk-taking, or fantasy, than in another. These dispositions in turn will typically feed back to, and influence, earlier steps; thus the typical content of the paratelic state may come to depend on the actions an individual prefers to use in order to achieve intense experiences.

It can therefore be seen, in the light of the analysis of individual differences presented in this chapter, that individuals may differ in a wide variety of inter-related ways with regard to metamotivation. To study this aspect of personality empirically, a range of different psychometric tests will be need. The Telic Dominance Scale represents a start in this direction.

Notes on Chapter 10

1. There is, however, increasing unease about the concept of consistency, as evidenced by the collection of papers edited by Magnusson and Endler (1977).
2. For a good discussion of these two 'schools', see for example Eysenck (1970).
3. Developmental theorists have also of course concerned themselves with innate changes in personality over time, but these gradual and generally irreversible changes are clearly different from the reversals of reversal theory.
4. In any case, 'bias' has a technical meaning in cybernetics which is rather different from the everyday sense implied here, and its use would therefore be a little confusing.
5. This does not preclude the possibility that in a minority of individuals there may be marked discrepancies between subscale scores; there may indeed be certain patterns of discrepancy which characterize certain personality types, including pathological types. This is obviously worth investigating further.
6. This approach is currently being developed by L. Bradford, working with adolescents.
7. Informal clinical observation by Dr K. C. P. Smith suggests, following Blau (1946), that domin-ance of the negativistic state may be related to lefthandedness. It will be possible to test this hypothesized relationship when a satisfactory measure of negativism dominance becomes available.
8. It will be recalled that it was argued in Chapter 4 that felt arousal, if left to the regulation of the arousal system itself, would be likely to be homeostatic, but that it is 'overlaid' by the bistability deriving from the operation of the excitement-seeking and anxiety-avoidance meta-motivational systems.

11 Psychopathology and Metamotivation

Psychopathology of Arousal

The analysis in the preceding chapter provides a way of putting various types of individual psychopathology within a framework which is different from any currently in use in psychiatry and clinical psychology. The whole area of psychopathology is an enormously complex one. But the way in which an approach to this area can be made through reversal theory will be shown here by looking at various psychological problems which might arise principally in relation to felt arousal. At the most general level, these problems fall into three categories; each of these will now be examined in turn.

1. Unpleasant arousal is experienced in an acute or chronic form

Of the six different types of felt arousal, four of these are unpleasant: apathy, boredom, anxiety and over-excitement. (Reference back to Fig. 4.5 may be helpful at this point). Everyone presumably experiences each of these from time to time, but some people appear to experience one or another of them in a more extreme or enduring form than others do.

If the curves governing the relationship between felt arousal and hedonic tone are more like those in the graph on the left in Fig. 10.2, rather than those in the graph on the right in the figure, then while these curves obtain it is possible for the extreme forms of these four disagreeable types of felt arousal to be experienced.[1] Should one of these be experienced in this extreme way over a reasonably short period, it would be said to be acute. Should this, or a slightly lesser intensity of the feeling, be experienced continually or regularly over an extended period, it would be said to be chronic.

Frequently recurring acute anxiety merges into chronic anxiety. As Levitt (1971) has pointed out:

"'Chronic', in the sense of constant or continual, is misleading when applied to an emotional state like anxiety. What is actually meant is a high proneness or predisposition to experience anxiety. The anxiety-prone individual is one who has a noticeable upsurge of feelings of anxiety on a relatively large number of occasions, under more circumstances and in a larger number of different situations than do his peers." (p.35)

This view translates well into reversal theory if one states that the person who suffers 'chronic' anxiety is one in whom the anxiety-avoidance state is highly dominant, but not necessarily exclusive, and in whom high arousal is for one reason or another experienced more frequently than low arousal. Such proneness to high arousal might be due to one or more of a number of different factors. For example, the individual's natural resting level of arousal, i.e. the level it would tend to return to if it were not operated on by either of the arousal-regulating metamotivational systems, may be rather high; arousal may be raised by an unusually wide range of different stimuli; or the individual may strive to achieve high felt significance which, unfortunately, in turn tends to maintain his arousal at a high level, since his every action comes to be seen by him as important. The most distressing anxiety conditions will be those in which this tendency to experience anxiety frequently, for whatever reason, is coupled with a tendency to experience it in an acute form; in such cases one would have a conjunction in the same individual of anxiety-avoidance dominance, a tendency for felt arousal to be elevated, and a typical anxiety-avoidance curve of the type approximating to that shown in the graph on the left in Fig. 10.2.[2]

The same kinds of considerations apply to boredom. Acute boredom *may* arise if the curves relating felt arousal to hedonic tone are like those in the graph on the left in Fig. 10.2; chronic boredom may arise if the individual is characterized by an excitement-seeking state which is highly dominant and in whom low felt arousal is, for one reason or another, a condition from which he finds it difficult to escape. Thus he may have a naturally low resting level of felt arousal; or there may be few stimuli which increase his levels of felt arousal; or he may be generally successful in lowering the feelings of significance which attach to his actions, so that this possible contributing source of arousal may be effectively blocked. Alternatively, in chronic boredom, a dominant excitement-seeking state may be coupled with curves, the peaks of which remain low on the arousal dimension, i.e. they may be more like those shown in the graph on the right in Fig. 10.1 than those shown on the left in this figure. As with anxiety, the acute form of the condition merges into the chronic form, and the most distressing conditions will be those in which these are combined. All this would seem to imply that, in principle, boredom is likely to be as much a pathological problem in a given population as anxiety. Consonant with this, Fromm (1977) has argued that "Chronic boredom . . . constitutes one of the major psychopathological phenomena in contemporary technotronic society, although it is only recently that it has found some recognition" (p.326).[3] Unlike anxiety, boredom generally presents itself clinically as a problem in relation to the behaviour that stems from it, rather than in relation to the distress occasioned by the feeling itself. But the feeling of boredom itself can, and often does, reach desperate levels, causing an intensity of suffering in some people which is comparable to that generated by anxiety.

Although acute and chronic forms of apathy and over-excitement are perhaps not found as frequently as acute and chronic anxiety and boredom, one may in principle expect the same general considerations to apply to their genesis. Thus someone can reach a state of acute over-excitement (mania) only if he is in an excitement-seeking state and the curve is of the form shown in the graph on the left in Fig. 10.2; and chronic apathy can only arise in someone in whom the anxiety-avoidance state is highly dominant and who tends to experience particularly low levels of arousal.

In general then, saying that an unpleasant arousal state of whatever kind is chronic, implies that the person concerned is unable either to change his level of arousal sufficiently, within the prevailing metamotivational state, for that arousal to be felt as pleasant, or alternatively to reverse so as to make the prevailing level of arousal a pleasant one. The individual is restricted on both fronts: he can neither change adequately in respect of felt arousal nor can he change at the metamotivational level.

There is one other point about the characteristics of the felt-arousal/hedonic-tone curves which has a bearing on the theme of pathological states in relation to felt arousal. This is that the shape of the curves may be such that, for certain ranges of felt arousal, it is not possible to experience such arousal as anything but unpleasant, even if reversals occur. There are two ways in which this can arise:

(i) Suppose that the two curves are like those shown in Fig. 11.1, which is derived from Fig. 10.4 (right-hand graph). Then over the middle ranges of

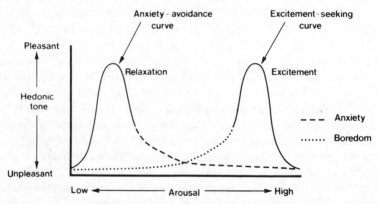

FIG. 11.1 *In the situation depicted here, arousal will be experienced as unpleasant over the intermediate range, even if reversals occur.*

arousal, reversal can only be between boredom and anxiety. Hence, an individual in whom these two curves are typical is likely to present a rather miserable picture.

(ii) If the curves are like those already shown in Fig. 4.5, reversal at extremes of the arousal range will still be likely to be between different unpleasant feelings of arousal: between apathy and boredom in one case and between anxiety and over-excitement in the other. If the curves are slightly different from those in Fig. 4.5 in shape and position, as shown for example in Fig. 11.2 in which the peaks of the two curves are nearer to each other, i.e. opposite in this respect to Fig. 11.1, and the tails are elongated, then this will be true over a greater range of the extremes of the felt arousal dimension.

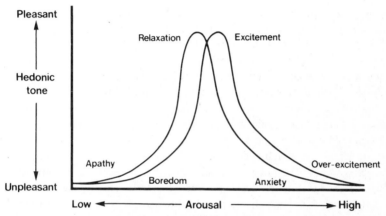

FIG. 11.2 *In this situation, arousal will be experienced as unpleasant overall, except a relatively small range of intermediate values, when either system is operative.*

For either of these reasons a person may find himself in a state of chronic unpleasant arousal, in which the nature of the unpleasant arousal changes, so that the state is what one might term a 'chronic mixed state'. If the typical curves are like those shown in Fig. 11.1 and the person concerned finds it difficult to obtain high or low levels of arousal, then he will be in a chronic mixed state of boredom/anxiety. If the typical curves are like those shown in Fig. 11.2, and he finds it difficult to escape from either high or low arousal, then he will be likely either to experience chronic apathy or chronic boredom, or to experience chronic anxiety or chronic over-excitement. In these chronic mixed states, the individual cannot escape through reversal, even for short periods, as he can in principle with such states as chronic anxiety or chronic boredom.

The question of chronic unpleasant arousal leads naturally to the topic of depression.[4] Depression takes many different forms and is expressed through a variety of combinations of symptoms. Perhaps the central feature, however, is that of a feeling of hopelessness, or what Becker (1967) has called 'negative expectation'. In Becker's study this symptom showed the highest correlation with clinical ratings of depression, and was the most frequently found single cognitive or motivational symptom in cases of severe depression (Becker, op.cit., Chapter 2). This is certainly consistent with Seligman's theory that depression arises from what he has called 'learned helplessness' (Seligman, 1975). Seligman's original experimental work on learned helplessness was carried out with dogs; more recent research with humans (reviewed in Kleinke, 1978, Chapter 8) has indeed provided evidence for a relationship between experimentally induced learned helplessness and depression. In relation to arousal, what this implies is that if one loses hope of escaping from a state of unpleasant arousal, of whichever kind, or of escaping from it for sufficiently long periods, and one feels helpless in this respect, then this cognitive feature becomes added to the chronic arousal pathology to produce depression.[5]

This implies that phenomenologically there are at least four different types of depression in relation to arousal, these types cutting across traditional distinctions like that between endogenous or reactive depression. These four types can be labelled anxiety depression, boredom depression, apathy depression, and over-excitement depression. Alternatively, it could be said that there are two types of anxiety-avoidance depression and two types of excitement-seeking depression.[6]

Is this kind of distinction one which can be sustained in terms of the descriptions of depression which one finds in the voluminous literature on the subject? We believe that it can be. Firstly, anxiety depression is already generally recognized as a distinct clinical syndrome. The term 'agitated depression' is also used for what appears to be essentially the same state, but one in which the anxiety is expressed in restlessness. Where the term 'depression' is used without any such qualification, then it would appear to refer usually to boredom depression, which is characterized by low arousal, although it might also be said to include apathy depression as well. But what about 'over-excitement' depression: does a state exist which corresponds to this odd-seeming designation? It may be supposed that the manic state is one in which the individual finds himself somewhere on the excitement-seeking curve between excitement and over-excitement. Now, as many standard texts on psychiatry attest, the manic state is on occasion accompanied by feelings of depression. As Curran and Partridge (1955) have said: "Many patients will say after a (manic) phase is over that, contrary to appearances, they experienced no real enjoyment, and an appreciable number will show a depressive content . . . even though their phase be a manic one." (pp.267–8). In terms of the analysis given here, whether mania is enjoyed will depend on the position arrived at on the excitement-seeking curve between the high point of excitement and the low point of over-excitement. Should an individual feel himself unable to escape from a state of chronic over-excitement, then one would expect him to experience depression along with this over-excitement.

If these forms of depression are seen in the wider context of the telic and paratelic metamotivational states which, in the manner described earlier in the book, are associated with the anxiety-avoidance and excitement-seeking states respectively, then these kinds of distinctions come into even clearer focus. Boredom depression, which is paratelic, might be characterized not just by low arousal, but also by a lack of interest 'in anything and everything' and, in general, a low intensity of experience. This is expressed typically by such symptoms as lack of appetite and lack of sexual drive, these symptoms being related to a loss of pleasurable sensation or gratification. Food seems to lose its taste for example. Over-excitement depression, which is also paratelic, might be a state in which the person is unpleasantly overwhelmed by strong sensations of all kinds which he feels he cannot avoid; all aspects of his experience are over-intense. Apathy depression, on the other hand, being a telic rather than a paratelic state, would mean that the individual is aware of essential goals to which his whole experience is oriented; but he feels no inclination to pursue them. This would fit exactly with the description of certain kinds of depressive state in which the depression is expressed principally as a feeling of futility. The reason for this lack of a disposition to pursue goals, despite the fact that they are seen as essential, may stem from one of a number of sources. One of these may be a form of self-negativism: the individual may not allow himself to pursue such a goal. Another may be that when arousal reaches a low enough point, the arousal is not adequate to imbue the goal with sufficient feelings of importance. This is rather like the situation in which a car battery has become so run down that it cannot ignite the engine which would recharge it. The person understands that the goal is essential from some point of view, but the emotional quality is lacking. Yet another reason for apathy may be success in attaining some important long-term goal, so that the remaining goals, although still seen to be essential, do not compare in importance with that which has just been achieved, and cannot, at least for the time being, elicit renewed efforts; this would be what might be called 'success depression'. The individual feels deprived of such goals as would galvanize him into action again. (A good autobiographical example of 'success depression' will be found in Pavarotti, 1981.) Apathy depression in turn contrasts with anxiety depression, which is also telic, but in which there may be no lack of phenomenologically essential goals to be pursued. Even if the anxiety is 'free-floating' the individual continually ties it down to first one goal and then another.[7] Here the depression relates to the feeling, often deriving from low self-esteem, that one will be unable to achieve any of these goals and reduce the anxiety, however hard one tries.

In Chapter 9, two types of frustration and their diverse effects were discussed. The first type consisted of frustration in achieving a goal, the second of frustration in achieving the preferred level of some variable specified by the meta-motivational state obtaining at the time in question. It can now be seen that depression is a further possible effect of frustration, especially if frustration systematically fails, for some reason, to lead to reversal. Although the discussion here has centred on the second type of frustration, it would appear that depression can arise from either type of frustration, or indeed both at the same time, as exemplified by anxiety depression which has just been discussed. Depression, however, rather than one of the other effects of frustration, occurs when the frustration of either type leads, usually over a length of time, to a recognition that the particular frustration will inevitably endure, however often the task or activity involved is returned to.

This discussion of depression in relation to frustration in obtaining the preferred level of a metamotivational variable has centred on the variable of felt arousal. But before leaving the topic of depression some reference should be made to the fact that it can also arise from frustration in achieving the preferred level of other metamotivational variables. Thus depression may result from chronic failure to achieve the preferred level of the felt significance variable. In the telic state this would take the form of a persistent inability to discern any significance in anything, the whole of life coming to seem pointless and lacking in any ultimate purpose which would give it structure and meaning. In the paratelic state the failure would be experienced as a continuing inability to escape from an ever-proliferating network of implications and complications. Similarly, repeated frustration in achieving the preferred level of the felt negativism variable may also give rise to feelings of depression. In the negativistic state this would be likely to be associated with feelings of lack of autonomy and personal distinctiveness, since, as will be argued further in Chapter 13, these depend on the individual's potential for negativism. In the conformist case, an inability to experience low felt negativism might be expected, among other things, to give rise to loneliness - not in the sense of actually being alone but in the sense of failing to feel any solidarity with others, or to experience group membership. In each of these types of failure, depression is of course particularly likely if it is associated with dominance of the metamotivational state in which failure continually occurs. In pathological cases this dominance may arise, at least in part, through a failure of the reversal mechanism to respond to frustration. It should also be pointed out, finally, that different types of depression related to different metamotivational variables can, in principle, be combined in the same person at the same time.

2. Reversals tend to occur inappropriately

A second type of pathology in relation to felt arousal arises when reversal is brought about inappropriately, i.e. the stimuli which induce the reversal do so only because they are in some sense incorrectly interpreted by the individual, or because he is over-sensitive to them. The result may be that in certain situations, instead of excitement or relaxation being felt, one of the unpleasant forms of arousal is experienced. Although such inappropriate reversals may occur only in certain situations, which perhaps arise no more than intermittently, the reaction can nevertheless be regarded as pathological, since it may systematically prevent the individual from performing adaptively in these situations and cause unnecessary distress.

An obvious example would be that of mild phobias, where certain specified objects, or situations, are threatening and induce anxiety. The reverse into the anxiety-avoidance state, and the resulting anxiety, is biologically unnecessary since it involves seeing a danger where no objective danger exists, or exaggerating some small risk into enormous proportions. Where the effects of a phobia seep into all aspects of the person's life, so that he spends large amounts of time and effort avoiding the situations which he feels to be threatening, then the state of anxiety-avoidance may become highly dominant and the problem a chronic one.

The field of sexual dysfunction also provides good examples of inappropriate reversals. It will be recalled from a discussion earlier in the book that normal, functional sexual behaviour is performed in the paratelic state of mind: it is enjoyed in its own rights, it is playful, and it is concerned with sensations of all kinds, as well as with the enjoyment of high arousal, which is experienced as sexual excitement. It is the arousal aspect of sexual behaviour which will be the focus of interest here, but the telic/paratelic context will not be lost sight of.

In the case of such problems as impotence or premature ejaculation in men, and frigidity in women, the problem appears to be one of a tendency for reversal to take place from (paratelic) excitement-seeking to (telic) anxiety-avoidance at some stage during the course of sexual behaviour. This reversal is inappropriate on two grounds. Firstly, instead of the sexual arousal being felt as excitement, it is subsequently felt instead as anxiety and the whole situation becomes dysphoric. Secondly, this resultant anxiety plays a part in interfering with normal sexual behaviour, or in inhibiting it altogether.

There is a wide variety of perceived threats which can bring about such reversals in different people. Most of these can be listed under four main headings:

(i) *Threat of non-completion.* This may arise in a number of ways. For example, where there is little privacy, there is the continual threat of discovery and interruption. Or with a new partner, there may be the threat that the partner will change his/her mind before intercourse has commenced, or before orgasm has been achieved.

(ii) *Threat to self-esteem.* If the situation is construed as one in which one has to 'prove oneself', or demonstrate one's masculinity or feminity, and particularly if there is a lack of confidence, then the situation can be highly threatening. Masters and Johnson (1970) refer to this as 'performance anxiety' and see it as the prime cause of sexual dysfunction. If such a threat leads to failure on one occasion, and to humiliation and embarrassment, then the sexual situation is to that degree more threatening on the next occasion, and failure even more likely. In this way a vicious circle is set up.

(iii) *Threat of partner's behaviour.* This may arise particularly where the partner is attempting to add to the arousal in the situation by various non-sexual techniques of the kind discussed in Chapter 5, e.g. by breaking taboos, as in oral–genital caressing, by becoming aggressive, or by introducing elements of unexpectedness and surprise. Although this may indeed raise arousal, it may also in particular cases be felt as threatening and induce a reversal to the anxiety-avoidance state.

(iv) *Intrinsic threats.* A number of possible perceived threats are more or less intrinsic to the sexual situation itself. These include the threat of loss of control, the threat of being dominated by one's partner, and the threat, especially in women, of physical vulnerability.

Other possible threats may include the threat of injury or pain, the threat of memory of early traumatic experiences from childhood, the threat of guilt and punishment, and the threat of pregnancy.

Remembering the telic and paratelic context of the anxiety-avoidance and excitement-seeking states, it will be realized that whatever triggers a reversal from the paratelic to the telic state will at the same time bring about a reversal into the anxiety-avoidance state. Now the telic state is induced not only by threats, but also by situations which individuals see as imposing some essential goal or duty on them. This introduces another set of possible sources of reversal which, from the point of view of sexual experience and behaviour, are inappropriate and can led to dysphoria and dysfunction. Here are a few examples:

(a) In marriage, particularly if the needs of one partner are considerably greater than those of the other, or if one partner imposes his or her needs on the other, then intercourse may come to be felt by the latter as an obligation.

(b) If the aim of the intercourse is that of conception and this goal over and beyond the behaviour itself remains in the forefront of attention, then the whole act will be felt as a duty at such a time.

(c) If the individual feels that he owes it to himself or herself to have intercourse and to achieve orgasm regularly and frequently, then again the sexual situation may come to be felt to be a duty. Here the liberalization of sex in advanced western society has had something of a paradoxical effect. To the extent to which it has produced an atmosphere in which sex is no longer highly repressed, it has doubtless helped to remove a powerful source of neurosis. To the extent to which it has made frequent intercourse and orgasm seem to be something of a right, however, it has put pressure on people to achieve this, even if they do not otherwise want to do so, or if circumstances do not permit. In other words, for many people sex has become not proscribed but prescribed, and sexual behaviour is approached in a telic state of mind as a right to be safeguarded, or a norm to be achieved. As a consequence, this feeling of duty, where it occurs, makes it difficult for people to enjoy sex, or perform satisfactorily. It may well be the case, therefore, that the problems of repressed sexuality which so concerned Freud are currently being replaced by a set of sexual problems which are of an opposite character.

In all such cases, the paratelic feeling that the sexual behaviour is freely chosen and entered into, becomes replaced by the telic feeling that it is an unavoidable and imposed necessity. Sexual dysfunction then becomes highly likely. Therapy, in relation to sexual dysfunction, therefore requires that the patient should learn how to maintain the paratelic state in sexual situations. This can be seen as the purpose of the Masters and Johnson technique of sensate focusing, which emphasizes the paratelic pleasures of the moment. It is also the purpose of techniques which encourage fantasy during sexual behaviour, and techniques which 'require' couples not to indulge in intercourse for a period, hence releasing them from obligation, so that if intercourse *is* indulged in during this period it is likely to be undertaken in a paratelic state of mind.

This analysis helps to explain certain aspects of sexual dysfunction which are difficult to explain in other terms. Firstly, it explains why the switch from excitement to anxiety at a particular moment in a sexual situation can be as rapid as it appears to be in many cases. This is possible, according to reversal theory, because the reversal from one interpretation of arousal to another can occur more rapidly than a change in the arousal level itself. Secondly, it is possible in terms of the theory to understand why a range of apparently heterogeneous factors underlie these dysfunctions: they are all factors which, for different reasons and in different ways, induce the telic state. Thirdly, reversal theory explains the apparent paradox that the dysfunctional person may feel highly sexually excited before he becomes anxious.[8] If, as suggested here, the anxiety is largely the sexual excitement misinterpreted, then the situation loses its paradoxical aspect: the greater the felt arousal, then the greater the sexual excitement which will be felt before the reversal and the greater the anxiety immediately afterwards. In turn, the greater the sexual excitement, the more the sexual behaviour is likely to be disrupted or inhibited after the reversal. In reversal theory, it is argued that it is not the case, as is commonly supposed, that anxiety inhibits sexual arousal; rather the anxiety is, to a large extent, *the sexual arousal interpreted differently.*

3.   Unsuitable methods are used to obtain the preferred arousal level

Here the problem is not so much with the felt arousal, which may well be experienced as pleasant for extended periods, but with the methods used to obtain the preferred level of this variable. These may be unsuitable because they have side-effects which cause either more problems than they solve for the person concerned, or problems and distress for other people. One thinks in particular of methods which are unusual or extreme, and which tend to be used in desperation by people who would otherwise be unable to achieve pleasurable levels of arousal, low or high.

This may be illustrated again from the field of sexual behaviour. If, for any reason, an individual has difficulty in experiencing adequately high arousal in sexual situations, then he may try to obtain additional arousal by using any of the variety of techniques for obtaining arousal discussed in Chapter 5. For the most part, these techniques, such as risk-taking, or the use of negativism, are not necessarily sexual but may take a sexual form. If they do, or if they are used in a way which integrates them with foreplay, intercourse, or other sexual behaviour, then any arousal which results is likely to be felt specifically as sexual arousal.[9] A number of these techniques normally cause no problems, e.g. the negativistic breaking of mild taboos, as in fellatio or cunnilingus; or the use of surprise and novelty, e.g. in context, clothes, time of day, or types of foreplay. Problems can arise in two ways from the use of such initially extrinsic sources of arousal, however. Firstly, there may be incompatability between the partners in that the methods which one partner needs to use to obtain arousal are exactly those which switch his or her partner into a telic state of mind. So one partner may need the arousal produced by breaking a mild taboo, whereas the other may feel threatened by this. The second, and more serious kind of problem which arises, is that in which the techniques used are more desperate and extreme. One thinks here, for example, of the way in which some people can only obtain sufficiently high arousal by breaking a strong taboo, as in pederasty, bestiality, or necrophilia. This is clearly very different from breaking a taboo like that against oral–genital caressing, which, from the frequency with which it appears to be broken, as noted earlier, may be suspected of being a pseudo-taboo whose very purpose is to be broken. The arousal associated with aggression may also be harnessed to obtain excitement in the sexual situation, as in sadistic and masochistic sexual behaviour. Although in all such cases the individual may succeed in obtaining temporary excitement, the side-effects of such perversions for himself or others are such as to make the behaviour thoroughly maladaptive.

Like the sexual deviant, the psychopath can also be understood from the point of view of reversal theory to be someone who is willing to go to extremes and perform all kinds of unsuitable and anti-social behaviour in order to obtain excitement; but the excitement which the psychopath seeks out is not confined to sexual excitement.

In the light of reversal theory, it is possible to characterize the psychopath in terms of three features.

(i) *The first feature is that of paratelic dominance.* That is, most of the time the psychopath would appear to be in the paratelic state of mind in which there is no inclination to take anything seriously; behaviour tends to be spontaneous, impulsive and unplanned; there is little awareness of the significance which this behaviour might have for self or others in the longer term; there is much concern with immediate sensation, through drugs and music, for instance; and the search is generally for arousal and excitement.[10] Events and situations which would bring about a reversal into the telic state in most people, such as threat of pain or injury, social obligations, risk of loss of money and other possessions, tend to have little chance of dislodging the entrenched nature of the paratelic state in psychopaths. In extreme cases, almost any kind of threat or danger is felt as exciting, and few consequences of behaviour are severe enough to induce the telic state. In short, the psychopath treats life like a game, taking little seriously. Factors like the disapproval of others, the risk of loss, pain, or injury have little effect. In extreme cases even the risk of death may fail to induce serious concern. From this point of view it is not so much as Eysenck would have it (e.g. Eysenck, 1970), that the psychopath is difficult to condition, but rather that he tends to construe the world in a way which, because of his paratelic dominance, makes only rare reference to essential goals: he has an innate tendency to *see* the world in one way rather than another.

(ii) *Extreme measures must be taken to obtain satisfying arousal,* and these may be inappropriate from various points of view. Thus the individual may need to gamble large sums of money, or get into fights, or take inordinate risks of one kind or another. There are a number of possible reasons why such powerful if unsuitable methods should be needed in the attempt to raise arousal to pleasant levels and maintain it there:

(a) the individual may have a low resting level of felt arousal;[11]
(b) there may be few stimuli which raise his resting level of arousal;
(c) arousing stimuli may need to be particularly strong to raise arousal substantially;
(d) the effects of arousing stimuli may habituate quickly;
(e) exceptionally high arousal may be needed before it is experienced as pleasant because of the shape and position of the excitement-seeking curve;
(f) the excitement-seeking curve may peak at a rather low level. In this case, of course, unlike the preceding four, it may be impossible for the individual to experience a satisfying level of arousal, whatever methods he uses, unless these have the effect of shifting the curve in a suitable way.[12]

Some of these reasons for experiencing difficulty in obtaining pleasant high arousal were mentioned above in relation to chronic boredom and boredom depression. The psychopath is someone who has a tendency to chronic boredom, but who attempts to overcome it through extraordinary forms of behaviour.[13] In other words, he finds or constructs stimulus situations which he hopes will be powerful enough to raise and maintain adequately high levels of arousal. These methods do not guarantee that he will achieve satisfying arousal, but he may have learned that they often do. In the process of behaving in these ways, however, the psychopath creates new problems for himself or, perhaps more often, for others.

One conclusion to be drawn from this analysis is that, although psychopaths are similar to each other in that they have to 'over behave' in order to achieve satisfyingly high levels of arousal, there may be many *different* reasons for this. One psychopath may have an unusually low resting level of felt arousal; another may have quite a high resting level, but require abnormally high levels of arousal before it is felt as satisfying; yet another may have a normal resting level and a normal peak on the excitement-seeking curve, but have great difficulty in changing the level of felt arousal sufficiently in the desired direction. It is therefore not surprising, if physiological arousal is indeed closely related to felt arousal, that contradictions have arisen in the research literature on the physiology of psychopathy. Hare (1973), for example, has concluded from his review of a number of studies, including his own, that psychopaths are charac-terized by reduced sympathetic reactivity, whereas Schachter has demonstrated hyper-reactivity in terms of a number of physiological variables (see Schachter, 1971).

(iii) *There is a tendency to attempt to obtain excitement through negativism*, especially through destructive and antisocial behaviour, rather than by means of any of the other possible techniques which might be used. To put this in a different way, of those people who have to go to abnormal lengths to obtain excitement, those who can be most suitably labelled as psychopaths are those who have a predilection for using negativism for this purpose. This is certainly consistent with the way the term 'psychopath' is generally used. People who enjoy dangerous sports, for example, are not usually labelled as psychopathic, even though they may be highly paratelic dominant and may require high levels of arousal when they are in the paratelic state. Similarly, soldiers, sailors, saints, and stuntmen may have much in common with psychopaths; but their supposed conformism typically precludes their classification as psychopaths.

Following Henderson (see Batchelor 1969), a distinction is commonly made between inadequate and aggressive psychopaths. In the light of the present analysis it can be seen that this distinction is related to the way in which negativism typically arises and is utilized by each of these two psychopathic types. The inadequate psychopath tends to be negativistic to whatever requirements present themselves to him and is easily displaced from one to another in the search for excitement. He may use prohibited drugs, dress in outlandish ways, and indulge impulsively in various types of petty crime. He tends not to think through the consequences of his actions, and has difficulty in sustaining any line of activity. He therefore achieves little, and even the excitement he experiences may for long periods be no more than spasmodic. By contrast, the aggressive psychopath, being self-confident, tends to choose goals which are highly ambitious, even unrealistically so, and to persist in their pursuit. The failure to reach them induces negativism to whatever obstacles or barriers he perceives preventing their attainment. (The argument at this point is a development of the analysis of the relationship between negativism and frustration which was presented in Chapter 9). Unlike more normal people, however, the paratelic state is still maintained, the pursuit of the goal remaining a kind of game. Acting against these barriers then provides the satisfaction of both excitement and high felt negativism, which, in combination with the continuing paratelic state, are experienced as parapathic anger. The frustration is less likely to bring about an eventual reversal to the conformist or telic states than it would in normal people, so that the "angry" negativistic behaviour can be sustained, and the related feelings enjoyed for relatively long periods. Indeed, if it is eventually accepted that the goal is unattainable, instead of reversing to the conformist and telic states, this type of psychopath often uses this failure in order to achieve high arousal in a different negativistic way: by accusing, demanding or blaming, and in general by becoming a 'pest'. On the other hand he may at this stage switch to the telic state and experience real, i.e. non-parapathic, anger and bitterness.

The use of negativism certainly seems to be a reasonable way in principle to mark off psychopaths from other excitement-seekers, although determining whether someone is negativistic or not by means of judgements about his overt behaviour may on occasion be misleading. Some people whose behaviour is conventionally regarded as conformist may in fact be behaving in a negativistic state of mind, and some people whose behaviour is commonly taken to be negativistic may be behaving in a conformist state of mind. So some people who might appropriately be classified as psychopathic fail to be labelled in this way, while others are labelled as psychopathic misleadingly. Delinquents, for example, are often seen as psychopathic. It is true that, from the classic studies of the Gluecks (1952) onwards, the delinquent's frequent and strong need for excitement has been noted as a major characteristic; and studies such as that of Farley (1973) have clearly linked delinquency with sensation-seeking. It is far from clear, however, that all delinquents necessarily perform their antisocial behaviour in a negativistic state of mind. Thus participant studies carried out in the United States and reported by Miller (1958), lead him to conclude that ". . . the relative impact of 'conforming' and 'rejective' elements in the motivation of gang delinquency is weighted preponderantly on the conforming side" (p.19). Similarly, interviews with delinquents carried out recently in Britain by Jones and Walter (1978), and Walter (1978a, 1978b) disclose that in many cases the children simply see their activities as 'fun', and enjoy them in the same sort of conformist way as other children might enjoy playing football.

Just as one individual may go to abnormal lengths to raise arousal, so another may go to abnormal lengths to lower it, and again the behaviour may in itself present various kinds of problems. This condition is represented by the obsessional personality. If the psychopath is paratelic dominant, the obsessional personality is characterized by high telic dominance: he tends to be serious and to organize his life rigidly around various goals and plans towards these goals. Indeed, he tends to take seriously even those small things in life which the normal person takes as part of the background of living: tidiness, cleanliness, doing things in the 'proper' way, formality, punctuality, and so on, and the accomplishment of each of these may become a telic goal in itself. In organizing his life to this degree and leaving little to risk or chance, the obsessional personality may avoid anxiety and depression,[14] but he does so at the expense of behaviour which, in its rigidity, may be maladaptive from the point of view of enjoying life fully, or of achieving major goals or fulfilments. Such behaviour will in any case be likely to cause great irritation, if not distress, to members of his family and others.

An even more interesting picture is presented by the obsessional *neurotic*, using Freud's (1926) distinction between the obsessional personality and obsessional neurosis, i.e. between obsessional traits and obsessional symptoms. If Freud is right, then the obsessional personality results from the workings of successful reaction-formation, while in the obsessional neurotic these reaction-formations are in the process of breaking down. The result, in the neurotic form of obsessionality, is that there is ambivalence and alternation between, on the one hand the traits of orderliness and control, represented by irrational obsessional thoughts, compulsions, and rituals, and on the other hand a dislike of order and control which are felt as ego-dystonic. This translates well into reversal theory, as Fontana (1978) has pointed out. If the obsessional personality is one possible consequence of high telic dominance, the individual reversing into the paratelic state only rarely, then the obsessional neurotic may be regarded as someone who reverses between telic and paratelic states abnormally frequently, the ambivalence that Freud refers to being a result of this abnormal lability. In the one case reversal is over-inhibited, in the other it is over-facilitated. It may be supposed that, under the conditions of frequent reversal, it becomes increasingly difficult for the individual to achieve the preferred levels of arousal in each state: he may reverse before he has had time to bring the level of arousal into the preferred state, and his actions taken in the previous state may continue to affect his arousal level in the wrong direction in his current state. Under these circumstances it is hardly surprising that, in the telic state, the obsessional strategies he has been using to lower arousal become exaggerated, and that the strategies he uses in the paratelic state to raise arousal become somewhat frantic. In short, the individual finds it increasingly difficult to optimize arousal in these circumstances, his behaviour becoming increasingly abnormal, and his condition one which eventually requires therapeutic intervention.

One of the implications of this discussion of different forms of psychopathology, is that a number of the conventional psychiatric labels relate to conditions each of which may be associated with more than one type of experiential state. In certain respects therefore these psychiatric labels may be misleading. Thus according to the reversal theory analysis, depression is a blanket term which, despite certain common symptoms, covers a number of states which differ fundamentally in experiential terms; the common appellation 'depression' may lead one to overlook these basic differences. Similarly, although psychopaths may be similar to each other in that they have difficulty in obtaining pleasant high arousal, and have to behave in extraordinary ways to achieve it, their experience of arousal as suggested by reversal theory may vary widely. In one case the psychopath may find moderate levels of arousal pleasurable but have difficulty in obtaining these moderate levels; in another case he may need to feel high arousal before it is experienced as even moderately pleasant; in yet another case he may have the capacity to feel very high arousal as extremely pleasant and go out of his way to achieve this. Again this brings out the point that one cannot necessarily equate behaviour, here 'symptoms', in any simple one-to-one way with experiential states. Overall, the generally confused state of the field of psychophysiology in relation to psychopathology, and its failure to establish clear and unequivocal relationships between physiological variables and standard psychiatric diagnostic categories, appears inevitable in the light of this analysis.

Psychotherapy

The implications for therapy are twofold. First of all, it may be essential to know something about the experiential aspects of the condition to be treated, otherwise the choice of treatment may be inappropriate. Indeed, the treatment may have exactly the opposite effect to that intended. For example, if a depression is of the boredom type, then any treatment which reduced arousal would be likely to exacerbate the condition, whereas reducing arousal in the case of anxiety depression would be helpful. Similarly, attempting to increase the sexual excitement felt by someone suffering from some form of sexual dysfunction may have the reverse effect to that intended, and only increase his anxiety in the sexual situation. In a related way, in using behaviour modification techniques in therapy, the choice of reinforcer may be crucial: use of a 'reinforcer' which increased arousal would be quite inappropriate with someone for whom a low level of arousal constituted the preferred level at the moment in question, while using a 'reinforcer' which lowered arousal would be inappropriate with someone who, at that moment, was attempting to increase arousal to a high level. Which type of reinforcer is appropriate may also be expected to change over short lengths of time with some patients.

The second general implication for therapy is that there may be alternative ways of dealing with a variety of conditions, not just in the weak sense of different ways of achieving the same effect, but in the strong sense of achieving different effects which may nevertheless be equally therapeutic. Thus for a range of conditions one can attempt either to change the level of arousal, or to change the metamotivational state so that the prevailing level of arousal is felt as relatively pleasant. In the case of chronic anxiety, for instance, one can attempt either to find ways in which the patient can learn to lower his arousal, or avoid arousal being raised, or one can attempt to set up conditions whereby he can reverse into the paratelic state if the arousal level becomes unpleasantly high, so that the arousal can instead be enjoyed at such times. Similarly, if the problem is that of chronic boredom, one can either try to make the telic state more easily accessible, so that the boredom is felt frequently as relaxation, or one can try to teach techniques for achieving higher arousal, without harm to others. Again, one can approach the problem of phobia either by looking for ways in which the arousal felt in response to the phobic situation can be reduced, or by looking for ways in which the paratelic state can be induced in the phobic situation so that the resulting arousal is experienced as excitement or "fear", rather than as fear. What all this comes to is that, for a range of conditions, the therapist has the advantage of a choice of approaches. With a given patient, and under given conditions, one of these may be more appropriate or more effective than the other. In any case it also means that if one approach fails, then the other may work. There may also be a third chance of success, through attempting to shift the shape and position of the relevant curve, e.g. the anxiety-avoidance curve, or the felt negativism curve. It may be that this is the typical effect of some forms of chemotherapy, although other factors, like fatigue, may play at least a transitory part. In principle, then, there are three chances of success for these conditions.

If one looks at the variety of psychotherapies that are currently fashionable, it can be seen that some are oriented primarily towards changing levels of arousal, and others towards changing the metamotivational state. Of the former, one thinks in particular of all the different techniques which have been developed to help patients to relax: these include Jacobson's technique of progressive relaxation (1938), the technique of systematic desensitization as developed by Wolpe (1958) and others, Luthe's autogenic training (Luthe, 1969-73) based on the work of Schultz (1932), and the technique of biofeedback which appears to have been used more to help people to relax than for any other purpose; Transcendental Meditation may also be regarded as a technique of this type. At the same time, some other therapeutic techniques clearly involve increasing arousal to a high level during the therapy itself, although with the ultimate aim of bringing the level of arousal felt by the patient during the course of everyday life down to a generally lower level. These include primal therapy (Janov, 1970), implosive therapy (Stampfl, 1970), and the use of abreaction (see especially Sargant, 1957). In these cases it would seem that 'offence mechanisms' (viz. Chapter 5) are being used, since they all involve releasing rather than inhibiting arousal-increasing memories and ideas.

Other therapeutic procedures can be seen to involve inducing a reversal of metamotivational state, typically in the paratelic direction, and helping the individual to find ways of inducing the appropriate state, or predisposing him to do so relatively automatically, in 'problem situations'. For example, Albert Ellis' Rational-Emotive psychotherapy involves helping people to relabel their bodily states (Ellis, 1962), particularly so as to interpret their anxiety in a more positive way, and feel stimulated rather than threatened by those stimuli which increase their levels of arousal. Gestalt therapy interprets anxiety as 'blocked excitement' (Perls, Hefferline and Goodman, 1973, p.169) and teaches that excitement will be felt rather than anxiety if the individual learns correct breathing: an actor, for example, may experience excitement rather than anxiety if he breathes properly (ibid., p.165). The reversal theory notion that excitement is felt as part of a state which involves other characteristics like spontaneity and a tendency to focus on the present moment, i.e. the paratelic state, is consistent with various statements by Perls and others, e.g.: "If you are in the now, you can't be anxious, because the excitement flows immediately into ongoing spontaneous activity" (Perls, 1971, p.3).

Another example of a therapy which involves changing the metamotivational state, is Victor Frankl's technique of paradoxical intention (Frankl, 1973a) which is one of the key techniques of his Logotherapy.[15] In this technique, the patient is instructed to exaggerate his symptoms rather than fighting them (see example case histories in Gerz, 1973a). This is seen by Frankl as a way of removing the anxiety associated with the symptoms, so that at least that part of the neurosis which derives from the patient's fear of the neurosis is neutralized. In reversal theory terms, it allows the patient to think of his symptoms in a paratelic rather than a telic frame of mind. In turn, of course, 'performing' the symptoms in an exaggerated way can make them seem rather pointless, and help the patient to overcome them. So, where the symptoms are ones which occur in a telic state of mind, e.g. obsessional ritual, or nervous reactions to a phobic situation, performing them in an exaggerated way can itself induce the paratelic state. The self-dramatization involved may also help to convert the associated emotions into their parapathic counterparts. As a consequence, this may remove the distress involved in the situation and perhaps eventually allow the patient to dispense with the sympoms altogether. Frankl brings this to a point by asserting that ". . . the purpose (of paradoxical intention) is to enable the patient to develop a sense of detachment towards his neurosis by laughing at it . . ." (Frankl, 1973b, p.209). Since humour, as has been argued earlier, occurs in the paratelic state of mind, this is clearly an excellent way of inducing the paratelic state for therapeutic purposes.

The various techniques associated with encounter groups of different kinds can also be seen as methods used to induce the paratelic state in participants. The whole encounter situation is typically presented as a kind of 'game' which is bracketed off from the pressures of everyday life; playfulness is generally encouraged, especially through reversing many of the rules of normal conduct (paratelic negativism), as in touching people with whom one is not intimate, saying what one really thinks rather than 'dressing it up', and showing emotions openly. There is usually an emphasis on immediate sensations, on spontaneity, and on expression for its own sake; and self-dramatization may be encouraged, and parapathic emotions elicited. The same is generally true of the technique of psychodrama, stemming from the work of Moreno (1934), especially in relation to self-dramatization. This may all help the individual, in the same way as Frankl's technique does, to overcome certain problems which occur in the telic state by increasing the likelihood of his approaching these problems subsequently in a paratelic state of mind. But the advantage of inducing the paratelic state during therapy itself may not rest here. If the paratelic state is more spontaneous, then it may be easier to induce at least some kind of change in this state than in the telic state. In this case, the induction and maintenance of the paratelic state during therapy, through encounter groups or in some other way, would be a helpful first step in dealing with a whole range of clinical problems.

From the reversal theory point of view, a variety of different therapeutic procedures which are already in widespread use can be seen as essentially complementary, in that they involve either trying to achieve the same ends in different ways, or trying to achieve different ends which, in the light of the theory, are nevertheless equally viable. To some extent therefore, which therapy one chooses as a psychiatrist or psychotherapist can justifiably be a matter of taste or personal ability. Choice of therapeutic approach may also depend on the therapist's judgement of what would be most effective and convenient for a particular patient at a particular time. Reversal theory implies that adopting an eclectic approach is not something about which a therapist needs to feel apologetic. It does, however, also indicate that some forms of therapy may be counter-productive for some types of pathology. The contribution of reversal theory to therapy therefore is primarily the provision of a framework within which decisions can be made about which therapeutic techniques to use. In fact, it provides a *framework for eclecticism*.[16]

Problems in Family Relationships

Up to this point, psychological problems have been discussed in purely individual terms, but often such problems can be more appropriately viewed as problems of relationships, i.e. as having their genesis in interactions between people. This is a broad topic, but one which is worth pursuing here so as to bring out several of the social psychological implications of reversal theory. Relationship problems often arise in the context of the family, which will be the focus of attention for the rest of this chapter. But in many respects the family may be taken as a model for other social groupings.

Relationship problems often involve incompatibilities, people 'pulling in opposite directions' so that if one is satisfied then, *ipso facto*, the other is dissatisfied.[17] In reversal theory terms, such incompatibilities can arise in relation to metamotivational states. Of course, the co-existence of opposite metamotivational states in people interacting at a given time does not necessarily lead to incompatibility: for example two people may be able to play golf quite satisfactorily when one is in a telic and the other in a paratelic state. Nevertheless, if two interacting people are in opposing metamotivational states, this gives rise to the possibility of certain kinds of incompatibility. For example, when two people interact closely there would seem to be a tendency for their arousal levels to approach each other, but if one person is in an excitement-seeking state and the other in an anxiety avoidance state at the same time, then incompatibility would appear to be almost inevitable. If two people, e.g. husband and wife, interact frequently, and they have metamotivational states of opposite dominance, then one would expect problems to arise with some regularity; should the dominance be extreme in opposite directions, then incompatibility between the two may become chronic. Thus, if one or other, or both, members of the dyad find themselves regularly at a level of felt arousal which is not the preferred level for their own prevailing metamotivational state, then every attempt to change their level of arousal will cause a reaction in their partner which will tend to work against this change. This situation may arise in two people who would not otherwise individually have problems, and the problem therefore derives essentially from the interaction between them. For example, it may frequently be the case in a particular marriage that when the wife is excited her husband is anxious, and when he is relaxed she is bored. If she attempts to raise her own level of arousal, for instance by talking excitedly, then this raises her husband's level of arousal and he feels some irritation and anxiety; if he manages to calm things down, then she starts to feel bored again. Obviously, they are not always going to be in opposite metamotivational states with respect to arousal but, if their dominance is opposite, then this kind of incompatible interaction may nevertheless occur regularly enough to cause marital problems.

This problem is exacerbated, in the case illustrated, if the wife's behaviour in raising arousal also simultaneously induces, or helps to maintain, her husband's telic state, and her husband's attempt to lower arousal also induces, or helps to maintain, his wife's paratelic state. Indeed if this kind of situation occurs with some regularity, then chronic incompatibility may arise even in partners whose dominance in relation to arousal is not opposite. Suppose for example that a typical strategy of the wife to raise arousal is to start an argument with her husband; the argument may only be playful, but if the husband does not understand this and takes it seriously, he will feel threatened and his telic state will be maintained, or this state will be induced if he was in the paratelic state at an immediately preceding time. Conversely, if the husband attempts to find some way of resolving the argument and reaching agreement, this may have the effect not only of lowering both his arousal, which is then felt as relaxation, and his wife's arousal but, since his attempt to reach agreement makes his wife feel more secure in their relationship, it may help to maintain her paratelic state and consequent need for high arousal, which is now unsatisfied.

A general level of incompatibility may arise out of opposing dominance of metamotivational state, or it may arise out of communication problems in which opposite metamotivational states tend to be induced in the course of interaction. Both of these may also apply at the same time. Many family problems involve incompatibilities between parents and their children and these may derive in either, or both, of these ways. Let us look at each of these in turn.

Normally, young children spend more time in the paratelic than in the telic state, whereas, at least in comparison, parents spend relatively long periods in the telic state. This may be because children's needs, such as the need for food and the avoidance of danger, are normally met by their parents: hence children tend to feel themselves to be secure and no telic need imposes itself. Parents, on the other hand, because the duty to look after and be responsible for the children is imposed on them, are likely to be in a telic state of mind while they are caring for their children. In other words, children do not need to be goal-oriented in the telic sense, because normally their parents pursue essential goals on their behalf. It seems likely that maturational processes are involved too, and that children are programmed to be paratelic dominant and adults to be relatively telic dominant; this would then provide biological underpinnings for the adaptive relationship between parents and children just described.[18]

This difference of state does not in itself necessarily lead to incompatibility. Thus a mother may be relaxed and happy when her children are playing, if her telic goal is that her children should be enjoying themselves. But if her goal changes, then incompatibility may arise. For example, if she needs to prepare food, write a letter, or make some clothes, and she is still aware of the children playing, then in this telic state of mind she might find that their play becomes irritating. Should their play be rowdy, then the arousal which this induces in her is likely to be felt as anxiety. If she forces the children to quieten down, this may temporarily reduce her own anxiety, but in the process the children may become bored and unhappy, and in due course find some new and even more anxiety-provoking outlet.

There is nothing unusual about this kind of incompatibility, which is usually accepted in most families as part of the 'ups and downs' of normal family life. But in some families such incompatibility takes a more serious turn. This may well occur if the parents are *too* telic dominant. Father, for example, may be extremely ambitious and mother a career woman, the children being made to conform to strict rules so that they do not interfere unduly with their parents' purposeful activities. Children may also be treated in this way if there are severe external pressures on one or both parents, such as the threat of bankruptcy. Or the parents may attempt to express their telic purposefulness *through* their offspring rather than in spite of them: they may set high scholastic goals, or force them to develop such talents as they possess, e.g. in music or sport. This should have the effect of regularly inducing the telic state in their children. But if it does not, then in the paratelic state their children may find it difficult to experience the pleasures which should be available in that state: to behave spontaneously and impulsively, to obtain excitement, and so on. Over a period this may lead to the children responding with various forms of disturbance. Alternatively, if such parents do succeed in inducing the telic state regularly, and also tend to bring about a high level of anxiety in their children in that state, then their children may become 'nervous', and develop various neurotic symptoms, possibly including problems of a psychosomatic nature.

Serious problems may also arise in a family for the opposite reason, i.e. when the children are extremely paratelic dominant. Furthermore, in the most difficult cases, the child may not only be paratelic dominant, but in need of abnormally high levels of arousal while in the paratelic state. The discussion earlier in the chapter on the use of unsuitable methods to obtain high arousal is relevant here. In this case one is thinking of children who are generally wild and disruptive beyond the normal degree, and who go to extremes in the search for excitement: they may be rowdy and uncontrollable, and expose themselves quite unnecessarily to dangers of various kinds. At the same time they are likely to have difficulty settling down to any kind of serious work at school, and are generally restless and distractable. In some cases a tendency to be negativistic, and to find excitement through negativism, also accompanies the paratelic dominance. This negativism may be expressed in a variety of ways. A young child of this type usually finds that shouting, or having a temper tantrum in a public place can, especially through the embarrassed reaction of his or her parents, cause a great deal of excitement. So too can doing those things which parents, or other adults, have specifically prohibited, e.g. swearing, or chewing gum, or having dirty shoes. Indeed, such children typically indulge in a great deal of 'testing out' behaviour, in which they try out different actions to see which of them parents get upset about and prohibit. This provides them with an armoury of negativistic weapons which they can use to gain excitement as and when needed. The psychological characteristics of such children are essentially the same as those of psychopaths, as discussed earlier, although it must be emphasized that this may be no more than a passing phase which the child will grow out of, especially when he becomes less paratelic dominant in the course of normal development. But during this phase the child can cause a great deal of distress to parents, school teachers, and other supervizing adults.

Incompatibility may also arise out of inappropriate communication and interaction between parents and children. Just as a husband may not understand that
his wife's argument is a playful attempt to raise excitement, so parents may not
realize that some statement or piece of behaviour on the part of their child should
not be taken at face value. Thus a child may say to his mother "I hate you", or
even "I wish you were dead", and this may considerably upset her, so that as a
result she experiences a state of telic high arousal. Yet the child may not really
mean what he says, and may not even appreciate the fact that his mother thinks
he does; mother's anguished self-examination may therefore be quite unnecessary.
Or the child may, in a playful spirit, temporarily refuse to obey his father, who
takes this as a serious affront to his authority, sending him into a paroxysm of
fury, instead of entering into, or at least understanding, the game which is being
played. Such problems tend to involve not only a species of misunderstanding,
but also a reaction which further compounds the problem. For example, in the
illustration just given not only does father misjudge the spirit of his son's
defiance, but his reaction may have the opposite effect to that intended: if it
increases his son's level of felt arousal without inducing the telic state, then this
arousal will be pleasurable, and the son will attempt to keep up the excitement
with further defiance. In any case, the defiance will have been reinforced and
will doubtless be repeated on later occasions. Such a reaction is an example of
what may be termed a 'reversal-of-effect' communication. This is defined as a
communication which has the opposite effect to that intended. In general terms,
if a child is in the paratelic state and is difficult to dislodge from that state,
because highly paratelic dominant, and if he or she needs particularly high
arousal in that state, then shouting, threatening, or punishment, indeed over-
reaction of any kind, may have the effect of aggravating matters because it simply
provides the child with what he or she needs. Similarly, if the child is in a
negativistic state of mind, an order by a parent may give the child something on
which to focus his negativism. If the order is a response to some preceding act by
the child which was intended to be negativistic, then this only serves to validate
that act by affirming that it has exactly the meaning intended by the child. All
this should not be taken to imply that parents should be permissive, but rather
that they should try to be sensitive to the states of mind of their children, and not
overreact at the wrong moments.

Not infrequently, a family in attendance at a child guidance clinic or family
therapy centre has problems which have arisen through a combination of the
factors mentioned. One or more of the children may be highly paratelic
dominant, expressing this through uncontrollable 'naughtiness'; mother may be
highly telic dominant and have become chronically anxious as a result; and
father may express his goal-oriented telic dominance through an attempt to
dictate solutions to the rest of the family. In turn the resulting pattern of interaction typically displays various forms of reversal-of-effect: e.g. father's authori-

tarianism reinforces his child's unruliness, and causes further anxiety in mother, who now worries about her husband's reactions as well as the child's behaviour; mother's anxiety further reinforces the child's behaviour while making father even angrier, and so on. This pattern, or some variant of it, will be familiar to many clinicians.

One other strategy which the paratelic dominant child may use to raise the level of arousal in his family, and hence to raise his own arousal to pleasurable levels, is to set other members of the family against each other. This game can be played using any pair of members of the family, but most frequently it is played by manipulating the parents. Wherever parents disagree, the child notes this and attempts to bring about the conditions of disagreement on later occasions. This is particularly easy to accomplish where the disagreement between parents is about how he should himself be handled: if mother is protective and father is punitive, for example, then almost any act of naughtiness can provoke disagreement. But disagreement can also be brought about in more subtle ways; for instance the child may self-effacingly draw parents' attention to topics on which he has observed them to disagree. Disagreement between parents also tends to have a synergic quality which is pleasant in the paratelic state: the parents are seen simultaneously as both a unity, and as divided; they are a team, but they are also playing against each other.

This strategy only works, of course, where the child remains in the paratelic state. It can 'backfire' when the family becomes so divided against itself, that the feeling of security which the healthy family provides for the child disappears, and the child finds himself increasingly in a threatened telic state. There is, however, a modified way of playing the game which can overcome this. The child, in bringing about a division, can do so in such a way that parents take sides, one parent siding with him and the other against him. If this strategy is successful it means that the child has the security of one parent, and this may be sufficient for him to be able to maintain the paratelic state. The disagreements and arguments, together with the opposition of the other parent to him, then have the function of producing arousal within this secure context. So the child makes sure of the protection of one parent, by obedience and displays of affection, and he is wise to choose the 'stronger' parent for this purpose, and then engineers disagreements between this parent and the other. He can also go out of his way to upset the other parent deliberately, especially through behaviour which is negativistic.[19] As well as obtaining excitement as a result, he will be able to enjoy a new kind of synergy: the feeling of being both weak, because a child, and strong, because there is a two-to-one coalition in his favour. The resulting situation is obviously a form of triangle, a configuration which has received attention from a number of writers on family pathology (e.g. Bowen, 1966; Haley, 1967b; Zuk, 1971; Freeman, 1976). In the light of reversal theory, however, such triangles take on a new significance.

One cannot avoid wondering whether the sorts of family situations which psychoanalysts automatically interpret in Oedipal or Electral terms, may not in fact be triangles set up by the child for the reasons just outlined. In situations in which a child clearly establishes close ties of affection with one parent, but displays hostility, or masked hostility, to the other, reversal theory would suggest that this is likely to be a result of the child's need for excitement rather than deriving, as Freudians would claim, from his need to express his sexuality. Since the expression of sexuality normally involves excitement, there would appear to be some degree of overlap between these two interpretations, allowing that one can meaningfully talk of sexuality in children at all. But fundamental differences between the two theories remain. One of these is that, in Freudian terms, the sexuality is directed towards the parent with whom the child has a tie of affection, whereas in reversal theory the excitement derives largely from interaction with the 'resented' parent. In other words, in reversal theory the affection and excitement relate respectively to different parents, in psychoanalytic theory they could be said to relate to the same parent. A second difference is that if one parent is resented, then according to Freudians this is ultimately *because* the other is loved; in the 'pathological triangles' described in reversal theory, one parent is loved *in order to* set up a situation of hostility in relation to the other. Thirdly, in psychoanalysis the loved parent is of the opposite sex and the resented parent of the same sex; in contrast, reversal theory suggests that there is no necessary connection between the sex of the child and the sex of the parent with whom the child relates positively. The evidence therefore that daughters frequently prefer their mothers to their fathers, and sons their fathers to their mothers (e.g. see Valentine, 1956), presents no problems for reversal theory; but it is more difficult for Freudian theory to deal with convincingly and requires further explanatory principles such as 'identification with the aggressor'. Finally, it should be noted that in Freudian theory the Oedipal situation is supposed to be universal, whereas in reversal theory the setting up of a coalition by a child with a parent simply constitutes one possible strategy, albeit a common one, which a child may utilize in the pursuit of excitement.

Reversal theory provides a new perspective on a number of frequently occurring family problems, and this in turn suggests ways in which such families may be helped. Initially, the therapist must attempt to identify the nature of the problem, and one major difficulty here is that symptoms presented by members of the family do not fall in any simple way into categories which relate unequivocally to operative or dominant metamotivational states. Thus the same symptom may be generated in the telic or the paratelic state; e.g. a child who refuses school may do so because school is boring and he needs the excitement of truancy, or because he is afraid of school and wishes to avoid the anxiety associated with it. Soiling may occur as a psychosomatic response to stress in the telic state, or alternatively as a way of gaining attention, and hence excitement, in the paratelic state. Similarly, an apparently negativistic act, like wearing some article of clothing which parents prohibit, may actually be negativistic towards parents' requirements, but it may also be performed in a conformist state of mind, for instance by reference to the requirements of the child's peers. The therapist has to be sensitive to cues which can help him to decide on the states of mind of members of the family during problem episodes, but he may also have to probe in various ways in order to build up an accurate model of what is happening during these episodes. One further problem for the therapist is that the same symptom in the same person may at different times relate to different metamotivational states. For example, a child in a telic state of mind may steal from his parents because he is insecure and hopes that if he is found out this will allow him to test how much his parents really love him. Having gained a feeling of security in this way from the concern and forgiveness of his parents he may then later on steal for the excitement. On this later occasion it is possible that his parents will react in a different and less understanding way, which makes him insecure and anxious again, i.e. telic, and he then has to steal once more to prove that he is really loved. Fig. 11.3 represents this kind of situation, with the child alternating between an inner (paratelic) and outer (telic) loop. A similar diagram could of course be drawn up for parents as well as children, with inner and outer loops for the parent concerned. To give appropriate guidance, therefore, the therapist has to decide which loop is primarily operative for the member of the family in question, during the period in which he is dealing with the family.

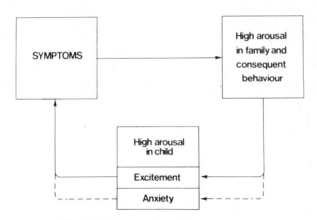

FIG. 11.3   Two related family-interaction cycles.

Having made judgements of this kind, and constructed a conceptual model of the dynamics of the family, the therapist is in a position to attempt to guide the family into a new and healthier pattern of interaction. A number of ways of doing this may suggest themselves, depending on the nature of the problem.

He may, for example, see the problem as largely a result of communication difficulties, and attempt to counter these through teaching the members of the family new communication skills. The aim of this would be to teach family members to give clearer metacommunicative signals about their metamotivational states, and to be more sensitive to the cues which others give about which state they are in. Thus a wife who starts arguments for the sake of excitement might be taught to give certain cues, or the husband to become more aware of cues which she gives involuntarily, and which disclose that she is in the paratelic state; this would then allow the husband to avoid feeling threatened and anxious in such situations. Similarly a mother might be taught not to interpret literally her child's statement that he hates her. The therapist may also be able to teach parents how to prevent themselves communicating in a way which produces the opposite effects to those intended, i.e. how to avoid 'reversal-of-effect'. Such attention on the part of the therapist, or counsellor, to communication aspects of the family would be thoroughly consistent with the emphasis which the influential Palo Alto school of family therapy has placed on communication.[20] Reversal theory, however, provides a rather different theoretical underpinning for this emphasis.

Furthermore, reversal theory is not restricted to the level of communication, and some family problems may be most appropriately construed, at a more fundamental level, as stemming from different degrees and directions of metamotivational dominance among the members of the family. In this case, the therapist working on the basis of reversal theory would not make problems of communication his prime target, although he might still profitably pay some attention to this aspect. Rather, such a therapist would direct his attention to an attempt to change the problem behaviour itself, or to intervene in some way in relation to the metamotivational states in the family. On the one hand he may attempt to change the behaviour which derives from the different metamotivational states so that it is less disruptive in the family setting. On the other hand, he may attempt to counteract the underlying dominance of one metamotivational state or another, in one or more members of the family, by searching for those stimuli which induce a reversal away from the dominant state for those members, and then trying to organize family life so that these stimuli occur more frequently, or can be brought to bear at crucial moments. So, if the problem is that of a paratelic dominant child achieving excitement in ways that upset other members of the family, the attempt might be made to help the child to find other ways of achieving excitement which are not disruptive, e.g. he might be encouraged to achieve this through sporting activities. In this case, one would be attempting to *displace* the content of the metamotivational state and the behaviour which derives from it. Such an attempt must of course be closely monitored, otherwise there is a danger that new activities will become even more disruptive than the previous ones were. The alternative way of dealing with such a child might be to identify the stimuli which, for that particular child, induce the telic state; certain of these could then be used by the child's family when the child's disruptive behaviour threatens to cause a family crisis. For example, there may be certain events in the future which the child takes seriously enough to plan and work for, and it may be possible to bring these to the forefront of his attention at crucial times and induce the telic state in this way. More generally, if the therapist can impress on the child the serious consequences of his disruptive behaviour for the future of his family, then his parents may be able to remind the child of these, and induce the telic state in this way at appropriate moments in the course of family interaction. Clearly one would have to avoid inducing the telic state in ways which might be detrimental to the child, through over-severe threats, or frequent and harmful punishment, for example. At the same time one would also have to be careful that, in inducing a change to the telic state, one was not doing so in a way which provided immediate reinforcers in that state, thus encouraging the immediately preceding problem behaviour. Great care is required therefore in using strategies involving the induction of the telic state.

There can be no doubt about the enormous complexity of family relations and the intricacy of family pathology, and this is emphasized in reversal theory. Neither can there be any doubt from the perspective of reversal theory about the qualities which a therapist needs to be able to guide problem families towards healthier patterns of interaction. He must be sensitive to the metacommunicative signals of all the members of the family, and be able to build up a picture of their underlying metamotivational states at different times; he must have insight into the way in which different configurations of states in the family evolve over time; he must display ingenuity and improvisatory capacity in constructing suitable therapeutic strategies for each individual problem family; he must be quick to spot when his own intervention has reversal-of-effect properties, so that he can take immediate corrective action; he must be flexible enough to cope with unexpected twists in the development of the family's interactions; and he will need patience. As with all forms of therapy therefore, the successful therapist requires a variety of abilities and skills. Given these, we believe that guidance along the lines suggested by reversal theory can be highly effective.[21]

Notes on Chapter 11

1. The curves in the graph on the left in Fig. 10.2 are of course not necessarily individually symmetrical, nor are they necessarily mirror-images of each other as they are in this hypothetical graph, so that at any given time the number of ways in which arousal may potentially be experienced as extremely unpleasant may be less than four.
2. The fact that increased arousal is generally part of stress reactions, reminds us that stress researchers (following Selye, 1956) typically do not distinguish between 'threats' which elicit anxiety, and other forms of demand, including freely-chosen 'challenges' which elicit

excitement. In terms of reversal theory, either telic or paratelic states of mind and forms of arousal, may therefore be involved in different forms of what these researchers refer to in a global way as 'stress'. In phenomenological terms there is clearly a difference between threat and challenge, just as there is between anxiety and excitement, and the normal everyday meaning of the word 'stress' would relate only to situations involving the experience of threat and anxiety. Since researchers working on stress generally do not make this kind of distinction, it is difficult to know whether the pathological somatic consequences which are supposed to follow from stress really do apply equally to both types of situation. One suspects, however, that they do not.

3. It should however be made clear that Fromm's use of the term 'boredom' is a little different from its use in reversal theory, as is his analysis of the boredom phenomenon; nevertheless there is enough similarity in the two uses of the word for his emphasis on the prevalence of chronic boredom to provide some support for the point being made here.

4. The author is grateful to Mr S. Murgatroyd for discussions which helped to clarify the nature of depression in relation to arousal from the perspective of reversal theory.

5. This cognitive feature itself is not necessarily long-lasting, so that although depression may be related to chronic arousal problems, the depression itself is not necessarily chronic but lasts for whatever length of time the cognitive interpretation remains of this type, which in some cases may be only momentary; i.e. depression itself is not necessarily long-lasting, but it arises from the cognition that some unsatisfactory state of affairs *is*.

6. In these terms it is hardly surprising that Zuckerman and Neeb (1979) found no significant difference between depressives, as a global category, and non-depressives on the Sensation-Seeking Scale.

7. What is called 'free-floating anxiety' may in some cases turn out to be 'tension' in the sense defined in reversal theory. Tension in this sense will always be a concomitant of depression of whatever kind, since tension is always experienced when an individual is unable to achieve the preferred level of some variable specified by the prevailing metamotivational state.

8. See, for example, cases 1, 15, 25 and 29 in Kaplan (1978).

9. That is, it seems that in the sexual situation, the sexual interpretation of the arousal normally predominates. Not only is excitement felt as specifically sexual excitement, but such parapathic emotions as "anger", which one would expect when negativism is used in the paratelic state to increase arousal, or "fear", in response to surprise in the paratelic state, are also felt as forms of sexual excitement.

10. Evidence that psychopaths and sociopaths score highly on the Sensation-Seeking Scale is consistent with this (Emmons and Webb, 1974; Blackburn, 1978; Zuckerman, 1978).

11. By 'resting level' here, as in the earlier discussion of anxiety and boredom, is meant the homeostatic preferred level to which arousal would tend to return if the arousal system were not operated on through the activities of the excitement-seeking or anxiety-avoidance systems.

12. The first four of these reasons are of the type to which Eysenck in particular has had recourse in explaining psychopathy. The final two are more specific to reversal theory, since they deal essentially with characteristics of metamotivational states.

13. His behaviour should of course not be confused with that of someone in an anxious or agitated state whose hyperactivity relates to an attempt to lower rather than to raise arousal.

14. On the other hand the high felt significance which he may experience as a result of all his planning and self-organization, while pleasurable in itself, may well play a part in keeping his level of anxiety uncomfortably high, since the possibility of failure in any particular action will be seen to have many repercussions.

15. This bears a close relation to the use of paradox or 'Symptom prescription' in therapy as described by such writers as Jay Haley (1967a), Watzlawick *et al.* (1967, 1974) and Cade (1979).

16. I am indebted to Mr S. Murgatroyd for this felicitous turn of phrase.

17. The kinds of problems which arise when systems with their own preferred states are 'coupled', so that the output of each is the input to the other, are well known in cybernetics; viz Ashby (1956) Chapter 4.
18. The biological advantage of genetic programming of paratelic dominance in children will be discussed further in Chapter 13.
19. The behaviour of people in groups often follows the same pattern: in the context of the security provided by group membership it is possible to search for excitement by opposing outgroups.
20. As is well known, this school developed under the influence of the ideas of Gregory Bateson, Don D. Jackson and Milton Erickson, and leading members include Paul Watzlawick, John Weakland, Janet H. Beavin and Richard Fisch. The School's approach is well described in Watzlawick *et al.* (1967 and 1974).
21. Reversal theory has already demonstrated its usefulness in several child guidance clinics in the West of England; in particular, it has been used regularly by Dr K. C. P. Smith for a period of some six years at the time of writing.

12 Religion and Reversal Theory

Any serious attempt to develop a psychological theory of human motivation must sooner or later confront the problem proposed by man's religious quest, and any theory which fails to address itself to this problem must be regarded as necessarily incomplete. Furthermore, to regard religious behaviour and thought as in some way 'peripheral' is to fail to recognize the central part which religion has played in man's behaviour across all known cultures throughout recorded history.

The beliefs and behaviours associated with religion, and the scriptures, buildings, ritual objects, and other trappings, have all evolved throughout history in an enormous variety and complexity of forms. Yet there remain such fundamental similarities between different religions in different cultures and at different times, that it is reasonable to assume that all religions serve a common core of psychological and sociological functions for those who practise them, and that all the phenomena of religion are generated in essentially similar ways. The aim of this chapter is to see how far the concepts of reversal theory can help to elucidate some of the complexities of religious behaviour and thought, and in particular to make some suggestions about the aetiology of religious phenomena. Much of the argument will centre on Christianity, but other religions will also be referred to at various points in order to bring out the generality of the discussion.

The Genesis of Religion

In order to understand the genesis of religious material of all kinds, it is necessary to bear in mind two features of thinking. The first is that thinking may produce material which is independent of the individual thinker and which becomes part of the public rather than the private domain. This includes linguistic 'material', solutions to problems, ideas, stories, programmes of action, etc. and also other kinds of structures 'in the real world', including various types

276

of artefact. These materials are experienced by people other than those who produced them; indeed, if the materials are reasonably permanent, which implies in the case of linguistic materials that they must either be transmitted orally from generation to generation, or written down, they may be experienced by *many* other people. They may then stimulate further thinking by others, and possibly the development of the materials themselves as a result of this thinking.

The second feature is that style of thinking, and the products of thinking, are typically rather different in the telic and paratelic states. In the telic state, the achievement of an essential goal may require the solution to a problem, and the aim of the thinking in such a case is to solve the problem as soon as possible, since lack of a solution is likely to be associated with rising anxiety. Progress will probably be monitored continually in the attempt to ensure that the thinking is progressing satisfactorily towards the solution of the problem. The thinking need not be logical, although it often is; but the solutions must normally be tested against certain requirements which are usually empirical, i.e. there are criteria which must be satisfied in the real world. In the paratelic state, the thinking may be enjoyed for itself, or for the excitement it can provide. This excitement may be generated from solving puzzles, mysteries, and intellectual challenges of different kinds which the individual sets himself; but the solution is in an important sense its own reward, and the criteria for solution are often subjective rather than objective. Paratelic thinking is characterized above all by the use of a number of the techniques for gaining excitement which were listed in Chapter 5. In particular one will expect to find paratelic thinking at a given time characterized by one or more of the following features: the invention of cognitive synergies, including especially those of a make-believe type; the search for unexpected and novel insights; the construction of surprising and original objects; the playful and negativistic denial of generally accepted ideas or beliefs; an overriding interest in situations and events which are normally arousal-producing, such as birth, death, violence, catastrophe, sex, and every type of taboo topic; the attempt to induce parapathic emotions, especially through the invention of stories; and, in general, the use of imagination and fantasy. These techniques tend to be used in a variety of combinations, as they are for example in the thinking that underlies the creation of art and of entertainment of all kinds.

Taken together, these two general features of the process of thinking imply that some materials may be produced in the course of telic thinking, and others in the course of paratelic thinking, and that these materials will have different characteristics. Furthermore, if the material exists in the public domain, it is possible that the same material may be developed not only by the same person in different metamotivational states at different times, but also by different people, and these people may also be in different states during the time they are in creative contact with the material. In this way it may, in the course of evolution, acquire a considerable richness and complexity.

One usually knows whether one is experiencing the results of imaginative paratelic thinking or serious telic thinking. Generally, one does not take materials which have been produced by paratelic thinking as literally true, unless it is quite clear that no imaginative invention has been involved in their creation. There are exceptions to this, however, and one of the special characteristics of the process which leads to the production and development of religious material, would seem to be that this form of 'mistake' does occur. That is, people occasionally do not recognize the imaginative origin of paratelic material, or the fantasy manipulation of material which was originally telic, by paratelic thinking processes. Such mistakes can accumulate, so that a whole body of material may be built up which is taken seriously and believed to be true but which in fact, in its origins, contains large elements of make-believe, as well as reflecting other characteristics of paratelic thought. Religious material is perhaps one of the prime examples of this type of confusion. The term 'religious material' here is intended to include religious ideas, ethical injunctions, symbols, stories, ritual, architecture, priestly costume, sacred objects, and so on. Clearly, it will not be possible to go into details concerning all of these types of material individually, or to suggest how the development of each might interact with each of the others. But examples of particular kinds of materials will be given in the course of the argument where these are deemed to be most appropriate by way of illustration.

The confusion between the products of telic and paratelic thinking is part of just one step, albeit a crucial one, in the development of religious material. The whole process can be analyzed into three steps, although it may be supposed that in reality all three of these steps are continuing to take place concurrently in relation to different parts of the same body of material. Furthermore, the steps may continue through many cycles. The material or any part of it, however, does not become what one might call 'religious material' until it has been through at least one complete cycle. The steps are as follows.

(i) Human beings face certain problems which are not faced by animals. In particular, as Hobbes, Rousseau, and many others have argued, the fear of death is special to human beings alone. Knowledge of personal death, together with other specially human attributes, including the ability to abstract and to use language, lead to a range of related abstract problems concerning the purpose of life, the meaning of death, and the nature of the universe. These problems are, at least in their origins, telic: they are serious, they cannot be avoided, and the lack of solution causes anxiety. The first step consists of thinking about these problems. They are, however, ones which cannot be solved by the methods of thinking which are commonly used in the telic state.

(ii) One of the main aims of paratelic thinking may be to increase arousal and maintain it at a high level. Such thinking often starts with real problems and factual information, but then develops them by means of the various techniques listed. So problems which lead to anxiety in the telic state are exactly the problems which appeal in the paratelic state, because the high arousal which they provoke is now felt as pleasant excitement. These problems include those just described which relate to the fact of personal death. Thinking about these problems in the paratelic state, which constitutes the second step in the development of religious materials, may involve imaginative answers being given, e.g. in terms of the notion of 'God'. It may also involve the playful development of elaborate sets of materials displaying cognitive synergies, narrative (mythology), unexpectedness, and negativism.[1] Negativism here is especially likely to take the form of denial, as in the denial of the inevitability of personal death or the denial of the laws of science (as exemplified by miracles). Synergies are so prevalent in religious materials of different kinds that they will be considered in more detail later in the chapter.

(iii) The playfully invented answers, and other materials produced in the paratelic state, become part of the public domain and immediately or eventually become treated by the individual who produced them, or by others, as 'telic materials', i.e. as if they had been produced and validated by telic thinking processes. The acceptance of these solutions, having 'faith' in them, constitutes the third step, and leads to a lowering of anxiety. This is the point where confusion occurs: the imaginative and even fanciful origin of the materials in the paratelic state is lost sight of, and the materials are taken as serious, veridical, and revelatory.[2] In short, religious phenomena derive, mistakenly, from playful thinking.[3]

It must be emphasized that this analysis is basically at the individual, and inter-individual, rather than the collective level. There is no such thing as a collective telic or paratelic state, except in the sense that a body of people may happen to be together in the same state at a given time. So what is being suggested is that religious ideas, stories, symbols, and so on, originate typically from individuals who are thinking about certain problems in a paratelic state of mind; then other individuals mistake the origin of the ideas and materials, and take them seriously. In due course this material comes to be taken seriously by large numbers of people and is eventually assimilated to the whole of a culture. But this large-scale sociological effect stems from individual and small-scale social psychological processes. The point at which the confusion occurs, when paratelic materials are mistakenly taken 'at their face value' rather than being seen to be the results of playful intellection, vary: at one extreme the confusion may occur on the very first occasion when an individual communicates his thoughts to someone else; at the other extreme a large number of people may understand the playful nature of the material and develop it in the same spirit for a long time, until others start to misinterpret its nature and come to 'believe in it'.

Several question will no doubt already have occurred to the reader about this analysis. The first is that if such problems as the problem of death cause anxiety, how is it that they can ever be thought about by an individual in the paratelic state? Surely the threat posed by these problems will always serve to maintain the telic state while they are being thought about, or induce a reversal to the telic state if the paratelic state is operative when the problems arise? The answer to this requires reference to the ways in which reversals can be brought about.

Each of the three classes of reversal-inducers discussed in earlier chapters may function in such a way as to allow problems which are telic and threatening to be thought about for periods in the paratelic. First of all, take contingency: the opposite of threat is security, and sometimes the environment, including especially the social environment, may create such strong feelings of security that threatening situations can be thought about with equanimity for certain lengths of time. Secondly, there is the effect of frustration. The inability to solve the problems related to death and the meaning of life, while in the telic state, may itself eventually bring about reversal to the paratelic state, where the problems may be solved in fantasy. So, paradoxically, the inability to solve the problem, which is part of the reason why it is threatening, may cause reversal to the paratelic state in which it is temporarily not seen to be threatening, or in which the 'threat' can be enjoyed. Thirdly, there is satiation. If serious telic thinking goes on for too long, a reversal will eventually occur 'spontaneously', and the individual may well continue to think about the same problems, but to do so using the paratelic techniques which have been outlined. It has been assumed here that the individual is thinking about problems related to the meaning of life and death and, while thinking about them, reverses into the paratelic state. However, it may also be the case that the individual is thinking about other kinds of problems while in the paratelic state but, because of the way the train of thought leads or because of some communication to him, problems related to the meaning of life and death may arise in such a way that he does not reverse back to the telic state. Perhaps reversal does not occur in such a case because the context is secure enough to maintain the paratelic state, or the problem of death is only peripheral to the paratelic problem being thought about.

A second question which arises in this: why, if the paratelic material causes *increased* arousal, does it *reduce* the arousal when the material is dealt with in the telic state at the third step of the cycle? The answer is simply that when the ideas involved are believed to be true, they then serve as answers to the questions which originally caused the anxiety at the first step of the cycle; and this reduces the anxiety. Of course, some of the aspects of the material, including its unexpectedness, and use of denial and cognitive synergy, may continue to cause increased arousal. But this is generally a relatively short-term effect. As the material becomes increasingly familiar, so it loses its quality of unexpectedness, and frequent reference to the synergies will eventually reduce their arousal-producing properties so that they become rather like dead metaphors; the opposites in the synergy may no longer even be noticed as being opposite.[4]

The telic development of the material will also be carried out so as to disguise those features, like the synergies, which might cause increased arousal. Finally, when denial of 'obvious truth' becomes the statement of 'obvious truth', which it does when the ideas are believed to be literally true, then the arousal-producing negativistic properties of the ideas no longer exist.

A third question which may have occurred to the reader is this: how is it that the confusion between the results of telic and paratelic thinking occurs in the case of the kind of material that is being discussed here? Why is it that invented paratelic solutions to serious problems *are* taken as being genuine solutions?

One way in which this may occur is that various ideas and other material produced in the paratelic state, in response to telic questions such as those relating to the meaning of death, and displaying synergy, narrative, and so on, are produced by a person or group of persons at one time. These then spread in time and space, over generations, or from one geographical region to another,[5] until the original paratelic genesis is not clear and may even no longer be recognized at all. The material can now be treated in a 'telic fashion' and taken to be true. So the poetry of one generation may become the sacred scripture of the next, the speculative ideas of one groups of scholars the unquestioned doctrines of another, the mythology of one people the accepted truth of their neighbours. It is small wonder that "A prophet is not without honour, save in his own country, and in his own house" (St. Matthew, Chapter 13, verse 57).

In this context it is relevant that people appear to be able to come to believe the most extraordinary invented material when its imaginative origin is not clear to them. An excellent example of this is the panic reaction which occurred in America to the broadcast of H. G. Wells' "War of the Worlds", as dramatized by Orson Welles, and which was studied by Hadley Cantril (Cantril *et al.*, 1940). This celebrated study showed how readily people believe what they are told, however unlikely it it, when paratelic cues are not made clear in the message.

Not only are the paratelic cues to the origin of religious material lost during the transmission of the material over time and space, but the material is frequently of a kind which in any case does not allow of testing when it is dealt with in the telic state. The non-refuteability of religious ideas is a point which, following the logical positivists, has been considered extensively by philosophers and so will not be pursued further here, except to note that many of the events referred to in religious material relate to another world, a supernatural world (Heaven, Olympus, etc.) in which events are not amenable to the sort of truth testing which is possible in the natural world. So the acceptance of the truth of the ideas of a given religion is generally not so much a case of believing that which is patently untrue, although this may occur, as of treating as true something whose truth value cannot be tested, unless the religion does make definite predictions and prophecies about events in the natural world.

The advent of systematic theology in the evolution of a religion represents a major step in the telic justification and development of the paratelic ideas. What theologians do is to rework the 'paratelic material' in such a way as to make it as rationally acceptable as possible. This includes emphasizing the factual, non-invented, part of the material if such exists, e.g. the Exodus of the Jews from Egypt, or the Crucifixion, and developing in a logically consistent way the paratelic ideas, some of which act as axiomatic starting points for the logical deductions. In this way the body of ideas as a whole comes to seem thoroughly reasonable and sensible. This further disguises the paratelic genesis of the material and makes it easier for people to believe: if the weight of prestige and authority which attaches to scholarship and to the written word is thrown behind the ideas, the resulting dogma becomes all the more difficult to reject. This is especially true when a tradition of scholarship and theology has developed over a prolonged period.

Once the material has become accepted by a substantial number of people, there are other forces which come into effect, and which tend to increase still further the acceptability of the material. Thus the more people there are who believe, the easier it becomes for others to believe. In this way a self-generating process is set up. This is no doubt one of the processes which tends to lead to institutionalization, in the form of the development of a church and a priesthood, and this development in turn makes it more difficult for people to question the truth of the ideas and the validity of the various related materials. This is especially true when these other materials, such as architecture, ceremonies, caste-systems, and festivals, have become a relatively permanent part of the way of life of a culture, and part of the 'set' which individuals in that culture unavoidably bring to bear in thinking about the meaning of life and the cosmos. As Berger (1969) among others has argued, religion legitimizes social institutions and socially defined 'reality'.

This would seem to be an example at the cultural level of a phenomenon for which there is now a substantial amount of experimental evidence at the individual psychological level and which has come to be called 'cognitive irreversibility' (viz. Lepper *et al.*, 1970). There is also a great deal of evidence to show that if people are forced to behave in certain ways, then their beliefs will change in such a way as to come into line with their behaviour (e.g. see Kiesler *et al.*, 1969). So if certain kinds of religious behaviour are encouraged in a given culture, e.g. taking part in religious rituals, then one would expect that the religious beliefs of people in that culture would come increasingly to conform to the encouraged behaviour. There are, therefore, many forces which tend to bring about belief in the truth and validity of religious materials, even if some of these materials are fictional in origin, once the development of the materials and their acceptance has reached a certain point. Of course, there are also natural limiting forces too, such as the presence of alternative, competing religions, and the negativistic need which people have occasionally to deny generally accepted ideas.

What has been presented so far in this chapter has been something of an oversimplification, due to the need to express the central argument concerning the genesis of religious material in as clear a way as possible. It is now necessary to add a little complexity to the picture.

(i) It has been argued that the starting point of the genesis of religion consists of certain rather abstract questions which relate to the meaning of personal death, and that these questions are essentially unanswerable in the telic state. There are, however, other problems which, while they are not unsolvable in principle in the telic state in the way in which the problem of the meaning of death is, nevertheless are effectively unsolvable for particular people at a particular time. These are practical problems such as those of how to deal with poverty, hunger, disease, hostile neighbours, and so on. Certain solutions to these can be generated by means of paratelic thought, including imaginative solutions, and these are 'transferred to the telic' where they take the form usually of rituals or observances of various kinds, which it is believed will solve or alleviate the problems concerned. Alternatively, the problems are given some kind of meaning in terms of a larger context, such as in terms of the idea of an after-life, or in terms of the principle of Karma. The three steps in the genesis of religious material in such cases are the same as those described before, the only difference being that the starting point consists of a rather different kind of problem from that indicated before, and that obvious criteria exist in the real world against which the materials produced may be required to be judged at the third step. The answers to such practical problems, as well as to the more metaphysical problems, are of course likely to get mixed together, so that the same ideas or mythology come to apply to both. The more primitive and insecure a society, the more one would expect the religious material to be generated by practical problems related to survival, rather than by more abstract problems of meaning.

If the religious material produced turns out to be inadequate, then this poses a new problem, which can become the first step of a new cycle of development. If new apparently unsolvable practical problems arise, then the materials must be extended to deal with them; if predictions have been made which have been disconfirmed, then the material must be altered in some way to deal with this (viz. Festinger et al., 1956, on disconfirmed prophecy as instanced by the case of Mrs Keech); if the rituals turn out not to solve the problem, such as bringing rain or curing an epidemic, then new rituals must be found, or new ideas developed to show why the ritual did not work in that particular case. Finally, especially with materials that relate to the more metaphysical problems, such material may be found to contain an idea which is difficult to interpret, this constituting a problem which may also become the first step of a new cycle of development. But the development of material in all these cases is not significantly achieved through purposeful telic thinking; it is achieved rather as a by-product of the mediation of paratelic thinking which occurs as part of the three-step process already described.

(ii) Since one of the aims of paratelic thinking may be to increase arousal, reference in narrative to actual events of an arousing nature will often be brought in and mixed with invented events,[6] even when the paratelic thinking has not developed in response to practical problems such as those of disease and poverty. The events of both kinds will then typically be woven into a cohesive narrative which also incorporates explanations for the events.[7] Such real events may include natural calamities like floods, earthquakes, volcanic eruptions, pestilence, famine; strange natural events like eclipses and the appearance of comets; man-made catastrophes like war and persecution; and other awesome phenomena such as the migrations of peoples, and the achievements of great leaders. In other words, part of the corpus of paratelic material may be factual rather than fictional, although the factual material will tend to become exaggerated for effect, especially for the excitement it produces. As already noted, the factual element may also be especially emphasized in the subsequent treatment of the material in the course of telic thinking, in order to increase the verisimilitude of the whole body of material.

(iii) One of the ideas used in the argument so far is that the 'paratelic materials' of one generation or country may become the 'telic materials' of another generation or country. But the reverse process can also occur: the 'telic materials' of one generation of country may become the 'paratelic materials' of another. Thus the genuine religious beliefs of one group of people may be taken as make-believe by another group of people and used playfully in the development of their own 'paratelic materials'. That is, they are not believed to be true by the second group of people, but the ideas, stories and other materials are stimulating and become incorporated, probably in modified form, in their own body of ideas and stories. So mythological and other ideas may not be invented entirely afresh during the paratelic phase of development of the material, but may involve the absorption of suitable stories and ideas from other cultures, including material which is already typically treated in a telic manner in those other cultures. This material may then become subject to the third step of the cycle as already described.[8] If not, then the result is material like much of that associated in our own culture with Christmas, such as Christmas trees, gift giving and decoration with holly, which are derived from genuine beliefs of other people but have, in our own culture, become a playful adjunct to the serious Christian beliefs.

Both of these processes are represented in Fig. 12.1, in terms of four geographical areas, with the 'reverse process' indicated by a dotted line. The problems are assumed to be the same in each area, which might be different regions of the same country, different countries, or even different continents. They might also be taken as representing different generations in the same area.

To give one example of exotic borrowing as part of the process leading to serious religious beliefs, a number of the materials of Christianity bear a striking resemblance to religious ideas already extant in other cultures, quite apart from the Hebrew culture out of which it directly arose. Such materials include the idea of Gods dying and rising again, which was part of the beliefs of ancient Egyptian religion; the idea of incarnation of God in human form in the Hindu religion, e.g. the incarnation of Vishnu as Rama and as Krishna; and the idea of a Saviour-God in Mithraism, a religion which arose in Persia and spread Eastward to India and Westward around the Mediterranean in pre-Christian times. The Christian ideas may well have arisen independently, but the resemblances do at least suggest the possibility that they are derivative. This becomes especially plausible when one considers some of the detailed resemblances of subject-matter. To give examples from Mithraism alone, it seems that there was a Mithraic myth foretelling the appearance of a star which would lead Magi to the birthplace of the saviour, and believers held a regular communion meal of bread and wine (Hinnells, 1971).[9]

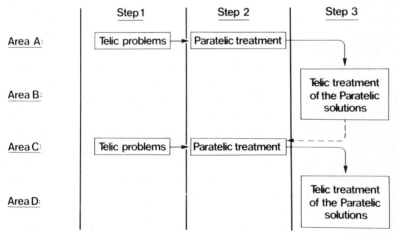

FIG. 12.1 Some ways in which interaction occurs in the development of religious materials in adjacent geographical areas.

(iv) The genesis of religious material has been discussed so far mainly as a social psychological phenomenon: it has been supposed that each of the steps involved in developing a body of material has been taken by people different from those involved at each other step. However, it is possible that all three steps may be taken by the same individual. Indeed some religions, including a number of the great world religions, have started from the ideas and teachings of individual religious leaders, who have personally developed the material through all three steps, even though the material has in each case undergone continuous subsequent evolution along the social psychological lines already outlined. So all three of these steps *can* be taken by one individual: he can invent ideas in a paratelic state in response to 'telic problems', and later treat them in the telic state as if they were true rather than imagined. Some people, therefore, can come to believe their own make-believe materials as well as convincing others of their legitimacy. This may seem to be a large claim, but there are several lines of evidence which suggest that such a phenomenon can or does occur in different forms.

For one thing, there are a number of pathological states in which a failure of what Freud called 'reality-testing' occurs; that is, there is an inability in these cases to distinguish between real and imaginary events. This is a symptom of a range of psychiatric syndromes including organic brain disease, epilepsy, and various functional psychoses in which the symptom takes the form of hallucinations and delusions. The sufferer attributes his experiences to external forces, and communicates them to others as if they had some correspondence in reality. Bodily malfunction due, for example, to fasting or drugs, may have the same kind of effect. So may a pathological loss of memory, e.g. due to concussion, since in many cases this results in confabulation: the patient fills the memory gap with elaborate fabrications which he is subsequently convinced actually occurred. What is being suggested here, then, is that at least some religious leaders may have suffered from certain psychiatric conditions for at least a period during their careers. This is an argument which has been put by a number of writers[10] but which remains controversial, since many people find the idea that major religious leaders have been psychotic or epileptic not only distasteful but also, in the relative absence of substantive data, totally unconvincing.

The reversal theory argument about the development of religious ideas by individuals does not *depend* on psychopathology, although this cannot be excluded as a possible explanation. A totally different line of evidence, but one which is equally relevant to the present argument, concerns the phenomenon of 'illumination'. This has been said by Wallas (1926), and many others since, to occur in much creative thinking. In illumination, an idea comes to the thinker with such suddenness and force that it appears to him as if it has come from outside, rather than being generated by his own thinking. Indeed, some creative thinkers have been convinced that they have simply acted as a medium for external forces. Such a one was Coleridge, who felt that his poem 'Kubla Khan' was dictated to him, and that all he had to do was to write it down. It is presumably easier for the thinker to believe in the truth of such ideas, because he does not feel with any conviction that he himself has invented them.

Finally, there is experimental evidence for self-persuasion in perfectly normal people (viz. Bem, 1965) and some experimental evidence which shows that under certain circumstances an individual can be induced to believe in his own 'false confessions' (Bem, 1966).

(v) Once a church has become established, the telic questions which are at the basis of the genesis of religion are answered by it and this generally reduces anxiety in its members in relation to these questions.[11] This security not only reduces anxiety, however, but may also help to induce the paratelic state, especially during its services or ritual events. This in turn may give rise in the individual to a need for high arousal, which would be felt as excitement, and the church may also attempt to satisfy this need. Therefore many churches tend to do opposite things in their services and in other ways, as through their architecture and art: they lower arousal by providing solutions to certain kinds of problems, and they subsequently raise arousal to provide pleasurable excitement.

How are these opposing aims achieved? One obvious way is by deliberately doing each of these things at different times. Thus during the service, at certain times the congregation is made to feel assured and safe, at other times feelings of excitement are created. This is seen most clearly in evangelical services, where a third mood is typically added at the beginning of the service by the evangelist deliberately producing telic feelings of fear, guilt and uncertainty as a prologue to reassurance: "If you trust in God, he will save you".

More generally, the materials of a successful and well-established church are so varied and rich that those taking part in its services, or otherwise coming into contact with it, will be able to attend to, and take from it, just what they need, hopefully at the moment they need it: feelings of security and lowered arousal from the message, from the assured confidence of the priests, from the expressed belief of the congregation, and from the slow and inexorable forward progression of the ceremony; excitement from the narrative, poetry, processions, music and costumes, and from the drama and sense of occasion which the service engenders. This does not always work, and may readers will no doubt have experienced church services in which anxiety or boredom were experienced rather than relaxation or excitement. But generally, for a thriving church, it must work. Put in a different way, a church is more likely to be successful and to endure as an institution if it is able to satisfy the opposing needs of the telic and paratelic states, rather than those of the telic state alone. Different churches may also, even within one religion like Christianity, have different degrees of emphasis in comparison with each other; some stressing more the basic telic aspects, others the paratelic aspects in which the generation of excitement is one of the main features.

A resemblance will have been noticed between one aspect of this description of a church service and the earlier description of a football match, since they can both generate arousal which is enjoyed within the secure context which they also provide. There is also a resemblance to such phenomena as joking and cigarette smoking, as analysed earlier, in that one aspect of the situation produces security, and the other pleasantly increased arousal. The argument here, however, is that a church service is one degree more complicated than these other situations in that this is only one way in which the situation is regularly experienced. The other is for satisfaction to be derived from experiencing solutions to real problems. In other words, while such events as football matches are generally experienced in the paratelic state, a church service is typically experienced in both the telic and the paratelic states at different times.

There is a final paradox in all this: the material which leads to a feeling of security in the telic state, and which may therefore help to induce the paratelic state, is itself derived from paratelic thinking.

Contrast and Synergy in Religion

The intensity of experience may be enhanced through contrast effects, as discussed in the chapters on synergy, and such effects are ubiquitous in religion. For example, contrast is often used as a rhetorical device in scripture: "But many that are first shall be last; and the last shall be first" (St Matthew, 19:30); "He that is not with me is against me" (Matthew, 12:30); "Blessed are the meek for they shall inherit the earth" (Matthew, 5:3). Contrast also enters frequently into religious narrative: for example the story of St Peter who was the most loyal of the disciples but who denied Christ three times; or the story of St Paul, a great unbeliever who became a great believer; or, to turn to another religion, the story of Gautama Buddha who started off as exceptionally ignorant, being shielded in childhood from knowledge of old age, sickness or death, but who became omniscient.[12] Such contrasts make the stories more striking and exciting. One can find similar contrasts in religious ceremonies and architecture, e.g. the way in which in Islamic mosques the minaret is as high as possible and believers make themselves as low as possible by abasing themselves below it within the mosque. Religious symbols often contain opposites, too, like the Star of David which consists of two overlapping triangles, one pointing to Heaven and one to Earth.

Such simple contrasts may be built into systems, for instance trinities of various kinds which occur in many different religions, especially trinities of Gods. Examples include: the Brahminic trinity of Brahma the creator, Vishnu the preserver, and Shiva the destroyer; the Babylonian trinity of An the Lord of Heaven, Bel the Lord of Earth, and Ea the Lord of the Underworld; the Ancient Egyptian trinity of Osiris the Father, Isis the Mother, and Horus the Son; the Christian trinity of Father, Son, and Holy Ghost. Whereas in a duality only one contrast is involved, in a trinity two, or even three, types of contrast may be brought together so that up to three different contrasts may be obtained from just three elements. Thus in the Egyptian trinity the following three contrasts are derived: male/female, protector/dependant, parent/child.[13]

Synergies as well as contrasts are found widely in religious materials and, indeed, several of the examples of contrast just given could also be interpreted as forms of reversal synergy. Thus in the story of St Paul, one of his characteristics undergoes a crucial reversal so that, especially immediately following the reversal, his identity is seen in two different ways. The same considerations apply to the way in which the stories of St Peter, and of the Buddha, are likely to be experienced.

Loader (1979) has carried out a detailed analysis of the book of Ecclesiastes in the Old Testament, in which he shows how the structure of the book is derived from a number of conceptual polarities resulting in an enormously complex hierarchical pattern of combinations and juxtapositions of opposites, some of which are of a clearly synergic nature. It would be difficult to find a better example of the way in which religious writing tends to make systematic use of contrast and synergy, and Loader's analysis could be said to show that, in reversal theory terms, the whole book is a single, highly elaborate, multiple synergy.

Heidegger's description of a Greek temple (quoted in Steiner, 1978) brings out nicely the way in which religious architecture can embody a variety of synergies. He points out that the building is earth-bound but links the earth to the sky: indeed, from some angles the sky can be seen through it. The colonnades make the temple simultaneously enclosed and open to the outside; and the god of the temple is both displayed and concealed. A gothic church is similarly synergic in a number of respects: the spires point to the sky while the tombs direct one's thoughts below ground; the masonry is made to seem light and soaring while simultaneously retaining the substantiality of stone; the stained-glass windows are at one and the same time windows and pictures, they allow the interior to be seen while drawing attention to themselves; the pulpit is both a piece of furniture and a piece of architecture, e.g. it frequently has a roof of its own and is a kind of building within a building; the altar and the space around it is both the most public and the most private part of the whole edifice.

Turning to the more conceptual level, here are a few examples of identity synergy in Christianity. Christ is seen as being both fully divine and fully human, divine and human forming an opposition pair; related to this he can be seen as the immortal made mortal, and the omnipotent made powerless. The Virgin Mary is a human who, at least to Roman Catholics, becomes super-human, the 'mother of God', while still remaining human. The Holy Ghost is an identity synergy of the personal (soul) and collective. Even the Godhead is a synergy: of unity and, in the form of the trinity, diversity. Christian services involve simultaneously lament, for the death of Christ, and rejoicing that mankind is saved by his death. According to the doctrine of transubstantiation, the bread and wine used in the Communion is not only bread and wine but, at the same time, flesh and blood of Christ. Communion is itself a small act with a profound significance, an everyday event, eating and drinking, with cosmological implications. Where prayer is silent it represents the inaudible made audible (to God); furthermore, all prayer is an attempt to 'control the controller'. These are some of the more obvious synergies in Christianity, but the careful observer should be able to identify many more.

Much of the material created in the paratelic state involves reference to another, supernatural, world. This gives rise to the possibility of having various synergies of the supernatural and natural world, and such synergies appear to occur in all religions. Indeed, there is a word which signifies all such synergies, the word 'sacred'. Something in the natural world is sacred if it also partakes of the supernatural world, and therefore constitutes a natural/supernatural identity synergy. This point of overlap can be a place, e.g. Mecca, or the Wailing Wall in Jerusalem; an object, e.g. a relic, or a sacred scripture; a time, e.g. for Christians, Christmas day; a person e.g. the Dalai Lama to Tibetan Buddhists; or even an animal, e.g. the cow to Hindus. All these synergies create special feelings of awe, reverence and 'magic'. There is a certain resemblance between 'sacredness' synergies and 'make-believe' synergies in that both involve bringing into one identity something which exists in the real world and something which does not; but, as noted in Chapter 7, in one case the non-real world is that of fantasy or imagination, in the other to believers it is that of the supernatural.[14]

Sometimes 'sacredness' synergies may be combined into multiple synergies. Thus the cow in India may represent to Hindus not just a natural/supernatural synergy but also a lower-status/higher-status synergy, since animals are generally taken as lower than humans, but in this case the animal concerned is given a higher status while still remaining an animal.

Another type of synergy which plays a part in religion would appear to be the type experienced by mystics, of a wide variety of religions, who describe their experiences in terms of combined opposites like 'learned ignorance', 'multiplicity in unity', 'the timeless moment', 'dazzling obscurity', and 'joyful pain'.[15]

It should, incidentally, be clear why the sacredness synergies which are experienced by believers are not generally felt to be comic. This is because the synergies of humour are of the real/apparent variety, whereas both parties to sacredness synergies are taken to be real, even if they partake of different forms of reality. Furthermore, synergies are much funnier if they involve an element of the unexpected. But to the adherents of a particular religion, there is such frequent reference to the synergies which enter into their religion that they become highly familiar. Indeed, they may even come eventually to lose their synergic phenomenological properties altogether. However, if a mystical synergic experience occurs of a type which involves 'seeing through' the more superficial aspects of 'reality', then one would expect there to be some element of felt humour in this experience, especially if the experience occurs in a way which involves suddenness and unexpectedness, even shock. It is interesting therefore that the typical response in just that religion which specializes in techniques to gain *sudden* mystical insight of this type and to transmit such insight to others by means of shock effects, namely Zen Buddhism, is laughter. "Zen and the Comic Spirit" by Hyers (1974) deals with this phenomenon in some detail, and does so in a way which would appear to be highly consistent with reversal theory.

Synergies also occur in certain kinds of religious argument. One such argument takes the following general form: if A has a relationship X to B, then B must have a relationship X to A. The second proposition is one type of opposite to the first, and these two opposite propositions are brought together in the argument through the supposition that the first in some sense 'means' the second, that the two are essentially the same. Of course, where a relationship is a symmetrical one, like the relationship 'being married to', then such an argument is valid. But it is used in religion in cases where it is not at all clear that the relationship is necessarily a symmetrical one; here the pattern of the argument, and its synergic quality, appears to give it a certain psychological validity. An obvious example is that of the principle of Karma in Eastern religions, which can be formulated as 'evil produces evil, good produces good'; thus if someone does something cruel to someone else, then something equally cruel will be done to him by someone else, if not in this life, then in a later one.[16] Another example of this type of argument is implicit in the idea of sacrifice, which occurs in many different religions. The general form is: If A gives something demanded by B to B, then B must give something demanded by A to A. Thus if a person sacrifices an animal to a god who demands this sacrifice, then the god must give to the person something which he in turn demands. The Christian interpretation of the crucifixion would seem to embody not only this synergic argument, but two others. If an innocent man (Jesus) can be found guilty, then guilty men (human beings) can be found innocent. If an immortal (God) can be made mortal (Jesus), then mortals (human beings) can be made immortal (have eternal life). The form of the latter two synergic arguments would appear to be somewhat different from that formulated above, and is of the form: if A becomes B, then B becomes A. In this type of synergic argument, in order to make an idea plausible, the reverse of the idea is stated and made a premise of an argument in which the idea that is wanted is the conclusion. Furthermore, if A and B are opposites, as they are in these two examples, e.g. a man is both innocent (A) and guilty (B), then the two separate statements which make up each argument are themselves synergic and the argument as a whole is a form of multiple synergy in each case.

Structural anthropologists like Leach (1976), have also analysed religious materials, including religious arguments, which display what Leach calls 'mythologic', in terms of oppositions and the 'confusion' of such oppositions. Much of reversal theory as presented here in relation to religion is fairly consonant with Leach's analysis. The reversal theory perspective, however, is psychological rather than social anthropological, and the intention in this chapter has been to show how the materials of religion may have arisen out of individual psychological needs and been generated by psychological processes.

Notes on Chapter 12

1. This argument is not intended to have any epistemological status but is purely psychological. Because ideas are produced playfully and imaginatively in the paratelic state, this does not mean that they are necessarily and automatically false in a philosophical or theological sense.

2. The development of contemporary religious cults, as described by Chris Evans (1973), exemplifies this particularly clearly, with the added twist that the fantasy solutions tend nowadays to be influenced by science. Thus the scientology cult stems from the ideas of L. Ron Hubbard, who was originally a science fiction writer, and the ideas of scientology step straight out of science fiction. Similarly, many modern cults are obsessed with pseudo-scientific gadgetry, like the E-meter used by members of the Aetherius society, Reich's Orgone Accumulators and the 'Black Boxes' of George de la Warr.

3. David Miller's book "Gods and Games" (1973) is relevant here since it discusses a variety of relationships which he perceives between religion and play.

4. This may not always be the case, of course, and some kinds of synergies which occur in religious contexts may be experienced by some people with fear and even dread. This is, perhaps, particularly likely to be the case with 'primitive' peoples.

5. A nice historical example of this will be found in Vansina (1973) pp.117-8.

6. Or to put it the other way: invented material is interpolated in factual narrative concerning arousing events. See Vansina (1973), pp.44-5, for a good example of this in relation to an oral tradition.

7. This process in the development of religious narrative has been referred to by Pruyser as 'fabulation' (Pruyser, 1970).

8. Such exotic material may also of course be adopted directly from the foreign culture at the third step, without the intermediation of the second, paratelic, step.

9. Many more examples of 'borrowing' by one religion from another will be found in Eliade (1963), Chapter IX.

10. The classic discussion here is that of William James (1902) in his "Varieties of Religious Experience" (especially lecture I.) For a more modern discussion see Argyle (1958), p.109ff.

11. For certain individuals, however, the church may be far from reassuring but provoke a continual struggle to believe which, during periods when belief is impossible, only compounds the anxiety.

12. An extended analysis of the way in which religious myths embody polarities like light/dark, life/death, good/evil, etc. has been made by Alan Watts in his book "The Two Hands of God" (1963). He gives examples from a wide variety of religious sources.

13. Further examples of the way in which polarity and contrast enter into religious thinking and belief will be found in Lloyd's (1966) discussion of ancient Greek philosophy and religion (viz. especially pp.41 ff), and Capra's (1976) discussion of Taoism (especially Chapter 8).

14. If Lévy-Bruhl's (1923) classic analysis of primitive thinking is correct, however, one would have to conclude that 'sacredness' synergies could not occur in primitive religion. He asserted that primitive people make no distinction between the natural and supernatural, so that forces which would otherwise be called supernatural are to them simply another part of the natural world. This is, however, a thesis which is far from being universally accepted by anthropologists.

15. This list of descriptions is taken from Clark (1972).

16. Other examples of similar arguments, from Indian religion, will be found in Canetti (1962) in a chapter (p.324 ff) suitably entitled 'The Reversal'.

13 The Biological Perspective

Little reference has been made in the course of this book to physiological and biological aspects of behaviour and experience. This 'bracketing out' has been deliberate in order to concentrate on the structure of experience, especially the experience of motivation, and its relation to behaviour. In this chapter, however, these 'brackets' will be 'removed' and the topics dealt with by reversal theory will be considered in a more biological context.

This will be done first of all by looking in a general way at the relationship between the level of physiology on the one hand and, on the other, the levels of mental life, conscious and unconscious, and behaviour. Following this the evolutionary perspective will be adopted and the question asked: What might the survival value have been for man of the processes dealt with by reversal theory? Finally the question will be considered of whether the metamotivational structures identified in the theory are unique to man or whether they cannot also be inferred, however tentatively, to exist in other species.

The Four Levels of Psychology

A complete human psychology would deal with four levels or streams which operate in parallel: behaviour, conscious mental life, unconscious mental life, and physiology, including neurophysiology. It would also deal with their inter-relations. Reversal theory as developed here has been concerned in the main with only two of these—conscious mental life and behaviour—and with the complexity of the relationship between them. But at this final stage all four levels will be considered from the perspective of the theory.

The discussion at this point necessarily takes a philosophical turn, since it cannot avoid dealing with the relationship between body and mind. In this respect the basic problem for reversal theory is that in asserting that experience is, in certain aspects, governed by the cybernetic principle of bistability, the assumption seems to be that mind is a kind of matter. Furthermore, by stating that reversals can be induced by environmental events, it appears to assume that mental events can have physical causes. However, neither of these assumptions is being made; any impression to the contrary, derives from the attempt to avoid making the argument unnecessarily convoluted at earlier points in the book. In fact, our supposition is that the cybernetic principle of bistability operates at the physiological level, and that when environmental events bring about reversals they do so at this level, the mental states being no more than concomitant.

This point needs to be developed a little. It is being assumed that physiological systems, including neurophysiological systems, are elaborate mechanisms which can be thought about cybernetically. Without entering into philosophical discussion about the nature of causality, it is reasonable at a certain level of analysis to see such systems as operating in a lawful, if complex, cause-and-effect manner. Sequences of events in consciousness, however, are difficult to conceive in this way: one mental event cannot be said in the same mechanistic sense to be the cause of another, and experience, as William James pointed out, has a 'flowing' quality. In any case, how can the concept of physical causality be applied to the relationship between non-physical events? The way of reconciling the two universes of discourse adopted here, is to suppose that causation occurs at the physiological level, and that conscious experience merely 'reflects' these physiological events; in other words, mental events are epiphenomena. The epiphenomenal position on the mind–body problem raises other philosophical problems concerning the way in which non-physical events can be 'projections' of physical events; but it is a convenient position to adopt when one is concerned, as a scientist rather than as a philosopher, with the structure and dynamics of conscious experience. One can then talk about experience as if it were directly governed by cybernetic principles, while remaining aware that the relationship is an indirect one, mediated by physiological mechanisms. Reversal theory, however, does not *depend* on this philosophical position; it would no doubt be possible to adopt other positions, including non-dualist positions, without this having any effect on the psychological substance of the theory.

Behaviour is generated by physiological processes in a way which is philosophically unproblematic, and the behaviour itself has a physiological aspect. So, although the way in which experience and behaviour are produced is fundamentally different, physiological processes may nevertheless be seen as underlying and generating both. Volitional mental events, e.g. the conscious decision to do something, may *appear* to generate behaviour, but this would be expected if such events were expressions of the physiological events which did in fact bring about the behaviour. Of course, only *some* central nervous system activities are reflected directly in experience; the other activities, taken together, may be said to constitute the unconscious, or, in the Freudian sense, the unconscious and the preconscious together.

The view being presented here contrasts strongly with that of phenomeno-logical psychologists like Snygg and Combs (Snygg, 1941; Snygg and Combs, 1949), since they argued that behaviour is completely determined by the phenomenological field of the individual. Our own view differs from this in two ways: firstly, we believe that much behaviour is determined by mechanisms which remain unconscious, and which therefore do not enter the phenomenological field; secondly, even that behaviour which *has* conscious concomitants is not seen as being determined by the phenomenological field, but by physiological processes which are reflected in this field.

If mental events *are* epiphenomena of physiological events, then meta-motivational states are epiphenomena of those physiological systems referred to as metamotivational *systems*. (The physiological aspect was implied when the term 'metamotivational system' was introduced in Chapter 2.) These systems have not yet been identified at the physiological level, their existence and their bistable mode of functioning being at present inferred from conscious experience. Metamotivational systems at the physiological level, then, are presumed to play a part in the generation of behaviour and are also partly reflected, epiphenomenally, in conscious experience where they can be recognized as distinct mental states. The behaviour which metamotivational systems play a part in generating, has consequences which feed back and may affect the metamotivational systems: they may change the way in which the system operates at a given moment (e.g. the curve which describes the relationship between arousal and hedonic tone in the arousal-seeking state may be shifted), and they may induce reversals. In contrast, the metamotivational *states* and other aspects of continuing experience, being epiphenomena, do not determine anything, although they may seem to do so to the individual experiencing them. Knowledge of metamotivational states however, allows one to infer which metamotivational systems are operative at a given time.

The situation as a whole is represented in the block diagram given in Fig. 13.1. Here the central block, inside the rectangle indicated with a broken line, represents the level of physiology, i.e. all bodily functioning, including that of the central nervous system (CNS). Some physiological functioning is associated at cortical level in the brain with conscious experience. Consider someone smoking a cigar. Among other things, certain taste buds will be activated, and this will set in motion a train of physiological events which will eventually bring about some activity in the brain, which will be accompanied by the sensation of taste. The same will apply to the generation of sensations in other modalities like smell and touch; other 'higher level' neurophysiological activities which stem from this may be accompanied by other kinds of experiences, like memories of previous occasions when a cigar was smoked. All these neurophysiological events can be presumed to operate in cause-and-effect terms, and are represented by arrows within the central block in the figure. The very last step, however, that of conversion of certain of the activities into their mental concomitants, i.e. of epiphenomenal reflection, is a mystery in the sense that it cannot operate in terms of cause-and-effect as it is generally understood in science. This last step is represented in the figure by dotted arrows which connect the level of physiology to the level of conscious experience. It should be clear that most of the train of physiological events in the CNS remains unconscious, and it is only some of these events—in the case of sensations, those which occur towards the end of the CNS processing—which are associated with conscious experience. In this respect it should be noted that the parts of Fig. 13.1 labelled 'Some cortical events' and 'Unconscious events' cannot be equated respectively with cortical and sub-cortical events, since many cortical processes are unconscious.

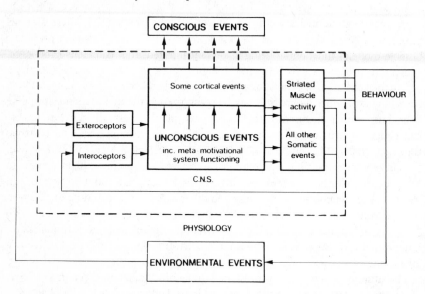

FIG. 13.1   The relationship between conscious events, unconscious events, behaviour and environmental events. All events shown within the rectangle depicted by means of a broken line are physiological events.

In performing the act of smoking, there are a number of parallel sequences of overt behaviour, each of which has a physiological aspect in the sense that it consists of the activities of striated muscles. For example, co-ordinated muscular activity in the arm, hand, and fingers constitute the cigar being put in the mouth; other muscles are involved in the smoke being sucked into the mouth; other muscular activities throughout the body are involved in the maintenance of posture, and so on. Many other somatic events, including those governed by the autonomic nervous system, will also be occurring in parallel. Much of this physiological activity will feed back directly into the CNS through intero-ception. The muscular activity constituting overt behaviour is in turn *brought about* by other sequences of physiological events which are unconscious, and these are represented, as before, by arrows within the central block of the diagram. The relationship between the striated muscular activity and the behaviour is, however, represented by straight lines rather than arrows, to signify that the behaviour is an *aspect* of the activity rather than caused by it. Both conscious events and behaviour then are aspects of certain physiological activities, although they are 'generated' in quite different ways.

To complete the picture shown in Fig. 13.1 the overt behaviour feeds back exteroceptively, through environmental consequences, to the physiological system in which a number of effects may be induced directly, or indirectly, including metabolic change and the changes underlying learning, as well as the processes already discussed underlying sensation and perception. The nature of these effects depends in some measure on environmental contingencies, e.g. in the case of the cigar, on such factors as its size and quality, and whether it remains alight or not. So behavioural events, in this way, feed back indirectly through environmental circumstances, into the physiological system. In contrast, conscious events do not feed back into the physiological system. If the cigar goes out, it may seem that a mental decision to relight it feeds back into the physiological system, which then generates the subsequent behaviour; but this decision is in reality mediated by brain processes, and not by the experience which merely reflects these neurophysiological processes. On this view conscious events do not play an integral part in the functioning of psychological systems, but are a type of by-product. This point is brought out by the structure of Fig. 13.1.

It should now be possible to see more clearly that out of the four parallel levels of analysis-the physiological including neurophysiological, the conscious, the unconscious and the behavioural-the pivotal level is the physiological. Conscious events are seen as epiphenomena of some, but not all, neurophysiological events; behaviour is seen as an aspect of some, but not all, physiological processes; and the unconscious simply consists of all the physiological functioning in the CNS which is not represented by conscious events.

Where do metamotivational systems fit into all this? As has already been argued, metamotivational systems are neurophysiological systems. Even if a system like arousal-seeking, or arousal-avoidance, involves an interpretation of *felt* levels of physiological variables, this interpretation is itself a physiological process, albeit one involving the higher levels of the brain. The functioning of metamotivational systems is itself unconscious, but the results of this functioning directly affect those brain processes which have conscious concomitants. In other words, as a result of unconscious metamotivational processes, the individual's phenomenal field has, for example, a certain structure with respect to goals and means-to-goals; or he is consciously aware that increasing arousal is pleasant, or decreasing felt negativism unpleasant. In this respect the operation of metamotivational systems is no different from that of other unconscious neurophysiological systems which affect conscious brain processes.[1]

It is worth remarking that an outside observer may be aware of many pieces of behaviour, or aspects of behaviour, of which the individual who is being observed is not aware at that moment: gesture, posture, facial expression, unnecessary movement, and the like. To this extent the observer may have an advantage over the person oberved, since he knows something which the latter does not know about himself. This knowledge may be trivial; on the other hand, especially if patterns are observed over time, it may give some insight into the individual's personality which is denied to that individual. This fact has been used in certain kinds of individual therapy, like Gestalt therapy, and in some kinds of family therapy. At the same time, however, the person being observed may be aware of much which may not be expressed in behaviour, or not expressed in behaviour in an unequivocal form. This includes in particular the metamotivational states which obtain at a given moment, of which he is aware in the sense that, for example, he knows if increasing arousal is pleasurable. In this respect the casual outside observer is at a distinct disadvantage, and understands much less about the individual, who has private access to this information, than the individual himself does. For reasons given in the earlier discussion of psychopathology and therapy, it may be necessary for the outside observer, especially if he is a therapist, to identify the individual's metamotivational states (and therefore operative metamotivational systems), at a given time, or in given types of situation. The most obvious way of trying to do this, at least in the clinic, is through appropriate questioning. In the psychological laboratory, other methods can be used to attempt to identify metamotivational states, such as the use of questionnaires or suitable mood-adjective check lists. It is also conceivable that certain physiological measures may turn out to serve as useful indices.[2] Furthermore, some of the aspects of behaviour of which the person behaving is unaware, like gesture or facial expression, may give clues to metamotivational states. All these approaches to the identification of metamotivational states/ systems are currently being investigated.

The Biological Function of Metamotivational Systems

Let us now take an evolutionary perspective and consider what biological advantage might derive from being equipped with pairs of opposite metamotivational systems. At this stage all reference will be to metamotivational *systems* rather than *states*, to avoid the awkwardness of seeming to imply that mental states can be operated on directly by external physical processes.

Although metamotivational systems are not related on a one-to-one basis to different kinds of behaviours, nevertheless there are tendencies for some kinds of behaviour to be performed more often in one system than another, or under given circumstances to be performed more successfully in one system rather than another. Thus it is reasonable to suppose that various classes of play behaviour are more likely to derive from the operation of the paratelic than the telic system. Similarly, behaviour which is deviant in terms of the norms of a group is more likely to be associated with the negativistic system than behaviour which clearly conforms to the norms. To the extent that a type of behaviour has survival value for the individual or his group, the system which tends to give rise to such behaviour will also have survival value.

Generally, of course, it is easy to see what the biological function of the telic system is for humans, since the pursuit of goals that are biologically essential, such as avoidance of danger, or search for food, are typically carried out by this system. Similarly, it is not difficult to understand the biological function of the conformist system, since it usually allows these essential biological goals to be pursued with more success through teamwork than would otherwise be possible; and in any case it minimizes dangerous and unnecessary conflict between individuals in a social group. Since each of these systems is paired with an opposite system which has survived through evolution, however, it is wise to assume that the opposite systems also have biological functions and, in certain circumstances, may aid survival. This is not to say that all biological systems which survive, necessarily have a useful biological role. Some systems may be vestigial remnants of systems which were useful once, but which no longer perform any useful role. Other systems may be irrelevant, or even harmful, but have evolved in a way which is inextricably linked with systems whose usefulness more than outweights their disadvantages. This may be the case with the paratelic and negativistic systems. Since these two systems seem to play such a central role in human activity, however, it seems more reasonable to suppose that on the whole they do directly contribute something to man's biological fitness. One is therefore forced to ask what the nature of this contribution might be. In so doing one is addressing the question, raised in the first chapter, of the purpose of gratuitous and paradoxical behaviour.

Let us turn first to the paratelic system. Although, when this system is operative, the individual may not feel that his behaviour is directed to essential goals, nevertheless, in a biological sense his behaviour may have a variety of functions which genuinely serve important biological purposes. (Conversely, of course, certain behaviours mediated by the telic system, although seeming essential to the individual, e.g. performing certain cultural rituals, may in fact be biologically inessential. In other words, the relationship between 'essentialness' in the experiential and biological senses is far from perfect.) Here are five different ways in which the paratelic system might be thought to confer biological advantages.

(i) Although it is not always correct to infer the operation of the paratelic system from the occurrence of behaviour of a type which is usually categorized as 'play', since the goals of 'play' can sometimes be experienced as extremely serious, nevertheless it can be assumed that play *is* more typically mediated by the paratelic than the telic system. Indeed, in its purest forms, play seems to be an obvious expression of the functioning of the paratelic system. So, if play serves any biological purpose, its production could constitute one of the functions of the paratelic system. One idea concerning play, which can be traced back at least as far as Karl Groos (1898, 1901), is that play allows the child to practise a variety of behaviours which will later be useful in adult life. This idea of the biological function of play has been taken up by a number of writers, and Piaget's (1951) interpretation of play extended it to practice with the manipulation of symbols, as well as objects. The general idea can be restated in terms of the paratelic system, by saying that if activities are undertaken for their own sakes, then they are more likely to be repeated continually than if they are used solely to achieve a goal; in the course of such repetitions, skills are developed which allow essential goals to be achieved more readily when the need to do so arises in later life. This would be true both for goals which require skilled behaviour and those which require skilled thinking. A further feature of paratelic activity is the construction of make-believe synergies, and the child may learn from this too; e.g. by pretending to be an adult, the child can begin to learn how to become an adult, as Claparède (1911) was one of the first to point out.

The paratelic dominance of children, then, would appear to have a biological justification, and be likely to be genetically programmed, rather than simply being a reaction to the security generally provided for children by their parents. This security, however, to the extent to which it is objectively real as well as subjectively experienced, does provide an additional advantage; this is that the skills that are learned in the paratelic state are perfected under conditions which minimize risk in the event of failure.

This 'practice function' of the paratelic system also applies to adults, and indeed the extent to which adults engage in play can be regarded as a form of neoteny which has proved advantageous for the human species as a whole.

(ii) Another function of the paratelic system, especially in adults, may be to provide an alternative mode of problem-solving which can be brought to bear on problems which have not found a solution during telic-based thinking. If the problem is one which requires a new approach for a successful solution to be obtained, then paratelic thinking may be more effective than telic thinking. There are a number of reasons for supposing this to be the case: the spontaneity of the paratelic thinking; the pleasure of playing with ideas for their own sakes, and following them wherever they lead; the cultivation of novelty and unexpectedness in interactions with the environment, and, for the same purpose of arousal-seeking, the openness to chance effects; and the relatively peripheral nature of goals in the phenomenal field making it easier to be sensitive to stimulation and information from a variety of sources. In all these ways the paratelic system is likely to throw up ideas of a more diverse and unusual kind than would be expected from the comparatively rigid goal-oriented approach characteristic of the telic system. Viewed differently, if the problem is one which needs some 'set' to be overcome, then one may suppose that this set is more likely to be overcome by the paratelic than the telic system. (The process of overcoming set has been studied and described in various ways by different writers, viz. Luchins, 1942, on Einstellung; Duncker, 1945, on 'functional fixedness'; Wertheimer, 1961, on 'recentering'; and more recently, De Bono, 1968, on 'lateral thinking'). Hence paratelic thinking is likely to be more original than telic thinking. The telic system, however, will still be necessary for the systematic amassing of information relevant to the problem, and for evaluating solutions thrown up in the course of paratelic thinking. As argued earlier in relation to 'brainstorming' (Chapter 3), the most effective problem-solving seems to require some kind of alternation between the telic and paratelic systems.

Another way in which the paratelic system may help in dealing with problems is by providing fantasy solutions to problems which are otherwise unsolvable. These fantasy solutions, as was argued in the chapter on religion, may then be adopted by the telic system as genuine. Although this may not directly aid survival, and in some cases will even turn out to be detrimental, especially if they bring to a premature end the search for answers to questions which *are* answerable, they may indirectly have some survival value by giving the individual a basis for making practical decisions, rather than vacillating in situations where any decision about which action to undertake is preferable to none.

(iii) If one considers the various techniques which adult or child may use to gain arousal in the paratelic system (see Chapter 5), it will be realized that many of them are likely to increase the individual's knowledge of the world or of himself, and to enrich his experience and broaden his outlook; in short, to provide him with information and insight which he would not otherwise have gained. This is clearly the case with deliberate risk-taking, and with the use of novelty and uncertainty to gain arousal. Similarly, in attempting to overcome his natural physical limitations, the individual is likely to discover much not only about the potentialities of his environment, but more importantly about his own abilities and capacities—much which otherwise might have remained unsuspected. In a rather different way, the use of empathy to gain arousal through parapathic emotions, e.g. through fiction of all kinds, brings the individual into contact with perspectives and experiences of which he would otherwise have remained ignorant, and may even give him special insight into the different needs and ways of thinking of other people, which will make him a more socially competent member of his community.

(iv) Perhaps the most general effect of paratelic activity is to promote change in the individual. Much of this change will involve improvement in the ways already noted: through practising skills, discovering novel solutions to problems, and learning new information. Much of it will also involve improving the individual's environment, through the invention of new techniques to overcome limitations, for example, which have the potential of enhancing his ability to survive. All this can occur in the telic system too, but the telic system is essentially conservative: if something works then there would be no reason for changing it, and hence no stimulus for further change or improvement. As Peckham (1965) has argued:

> "There must . . . be some human activity which serves to break up orientations, to weaken and frustrate the tyrannous drive to order, to prepare the individual to observe what the orientation tells him is irrelevant, but what may very well be highly relevant" (p.xi).

Peckham equates this with artistic activity, but it can be seen as applying to all activity generated in the paratelic system.

(v) Change in itself is not necessarily good, of course, and the paratelic system must often provoke problems for the individual which would not otherwise have arisen. The preference for uncertainty, for instance, may quite unnecessarily put previous accomplishments at risk; and playful risk-taking may bring about genuine danger which could have been avoided. In such cases, things may turn out badly for the individual. Nevertheless, the paratelic characteristic of inducing and amplifying change, be the effect good or bad in particular cases, does in general help the individual to become more 'familiar with novelty', and more accustomed to change than he otherwise would have been. In turn, this helps him to cope in environments that produce sudden, unexpected and uncontrollable changes, to which he must adapt quickly in order to survive.

The advantages of the paratelic system apply not only to the individual, but also to his community. The survival of the community depends among other things on its members being able to develop suitable skills, solve new problems, build up a common fund of knowledge, promote change, and cope with sudden environmental change when it occurs; special contributions to all of these are provided by the paratelic system in the five ways just discussed. Two further potential advantages accrue at the community level. The first is implied by Huizinga (1949), who suggested in his book "Homo Ludens" that play, by providing 'experiments in living', can be seen historically to have been essential to the development of cultural institutions. Secondly, it is useful for a community to number among its members some who are highly paratelic dominant, and whose preferred level of arousal in the paratelic state is extremely high. It is presumably from the ranks of such people that it finds most of its more daring professional hunters, warriors, explorers, and pioneers; and although the operation of the paratelic system may decrease the chance of personal survival for such adventurers, it increases the chance of survival for the community as a whole. (On the other hand, if there is nowhere left to explore, no animals to be hunted, and no wars to be fought, the presence of these people in the community may become a source of continual internal threat which will ultimately militate against its successful survival.)

Turning now to the negativistic system, one can see that this system too may have a number of important biological functions. The first of these is developmental. As discussed in Chapter 9, children generally seem to go through a period, some time between the age of one-and-a-half and three-and-a-half, which has been described as the 'negativistic period', and which is characterized by frequent negativistic behaviour. It is reasonable to assume that the negativistic system underlies such behaviour and that this system is dominant during this period. Since this period seems to occur in most children, one must infer that it has some biological significance, and that it contributes in some way to the process of normal psychological development.

One contribution of negativistic behaviour may be that it plays an essential part in the child's acquisition of a concept of himself as an entity distinct from the rest of the world, i.e. in the child's development of a concept of 'me' in the sense discussed in the chapter on negativism. Obviously, it is not through negativism alone that a child develops such a self-concept, and indeed it is not inconceivable that he is born with at least some kind of proto-concept of himself. A number of factors no doubt contribute to the full development of this concept. These include the early exploration of his own body and the recognition of a relationship between movement of the body and volition, an increasing ability to distinguish between external and internal sources of stimulation, a developing awareness of the skin surface as marking a boundary between himself and his environment, and later on the recognition of his own voice and of his self-image in reflecting surfaces, and his gradual mastery of the use of the words 'I' and 'You'. Negativism at about the age of two-and-a-half may play a part in completing this process by helping to establish three essential constituents of a sense of personal identity: namely, the feelings of personal autonomy, distinctiveness, and continuity. By refusal to do what is required by others, the child can demonstrate to himself in the clearest possible manner that in the last analysis he is an *autonomous* agent. Similarly, if understanding what something is depends on understanding what it is not (see Chapter 6), then oppositeness of behaviour can help the child to discriminate himself from others, and to define himself as a *distinctive* person. By occasionally opposing those forces for change which come from outside, he can help to establish a feeling of personal *continuity*.[3]

As a result of this, the child should, as well as feeling more autonomous, actually come to be more independent in the sense of starting to make deliberate decisions for himself about his behaviour. From the biological point of view there may be some significance in the age at which this occurs, since in the natural state there may on average be a two to three year interval from the birth of one child to the birth of the next, and following this it would be adaptive for the mother to be able to pay most of her attention to the newborn.[4]

There are normally limits to such independence at this age, and negativism may have the additional function of allowing the child to discover what these limits are. In terms of the child's developing sense of personal identity, it is important for him to discover just how powerful he is, and by testing his parents and other adults in a variety of situations, through negativistic behaviour, he can make a good assessment. If it is true that in order to feel secure the child must know what the limits to his behaviour are, then testing the limits through negativism might serve this function too. A totally different function of negativism arises where parents are behaving inadequately as controllers; in this case, by pushing them further and further, and increasingly provoking them, the child should eventually force them into an adequate parental, controlling, role. So negativism can also be a biological mechanism for releasing parental controlling behaviour in situations where this is insufficient, or even totally lacking. Paradoxically then, negativism may in different circumstances act in such a way as to help the child to be more independent, and also help to elicit parental control. There is no necessary contradiction here, since parents' injunctions can be clear and unyielding in some areas, e.g. in relation to potentially dangerous activities, while allowing the child to be independent in a wide range of other areas, e.g. in relation to how he or she chooses to dress.

Adolescence can also be considered to be a period of negativism, and the functions of negativism during this later period appear to be much the same as those in the earlier period. That is, it helps the individual to find out who he is, to establish a greater degree of independence from parents and other adults, and to test once again the limits of his powers. Both periods of negativism are similar in that they mark important stages of transition in psychological development, the first marking a transition between babyhood and childhood, and the second marking a transition between childhood and adulthood. If the argument here is valid, then it is not by chance that these two periods of transition are characterized by negativism; rather, the negativism plays an essential role in achieving transition in each case. The difference between the two periods is that at the earlier period the transition takes place at a relatively concrete level: the child learns that he is an autonomous physical entity, capable of acting independently in a variety of concrete situations, and he discovers the limits to his actions. At the later period, the transition takes place at a more abstract level. (Piaget has called adolescence the 'metaphysical age'.) The adolescent discovers, through negativism, a new kind of autonomy: that of being able to make up his own mind on a variety of issues. This independence becomes an important part of his sense of his identity. He is now able to define himself by making decisions as to where he stands in relation to values, morals, religious and political beliefs, attitudes and tastes of all kinds. In doing this he tends to take up exaggerated positions which, by making a strong contrast between what he is for and what he is against, allow him to define himself more clearly than he would otherwise have been able to do. Furthermore, through negativistic behaviour, he is able to discover the limits to his freedom to think and say what he likes. In this respect, the extremeness and contrariety of his views allow him to test just how far he has the ability and character to sustain an independent line both in abstract argument and, more importantly, in the course of everyday life where such views place him in conflict with parents and other authorities.

So the negativistic system, like the paratelic system, may be said to play an essential role in normal psychological development. Like the paratelic system, however, the negativistic system continues to be available to the adult, perhaps as a form of neotony, and, like the paratelic system, it is possible to discern some advantages to the adult in the possession of such a system. For example, if the negativistic system helps the individual during development to gain a sense of personal identity it may, in the same way, help him as an adult to maintain this sense when it is threatened for some reason.

Perhaps the main advantage to the adult, however, is that it helps him to behave on occasion in an original and creative way, and in the process to solve problems which might otherwise remain resistant to solution. As Picasso is said to have remarked: "Every act of creation is first of all an act of destruction."[5] In other words, implicit in any new approach to a problem is a rejection of previous approaches and previous assumptions; by the same token, a tendency to reject accepted ideas in a given problem area must increase the chance of originality. A similar argument concerning the importance of negativism in original thinking has been put by Dreistadt (1970) in a paper entitled "Reversing, using opposites", negativism, and aggressiveness in creative behaviour in science and philosophy". He points out that originality in science and philosophy can arise not only from originating an idea which is the opposite of one that is widely accepted at the time, but also from originating an idea which is the reverse or opposite of the thinker's own previous ideas; in other words, as a form of self-negativism. He gives many detailed examples of such negativism and self-negativism from the fields of physics, mathematics, psychology and philosophy. He also extends his argument in a rather Hegelian way by pointing out that, having generated a reverse idea, the creative thinker often attempts to synthesize this idea with that which it negates in a new, more global, concept or theory.

From this point of view, the negativistic and paratelic systems supplement each other as 'amplifiers of originality'. Since negativism is often used as a technique to gain arousal, the negativistic and paratelic systems frequently occur in conjunction; for instance, the individual playfully denies common assumptions and asks himself what would happen if such-and-such were *not* the case. In this way ideas may be thrown up which would not otherwise have occurred, and some of these may occasionally constitute the solutions to problems, or lead to new and viable ways of looking at various problem areas. The production of synergies by the paratelic system might also occur at times through negativism. Thus the construction of a make-believe synergy might occur by the individual playfully *denying* what he perceives and substituting in imagination some opposite quality, e.g. imagining that something small is very large, or that something cheap is very expensive. This is not to say that all make-believe synergies, or all synergies of all kinds, derive from negativism; no doubt synergies are generated in a variety of ways.[6] But this points to a role which negativism might be expected to play on occasion, and which bears at least some similarity to the process discussed by Dreistadt (cited above) in which opposites are synthesized in creative thinking. This process may also be related to what Rothenberg (1971) has named 'Janusian thinking', which he defines as "the capacity to conceive and utilize two or more opposite or contradictory ideas, concepts, or images simultaneously" (p.197).[7]

The negativistic system, like the paratelic, also helps to initiate and maintain change in the individual and his community. From a more sociological and historical perspective, it can be argued that negativism has been one of the motive forces behind cultural evolution, and, by continually providing alternative directions for development, has helped many cultures to adapt to changing needs and, therefore, to survive. In this respect, negativism may have played something like the role in the evolution of different cultures which mutations are supposed, by evolutionists, to have played in the evolution of different species: in both cases variation is produced which then becomes subject to selection by a changing environment. The anthropologist Victor Turner (1969, 1978) has suggested that certain symbolic and ritual activities which involve reversals of normal ways of doing things, activities which he refers to as 'anti-structural', have an innovative potential for society. Sutton-Smith (1972) has further emphasized the creative role of such activities by referring to them as 'proto-structural' rather than 'anti-structural'; the similarity of all this to the view of Huizinga on play is notable. What is being suggested here is that not only anti-structural but all negativistic behaviours and ideas serve a purpose in the evolution of society. By initiating change of various kinds within a society, negativism can help that society to adapt to change which comes from without.

This can all be stated concisely in terms of a cybernetic law, due originally to Ross Ashby (1956), which is known as the Law of Requisite Variety. This says that for a system to be able to adapt to disturbance, it must have at least as much variety as the source of the disturbance. (Variety is defined rigorously within cybernetics, but the meaning remains essentially the same as the everyday meaning.) The negativism of individuals helps to ensure that there is, in the society which they constitute, a variety of opposing opinions, ways of doing things, and organizations. The effect of this is that their society has sufficient richness and complexity to meet and adapt to the challenge of a changing environment.

None of this means that the negativistic system always generates behaviour which is functional, directly or indirectly, for the individual, his family, social group, or society. Much negativistic behaviour is undoubtedly detrimental. This is especially true when the individual displaces his negativism onto himself, as in masochism or asceticism for example; and it is ironic that the development of the self-concept, the existence of which is a necessary prerequisite for self-negativism, is itself brought about at least in part through negativism. This analysis removes some of the mystery from certain kinds of paradoxical behaviour, by showing how two features of human nature, the possession of a self-concept and a negativistic system, both of which have individual biological utility, may on occasion become maladaptive in conjunction. Similar considerations apply to the paratelic system: although on balance this system has proved itself to be advantageous and, indeed, has made an essential contribution to man's adaptiveness, nevertheless much behaviour performed by the paratelic system may be totally irrelevant to biological needs, either in the short or long term. Furthermore, behaviour produced by the paratelic system, especially in connection with risk-taking, and with the use of novelty and uncertainty to gain arousal, may on occasion be more harmful than helpful to a given individual or his group. Much paradoxical behaviour arises in this paratelic way, including playing dangerous sports, gambling, and many forms of hooliganism. Gratuitous and paradoxical behaviour, therefore, are the price which has to be paid for the availability of two systems which in other respects appear to have conferred important advantages on mankind. Both the negativistic and the paratelic systems have made contributions, in the various ways outlined here, to the survival of the human species and to the unique development of human culture. However, whether they will continue to be advantageous in an age of dwindling resources and space, and of the continuing threat of nuclear annihilation, must be open to some doubt.

Metamotivational Systems in Animals

Since metamotivational states are defined in terms of subjective experience, one can never know for sure whether such states exist in animals other than man. However, despite the difficulties already emphasized of making inferences about metamotivation from behaviour, it is still possible to look at animal behaviour to see if there are any signs that the pairs of states postulated by reversal theory might be inferred, however tentatively, to exist in species other than man. In doing so, one is inverting the usual question in psychology of how far one can generalize from animals to humans, and asking instead how far one can generalize, in this respect, from humans to animals.

Since it is not intended to raise the question of whether animals may be said to have conscious experiences,[8] the question will be put in terms of the possible existence of pairs of metamotivational *systems* in animals. Formulating the question in terms of systems which are assumed to be physiological, has the potential advantage that if metamotivational systems are ever identified at the physiological level in man, it will be possible to search for analogous physiological systems in animals. Then if animals *are* assumed to have conscious states, the existence of metamotivational states based on such physiological systems would be a reasonable, if untestable, inference.

For the present, however, one is restricted to evidence from behaviour alone. Obviously it will not be possible to reach any definite conclusions, but it is possible to give examples of some types of animal behaviour which at least give pause for thought. Of most interest is evidence which might conceivably be taken to imply the existence of the paratelic system and the negativistic system, since the existence of something like a telic system and a conformist system seems already to be implicit in most studies of animal behaviour.

Firstly, let us consider possible evidence for the paratelic system and the related arousal-seeking system, and then turn to the question of negativism.

1. Activity for its own sake

If an animal persists in behaving in a given situation in a way which does not appear to be instrumental in achieving some end beyond itself, and which cannot be construed as consummatory behaviour in any obvious biological sense, then the behaviour may be said to be performed for its own sake, and to be 'self-reinforcing'. One way of interpreting such behaviour would be to say that it occurs when the paratelic system is operating.

Examples of such behaviour come in a number of forms. Perhaps the simplest case is that of behaviour which is performed in the apparent absence of any extrinsic reward. A well-known example here is that of Harlow (1950) who showed that monkeys will learn to disassemble mechanical puzzles without any reward other than that deriving from the task itself. In other words, manipulative activity in this case is self-reinforcing. Interestingly, he also showed that if a food reward is added to the situation the learning is not more efficient, but the general behaviour displayed by the monkeys changes: little interest is shown in the puzzles themselves, and they are now used solely as means for obtaining food. In reversal theory terms, it looks as if a paratelic to telic reversal might have occurred.

There are also experiments which show that one kind of behaviour can function as a reward for some other, instrumental kind of behaviour. For example, Kagan and Berkun (1954) showed that rats will learn (in this case to press a Skinner-type bar) in order to be able to run for half a minute in an activity wheel; this running activity is therefore reinforcing in itself.

Another line of evidence which points to behaviour being performed for its own sake comes from experiments which were not designed to show this, but in which the experimenter reports that the animal tends to disregard the supposed 'reinforcer', e.g. food, but continues with the 'instrumental' activity. In these cases the consummatory behaviour occurs perfunctorily, or is delayed, despite deprivation, and the conclusion must be that the 'instrumental' behaviour is more reinforcing than the primary reinforcers provided on these occasions. In Köhler's classic work on insight learning in chimpanzees (Köhler, 1926), for instance, the impression is imparted that when his experimental animals had learned a new skill, they were often more interested in trying it out than in eating the fruit obtained by it. Another more definite example of this kind is provided in the work of Liddell, on the effects of thyroid removal on the performance of sheep learning an alternating maze. He reported that his non-thyroidectomized sheep, on reaching the food box at the end of the maze, would often eat little or nothing and then rush off for the next trial. "We may conclude that the running of the maze was a self-rewarding activity which was also self-perpetuating" (Liddell, 1954).

A similar kind of behaviour has been drawn to the author's attention by Susan Sara of the University of Louvain. She has noticed in her work that when a rat has learned a maze, it sometimes refuses to enter the goal box and eat the food but, having assured itself that the food is there, returns down the maze and runs around for a period. For example, in one experiment she carried out with Wistar rats using a 6-unit binary choice modified K maze, just over 10% of the rats (7 out of a batch of 60) performed in this way on the fourth or fifth trial (pers. comm.). It is difficult to find any explanation for this gratuitous maze-running behaviour, other than that the rat is performing it for its own sake. It is notable in these cases that the rat appears to assure itself first that the food is there. A reversal theory interpretation might be that the paratelic system is induced in the rat through the assurance that there is food available and that the situation is in this respect 'safe', with the result that the maze-running behaviour is enjoyed in itself.

Some writers have noticed what appears to be a similar phenomenon in operant situations. For example, as Jensen (1963) found originally, and as Carder and Berkowitz (1970) and Davidson (1971) have also reported, rats who have learned to press a lever for food reward continue to press the lever when a supply of 'free food' (which is not dependent on lever pressing) is also made available to them. This differs from the examples of the last two paragraphs in that here the availability of food is independent of the activity; but the similarity lies in the fact that the animal performs more than is necessary. Morgan (1974) has pointed out that there are difficulties in claiming that such behaviour as that reported by Jensen and others demonstrates that bar-pressing is rewarding in its own rights since, among other things, if the response is not rewarded by the delivery of a pellet the rat quickly gives up. But it is perhaps misleading to conceive of the rat's activity as consisting just of bar-pressing; it would be more meaningful to think of it as 'pellet-obtaining by means of bar-pressing', the whole cycle being an end in itself rather than the isolated bar-pressing alone. Similarly, in the Liddell experiment it is presumably not running itself which is more rewarding than food eating, but running-through-the-maze. In arguing this way one is adopting the action theory perspective referred to in Chapter 1, and asserting that the rat's behaviour consists in actions which are meaningful to the animal, rather than in a series of isolated responses which can be abstracted from their context.

A further type of evidence comes from studies which show that instrumental behaviour will continue in rats and some other animals even when the animal is satiated, e.g. is no longer hungry. (Such satiation can be defined in operational terms as the animal not performing the consummatory behaviour of eating, even in the presence of food.) This evidence has been reviewed by Morgan (1974) in the paper already cited. He describes the phenomenon as 'resistance to satiation'. This differs from the situations described in the last three paragraphs in that, in the situations described there, the animal typically does engage in at least some consummatory behaviour, even if it is delayed, less than it might have been, or temporarily rejected in favour of instrumental activity. In the 'resistance to satiation' situations the animal, by definition, carries out no consummatory behaviour at all. In one class of experiments which Morgan reviews (e.g. Kimble, 1951) the animals are taught a particular instrumental behaviour when deprived, and then tested when satiated. In another class of experiments (e.g. Anderson, 1941) the instrumental behaviour is itself learned under satiation. Morgan argues that the instrumental behaviour in such cases continues, because of the previously reinforcing effects of consummatory *behaviour*. That is, the instrumental behaviour continues because the reinforcement of the lever-pressing, say, has previously come from the consummatory behaviour of eating rather than from the food. Satiation of hunger is then not directly relevant, although non-reinforcement by the consummatory behaviour should lead, eventually, to extinction of the instrumental responses. The alternative explanation which might be suggested by reversal theory, is that in the absence of an overriding biological need, such as the need for food, there is a reversal from the telic to the paratelic system, and while the latter system is operative the animal performs instrumental behaviour for its own sake, choosing that behaviour which is suggested by the facilities available, and the skills which have been acquired. From this point of view, use of the term 'instrumental behaviour' would be misleading to refer to such cases: the activity would be self-justifying and self-reinforcing and not the instrumental means to some reinforcement over and above itself. One part of Morgan's argument which is consonant with reversal theory, however, is that consummatory and instrumental activities are not necessarily determined by a single intervening 'drive' variable.

As well as all these lines of evidence from the laboratory, there is also evidence from ethology concerning activities which appear to be irrelevant, at least to immediate biological goals, and which some ethologists have been prepared to label as 'play'. Lorenz (1966), for example, studied hunting cats given one mouse after another. He noted that as satiety built up, the instrumental behaviour of killing the mice continued for a time, even though the killed mice were not eaten; later, even the act of killing ceased, but the instrumental behaviour of stalking continued. This behaviour seems similar to the 'resistance to satiation' behaviour found in laboratory studies. Often behaviour categorized by ethologists as 'play', occurs in situations in which consummation is not possible. For example, the animal is incapable of completing the behaviour: thus segments of mating behaviour may be performed by some mammals before they are sexually mature (Beach, 1951). Or the animal performs the behaviour in a context which does not provide any obvious immediate biological goal towards which the behaviour could be directed, as in the locomotor play of chimpanzees described by Lawick-Goodall (1976). As Loizos (1966) has pointed out, play in animals typically involves a fragmentation of behaviour in which segments of complete sequences are performed, often repetitively, and sometimes combined in non-functional sequences, so that the behaviour cannot lead to an outlet in normal consummation. A further feature of play in animals has been noted by some ethologists. This is that special metacommunicative signals are used to make clear to other members of the same species that the behaviour should not be taken in its 'normal' sense but is only 'playful'. Bateson (1954), who originally introduced this idea, based it on his own observations; but many examples have subsequently been catalogued by other investigators. For example, a number of signals of this type have been observed in monkeys, including a special 'play face', and actions like a slap and a quick retreat (Dolhinow, 1976). A 'play face' has also been noted by Loizos (1976) in the chimpanzee, together with panting behaviour. From the point of view of reversal theory, the function of these play signals would be to induce or maintain the paratelic system in all participants during the course of interactions which would otherwise, in the absence of these signals, involve the induction or maintenance of the telic system in one or more of them.

2. Arousal-seeking activity

All the work which has been taken to demonstrate curiosity and exploration in animals may be interpreted as involving behaviour which increases arousal, and which is even undertaken for this purpose. Indeed, as noted in Chapter 5, this evidence was one of the factors in the development of the notions of both optimal arousal and sensation-seeking. Among the many examples of such work was that of Myers and Miller (1954), which showed that rats would learn to press a bar in a shuttle box in order to gain entry into a black compartment from a white one, or vice versa, and of Montgomery (1954) which demonstrated that female rats would learn which arm of a Y maze to use in order to be able to go on to explore a Dashiell (chequerboard) maze.

Even a simple stimulus change seems to be reinforcing. A number of investigators (e.g. Girdner, 1953; Hurwitz, 1956) have shown that rats will learn bar-pressing when it is followed by a weak light coming on. Others (e.g. Roberts et al., 1958; Robinson, 1961) have shown the same effect in relation to a weak light being turned off. Similarly, Kish and Antonitis (1956) showed that lever pressing in mice could be reinforced by microswitch clicks and relay noises. One inference that can be made from evidence of this kind is that even the small amount of arousal consequent upon minimal change can be rewarding to the animal.

The 'spontaneous alternation' phenomenon in maze running is also relevant here. This phenomenon was originally described by Tolman (1925) who found that when rats were being run in a simple T-maze in which either route led to the goal box, they would tend to alternate the arm of the maze which they chose to reach the goal box. Dennis (1939) reported that under a large number and variety of experimental conditions, the rat's characteristic frequency of alternations was 80% against a chance level of 50%. This phenomenon has subsequently been investigated by many other researchers. In particular, Whiting and Mowrer (1943) found that even when the two alternative routes were considerably different in length, rats would still regularly, if occasionally, take the longer route. There are a number of ways in which attempts can be made, and have been made, to explain the alternation phenomenon. One way is clearly in terms of the animal's need for change, and therefore presumably for stimulation and a higher level of arousal than would otherwise have been obtained.[9] From the reversal theory point of view, a particularly interesting experiment on alternation is that of Syme and Syme (1977). Working with mice, they showed that a preference for either novelty (higher than chance alternation), or familiarity (lower than chance alternation), could be induced in the same batch of animals, by confining them to one arm of the T-maze for different lengths of time. From the perspective of reversal theory, the experimental manipulations could be interpreted as inducing reversals between the telic and paratelic systems.

In Harlow's well-known experiments on 'love' in infant monkeys (Harlow, 1959b; Harlow and Zimmerman, 1959) he found that the infants were willing to explore unfamiliar environments, or to approach previously avoided anxiety-provoking objects, provided they were given access to suitable surrogate mothers, consisting of wire frames covered in terry towelling, to which they could periodically cling. Harlow's explanation was that the contact comfort derived from these surrogates provided enough security for the infants to overcome their anxiety; in reversal theory terms, it might be suggested that the presence of a mother surrogate induced the paratelic state so that exploration was now exciting rather than frightening. A similar explanation in terms of increased security could be provided for Whiting and Mowrer's (1943) observation that rats placed in a maze without prior habituation showed anxiety, as indicated by urination and defaecation, but that after a time they engaged in considerable exploration, during which they ignored food even though food-deprived. Nevertheless, the possibility always remains that these rats, and Harlow's infant monkeys, were exploring, when they felt bold enough to do so, in order to reduce anxiety.

Halliday (1966) has reported that exploration of the striped section of a maze was increased by shocking rats in a box with striped walls, the inference which he drew being that, at least in these circumstances, exploration is undertaken to reduce fear. However, an equally valid explanation is that the rat is enjoying the arousal which comes from the threat of a mild shock. Bernstein (1976) provided various groups of monkeys with a set of vertical poles, one of which was fitted towards the top with an electric grid, by means of which animals could be shocked when they climbed the pole. He found, much to his own surprise, that in all four of the macaque groups used there was an *increase* in the use of the pole during the shock phase of the experiment, but interest declined when the power was disconnected. This experiment, and the evidence from it, is very similar in obvious respects to that of Halliday, but Bernstein, unlike Halliday, concluded that "the evidence was overwhelming that we had created an attractive toy rather than a taboo" (p.197); in other words, for the macaque groups, the possibility of a shock, in Bernstein's interpretation, made the pole in question an exciting one to explore. The difference between Bernstein's and Halliday's interpretation of their results demonstrates particularly clearly how difficult it is, from the evidence of behaviour alone, to determine whether an animal is attempting to gain excitement or to avoid anxiety.

All this work on exploration, stimulus change, spontaneous alternation, and the effects of shock, is therefore subject to a variety of interpretations and explanations. Although it is possible to make informed guesses, it is impossible to ascertain definitively on a given occasion whether an animal is attempting to raise or lower arousal to a preferred level, and whether this preferred level is intermediate or extreme on the arousal dimension. In the absence of phenomenological evidence, there are simply too many unknowns. Nevertheless, the evidence is at least suggestive that some animals might on occasion seek high arousal.

3. Negativism

On the face of it, it would seem that a good case could be made for the existence of negativism in at least some animals: after all, 'mavericks' are well known to farmers and others who have to deal with animals as part of their everyday work.

However, the whole question of negativism in animals is fraught with difficulties. The existence of a negativistic system would imply that the animal recognized and could identify requirements, expectancies, pressures, etc., from some source, and could then deliberately choose to act against them. Thus aggression on the part of an animal may seem to be negativistic to an observer, but this would not constitute negativism in the sense used in reversal theory, unless one could be sure, which in the case of animals one cannot, that the animal also conceived its action in this way. After all, a particular act of aggression may be a relatively simple automatic act, not essentially different from eating or drinking.

Several lines of evidence might be taken to suggest the existence of a negativistic system in animals, although in each case other explanations are perhaps more convincing at the present time.

(i) Dogs in the 'ultraparadoxical' stage of response to stress, as reported by Pavlov (see Chapter 2), were said to behave negativistically (e.g. viz. Cuny, 1964, pp.113-14). The dogs may, however, have been confused, or automatically responding to stimuli which they misperceived.

(ii) Breland and Breland (1961) observed animals of various species 'misbehaving' during the experimenters' attempts to shape their behaviour on Skinnerian principles. Since the 'misbehaviour' consisted of a tendency to revert to instinctive behaviour patterns related to the learned response, Breland and Breland explained it in terms of what they called 'instinctive drift'.

(iii) Sadowski (1974) obtained a negativistic response to food by food-deprived dogs who were self-stimulating with electrodes implanted in the anterior part of the basal forebrain. Of most interest was the fact that, when the current was switched on by the experimenter, rather than through self-stimulation, the dogs typically gave up attempts to reach the food, or even ejected it if it had already been taken into the mouth. Sadowski suggested that this might be due either to an aversive effect, or to the excitation of another drive concurrent with hunger, or to the excitation of a satiety system. He did not consider that a negativistic system might have been activated, although this must also remain a possible explanation.

(iv) Best and Rubinstein (viz. Best, 1963) trained planarian worms to choose the correct arm of a Y-maze, but found that, on achieving a certain success ratio, the worms would consistently and perversely discriminate *against* the correct choice. It seems likely, however, that this was due to the aversiveness of the lack of space in the water wells used for reinforcement, since when the wells were made more spacious the worms made the correct choice once more. Interestingly, in terms of arousal-seeking, when the task was made more difficult, those worms which succeeded in solving it, about one in three, continued to make the correct choice even when the original supposedly aversive wells were used, as if the increased challenge made the situation more stimulating again.

(v) Harlow (1959a) reported in his well-known 'learning set' experiments with monkeys, that some 'deviant' monkeys insisted on playing with the experimental stimulus objects by chewing them, tearing them and so on, rather than attending to the incentives offered for solutions to the problems posed.

"The difficulty encountered in training infant monkeys, most chimpanzees, and all human children is their persistent tendency to disregard both appetite and hunger and to respond to the stronger motives afforded them by the impedimenta" (p.530).

This may, of course, be evidence, not so much for the functioning of a negativistic system, as for the pursuit of activity for its own sake.

Perhaps the best evidence for a negativistic system is, oddly, evidence which is not normally reported at all: namely evidence concerning 'refusal' in laboratory animals, such as refusal to run in a maze. This may be related to the phenomenon reported by Harlow, but the explanation in terms of 'activity for its own sake' is no longer fully applicable, since the animal may produce little overt behaviour of any kind. There is at present no way of knowing how prevalent such refusal is, since animals which refuse to behave are typically rejected from the experiment, or the trials on which refusal occurs are simply discounted. Either way, it seems to be an accepted convention that no reference need be made to 'refusal' in written accounts of experiments. Nevertheless, the author, on the basis of informal discussions with psychologists working with laboratory animals, is convinced of the existence of this phenomenon. Refusal in animals used in experiments would seem to be a topic worth investigating in its own rights and should play a part in any complete 'ethology of the laboratory animal'.

What this discussion of the evidence for metamotivational systems in animals has emphasized predominantly, has been the difficulty of understanding behaviour, and the impossibility of understanding it fully and unequivocally, from the evidence of the behaviour alone. In the nature of things, the lines of evidence adduced here can therefore be no more than hints and clues from which it is possible to make tentative inferences about the existence, or non-existence, of metamotivational *systems* in animals – although hopefully, in due course, physiological evidence may throw additional and independent light on the question. What neither physiological or behavioural evidence can do is to disclose anything definitive about the *mental states* of animals, even if mental states may be said to exist at all in any sense analogous to the way in which the term would be used in relation to human experience. There is no way in which one can ever know for sure whether an animal actually feels serious or playful in anything like the human sense, or whether an animal ever experiences what a human being might call 'bloody-mindedness'. Unfortunately, the study of animal behaviour has to remain just that: the study of animal *behaviour*.

Notes on Chapter 13

1. For a recent review of experimental psychological evidence concerning such systems, see Shevrin and Dickman (1980).
2. Professor Sven Svebak, at the University of Bergen in Norway, is investigating physiological correlates of metamotivational states and dominance; the results of these interesting experimental studies will be published in due course.
3. Evidence for a relationship between negativism and the emerging self-concept of the child will be found in the writings of Henri Wallon, in whose work it is a central theme: viz. Wallon (1959, 1963, 1976). The importance of negativism to self-awareness has also been argued particularly strongly by Lowen (1975). This whole theme has been discussed at more length by the present writer elsewhere (Apter, in press b). For a contrary view on the need for negativism in development see L'Abate (1976) who sees it as essentially pathological.
4. But Cf. Busemann, cited in Kanner (1948) p.40. Busemann argues that negativism is brought about by a mother being too attentive towards a child if the next child fails to appear 'on schedule'.
5. Quoted in Rollo May (1976), p.60.
6. The factors, other than the induction of the paratelic state, which tend to encourage the creation of synergies, still have to be elucidated. It is possible of course, in this connection, that there are people whose thinking is much more dominated by an awareness of opposites than other people, and that this is a personality dimension in its own right. People for whom everything immediately suggests its opposite may well be more creative than others in the production of synergies of various types, including make-believe synergies and humour synergies.
7. In Rothenberg (1980), in discussing creativity in visual art, he refers to the process as 'homospatial' thinking. See also Rothenberg (1969, 1979).
8. This question has been particularly ably discussed by Griffin (1976).
9. Catania (1972) cited in Thoresen and Mahoney (1974) reported an operant phenomenon which seems to bear a relationship to alternation in maze running: pigeons apparently preferred a condition in which they could earn reinforcement on either of two keys, over a condition in which only one key was available (the reinforcement schedules being identical in both conditions).

14 Beyond Homeostasis and Consistency

The Dynamics of the Reversal Process

It may be helpful at this final stage to review the central theme of reversal theory, which is that of reversal between metamotivational systems/states, and of the experiential and behavioural consequences of such reversal.

It will be recalled that the complete reversal process can be analysed into three sequential components. First of all there is the 'reversal proper' from one meta-motivational system to the opposite member of its pair. Secondly, the newly operative metamotivational system must acquire a 'content'. Thirdly, this 'content' suggests, and typically leads to, action. It is possible for this sequence to be inverted at the first step since the 'content' may be what has precipitated the reversal in the first place, so that immediately following reversal the 'content' is already fixed. But when this is *not* the case, the metamotivational system will be momentarily 'pre-intentional', i.e. 'contentless', until the completion of the second component of the sequence. The reversal itself may be precipitated by some contingent event, often environmental, by frustration, or simply through satiation. It may also be instigated by some combination of these. Because of the factor of satiation, reversals will still tend to occur from time to time, even in the absence of other precipitating factors. The three steps involved in the whole reversal process can be described in terms of experiential variables. The first step involves a switch from one preferred level of such a variable to another; the second involves the choice of a particular content in relation to the variable; the third involves the attempt to bring the value of the chosen variable into the range of values which constitute the preferred level.

In the case of the pair of metamotivational systems labelled 'telic' and 'paratelic', two such experiential variables are involved: 'felt significance' and 'intensity of experience'. In the telic system the preferred level of the first of these is high, and the second low, and vice versa in the paratelic system.

In the case of a reversal into the telic system, therefore, the first step consists of the adoption of a new preferred level for each variable, this level being different from that previously obtaining. The second step involves the choice of a particular goal to be pursued, and this is the 'content' of this state at that time. Thus, if the reversal is brought about by some particular threat, then the 'content' of the state is the goal of removing this threat. The third step consists of thinking about and pursuing this goal, the effect of which should be to increase its felt significance and/or eventually to lower the intensity of the experience related to it, especially the associated arousal. In the case of a reversal into the paratelic system, the first step consists of the adoption of the appropriate preferred level for each of these two variables. The second involves acquiring some 'content' for the state in the form of a type of experience or activity which can be pursued, e.g. to play a particular game. This choice will also imply which variable or variables, that contribute to the intensity of experience, will be at the centre of attention, and optimized. Felt arousal is typically one of these, but some other variable like a specific form of sensation, or the degree of awareness of one's bodily movements, may take precedence at a particular time. At the third step the activity or experience is entered into, and this should have the effect of lowering the felt significance, and increasing the intensity of the experience in the form chosen. In both the telic and paratelic systems a choice may also have to be made about which variable, felt significance or intensity of experience, takes priority at a given time, since it may not be possible to optimize both, i.e. to bring both simultaneously into their respective preferred levels.

It is possible to regard the pursuit of preferred level of *arousal* as being mediated by a pair of systems which themselves constitute a pair of meta-motivational systems in its own right; these are referred to as the arousal-seeking and arousal-avoidance system respectively, or the excitement-seeking and anxiety-avoidance systems. The first step of a reversal here involves a switch from a preferred level of arousal, which is usually towards one end of the felt arousal dimension, to a preferred level which is usuall towards the other end of the dimension. With this particular pair of systems, however, the experiential variable is already predetermined, and so the second step, the choice of 'content', is auto-matic. For this reason neither of these systems can be pre-intentional at any stage, since the 'content' is specified by the nature of the states themselves. At the third step, behaviour is chosen and performed which should result in movement towards the preferred level of the variable for the system that is operative.

The third pair of metamotivational systems considered in this book were the negativistic and conformist systems. Here the crucial variable is that of 'felt negativism'. A reversal in the negativistic direction occasions a search for some requirement, if it is not already salient in experience, towards which it is possible to act negativistically. The 'content' is then the chosen requirement, and the resulting behaviour is intended to bring the value of the 'felt negativism' variable into its high preferred level, by behaving in such a way that one can see oneself to be opposing the requirement. A reversal into the conformist system involves the search for some requirement towards which it is possible to act in a way which one construes as being conformist, this constituting the 'content' of the system, when it is identified. The intention of the resulting behaviour in the conformist system is to bring the variable 'felt negativism' into its low preferred level. (In the conformist system, however, a simple lack of perceived negativism in one's own behaviour may be felt to be satisfactory, so that a positive search for requirements towards which one can act in a conformist way is not always required in this state.)

TABLE IV   A summary of the main characteristics of the three pairs of metamotivational systems dealt with in this book.

METAMOTIVATIONAL SYSTEM	VARIABLE	PREFERRED LEVEL	FOCAL CONTENT
Telic		High	A goal
	Felt significance		
Paratelic		Low	An activity
Arousal-avoidance		Low	
	Felt arousal (or intensity of experience)		Arousal or sensation
Arousal-seeking		High	
Negativism		High	A requirement
	Felt negativism		
Conformity		Low	(A requirement)

This is all summarized in Table IV. It will have been noticed, incidentally, that each of the three metamotivational variables, i.e. each variable acted on by a pair of metamotivational systems, are of quite different character. Felt significance is about the complexity of meaning which one assigns to a goal situation, felt intensity of experience and felt arousal about the strength of immediate sensations and perceptions, and felt negativism about how one sees oneself to be behaving, in a certain respect. There is a sense, therefore, in which felt significance is about how one sees the *external world* and its possibilities; felt intensity of experience and arousal as how one sees one's *internal bodily world*, including its reactions to the external world; and felt negativism about how one sees one's own *overt behaviour* in the external world. Although the strength of each variable at a given time depends on the interpretation of experience, the aspect of experience is not just different, but of a different *type* in each case. The kind of action which is taken to alter the strength of each variable, therefore, also tends to be rather different. In relation to felt significance, interaction with the outside world can bring to light different possibilities and meanings which can enhance this variable; or it can emphasize the way in which certain types of activity lead nowhere beyond themselves and are therefore 'encapsulated'. Intensity of experience and felt arousal are typically changed by the individual behaving in such a way as to place himself in situations which produce different levels and types of stimulation. In the case of felt negativism, the strength of this subjective variable derives from the experience of the behaviour itself, although the effect of the behaviour on the external world, especially other people's reaction to it, may play a large part in determining its strength. The value of all three variables can also be altered by cognitive processes, felt significance being perhaps most prone to the effects of thinking alone.

In all cases, attainment of the preferred level of the variable concerned is accompanied by some degree of pleasure, whereas a discrepancy between the preferred and actual level of the variable is associated with a feeling of tension, (which is defined in reversal theory as the experience of such a discrepancy); displeasure arises here both from the unsatisfactory level of the variable itself, e.g. boredom in the arousal-seeking state, and from the tension which accompanies it.[1] If the tension is prolonged, then a type of frustration will also be experienced. It should be noted that if step two of the reversal sequence is not successfully completed then the variable cannot be brought into its preferred level; and so tension, and possibly frustration, can arise as a result of a lack of success at step two, as well as step three. Thus an inability to *find* an essential goal to pursue will make it impossible to attain high felt significance in the telic system, just as an inability to find a salient requirement in the negativistic system will make it impossible to act negativistically, and achieve high felt negativism.

The reversal process as described here involves bistability and does so at two levels, the second being consequent on the first. The first level is that of the metamotivational systems themselves. Each such pair of systems is bistable since it consists of two stable states; or more strictly, since for each state there is always the possibility of reversal to the opposite stable state, two *relatively* stable states. The bistability at this level can also be described in terms of relatively stable preferred levels, i.e. ranges of values, of the variable concerned (e.g. felt arousal, or felt negativism). This leads to bistability at the level of the values of the variables concerned, since they tend to be brought into the preferred range of values specified by one metamotivational system, or into the preferred range specified by the opposite system. Bistability at this second level, however, may not always be as evident as it is at the first level. For one thing, at the first level the situation is of a discrete 'either/or' type, whereas at the second level the values of the variable constitute a continuous dimension, and movement from one value to another can only occur through the variable taking all the intermediate values in succession. For another thing, at the second level, environmental and other types of disturbance may be strong enough to prevent the preferred value of a variable being obtained at a given time. So a frequency curve of the values of the variable over time will not necessarily be bimodal, even though the underlying mechanism is bistable. (In the same way, environmental disturbance may be sufficiently strong to prevent a homeostatic system from displaying its homeostasis.)

Reversal between metamotivational systems therefore involves two types of related change: change in which of the two systems is operative and, typically, change in the actual value of an experiential variable. In reversal theory, however, two other possible types of change have been noted in relation to metamotivational systems, and these can occur without a reversal taking place at all. The first is that of change in the relationship between each value of the experiential variable and hedonic tone: this type of change has been referred to as a 'shift'. For example, a shift might occur for some reason in the telic system, such that each value of the variable 'felt significance' is associated with less pleasure, or more displeasure, than before the shift took place. The second is that of 'displacement': here the focal 'content' in a given metamotivational system at a given time changes, e.g. in the telic system from one essential goal to another. Although reversals have received most attention in this book, consideration has also been given at relevant points to the other two types of change in relation to metamotivational systems.

The Phenomenology of Reversal

The summary of the reversal theme just presented, emphasized the structural/ cybernetic aspects. Let us now review the theme in such a way as to make the phenomenological aspect more prominent. In doing so the reference will be to 'metamotivational states' rather than 'metamotivational systems'.

Just as the visual field is made up of figure and ground, so the phenomenal field as a whole is made up of what William James called 'focus' and 'fringe' (James 1890, vol. 1, p.478). Although one is by definition aware of everything in the phenomenal field, one is primarily aware of those 'phenomena' at the focus, the rest being peripheral and forming the context for the focal phenomena.

In saying that the individual is oriented towards essential goals rather than behaviour in the telic state, one is saying that the goals are focal and that the behaviour is experienced in a way which is relatively peripheral. Of course the goals and behaviour are closely integrated in experience, just as figure and ground are closely integrated in the visual field. But in the telic state the goal is part of the figure, the behaviour-towards-the-goal 'fitting in around it'. One is nevertheless always aware of the behaviour, and it is always possible that some aspect of the behaviour and related experience will 'take the centre of the stage', thus constituting a telic-to-paratelic reversal. In the paratelic state, conversely, it is the behaviour which is at the focus and any essential goals are at the fringe. More accurately, it is *activity* which is at the focus in the paratelic state and activity frequently implies goals which give it meaning: but in the paratelic state these goals do not have any 'existence' over and above the activity. Thus in playing football, part of the meaning of the activity is that it is directed towards goal-scoring. But this playing-and-goal-scoring is an activity which has no unavoidable essential goal beyond itself, for as long as the paratelic state is maintained. There are, however, always essential goals in the background, goals which exist in their own right quite apart from the game, and of which there is always at least minimal awareness. It is possible at any time that one of these will shift into the focus of the phenomenal field and constitute a reversal into the telic state. For example, in playing football there are always in the background such essential goals as those of avoiding serious injury, and maintaining self-esteem, and these essential goals are never entirely absent from the phenomenal field.

In the negativistic and conformist states the situation is more complicated since reversal can occur in one of two different ways, as represented schematically in Figure 14.1. Often negativism to the requirements from one source implies conformity to opposite requirements from another source. For example, destructive behaviour by a member of a gang of hooligans, while being negative to the requirements of society, may be conformist to the requirements of the gang. In a logical sense, therefore, many actions are both negativistic and

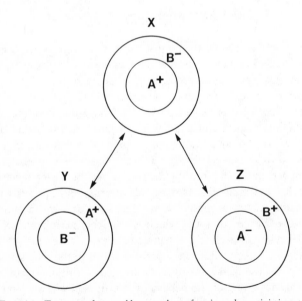

FIG. 14.1   *Two types of reversal between the conformist and negativistic states.*

conformist. Phenomenologically, however, whether an action is negativistic or conformist depends on which requirement is at the focus of the phenomenal field, and which is at the fringe. If a member of the gang at a particular moment is behaving in a way which, as he sees it, is conforming to the gang, then his behaviour is performed in the conformist state at that moment, even though he is peripherally aware that the behaviour also has a negativistic component. If on the other hand the negativistic requirement is at the focus, and the conformist requirement no more than a peripheral implication, then he is in the negativistic state. In Fig. 14.1 these two different ways of seeing a particular action are represented at X and Y. At X, requirement A which is being conformed with (represented by a '+' sign) is at the focus of the phenomenal field, while the opposite requirement (B) against which negativistic action is being taken (this being represented by a '-' sign), is at the fringe. At Y the situation is reversed, with requirement B being at the focus, and A at the periphery. A reversal between X and Y would therefore be, as it were, a type of 'figure-ground' reversal. If such a reversal takes place it has no effect on the continuing behaviour which remains the same, but only on the way the behaviour is interpreted by the individual who is performing it. However, another type of reversal is also possible: requirement A can stay at the focus and B at the fringe but the 'signs change' so that requirement A is now being acted against rather than conformed with, and requirement B conformed with rather than acted against. In terms of the example of the gang of hooligans, the member of the gang might now decide to act against the requirements of the gang rather than conforming to them. This new phenomenological situation is represented by Z in the figure. The type of metamotivational reversal represented by X←→Z, unlike that represented by X←→Y, *does* involve a change of behaviour.

Just as one action implies a rejection of an opposite action, or requirement, so the assignment of one characteristic to a perceived identity implies the non-assignment of an opposite characteristic. Hence, to see something as small means that it is *not* seen as big. The meaning of an identity in the focus of the phenomenal field therefore depends on a fringe awareness of what it is *not*. However, unlike the situation with respect to the experience of motivation, the 'rejected' characteristic can instead be both accepted and brought to the focus. It is this which constitutes an 'identity synergy'. Thus a small object may under certain circumstances be seen simultaneously as in some sense large, as in the small toy which represents a large motor car. This bringing together of cognitive opposites at the focus of attention is avoided as far as possible in the telic state, where it is experienced as in some measure threatening and unpleasant, and welcomed in the paratelic state, where it is experienced as a kind of 'magic' which is exciting and pleasurable.

Sometimes the perceived characteristic of an identity changes suddenly into its opposite - as when a pompous man falls down, or an alarm turns out to be false -

so that when the new perceived characteristic becomes evident in the focus of the phenomenal field, there still remains some trace of the original characteristic. As long as this temporary situation lasts, a 'reversal synergy' is experienced. It should be noted that 'reversal' here does not refer to a reversal of metamotivational state but to a reversal of some characteristic of an identity; this may or may not be *accompanied by* a reversal at the metamotivational level. In some cases, in conjunction with the appropriate metamotivational state and level of arousal, a reversal of meaning gives rise to an identifiable emotion such as humour, embarrassment, relief, or sorrow. This occurs in the case of an 'identity synergy', at those moments when one interpretation of a situation gives way to a different interpretation at the focus of the phenomenal field.

In general, different emotions can be related to particular conjunctions of metamotivational state, arousal level and, in some cases, type of synergy. This is shown in Table V where a number of emotions discussed in earlier chapters are listed alphabetically, and described in terms of these features. For simplicity,

TABLE V   The different combinations of characteristics displayed by a variety of emotions discussed in this book, but excluding parapathic emotions.

	METAMOTIVATIONAL STATE	AROUSAL LEVEL	SYNERGY
Anger	Telic, negativistic	High	
Anxiety	Telic	High	
Boredom	Paratelic	Low	
Embarrassment	Telic	High	Real/apparent
Excitement	Paratelic	High	
Humour	Paratelic	High	Real/apparent
Relaxation	Telic	Low	
Relief	Paratelic	High	Unacceptable/acceptable
Sorrow	Telic	High	Acceptable/unacceptable

parapathic emotions are not included in this table. A more extended phenomenological investigation of the full range of emotions would show how each emotion is characterized in relation to each of these features, although in some cases it is possible that further cognitive features would also be required for a complete and unique specification.

Two types of reversal process have been discussed in the last few paragraphs: metamotivational reversal and reversal synergy. It should now be clear that these differ not just in content, but also at the structural, or cybernetic, level. Metamotivational reversal may occur in such a way that, immediately following the reversal, there is momentarily *no* appropriate content at the focus of the phenomenal field. In reversal synergy, on the contrary, immediately after a reversal has taken place the content 'doubles up' in the sense that *two* different meanings temporarily co-exist at the centre of awareness.[2]

Conscious Control of Reversal

It has been argued that it is not possible to bring about a metamotivational reversal directly through a deliberate conscious decision as such, but that such reversals occur automatically when a threshold for reversal is reached.[3] So the combined strength of factors working in favour of a reversal has to be greater than the combined strength of factors working against it at a given time, for a reversal to take place at that time. In other words, there is an independent reversal mechanism through which satiation, frustration, and relevant contingent events operate. This mechanism functions unconsciously, although of course the results directly affect the structure of conscious experience in the way described. So although it may seem, for example, that a conscious decision is made to attend to an essential goal of some kind, the conscious decision is normally only the second step of the whole three-step reversal process, the meta-motivational reversal itself, i.e. the first step, having already been brought about by the reversal mechanism. This is not to deny that the likelihood of a reversal occurring can be decisively affected by conscious processes,[4] such as the cognitive interpretation of some event as threatening rather than non-threatening;[5] it can even be indirectly affected, as will be discussed shortly, by a conscious decision which is effectively a decision to reverse, since it brings about the appropriate antecedent conditions. What it does seem to mean, however, is that the individual cannot consciously, directly and voluntarily induce a reversal when he wants to in quite the straight-forward way that, for instance, he can voluntarily raise his own arm.

In a similar way the functioning of the arousal system, which results in different levels of felt arousal being experienced at different times, is itself not directly dependent on conscious decisions, although again the level of felt arousal may depend on the way certain events happen to be interpreted within experience. It is also in a sense independent of the arousal-seeking and arousal-avoidance meta-motivational systems: these govern the way in which the arousal is interpreted, but they do not *directly* govern the level of arousal. They do affect it *indirectly*, of course, through their influence on conscious decisions which result in behaviour intended eventually to have the effect of increasing or decreasing felt arousal. The arousal system itself is probably homeostatic, with its own stable resting level of arousal; bistability is normally imposed on this through the indirect effect of the operation of the arousal-seeking and arousal-avoidance systems, which tend to bring the organism into contact with arousing or de-arousing situations.

In Fig. 14.2, the reversal mechanism and the arousal system are shown as parallel systems which govern reversal and arousal level respectively. Both of these have an effect on conscious awareness, reversals changing the way in which events are interpreted within consciousness, and the level of arousal constituting one of the types of event interpreted within consciousness. The resulting experience in turn leads to activities being undertaken which have consequences, mediated by the environment's response to the actions, for the reversal mechanism (through facilitating or inhibiting reversal), and for the arousal system (by raising or lowering the felt arousal level). In other words, a feedback loop is involved in each case as part of a cycle which includes unconscious, conscious, behavioural, and environmental components.

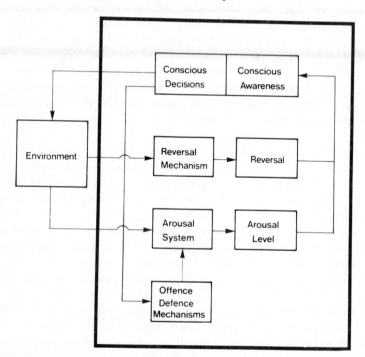

FIG. 14.2   The relationship of conscious decision-making processes to reversal mechanisms and to the arousal system.

Whether or not there is an essential goal in the focus of the phenomenal field (or a search for such a goal), primarily depends on whether the telic or paratelic state is already operative. Similarly, whether a requirement is being consciously acted against, or conformed with, depends in a prior way on whether the negativistic or conformist state is operative. In this respect, conscious decisions do not determine which of each pair of metamotivational states is operative.

What conscious decisions do normally determine, if this is not imposed by contingent events, is which particular goal or activity to pursue, which particular requirements to act with or against, and which particular means to adopt in relation to these choices and in relation to the attainment of the currently preferred level of arousal.

How does the phenomenon of displacement fit into all this? Displacement would appear to be under voluntary control in some circumstances, and to be involuntary in others. For example, where some contingent event like an unexpected threat imposes itself on the individual's phenomenal field, then the displacement involved is involuntary. (It should be noted, incidentally, that it will only count as a displacement, by definition, if the metamotivational state remains the same; so in this example the individual would have to have been in the telic state immediately prior to the contingent event occurring, otherwise a reversal would be said to have taken place rather than a displacement.) On the other hand the individual, as a response to frustration for instance, may take a voluntary conscious decision to change the content of his focus of awareness, and attend to something else. Since the content of conscious awareness *may* be determined voluntarily, therefore, it might seem that this could be used in the service, not only of displacement, but also of reversal. However, although a reversal often brings about a change of content, a change of content *cannot* itself directly bring about a reversal. For a reversal to occur, other factors over which the individual has no control (e.g. satiation) also play a part in combination with any effects which the content change may incur. Even though the new content is one which would seem to specify an opposite metamotivational state, there will not necessarily be a reversal to this state.[6] For example, should an individual in the paratelic state of mind deliberately focus his attention on a goal which he normally treats as serious, if the conditions are not as a whole suitable for a reversal to occur he will experience the goal on this occasion as something to be pursued playfully.[7] Of course a decision to replace one focal content by another may *lead to* the environment having a different effect from that which it would otherwise have done, and part of this effect may well be to bring about a rapid reversal. But again it must be emphasized that the effect is an indirect one. . . .

None of this should be taken to mean that conscious *decisions* to reverse to the opposite state cannot be made. What it does mean is that these decisions cannot be implemented in a direct voluntary way, but have to be induced indirectly. But is there not something puzzling, in the light of this analysis, about the very notion of a decision to reverse, whether it can be implemented directly or not? For example, how can an individual in the paratelic state decide to reverse to the telic state? Surely an attempt to be telic is itself telic, in which case such a decision is not possible in the paratelic state. The answer is that a situation may arise in which a decision made at the second step of the full reversal sequence, i.e. a decision about content, is *ipso facto* a decision which may have the effect of inducing a reversal in due course. This can be made clear by means of some examples. In the paratelic state a conscious decision may be made to undertake some activity, the end-product of which is inevitably and knowingly to induce the telic state. For example, one might playfully accept a wager that one cannot perform some task, and enjoy the excitement of the challenge, while being fully aware of its seriousness; but as soon as one commences to undertake it, its seriousness induces a reversal into the telic state. Conversely, in the telic state one may decide, for example, that for the sake of one's health one should 'take it easy' and enjoy oneself; in this sense the essential goal of the telic state may itself be the induction of the paratelic state. In the conformist state a deliberate decision may be made to conform to a requirement from some source to be negativistic. Although the decision itself is made in the conformist state, consequent action is likely to lead to the negativistic requirement coming to the focus of the phenomenal field at some stage, thus constituting a reversal to the negativistic state. Similarly, but with opposite effect, in the negativistic state a decision may be consciously made to oppose a negativistic requirement from some external source, e.g. a politician *opposes* his leader's requirement to vote *against* a certain bill; again, although this decision is itself negativistic, and undertaken in the negativistic state, the resulting activity is, logically, conformist, since it involves a 'double-negative'. In the example just given the politician votes *for* the bill. This does not necessarily mean that it will be seen by the individual as conformist, but the conformist aspect is nevertheless quite likely to come to the focus of the phenomenal field at some stage and to induce a reversal to the conformist state.

Phenomenologically, there is a difference between some of the examples just given, in that perhaps only in the case of the example of the induction of the paratelic state is the reversal itself actually desired. In the other cases the reversal is more of a by-product, and there would presumably be no feeling of disappointment if, after all, it did not occur. Either way, it should again be emphasized, the reversal does not occur automatically as the result of the decision, but depends on the behaviour which is chosen, and the effect this has on the environment. A reversal will only occur it seems, other things being equal, if the consequences of the behaviour are of a type and strength sufficient to induce it. To induce the paratelic state, for example, the individual may need to move into an environment which provides a context powerful enough to impose itself on the reversal system. Any control exerted on the reversal system by the conscious decision-making part of the system therefore, can normally only be exerted through the mediation of an unpredictable environment (as made clear in Fig. 14.2) and often mistakes will be made. In cybernetic terms, therefore, the control takes place through a 'noisy channel'. For example, one may, in a telic state, decide to watch television in order to induce the paratelic state, but for some reason, such as that one cannot forget that one has some urgent and unavoidable work to do, the paratelic state is not induced. In this case, the arousal from the television will be added to the arousal level already present, and even more anxiety will be experienced than before. One will also as a result of this feel more tension than before.[8]

Similarly, in attempting to control the arousal system, the conscious decision-making part of the system can do so by means of behaviour which has consequences that in turn increase or decrease felt arousal. For example, risky behaviour may be performed or avoided. But in attempting to control arousal there is also a more direct and less 'noisy' channel of control, through the use of offence and defence mechanisms: arousal can be increased or decreased by avoiding or by calling up suitable memories, ideas, fantasies, and so on. This is not meant to imply that all offence and defence mechanisms are, or can be brought, under conscious control, but some offence mechanisms at least would certainly appear to be voluntarily available to most people.

Of course, in trying to change the level of arousal, an action may be undertaken which has the effect of inducing a reversal; and in attempting to induce a reversal, through behaviour of different kinds, the level of arousal may be altered. The situation as a whole, as represented in simple outline in Fig. 14.2, is therefore a complicated one, in which the conscious decisions taken will often turn out to be inappropriate for one reason or another. This is not because the various subsystems are in conflict with each other, as is the case in the psycho-analytic model, but rather because the system is composed of relatively autonomous units, which interact in such a way that the result is not always the one intended by the conscious decision-making part of the system. Rather than being a 'conflict theory', reversal theory is more what one might term an 'ecological theory'.

In many respects the conscious decision-maker will have a larger role to play than that suggested by this discussion of its specific role in relation to the control of reversal and arousal, and to the choice of content for each operative meta-motivational state. In particular, in attempting to optimize overall hedonic tone, a number of choices and decisions are regularly required. For example, negativistic behaviour at a given time may give rise to high felt negativism and the pleasure associated with this, but at the expense of physical pain (during a fight, for instance); a decision must therefore be made about whether the pleasure of high felt negativism is worth the physical suffering. The pursuit of a career goal in the telic state may provide the pleasure of goal anticipation, but at the cost of punishing degrees of effort, or of the continuing experience of some physical need, like hunger. Alternatively, an easy goal may be pursued which provides immediate satisfactions, but without the prolonged pleasure of goal anticipation. In the paratelic state a sensation may be experienced which is intense, and which gives rise to pleasant high arousal, but which is also intrinsically unpleasant. Or a choice may have to be made in this state between an activity which gives rise to high arousal, but is experienced as low in terms of physical sensation, or vice versa. Examples could be multiplied of cases in which decisions are needed about which variable, or variables, are to be optimized in terms of hedonic tone: the preferred level of one variable is typically achieved only at the expense of suboptimal levels of other variables. This is particularly the case in relation to the contradictory demands of felt significance and felt arousal in the telic and paratelic states, since high felt significance often plays a part in increasing arousal; but in both the telic and paratelic states the preferred level of one of these variables is high, and of the other low.

Considering the inter-relatedness of the system as a whole, the unpredictability of the environment, the element of instability introduced through the effects of metamotivational satiation, and the tenuousness of much of the conscious control, it is hardly to be wondered at that high levels of positive hedonic tone are not typically maintained for extended periods. To put this in everyday terms, it is not surprising that people have difficulty in remaining happy for very long.

Final Remarks

Looking back at reversal theory as a whole, there are four points which it might be useful to re-emphasize.

The first concerns the nature of the explanation which reversal theory provides. All science is a search for pattern, for simple principles underlying complex phenomena. In developing reversal theory the attempt has been to search for patterns underlying the complexity of experience, especially the experience of motivation. The resulting theory has identified certain relatively simple structures, and related dynamics, underlying this aspect of experience. This does not mean that the richness and complexity of experience has been *reduced* to these structures, but rather that a new dimension, that of metamotivation, has been discerned and added to what is known of our conscious awareness of motivation. By adding this extra dimension, it has been possible to make sense of certain motivational phenomena which would otherwise remain mysterious; an analogy would be to the way in which three-dimensional geometry allows one to explain changes in two dimensions that would remain obscure without reference to change in a further dimension. This way of arriving at clarification is quite different from that type of simplifying practised by dogmatic behaviourists when they limit the study of man to the study of behaviour alone, and in this sense make man a one-dimensional being. Reversal theory does not, in principle, exclude reference to any aspect of human experience and behaviour, but rather adds a new perspective of its own.

The second point concerns the nature of the general approach adopted, which has been designated 'structural phenomenology'. Although reversal theory does not regard it as in any way illegitimate to refer to physiological and unconscious processes, as well as to behaviour and to conscious experience, it is conscious experience which is taken as the starting point in its investigations; and it is conscious experience which in many respects remains the centre of interest throughout. It is in this sense that the theory is phenomenological. Describing it as a form of *structural* phenomenology brings out the fact that it is concerned with the structure of experience, with different 'types' of experience and the way in which these different types, or ways of interpreting experience, are related to each other. In doing this, the theory addresses itself primarily to the experience of motivation, and it could therefore be called a structural phenomenological theory of motivation. But it should also be possible to apply the structural phenomenological approach to other aspects of experience. Hence, reversal theory cannot be equated with the whole of structural phenomenology: rather, it is an illustration of it, and an indication of how it might be brought to bear on other psychological topics. It would be quite possible to disagree with the assertions of the theory while supporting the general approach.

The third point concerns the status of reversal theory as science. At one level the theory provides a way of looking at, and interpreting, a wide range of types of experience and behaviour, including behaviour that would otherwise remain enigmatic, especially paradoxical behaviour of different kinds. It also provides ways of attempting to interpret particular pieces of behaviour, for instance behaviour which is seen as problematic in terms of the interactions in a particular family with which the therapist must deal. In other words, the theory suggests a systematic way in which meaning can be assigned to people's experience and behaviour. In this respect the theory may be depicted as an 'interpretative' or 'hermeneutic' theory (Gauld and Shotter, 1977; Bauman, 1978). Whether, and in what sense, a hermeneutic theory may be said to be scientific is a matter of some debate, but undoubtedly such a theory must meet certain kinds of criteria, and to the extent to which reversal theory is of this type it must satisfy these criteria. The minimum criterion is that of plausibility, and it is hoped that the reader will be convinced in the light of his or her experience that reversal theory meets this criterion. Furthermore, a hermeneutic theory should be coherent in the sense of being self-consistent, and it should have some degree of generality: ideally it should give meaning to a range of events of apparently different kinds, thus demonstrating unity in diversity. We believe that reversal theory meets both of these criteria too. A rather different kind of criterion is that of practical usefulness: a good theory should provide a helpful guide to action in situations where action is necessary. Here reversal theory is beginning to prove itself, and it is already being used with some measure of success in counselling and therapy. Because a theory is hermeneutic at one level, however, it does not mean that it cannot go beyond this to become, at least in certain of its aspects, a fully scientific theory amenable to experimental testing. In fact, research has already commenced on various hypotheses derived from reversal theory, and these experimental results will be presented in later publications. As a result of this research, and in the light of continuing clinical experience, the theory will no doubt undergo refinement and elaboration.

Fourthly, and finally, it will be realized that reversal theory embodies a number of denials of assumptions which are common in psychology, anthropology, and sociology. The theory denies that people automatically attempt to avoid ambiguity, incongruity, high arousal, disagreement, confrontation; rather, in certain states, they will seek out and enjoy all of these. It denies that all aspects of personality remain consistent, even over the short length of time of a laboratory experiment. It denies that people always act purposefully towards future goals, as learning theorists, cyberneticians, and others seem to imply; instead, it suggests that people often do things 'for the hell of it', and undertake activities *because* they have no point. In making such denials it should not be supposed that reversal theory is necessarily saying anything original, but rather that it is simply returning to what people already know in a commonsense way.[9] Going 'back to the things themselves', to use Husserl's famous rallying cry, can mean becoming aware again of things which have become overlooked in the course of previous abstraction, formalization, and systematization. Going backwards can in some circumstances be an excellent way of going forwards. At least it is a beginning.

Notes on Chapter 14

1. This statement applies to all three pairs of metamotivational systems. At any one moment tension may be high or low in relation to the operative system in each pair, and the tension from each presumably contributes to a single overall degree of experienced tension at a given time.

2. It will also be noted that, while metamotivational bistability and reversal are always of the externally-controlled type, reversal synergy (as remarked in Chapter 6, note 7 in relation to ambiguity) may be of either the value-determined or the externally-controlled type.

3. It is not inconceivable, however, that at some stage in the future, a training technique will be discovered that will help people to bring reversals under direct conscious control to some extent, just as other normally involuntary processes can be brought under conscious control through biofeedback.

4. It will be appreciated from the previous chapter that by 'conscious processes' here is really meant neurophysiological processes with conscious concomitants. This should be borne in mind throughout the following discussion.

5. Influencing cognitive interpretation provides perhaps the best opportunity for an outsider, e.g. a therapist, to help the individual to induce reversals in different situations.

6. This is consistent with the notion that, in the cybernetic terms introduced in Chapter 2, metamotivational reversal is externally controlled and not value-determined.

7. It might seem that switching attention from a negativistic requirement to a logically

complementary conformist requirement, would bring about an automatic reversal between the negativistic and conformist states and that reversal between these states could be brought under conscious control in this way. However, such a decision to switch attention implies that a reversal has already taken place, as discussed on pp.213-215 above.

8. Conversely, if the paratelic state *is* induced in this example, then a peripheral awareness that there is some important work to do may add to the arousal and increase the pleasure of watching the television.

9. Cf. Joynson (1974).

References

Aldis, O. (1975). "Play Fighting". Academic Press, London and New York.

Aldrich, V. C. (1971). Form in the visual arts. *British Journal of Aesthetics*, **11**, 215.

Allport, F. H. (1924). "Social Psychology". Houghton Mifflin, Boston.

Allport, G. W. (1937). "Personality: A Psychological Interpretation". Holt, New York.

Anderson, A. R., and Moore, O. K. (1960). Autotelic folk-models. Paper presented at the American Sociological Association, New York, September, 1960.

Anderson, E. E. (1941). The externalization of drive. III. Maze learning by non-rewarded and by satiated rats. *Journal of Genetic Psychology*, **59**, 397-426.

Angyal, A. (1941). "Foundations for a Science of Personality". The Commonwealth Fund, New York and Harvard University Press, Cambridge, Massachusetts.

Anscombe, G. E. M. (1966). "Intentions". Cornell University Press, Ithaca.

Apter, M. J. (1966). "Cybernetics and Development". Pergamon Press, Oxford.

Apter, M. J. (1969). Cybernetics and art. *Leonardo*, **2**, 3, 257-265.

Apter, M. J. (1970). "The Computer Simulation of Behaviour". Hutchinson, London. (U.S. edition, Harper and Row, New York, 1971).

Apter, M. J. (1972a). Cybernetics: a case study of a scientific subject-complex. *The Sociological Review Monograph No. 18*, 93-116.

Apter, M. J. (1972b). Systems and structures. *Technology and Society*, **7**, 2, 55-58.

Apter, M. J. (1973). The computer modelling of behaviour. *In* "The Computer in Psychology". (M. J. Apter and G. Westby, eds), Wiley, London, 245-279.

Apter, M. J. (1976). Some data inconsistent with the optimal arousal theory of motivation. *Perceptual and Motor Skills*, **43**, 1209-1210.

Apter, M. J. (1977). Can computers be programmed to appreciate art? *Leonardo*, **10**, 1, 17-21.

Apter, M. J. (in press a). Fawlty Towers: a reversal theory analysis of a popular television comedy series. *Journal of Popular Culture*.

Apter, M. J. (in press b). Negativism and the sense of identity. *In* "Threatened Identities" (G. Breakwell, ed.), Wiley, Chichester, U.K.

Apter, M. J. (1981). On the concept of bistability. *International Journal of General Systems*, **6**, 225-232.

Apter, M. J. and Smith, K. C. P. (1976) Negativism in adolescence. *The Counsellor*, Nos. 23-24, pp.25-30.

Arbib, M. A. (1972). "The Metaphorical Brain: An Introduction to Cybernetics as Artificial Intelligence and Brain Theory". Wiley-Interscience, New York.

Ardrey, R. (1976). "The Hunting Hypothesis". Collins, London.

Argyle, M. (1958). "Religious Behaviour". Routledge and Kegan Paul, London.

Arieti, S. (1959). Schizophrenia: the manifest symptomatology, the psychodynamic and formal mechanisms. In "American Handbook of Psychiatry, Vol. I." (S. Arieti, ed.). Basic Books, New York, pp.455-484.

Ashby, W. R. (1950). The cerebral mechanisms of intelligent action. In "Perspectives in Neuropsychiatry" (D. Richter, ed.). H. K. Lewis, London, pp.79-94.

Ashby, W. R. (1956). "An Introduction to Cybernetics". Chapman and Hall, London.

Ashworth, P. (1976). Some notes on phenomenological approaches in psychology. Bulletin of the British Psychological Society, 29, 363-368.

Averill, J. R. (1969). Autonomic response patterns during sadness and mirth. Psychophysiology, 5, 399-414.

Ayllon, T. (1963). Intensive treatment of psychotic behaviour by stimulus satiation and food reinforcement. Behavior Research and Therapy, 1, 53-61.

Babcock, B. A. (ed.). (1978). "The Reversible World: Symbolic Inversion in Art and Society". Cornell University Press, Ithaca.

Badcock, C. R. (1975). "Lévi-Strauss: Structuralism and Sociological Theory". Hutchinson, London.

Baldwin, J. M. (ed.). (1902). "Dictionary of Philosophy and Psychology". Macmillan, New York & London.

Ban, T. A. (1964). "Conditioning and Psychiatry". Allen and Unwin, London.

Bancroft, J. (1970). Disorders of sexual potency. In "Modern Trends in Psychosomatic Medicine". (O. Hill, ed.). Appleton-Century-Crofts, New York.

Bandura, A. (1973). "Aggression: A Social Learning Analysis". Prentice-Hall, Englewood Cliffs, New Jersey.

Bandura, A., Ross, D., and Ross, S. (1961). Transmission of aggression through imitation of aggressive models. Journal of Abnormal and Social Psychology, 63, 575-582.

Bandura, A., Ross, D., and Ross, S. (1963a). A comparative test of the status envy, social power, and secondary reinforcement theories of identificatory learning. Journal of Abnormal and Social Psychology, 67, 527-534.

Bandura, A., Ross, D., and Ross, S. (1963b). Vicarious reinforcement and imitative learning. Journal of Abnormal and Social Psychology, 67, 601-607.

Barclay, A. M. (1969). The effect of hostility on physiological and fantasy responses. Journal of Personality, 37, 651-667.

Barclay, A. M. and Harber, R. N. (1965). The relation of aggressive to sexual motivation. Journal of Personality, 33, 462-475.

Bartlett, F. C. (1916). An experimental study of some problems of perceiving and imaging. British Journal of Psychology, 8, 222-266.

Bartlett, F. C. (1932). "Remembering". Cambridge University Press, Cambridge.

Batchelor, I. R. C. (1969). "Henderson and Gillespie's Textbook of Psychiatry", 10th edition. Oxford University Press, London.

Bateson, G. (1954). A theory of play and fantasy. Paper given at the A.P.A. Regional Research Conference in Mexico City, 11 March, 1954. Reproduced in Bateson, G. (1973) op.cit., pp.150-166.

Bateson, G. (1973). "Steps to an Ecology of Mind". Paladin, St. Albans (U.K.).

Bauman, Z. (1978). "Hermeneutics and Social Science: Approaches to Understanding". Hutchinson, London.

Beach, F. A. (1951). Instinctive behavior: reproductive activities. *In* "Handbook of Experimental Psychology". (S. S. Stevens, ed.). Wiley, New York, pp. 387-434.

Becker, A. T. (1967). "Depression: Clinical, Experimental and Theoretical Aspects". Staples Press, London.

Beer, S. (1959). "Cybernetics and Management". English Universities Press, London.

Beishon, J. and Peters, G. (eds). (1972). "Systems Behaviour". Published for the Open University by Harper and Row, London.

Bem, D. J. (1965). An experimental analysis of self-persuasion. *Journal of Experimental Social Psychology*, **1**, 199-218.

Bem, D. J. (1966). Inducing belief in false confessions. *Journal of Personality and Social Psychology*, **3**, 707-10.

Bem, D. J. (1972). Self-perception theory. *In* "Advances in Experimental Social Psychology (Vol. 6)". (L. Berkowitz, ed.). Academic Press, New York and London.

Benedict, R. (1946). "The Chrysanthemum and the Sword". Routledge and Kegan Paul, London.

Berger, P. R. (1969). "The Social Reality of Religion". Faber and Faber, London.

Bergson, H. (1901). "Le Rire", Alcan, Paris. (English translation by Brereton, C. and Rothwell, F. as "Laughter", Macmillan, London, 1911).

Berkowitz, L. (ed.). (1969). "The Roots of Aggression: A Re-examination of the Frustration-Aggression Hypothesis". Atherton, New York.

Berlyne, D. E. (1950). Novelty and curiosity as determinants of exploratory behaviour. *British Journal of Psychology*, **41**, 68-80.

Berlyne, D. E. (1960). "Conflict, Arousal and Curiosity". McGraw-Hill, New York.

Berlyne, D. E. (1967). Arousal and reinforcement. *In* "Nebraska Symposium on Motivation, 1967". (D. Levine, ed.). University of Nebraska Press, Lincoln, Nebraska.

Berlyne, D. E. (1968). Laughter, humor and play. *In* "Handbook of Social Psychology" (G. L. Lindzey and E. Aronson, eds). Addison-Wesley, New York, pp.795-853.

Berlyne, D. E. (1971). "Aesthetics and Psychobiology". Appleton-Century-Crofts, New York.

Berlyne, D. E. (1972). Humor and its kin. *In* "The Psychology of Humor". (J. H. Goldstein and P. E. McGhee, eds). Academic Press, New York and London.

Bernard, C. (1859). "Leçons sur les Propriétés Physiologiques et les Alterations Pathologiques des Liquides de l'Organisme". Vols. I and II. Ballière, Paris.

Bernstein, I. S. (1976). Taboo or toy? *In* "Play" (J. S. Bruner, A. Jolly and K. Sylva, eds). Penguin, Harmondsworth, pp. 194-198.

Berry, D. (1974). "Central Ideas in Sociology: an Introduction". Constable, London.

Bertlanffy, L. von (1968). "General Systems Theory: Foundations, Development, Applications". Braziller, New York.

Best, J. B. (1963). Protopsychology. *Scientific American*, February 1963, 54-62.

Bindra, D. and Stewart, J. (eds) (1966). "Motivation: Selected Readings". Penguin Books, Harmondsworth.

Binet, A. and Simon, T. (1905). Méthodes nouvelles pour le diagnostic du niveau intellectuel des anormaux. *Année Psychologique*, **11**, 191-336.

Blackburn, R. (1978). Electrodermal and cardiovascular correlates of psychopathy. *In*

"Psychopathic Behavior: Approaches to Research". (R. D. Hare, and D. Schalling, eds). Wiley, New York.

Blackmore, M. and Murgatroyd, S. (1980). Anna: the disruptive infant. *In* "Helping the Troubled Child in the School". (S. Murgatroyd, ed.). Harper & Row, London, pp.32-42.

Blau, A. (1946). "The Master Hand". American Orthopsychiatric Association, New York.

Bleuler, E. (1912). "The Theory of Schizophrenic Negativism". Nervous and Mental Diseases Monograph Series No. 11. The Journal of Nervous and Mental Disease Publishing Co., New York.

Boring, E. G. (1942). "Sensation and Perception in the History of Experimental Psychology". Appleton-Century, New York.

Boudon, R. (1971). "The Uses of Structuralism". Heinemann, London. (Translated by M. Vaughan and D. MacRae. Originally published in French by Gallimard, Paris, 1968).

Bowen, M. (1966). The use of family theory in clinical practice. *Comprehensive Psychiatry*, **7**, 345-374.

Braun, M. (1964). " 'Love Me Do': The Beatles' Progress". Penguin, Harmondsworth.

Brehm, J. W. (1966). "A Theory of Psychological Reactance". Academic Press, New York and London.

Brehm, J. W. (1974). "Freedom and Reactance". Wiley, Chichester.

Breland, K. and Breland, M. (1961). The misbehavior of organisms. *American Psychologist*, **16**, 681-684.

Bridges, K. B. (1931). "The Social and Emotional Development of the Pre-School Child". Routledge, London.

Browning, D. (1964). "Act and Agent: An Essay in Philosophical Anthropology". University of Miami Press, Miami.

Bruner, J. S., Goodnow, J. J. and Austin, G. A. (1967). "A Study of Thinking". Science Editions, New York. (Originally published by Wiley, New York, 1956).

Bruner, J. S., Jolly, A., and Sylva, K. (eds) (1976). "Play: Its Role in Development and Evolution". Penguin, Harmondsworth.

Buck, R., Miller, R. E., and Caul, W. F. (1974). Sex, personality, and physiological variables in the communication of affect via facial expression. *Journal of Personality and Social Psychology*, **30**, 587-596.

Buckley, W. (ed.) (1968). "Modern Systems Research for the Behavioral Scientist: A sourcebook". Aldine, Chicago.

Bullough, E. (1912). 'Psychical distance' as a factor in art and an aesthetic principle. *The British Journal of Psychology*, **5**, Part 2, 87-118.

Bunney, W. E. Jr., and Murphy, D. L. (1973). The behavioral switch process and psychopathology. *In* "Biological Psychiatry". (J. Mendels, ed.). Wiley, New York.

Burchard, J. and Tyler, V. Jr. (1965). The modification of delinquent behavior through operant conditioning. *Behavior Research and Therapy*, **3**, 245-250.

Butler, R. A. (1953). Discrimination learning in rhesus monkeys to visual exploration motivation. *Journal of Comparative and Physiological Psychology*, **46**, 95-98.

Butler, R. A. (1954). Incentive conditions which influence visual exploration. *Journal of Experimental Psychology*, **48**, 19-23.

Butler, R. A. (1957). The effect of deprivation of visual incentives on visual exploration motivation in monkeys. *Journal of Comparative and Physiological Psychology*, **50**, 177-179.

Cabanac, M. (1971). Physiological role of pleasure. *Science*, **173**, 1103-1107.

Cade, B. (1979). The use of paradox in therapy. *In* "Family and Marital Psychotherapy: A Critical Approach". (S. Walrond-Skinner, ed.). Routledge and Kegan Paul, London.

Cade, B. and Southgate, P. (1979). Honesty is the best policy. *Journal of Family Therapy*, **1**, 23-31.

Canetti, E. (1962). "Crowds and Power". Gollancz, London.

Cannon, W. B. (1929). "Bodily changes in Pain, Hunger, Fear and Rage". Appleton, New York.

Cannon, W. B. (1932). "The Wisdom of the Body". Norton, New York.

Cantor, J. R. and Zillmann, D. (1973). The effect of affective state and emotional arousal on music appreciation. *The Journal of General Psychology*, **89**, 97-108.

Cantor, J. R., Zillmann, D. and Bryant, J. (1975). Enhancement of experienced sexual arousal in response to erotic stimuli through misattribution of unrelated residual excitation. *Journal of Personality and Social Psychology*, **32**, 69-75.

Cantril, H., Gaudet, H. and Hertzog, H. (1940). "The Invasion from Mars". Princeton University Press, Princeton, New Jersey.

Capra, F. (1976). "The Tao of Physics". Fontana/Collins, London.

Carder, B. and Berkowitz, K. (1970). Rats' preference for earned in comparison with free food. *Science*, **167**, 1273-1274.

Catania, A. C. (1972). The pigeon's preference for free choice over forced choice. Paper presented to the Psychonomic Society, St. Louis, November 1972.

Chapman, A. J. (1976). Social aspects of humorous laughter. *In* "Humour and Laughter: Theory, Research and Applications". (A. J. Chapman and H. C. Foot, eds). Wiley, London, pp.155-185.

Chapman, A. J. and Foot, H. C. (eds). (1976a) "Humour and Laughter: Theory, Research and Applications". Wiley, London.

Chapman, A. J. and Foot, H. C. (1976b). Introduction. *In* "Humour and Laughter: Theory, Research and Applications". (A. J. Chapman and H. C. Foot, eds). Wiley, London, pp.1-7.

Chapman, A. J. and Foot, H. C. (eds). (1977). "It's a Funny Thing, Humour". Pergamon Press, Oxford.

Chomsky, N. (1957). "Syntactic Structures". Mouton, The Hague.

Chomsky, N. (1965). "Aspects of the Theory of Syntax". M.I.T. Press, Cambridge, Massachusetts.

Claparède, É. (1911). "Experimental Pedagogy and the Psychology of the Child". (Trans. by M. Louch and H. Holman). Arnold, London.

Clark, H. H. (1970). Word associations and linguistic theory. *In* "New Horizons in Linguistics". (J. Lyons, ed.). Penguin Books, Harmondsworth, pp.271-286.

Clark, J. H. (1972). A map of inner space. *In* "Six approaches to the Person". (R. Ruddock, ed.). Routledge and Kegan Paul, London.

Cohen, J. (1953). The ideas of work and play. *British Journal of Sociology*, **4**, 4, 312-322.

Corso, J. F. (1967). "The Experimental Psychology of Sensory Behavior". Holt, Rinehart and Winston, New York.

Csikszentmihalyi, M. (1975). "Beyond Boredom and Anxiety: The Experience of Play in Work and Games". Jossey-Bass, San Francisco.

Cuny, H. (1964). "Ivan Pavlov: The Man and his Theories". (Trans. by P. Evans.) Souvenir Press, London. (Originally published by Seghers, Paris, 1962.)

Curran, D. and Partridge, M. (1955). "Psychological Medicine: A Short Introduction to Psychiatry". Livingstone, Edinburgh.

Daniel, R. S. (1967). Alpha and theta EEG in vigilance. *Perceptual and Motor Skills*, 25, 697-703.

Darwin, C. (1872). "The Expression of the Emotions in Man and Animals". Murray, London. (Republished by Watts, London, 1934.)

Davidson, A. B. (1971). Factors affecting keypress responding by rats in the presence of free food. *Psychonomic Science*, 24, 135-137.

De Bono, E. (1968). "The Five-Day Course in Thinking". Allen Lane The Penguin Press, Harmondsworth.

Deci, E. L. (1972). Intrinsic motivation, extrinsic reinforcement, and inequity. *Journal of Personality and Social Psychology*, 22, 113-120.

Deci, E. L. (1975). "Intrinsic Motivation". Plenum Press, New York.

Dennis, W. (1939). Spontaneous alternation in rats as an indicator of the persistence of stimulus effects. *Journal of Comparative Psychology*, 28, 305-312.

Dodson, F. D. (1971). "How to Parent". W. H. Allen, London.

Dolhinow, P. (1976). At play in the fields. *In* "Play" (J. S. Bruner, A. Jolly, and K. Sylva, eds). Penguin, Harmondsworth. (This paper was originally published in 1971), pp.312-319.

Douglas, M. (1966). "Purity and Danger: An Analysis of the Concepts of Pollution and Taboo". Routledge and Kegan Paul, London.

Dreistadt, R. (1970). Reversing, using opposites, negativism and aggressiveness in creative behavior in science and philosophy. *Psychology*, 7 (Pt. 2), 38-63.

Duff, W. (1975). "Images: Stone: B.C.: Thirty Centuries of Northwest Coast Indian Sculpture". Oxford University Press, Toronto.

Duffy, E. (1934). The conceptual categories of psychology: a suggestion for revision. *Psychological Review*, 41, 184-198.

Duffy, E. (1941). An explanation of "emotional" phenomena without the use of the concept "emotion". *Journal of General Psychology*, 25, 283-293.

Duffy, E. (1957). The psychological significance of the concept of "arousal" or "activation". *Psychological Review*, 64, 265-75.

Duffy, E. (1962). "Activation and Behavior". Wiley, New York.

Duncker, K. (1945). On problem solving. *Psychological Monographs*, 58, 5, 1-111.

Durgnat, R. (1967). "Films and Feelings". Faber and Faber, London.

Dutton, D. G. and Aron, A. P. (1974). Some evidence for heightened sexual attraction under conditions of high anxiety. *Journal of Personality and Social Psychology*, 30, 510-517.

Eastman, M. (1921). "The Sense of Humor". Scribners, New York.

Eastman, M. (1936). "Enjoyment of Laughter". Simon and Schuster, New York.

Eccles, R. (1978). The central rhythm of the nasal cycle. *Acta Otolaryngol*, 86, 464-468.

Eckblad, G. (1981). "Scheme Theory". Academic Press, New York and London.

Ehrmann, J. (ed.) (1970). "Structuralism". Anchor Books, Doubleday, New York.

Eliade, M. (1963). "Myth and Reality". Harper and Row, New York.

Ellis, A. (1962). "Reason and Emotion in Psychotherapy". Lyle Stuart, New York.

Emmons, T. D. and Webb, W. W. (1974). Subjective correlates of emotional responsivity and stimulation seeking in psychopaths, normals and acting-out neurotics. *Journal of Consulting and Clinical Psychology*, **42**, 620.

Empson, W. (1930). "Seven Types of Ambiguity". Chatto & Windus, London. (Reissued by Penguin Books, Harmondsworth, in association with Chatto & Windus, London, 1972).

Evans, C. (1973). "Cults of Unreason". Harrap, London.

Eysenck, H. J. (1967). "The Biological Basis of Personality". Charles C. Thomas, Springfield, Illinois.

Eysenck, H. J. (1970). "Crime and Personality". Paladin, London. (Originally published by Routledge and Kegan Paul, London, 1964.)

Eysenck, H. J. and Wilson, G. (1975). "Know Your Own Personality". Temple-Smith, London.

Eysenck, S. B. G. and Eysenck, H. J. (1977). The place of impulsiveness in a dimensional system of personality description. *British Journal of Social and Clinical Psychology*, **16**, 57-58.

Farley, F. H. (1973). Implications for a theory of delinquency. *In* T. I. Myers (Chm.). The sensation seeking motive. Symposium presented at the 81st meeting of the American Psychological Association, Montreal, August 1973.

Farrell, B. (1963). Introduction. *In* "Leonardo" by Sigmund Freud, Penguin Books, Harmondsworth, pp.11-88.

Fechner, G. T. (1873). "Einige Ideen zur Schopfungs, und Entwicklungsgeschichte der Organismen". Leipzig.

Festinger, L. (1957). "A Theory of Cognitive Dissonance". Row, Peterson, Evanston, Illinois.

Festinger, L., Riecken, H. W. Jr., and Schachter, S. (1956). "When Prophecy Fails". University of Minnesota Press, Minneapolis.

Fisher, S. (1973). "The Female Orgasm: Psychology, Physiology, Fantasy". Allen Lane, Harmondsworth.

Fiske, D. W. and Maddi, S. R. (1961). A conceptual framework. *In* "Functions of Varied Experience". (D. W. Fiske and S. R. Maddi, eds). Dorsey, Homewood, Illinois, pp.11-56.

Flugel, J. C. (1955). "Man, Morals and Society: A Psychoanalytical study". Penguin Books, Harmondsworth.

Fodor, J. A., Bever, T. G. and Garrett, M. F. (1974). "The Psychology of Language: An Introduction of Psycholinguistics and Generative Grammar". McGraw-Hill, New York.

Fontana, D. (1978). An Investigation of Reversal and Obsessionality. Unpublished Ph.D. thesis, University of Wales.

Foot, H. C. and Chapman, A. J. (1976). The social responsiveness of young children in humorous situations. *In* "Humour and Laughter: Theory, Research and Applications". (A. J. Chapman and H. C. Foot, eds). Wiley, London.

Foster, M. LeCron (1974). Deep structure in symbolic anthropology. *Ethos*, **2**, 4, 334-355.

Fowler, H. (1965). "Curiosity and Exploratory Behavior". Macmillan, New York.

Fox, E. and Blatt, S. J. (1969). An attempt to test assumptions about some indications of negativism on psychological tests. *Journal of Consulting and Clinical Psychology*, **33**, 3, 365-366.

Franke, R. (1931). "Gang und Character". *Beihefte, Zeitschrift für angewandte Psychologie*, No. 58.

Frankl, V. E. (1973a). "Psychotherapy and Existentialism: Selected Papers on Logotherapy". Penguin, Harmondsworth.

Frankl, V. E. (1973b). "The Doctor and the Soul: From Psychotherapy to Logotherapy". Penguin, Harmondsworth.

Freedman, J. L. (1963). Long term behavioral effects of cognitive dissonance. *Journal of Experimental Social Psychology*, **1**, 145-155.

Freeman, D. S. (1976). The family as a system: fact or fantasy? *Comprehensive Psychiatry*, **17**, 6, 735-747.

Freeman, G. L. (1948). "Physiological Psychology". Van Nostrand, New York.

Frenkel-Brunswik, E. (1949). Intolerance of ambiguity as an emotional and perceptual personality variable. *Journal of Personality*, **18**, 108-143.

Freud, A. (1937). "The Ego and the Mechanisms of Defence". Hogarth Press, London. (Republished, 1968).

Freud, S. (1888). Hysterie. *In* "Handwörterbuch der gesamten Medizin". (A. Villaret, ed.). Stuttgart, **1**, 886-92. (Translated as "Hysteria", Standard Edition of the Complete Psychological Works of Sigmund Freud, Vol. I. ed. J. Strachey. Hogarth Press, London, 1966. pp.39-57).

Freud, S. (1900). "Die Traumdeutung". (Translated into English as "The Interpretation of Dreams". Standard Edition of the Complete Psychological Works of Sigmund Freud, Vols. IV-V, ed. J. Strachey, Hogarth Press, London, 1953).

Freud, S. (1905). "Der Witz und Seine Beziehung zum Unbewussten". Deuticke, Leipzig and Vienna. (Translated as "Jokes and Their Relation to the Unconscious". Standard Edition of the Complete Psychological Works of Sigmund Freud, Vol. VIII, ed. J. Strachey, Hogarth Press, London, 1960).

Freud, S. (1915). "Triebe und Triebschicksale". (Translated as "Instincts and their Vicissitudes". Standard Edition of the Complete Psychological Works of Sigmund Freud, Vol. XIV, ed. J. Strachey, Hogarth Press, London, 1957, pp.109-140).

Freud, S. (1920). "Jenseits der Lustprinzips". Internationaler Psychoanalytischer Verlag, Leipzig. (Translated as "Beyond the Pleasure Principle". Standard Edition of the Complete Psychological Works of Sigmund Freud, Vol. XVIII, ed. J. Strachey, Hogarth Press, London, 1955, pp.7-64).

Freud, S. (1923). Das Ich und das Es. *Gesammelte Schriften*, **6**, 353. (Translated as "The Ego and The Id", Standard Edition of the Complete Psychological Works of Sigmund Freud, Vol. XIX, ed. J. Strachey, Hogarth Press, London, 1961, pp.12-66).

Freud, S. (1924). Das ökonomische Problem des Masochismus. *Gesammelte Schriften*, **5**, 374. (Translated as "Economic Problem of Masochism". Standard Edition of the Complete Psychological Works of Sigmund Freud, Vol. XIX; 1961, ed. J. Strachey, Hogarth Press, London, pp.157-170).

Freud, S. (1926). "Hemmung, Symptom und Angst". Internationaler Psychoanalytischer Verlag, Leipzig. (Translated as "Inhibitions, Symptoms and Anxiety". Standard

Edition of the Complete Psychological Works of Sigmund Freud, Vol. XX, ed. J. Strachey, Hogarth Press, London, 1959, pp.77-174).

Freud, S. (1928). Humour. *International Journal of Psychoanalysis*, **9**, 1-6.

Freud, S. and Breuer, J. (1895). "Studien über Hysterie". Deuticke, Leipzig. (Translated as "Studies on Hysteria". Standard Edition of the Complete Psychological Works of Sigmund Freud, Vol. II, ed. J. Strachey, Hogarth Press, London, 1955).

Fromm, E. (1977). "The Anatomy of Human Destructiveness". Penguin Books, Harmondsworth. (First published in Great Britain by Jonathan Cape, 1974).

Frude, N. (1979). The aggression incident: a perspective for understanding abuse. *Child Abuse and Neglect*, **3**, 903-906.

Gardner, H. (1976). "The Quest for Mind: Piaget, Lévi-Strauss and the Structuralist Movement". Quartet Books, London.

Gauld, A. and Shotter, J. (1977). "Human Action and its Psychological Investigation". Routledge and Kegan Paul, London.

Geen, R. G. and O'Neal, E. C. (eds.). (1976). "Perspectives on Aggression". Academic Press, New York and London.

Gennep, A. van (1960). "The Rites of Passage". Routledge and Kegan Paul, London.

George, F. H. (1965). "Cybernetics and Biology". Oliver and Boyd, Edinburgh.

George, F. H. (1979). "Philosophical Foundations of Cybernetics". Abacus, London.

Gerz, H. O. (1973). The treatment of the phobic and the obsessive-compulsive patient using paradoxical intention, Sec Viktor E. Frankl. *In* "Psychotherapy and Existentialism: Selected Papers on Logotherapy" by V. E. Frankl. Penguin Books, Harmondsworth, pp.185-205.

Giddings, R. (1979). Something about a soldier. *New Society*, 27th September, 686-7.

Giles, H. and Oxford, G. S. (1970). Towards a multidimensional theory of laughter causation and its social implications. *Bulletin of the British Psychological Society*, **23**, 97-105.

Girdner, J. B. (1953). An experimental analysis of the behavioral effects of a perceptual consequence unrelated to organic drive states. *American Psychologist*, **8**, 354-355. (Abstract).

Glanzer, M. (1953). The role of stimulus satiation in spontaneous alternation. *Journal of Experimental Psychology*, **45**, 387-393.

Glover, E. (1949). "Psycho-Analysis. A Handbook for Medical Practitioners and Students of Psychology". Staples Press, London. (2nd edn.).

Glueck, S. and Glueck, E. (1952). "Delinquents in the Making: Paths to Prevention". Harper and Brothers, New York.

Godkewitsch, M. (1972). The relationship between arousal potential and funniness of jokes. *In* "The Psychology of Humor" (J. H. Goldstein and P. E. McGhee, eds). Academic Press, New York and London, pp.129-142.

Godkewitsch, M. (1976). Physiological and verbal indices of arousal in rated humour. *In* "Humour and Laughter: Theory, Research and Applications". (A. J. Chapman and H. C. Foot, eds). Wiley, London.

Goffman, E. (1969). "The Presentation of Self in Everyday Life". Allen Lane The Penguin Press, Harmondsworth. (Originally published by Anchor Books, New York, 1959).

Goffman, E. (1975). "Frame Analysis: An Essay on the Organisation of Experience". Penguin Books, Harmondsworth.

Goldstein, J. H. and McGhee, P. E. (eds). (1972). "The Psychology of Humor". Academic Press, New York and London.

Goodenough, F. L. (1929). The emotional behavior of young children during mental tests. *Journal of Juvenile Research*, **13**, 204-219.

Goodenough, F. L. (1931). "Anger in Young Children". University of Minnesota Press, Minneapolis.

Greenberg, R. (1973). Anti-expectation techniques in psychotherapy: the power of negative thinking. *Psychotherapy: Theory, Research and Practice*, **10**, 2, 145-148.

Greene, D. (1974). Immediate and subsequent effects of differential reward systems on intrinsic motivation in public school classrooms. Unpublished doctoral dissertation, Stanford University.

Greene, D. and Lepper, M. (1975). How to make play hard work. *Psychology To-Day*, **1**, 5, 28-31.

Griffin, D. R. (1976). "The Question of Animal Awareness: Expanding Horizons in Ethology". Rockefeller University Press, New York.

Groos, K. (1898). "The Play of Animals". Appleton, New York.

Groos, K. (1901). "The Play of Man". Heinemann, London.

Grossman, S. P. (1967). "A Textbook of Physiological Psychology". Wiley, New York.

Guilford, J. P., Christensen, P. R., Frick, J. W., and Merrifield, P. R. (1959). The relation of creative-thinking aptitudes to non-aptitude personality traits. *Reports of the Psychology Laboratory No. 20*. University of Southern California, Los Angeles.

Hagan, J. (1977). "The Disreputable Pleasures". McGraw-Hill Ryerson, Toronto.

Haken, H. (ed.) (1974). "Cooperative Effects: Progress in Synergetics". North-Holland Publishing Company, Amsterdam.

Haken, H. (ed.) (1977). "Synergetics: A Workshop". Springer-Verlag, Berlin.

Haken, H. (1978). "Synergetics: An Introduction" (2nd edition), Springer-Verlag, Berlin.

Haley, J. (ed.) (1967a). "Advanced Techniques of Hypnosis and Therapy: Selected Papers of Milton H. Erickson". Grune and Stratton, New York.

Haley, J. (1967b). Toward a theory of pathological systems. *In* "Family Therapy and Disturbed Families". (G. H. Zuk and I. Boszormenyi-Nagy, eds). Science and Behavior Books, Inc., Palo Alto, California, pp.11-27.

Hall, C. S. and Lindzey, G. (1957). "Theories of Personality". Wiley, New York.

Halliday, M. A. K. (1976). Anti-languages. *American Anthropologist*, **78**, 3, 570-584.

Halliday, M. S. (1966). Exploration and fear in the rat. *Symposium of the Zoological Society of London*, No. 18, 45-59.

Halpin, M. (1979). Confronting looking-glass men: a preliminary examination of the mask. *Occasional Publications in Anthropology*, Ethnology Series No. 33. (N. Ross Crumrine, ed.). Museum of Anthropology, University of Northern Colorado.

Hampshire, S. (1965). "Thought and Action". Chatto & Windus, London.

Hare, R. D. (1973). Autonomic activity and conditioning in psychopaths. *In* "Contemporary Abnormal Psychology". (Maher, B., ed.). Penguin, Harmondsworth, 224-251.

Harlow, H. F. (1950). Learning and satiation of response in intrinsically motivated complex puzzle performance by monkeys. *Journal of Comparative and Physiological Psychology*, **43**, 289-294.

Harlow, H. F. (1953). Motivation as a factor in the acquisition of new responses. *In*

344 THE EXPERIENCE OF MOTIVATION

"Current Theory and Research in Motivation: A Symposium". (M. R. Jones, ed.). University of Nebraska Press, Lincoln, Nebraska, pp.24-49.

Harlow, H. F. (1959a). Learning set and error factor theory. In "Psychology: A Study of a Science, Vol. 2". (S. Koch, ed.). McGraw-Hill, New York, pp.492-537.

Harlow, H. F. (1959b). Love in infant monkeys. Scientific American, 200, 6, 68-74.

Harlow, H. F., Harlow, M. K. and Meyer, D. R. (1950). Learning motivated by a manipulation drive. Journal of Experimental Psychology, 40, 228-234.

Harlow, H. F. and Zimmermann, R. R. (1959). Affectional responses in the infant monkey. Science, 130, (3373), 421-432.

Harré, R. and Secord, P. F. (1972). "The Explanation of Social Behaviour". Blackwell, Oxford. (Paperback edition, 1976).

Hawkes, T. (1977). "Structuralism and Semiotics". Methuen, London.

Hearnshaw, L. S. (1964). "A Short History of British Psychology, 1840-1940". Methuen, London.

Hebb, D. O. (1955). Drives and the C.N.S. (Conceptual Nervous System). Psychological Review, 62, 243-54.

Hebb, D. O. and Thompson, W. R. (1954). The social significance of animal studies. In "Handbook of Social Psychology". (G. Lindzey, ed.). Addison-Wesley, Cambridge, Massachusetts, pp.532-561.

Heider, F. (1946). Attitudes and cognitive organization. Journal of Psychology, 21, 107-112.

Heider, F. (1958). "The Psychology of Interpersonal Relations". Wiley, New York.

Helson, H. (1947). Adaptation-level as a frame of reference for prediction of psychophysical data. American Journal of Psychology, 60, 1-29.

Helson, H. (1964). "Adaptation-Level Theory". Harper and Row, New York.

Henderson, L. J. (1913). "The Fitness of the Environment". Macmillan, New York.

Hendrick, I. (1966). "Facts and Theories of Psychoanalysis". Dell (Laurel Edition), New York.

Hilgard, E. R., Atkinson, R. C. and Atkinson, R. L. (1975). "Introduction to Psychology". (6th Edition). Harcourt Brace Jovanovich, New York.

Hinnells, J. R. (1971). Iran. In "Man and his Gods: Encyclopedia of the World's Religions" (G. Parrinder, ed.). Hamlyn, London.

Hite, S. (1977). "The Hite Report: A Nationwide Study of Female Sexuality". Summit Books (Paul Hamlyn), Sydney.

Hobhouse, L. T. (1901). "Mind in Evolution". Macmillan, London.

Holenstein, E. (1977). "Roman Jakobson's Approach to Language: Phenomenological Structuralism". (Translated by C. Schelbert and T. Schelbert). Indiana University Press, Bloomington, Indiana.

Holly, D. (1971). "Society, Schools and Humanity". MacGibbon and Kee, London.

Hoon, P. W., Wincze, J. P. and Hoon, E. F. (1977). A test of reciprocal inhibition: are anxiety and sexual arousal in women mutually inhibitory? Journal of Abnormal Psychology, 86, 65-74.

Horney, K. (1936). The problem of the negative therapeutic reaction. Psychoanalytic Quarterly, 5, 29-44.

Hornsby, J. (1980). "Actions". Routledge and Kegan Paul, London.

Hudson, L. (1967). "Contrary Imaginations: A Psychological Study of the English Schoolboy". Penguin, Harmondsworth. (First published by Methuen, London, 1966).

Huizinga, J. (1949). "Homo Ludens: A Study of the Play Element in Culture". Routledge and Kegan Paul, London. (Reprinted by Paladin, London, 1970).

Hull, C. L. (1943). "Principles of Behavior". Appleton-Century-Crofts, New York.

Hunt, M. (1974). "Sexual Behavior in the 1970s". Playboy Press, Chicago.

Hurwitz, H. M. B. (1956). Conditioned responses in rats reinforced by light. *British Journal of Animal Behaviour*, **4**, 31-33.

Hyers, M. C. (1974). "Zen and the Comic Spirit". Rider, London.

Itten, J. (1975). "Design and Form: The Basic Course at the Bauhaus". Thames and Hudson, London.

Jacobson, E. (1938). "Progressive Relaxation". University of Chicago Press, Chicago.

Jaffe, Y., Malamuth, N., Feingold, J. and Feshbach, S. (1974). Sexual arousal and behavioral aggression. *Journal of Personality and Social Psychology*, **30**, 6, 759-764.

Jakobson, R. and Halle, M. (1956). "Fundamentals of Language". Mouton, The Hague.

James, W. (1890). "The Principles of Psychology", 2 Vols, Holt, New York.

James, W. (1902). "The Varieties of Religious Experience". Longman, Green & Co., London.

Janov, A. (1970). "The Primal Scream". Putnam, New York.

Jasper, H. H. (1958). Reticular-cortical systems and theories of the integrative action of the brain. *In* "Biological and Biochemical Bases of Behavior" (H. F. Harlow and C. N. Woolsey, eds), University of Wisconsin Press, Madison, Wisconsin, pp.37-62.

Jensen, G. D. (1963). Preference for barpressing over 'freeloading' as a function of number of rewarded presses. *Journal of Experimental Psychology*, **65**, 451-454.

Jones, R. and Walter, T. (1978). Delinquency is fun. *Community Care*, No. 225, 20-21.

Joynson, R. B. (1974). "Psychology and Common Sense". Routledge and Kegan Paul, London.

Jung, C. G. (1954). The aims of psychotherapy. *In* "The Practice of Psychotherapy", Collected Works, Vol. 16. Routledge and Kegan Paul, London.

Kagan, J. and Berkun, M. (1954). The reward value of running activity. *Journal of Comparative and Physiological Psychology*, **47**, 108.

Kanner, L. (1948). "Child Psychiatry". Blackwell, Oxford. (2nd Edition).

Kaplan, H. S. (1978). "The New Sex Therapy: Active Treatment of Sexual Dysfunctions". Penguin, Harmondsworth.

Keen, E. (1975). "A Primer in Phenomenological Psychology". Holt, Rinehart and Winston, New York.

Kelly, G. (1955). "The Psychology of Personal Constructs, Vols 1 and 2". Norton, New York.

Kiesler, C. A., Nisbett, R. E. and Zanna, M. P. (1969). On inferring one's beliefs from one's behaviour. *Journal of Personality and Social Psychology*, **11**, 321-7.

Kinsey, A. C., Pomeroy, W. B., Martin, C. E. and Gebhard, P. H. (1953). "Sexual Behavior in the Human Female". W. B. Saunders, Philadelphia.

Kish, G. B. and Antonitis, J. J. (1956). Unconditioned operant behavior in two homozygous strains of mice. *Journal of Genetic Psychology*, **88**, 121-124.

Kimble, G. A. (1951). Behavior strength as a function of the intensity of the hunger drive. *Journal of Experimental Psychology*, **41**, 341-348.

Kleinke, C. L. (1978). "Self-Perception: The Psychology of Personal Awareness". Freeman, San Francisco.

Klinger, E. (1971). "Structure and Functions of Fantasy". Wiley, New York.
Koch, S. (1964). Psychology and emerging conceptions of knowledge as unitary. In "Behaviorism and Phenomenology: Contrasting Bases for Modern Psychology". (Wann, T. W., ed.). University of Chicago Press, Chicago.
Koestler, A. (1949). "Insight and Outlook". Macmillan, London.
Koestler, A. (1964). "The Act of Creation". Hutchinson, London.
Köhler, W. (1926). "The Mentality of Apes". Routledge and Kegan Paul, London. (Reprinted by Penguin, Harmondsworth, 1957).
Krech, D. and Crutchfield, R. S. (1948). "Theory and Problems of Social Psychology". McGraw-Hill, New York.
Kruglanski, A. W. (1975). The endogenous-exogenous partition in attribution theory. Psychological Review, 82, 6, 387-406.
Kruglanski, A. W., Alon, S., and Lewis, T. (1972). Retrospective misattribution and task enjoyment. Journal of Experimental Social Psychology, 8, 493-501.
Kuenzli, A. E. (ed.). (1959). "The Phenomenological Problem". Harper & Row, New York.
Kushner, A. W. (1967). Two cases of auto-castration due to religious delusions. British Journal of Medical Psychology, 40, 293-8. Reprinted in: "Psychology and Religion" (L. B. Brown, ed.). Penguin Books, Harmondsworth, 1973, pp.366-375.
Kwakernaak, H. (1973). Dynamic Systems and Control. In "Process Models for Psychology" (D. J. Dalenoort, ed.). Rotterdam University Press, Rotterdam.
L'Abate, L. (1976). "Understanding and Helping the Individual in the Family". Grune and Stratton, New York.
La Fave, L., Haddad, J. and Maesen, W. A. (1976). Superiority enhanced self-esteem, and perceived incongruity humour theory. In "Humour and Laughter: Theory, Research and Applications". (A. J. Chapman and H. C. Foot, eds). Wiley, London. pp.63-91.
La Fave, L., Mannell, R. and Guilmette, A. M. (1977). An irony of irony: the left-handed insult in intragroup humour. In "It's a Funny Thing, Humour". (A. J. Chapman and H. C. Foot eds). Pergamon Press, Oxford. pp.283-285.
Lamb, C. W. (1968). Personality correlates of humor enjoyment following motivational arousal. Journal of Personality and Social Psychology, 9, 3, 237-241.
Landis, C. and Hunt, W. A. (1939). "The Startle Pattern". Farrar, New York.
Lane, M. (ed.) (1970). "Structuralism: A Reader". Cape, London.
Lange, K. (1907). "Das Wesen der Kunst". Grote, Berlin.
Langevin, R. and Day, H. I. (1972). Physiological correlates of humor. In "The Psychology of Humor". (J. H. Goldstein and P. E. McGhee, eds). Academic Press, New York and London.
Lawick-Goodall, J. van (1976). Chimpanzee locomotor play. In "Play" (J. S. Bruner, A. Jolly and K. Sylva, eds). Penguin, Harmondsworth, 156-160.
Leach, E. (1964). Anthropological aspects of language: animal categories and verbal abuse. In "New Directions in the Study of Language". (E. H. Lenneberg, ed.). Massachusetts Institute of Technology Press, Massachusetts, pp.23-63. Reprinted in "Mythology", (P. Maranda, ed.). Penguin, Harmondsworth, 1972, pp.39-67.
Leach, E. (1976). "Culture and Communication: The Logic by which Symbols are Connected". Cambridge University Press, Cambridge.
Leach, E. (1977). "Custom, Law and Terrorist Violence". Edinburgh University Press, Edinburgh.

Lepper, M. R., Zanna, M. P. and Abelson, R. P. (1970). Cognitive irreversibility in a dissonance-reduction situation. *Journal of Personality and Social Psychology*, **16**, 191-8.

Lepper, M. R., Greene, D., and Nisbett, R. E. (1973). Undermining children's intrinsic interest with extrinsic rewards: a test of the "overjustification" hypothesis. *Journal of Personality and Social Psychology*, **28**, 129-137.

Lepper, M. R. and Greene, D. (1975). Turning play into work: effects of adult surveillance and extrinsic rewards on children's intrinsic motivation. *Journal of Personality and Social Psychology*, **31**, 479-486.

Letemendia, M. P. (1977). Problems in phenomenological psychology. *Bulletin of the British Psychological Society*, **30**, 137-139.

Leuba, C. (1955). Toward some integration of learning theories: the concept of optimal stimulation. *Psychological Reports*, **1**, 27-33. Reprinted in "Curiosity and Exploratory Behavior". (H. Fowler, ed.). Macmillan, New York, 1965, pp.169-175.

Levi, L. (1963). The urinary output of adrenaline and noradrenaline during pleasant and unpleasant emotional states. *Psychosomatic Medicine*, **27**, 403-419.

Lévi-Strauss, C. (1955). The structural study of myth. *Journal of American Folklore*, **68**, No. 270, 428-44.

Lévi-Strauss, C. (1963). "Structural Anthropology". (Trans. C. Jacobson and B. G. Schoepf). Basic Books, New York. (Originally published in 1958 by Plon, Paris).

Lévi-Strauss, C. (1964). "Totemism". (Trans. R. Needham). Merlin Press, London. (Originally published in 1962 by Presses Universitaires de France, Paris).

Lévi-Strauss, C. (1965). Le triangle culinaire. *L'Arc*, No. 26. 19-29. (English version in *New Society*, 22 December 1966, 937-40).

Lévi-Strauss, C. (1966). "The Savage Mind". Weidenfeld and Nicolson, London. (Original publication, "La Pensée Sauvage", Plon, Paris, 1962).

Lévi-Strauss, C. (1968). "The Elementary Structures of Kinship". Eyre and Spottiswoode, London. (Originally published in 1949 in French by Presses Universitaires de France, Paris).

Levitt, E. E. (1971). "The Psychology of Anxiety". Paladin, London.

Levy, D. M. and Tulchin, S. H. (1923). The resistance of infants and children during mental tests. *Journal of Experimental Psychology*, **6**, 304-322.

Levy, D. M. and Tulchin, S. H. (1925). The resistant behavior of infants and children. II. *Journal of Experimental Psychology*, **8**, 209-224.

Lévy-Bruhl, L. (1923). "Primitive Mentality", translated by L. A. Clare, Macmillan, New York. (Originally published in 1922 as "La Mentalité Primitive", Paris).

Lewin, K. (1935). "A Dynamic Theory of Personality: Selected Papers". McGraw-Hill, New York.

Lewin, K. (1951). "Field Theory in Social Science: Selected Theoretical Papers". (Ed. D. Cartwright), Harper & Row, New York.

Liddell, H. S. (1954). Conditioning and emotions. *Scientific American*, January 1954.

Lipps, T. (1903). "Ästhetik Vol. 1". Voss, Leipzig. (Vol. 2 published 1906).

Lloyd, G. E. R. (1966). "Polarity and Analogy: Two Types of Argumentation in Early Greek Thought". Cambridge University Press, Cambridge.

Loader, J. A. (1979). "Polar Structures in the Book of Qohelet". Walter de Gruyter, Berlin.

Loizos, C. (1966). Play in mammals. *Symposium of the Zoological Society of London*, No. 18, pp.1-9.

Loizos, C. (1976). An ethological study of chimpanzee play. *In* "Play". (J. S. Bruner, A. Jolly and K. Sylva, eds). Penguin Harmondsworth. pp.345-351. (This paper was originally published in 1969).

Lorenz, K. (1950). The comparative method in studying innate behaviour patterns. "Symposia of the Society for Experimental Biology", Vol. 4. Cambridge University Press, Cambridge, pp.221-68. Excerpts from this paper are given in "Motivation: Selected Readings". (D. Bindra and J. Stewart, eds). Penguin Books, Harmondsworth, 1966, pp.23-27.

Lorenz, K. (1966). "On Aggression". Methuen, London.

Louch, A. R. (1966). "Explanation and Human Action". Blackwell, Oxford.

Lowen, A. (1975). "Pleasure: A Creative Approach to Life". Penguin, New York.

Luchins, A. S. (1942). Mechanization in problem solving: the effect of Einstellung. *Psychological Monographs*, **54**, Whole Number 248.

Lucio-Meyer, J. J. de (1973). "Visual Aesthetics". Lund Humphries, London.

Luthe, W. (1969-73). "Autogenic Therapy, Vols. I-VI". Grune and Stratton, New York.

Lyons, J. (1968). "Introduction to Theoretical Linguistics". Cambridge University Press, Cambridge.

MacLeod, R. B. (1947). The phenomenological approach to social psychology. *Psychological Review*, **54**, 193-210.

MacLeod, R. B. (1964). Phenomenology: A challenge to experimental psychology. *In* "Behaviorism and Phenomenology: Contrasting Bases for Modern Psychology". (T. W. Wann, ed.). Chicago University Press, Chicago, pp.47-78.

Macmurray, J. (1957). "The Self as Agent". Faber and Faber, London.

Magnusson, D. and Endler, N. S. (eds) (1977). "Personality at the Crossroads". Erlbaum, Hillsdale, New Jersey.

Maier, N. R. F. (1932). A Gestalt theory of humour. *British Journal of Psychology*, **23**, 69-74.

Malinowski, B. (1922). "Argonauts of the Western Pacific". Dutton, New York.

Malmo, R. B. (1958). Measurement of drive: an unsolved problem in psychology. *In* "Nebraska Symposium on Motivation". (M. R. Jones, ed.). University of Nebraska Press, Lincoln, Nebraska, pp.229-264.

Marsh, P. (1978a). "Aggro: The Illusion of Violence". Dent, London.

Marsh, P. (1978b). Life and careers on the soccer terraces. *In* "Football Hooliganism". R. Ingham, S. Hall, J. Clarke, P. Marsh and J. Donovan. Inter-action Inprint, London.

Marsh, P., Rosser, E. and Harré, R. (1980). "The Rules of Disorder". Routledge and Kegan Paul, London.

Martens, R. (1969). Palmar sweating and the presence of an audience. *Journal of Experimental Social Psychology*, **5**, 371-374.

Masling, J. (1966). Role-related behavior of the subject and psychologist and its effects upon psychological data. *In* "Nebraska Symposium on Motivation". (D. Levine, ed.). University of Nebraska Press, Lincoln, pp.67-103.

Maslow, A. H. (1954). "Motivation and Personality". Harper and Row, New York.

Maslow, A. H. (1973). "The Farther Reaches of Human Nature". Penguin Books, Harmondsworth.

Masters, W. H. and Johnson, V. E. (1966). "Human Sexual Response". Little, Brown and Co., Boston.

Masters, W. H. and Johnson, V. E. (1970). "Human Sexual Inadequacy". Little, Brown and Co., Boston.

May, R. (1976). "The Courage to Create". Collins, London.

McConnell, J. V. (1977). "Understanding Human Behavior". Holt, Rinehart and Winston, New York.

McLuhan, M. and Fiore, Q. (1968). "War and Peace in the Global Village". Bantam Books, New York.

Mead, G. H. (1934). "Mind, Self and Society". University of Chicago Press, Chicago.

Meadow, A., Parnes, S. J. and Rees, H. (1959). Influence of brainstorming instructions and problem sequence on a creative problem-solving test. *Journal of Applied Psychology*, **43**, 413-416.

Melden, A. I. (1961). "Free Action". Routledge and Kegan Paul, London.

Menninger, K. (1966). "Man Against Himself". Harcourt Brace Jovanovich, New York. (Originally published 1938).

Milgram, S. (1974). "Obedience to Authority: An Experimental View". Harper & Row, New York.

Miller, D. L. (1973). "Gods and Games: Toward a Theology of Play". Harper, New York.

Miller, G. A., Galanter, E. and Pribram, K. H. (1960). "Plans and the Structure of Behavior". Holt, Rinehart and Winston, New York.

Miller, N. E. (1941). The frustration-aggression hypothesis. *Psychological Review*, **48**, 337-342.

Miller, W. B. (1958). Lower class culture as a generating milieu of gang delinquency. *Journal of Social Issues*, **14**, 3, 5-19.

Mischel, T. (ed.) (1969). "Human Action". Academic Press, New York and London.

Mischel, T. (ed.) (1977). "The Self: Psychological and Philosophical Issues". Basil Blackwell, Oxford.

Mischel, W. (1968). "Personality and Assessment". Wiley, New York.

Mischel, W. (1969). Continuity and change in personality. *American Psychologist*, **24**, 1012-1018.

Misiak, H. and Sexton, V. S. (1973). "Phenomenological, Existential, and Humanistic Psychologies". Grune and Stratton, New York.

Montgomery, K. C. (1953). Exploratory behavior as a function of 'similarity' of stimulus situations. *Journal of Comparative and Physiological Psycholgy*, **46**, 129-133.

Montgomery, K. C. (1954). The role of the exploratory drive in learning. *Journal of Comparative and Physiological Psychology*, **47**, 60-4.

Moreno, J. L. (1934). "Who Shall Survive? A new approach to the problem of inter-relations". Nervous and Mental Disease Publishing House, Washington, D.C..

Moreno, J. L. (1964). Philosophy of the third psychiatric revolution. *In* "The Worlds of Existentialism: A Critical Reader". (M. Friedman, ed.). The University of Chicago Press, Chicago, pp.468-472.

Morgan, M. J. (1974). Resistance to satiation. *Animal Behaviour*, **22**, 449-466.

Moruzzi, G. and Magoun, H. W. (1949). Brain stem reticular formation and activation of the EEG. *EEG and clinical Neurophysiology*, **1**, 455-473.

Moyer, K. E. (ed.) (1976). "Physiology of Aggression and Implications for Control: An Anthology of Readings". Raven Press, New York.

Mukarovský, J. (1964). Standard language and poetic language. In "A Prague School Reader on Aesthetics, Literary Structure, and Style". (P. L. Garvin, ed.). Georgetown University Press, Washington, D. C. pp.17-30).

Murgatroyd, S., Rushton, C., Apter, M. J. and Ray, C. (1978). The development of the Telic Dominance Scale. *Journal of Personality Assessment*, **42**, 519-528.

Murray, H. A. (1938). "Explorations in Personality". Oxford University Press, New York.

Myers, A. K. and Miller, N. E. (1954). Failure to find a learned drive based on hunger; evidence for learning motivated by 'Exploration'. *Journal of Comparative and Physiological Psychology*, **47**, 428-436.

Needham, R. (ed.) (1973). "Right and Left: Essays on Dual Symbolic Classification". University of Chicago Press, Chicago.

Newell, A. and Simon, H. A. (1963). GPS, a program that simulates human thought. In "Computers and Thought". (E. A. Feigenbaum and J. Feldman, eds). McGraw-Hill, New York, pp.279-293.

Nuttin, J. R. (1973). Pleasure and reward in human motivation and learning. In "Pleasure, Reward, Preference. Their Nature, Determinants, and Role in Behavior". (D. E. Berlyne and K. B. Madsen, eds). Academic Press, New York and London.

Ogden, C. K. (1967). "Opposition: A Linguistic and Psychological Analysis". Indiana University Press, Bloomington. (First published, 1932).

Ogden, C. K. and Richards, I. A. (1923). "The Meaning of Meaning". Harcourt, Brace, New York.

Oettinger, A. G. (1969). "Run, Computer, Run: The Mythology of Educational Innovation". Harvard University Press, Cambridge, Massachusetts.

Osborn, A. F. (1963). "Applied Imagination" (3rd edition). Scribner, New York.

Osgood, C. E., Suci, G. J. and Tannenbaum, P. H. (1957). "The Measurement of Meaning". University of Illinois Press, Urbana, Illinois.

Osgood, C. E. and Tannenbaum, P. H. (1955). The principle of congruity in the prediction of attitude change. *Psychological Review*, **62**, 42-55.

Parnes, S. J. (1963). Education and creativity. *Teachers College Record*, **64**, 331-339.

Parnes, S. J. and Meadow, A. (1959). Effects of brainstorming instructions on creative problem-solving by trained and untrained subjects. *Journal of Educational Psychology*, **50**, 171-176.

Pask, G. (1961). "An Approach to Cybernetics". Hutchinson, London.

Pavarotti, L. (1981). "My Own Story". Sidgwick and Jackson, London.

Pavlov, I. P. (1960). "Conditioned Reflexes". (Translated by G. V. Anrep). Dover Publications, New York. (Originally published in 1927 by Oxford University Press).

Peckham, M. (1965). "Man's Rage for Chaos: Biology, Behavior and the Arts". Chilton Books, Philadelphia.

Perls, F. S. (1971). "Gestalt Therapy Verbatim". Bantam Books, New York. (Originally published by the Real People Press, Utah, 1969).

Perls, F. S., Hefferline, R. F. and Goodman, P. (1973). "Gestalt Therapy: Excitement and Growth in the Human Personality". Penguin Books, Harmondsworth. (Originally published in the U.S.A. in 1951).

Peters, R. S. (1958). "The Concept of Motivation". Routledge and Kegan Paul, London.

Piaget, J. (1951). "Play, Dreams and Imitation in Childhood". Routledge and Kegan Paul, London.

Piaget, J. (1957). Logique et équilibre dans les comportements du sujet. In L. Apostel, B. Mandelbrot and J. Piaget, "Logique et Équilibre: Études d'Epistemologie Génétique", Vol. 2. Presses Universitaires de France, Paris, pp.27-117.

Piaget, J. (1971). "Structuralism". Routledge and Kegan Paul, London. (Original French edition, "Le Structuralisme", Presses Universitaires de France, Paris, 1968).

Pruyser, P. (1970). Thought organisation in religion. In "Personality and Religion: The Role of Religion in Personality Development". (W. A. Sadler, Jr. ed.). S.C.M. Press, London, pp.57-72.

Radcliffe-Brown, A. R. (1952). "Structure and Function in Primitive Society". Cohen and West, London.

Reynolds, M. M. (1928). "Negativism of Pre-School Children: An Observational and Experimental Study". Contributions to Education, No. 288. Bureau of Publications, Teachers College, Columbia University, New York.

Reynolds, V. (1976). "The Biology of Human Action". Freeman, San Francisco.

Rickwood, L. V. (1978). The Arousal Mechanism of Humour Appreciation and its Interaction with Motivational Arousal, Muscular Tension and Stress-Related Arousal. Doctoral dissertation, University of Manchester.

Rivière, J. (1936). A contribution to the analysis of the negative therapeutic reaction. *International Journal of Psychoanalysis*, **17**, 304-20.

Roberts, C. L., Marx, M. H. and Collier, G. (1958). Light onset and light offset as reinforcers for the albino rat. *Journal of Comparative and Physiological Psychology*, **51**, 575-579.

Robey, D. (ed.) (1973). "Structuralism: An Introduction". Clarendon Press, Oxford.

Robinson, J. S. (1961). The reinforcing effects of response-contingent light increment and decrement in hooded rats. *Journal of Comparative and Physiological Psychology*, **54**, 470-473.

Rochlin, G. (1973). "Man's Aggression: The Defense of the Self". Delta Books (Dell), New York.

Rogers, C. (1951). "Client-Centred Therapy". Houghton Mifflin, Boston.

Rogers, C. (1964). Toward a science of the person. In "Behaviorism and Phenomenology: Contrasting Bases for Modern Psychology". (T. W. Wann, ed.). Chicago University Press, Chicago, pp.109-140.

Rook, K. S. and Hammen, C. L. (1977). A cognitive perspective on the experience of sexual arousal. *Journal of Social Issues*, **33**, 2, 7-29.

Ross, M. (1976). The self-perception of intrinsic motivation. In "New Directions in Attribution Research (Vol. 1)". (J. H. Harvey, W. J. Ickes and R. F. Kidd, eds). Lawrence Erlbaum, Hillsdale, New Jersey.

Rothbart, M. K. (1973). Laughter in young children. *Psychological Bulletin*, **80**, 247-256.

Rothbart, M. K. (1976). Incongruity, problem-solving and laughter. In "Humour and Laughter: Theory, Research and Applications". (A. J. Chapman and H. C. Foot, eds). Wiley, London, pp.37-54.

Rothbart, M. K. and Pien, D. (1977). Elephants and marshmallows: a theoretical synthesis of incongruity-resolution and arousal theories of humour. In "It's a Funny Thing, Humour". (A. J. Chapman and H. C. Foot, eds). Pergamon, Oxford, pp.37-40.

Rothenberg, A. (1969). The iceman changeth: toward an empirical approach to creativity. *Journal of the American Psychoanalytic Association,* **17**, 549-607.
Rothenberg, A. (1971). The process of Janusian thinking. *Archives of General Psychiatry,* **24**, 195-205.
Rothenberg, A. (1979). "The Emerging Goddess: The Creative Process in Art, Science and Other Fields". University of Chicago Press, Chicago.
Rothenberg, A. (1980). Visual art: homospatial thinking in the creative process. *Leonardo,* **13**, 1, 17-27.
Russell, B. (1903). "The Principles of Mathematics". Cambridge University Press, Cambridge.
Russett, C. E. (1966). "The Concept of Equilibrium in American Social Thought". Yale University Press, New Haven.
Rycroft, C. (1968). "A Critical Dictionary of Psychoanalysis". Nelson, London. (Republished by Penguin Books, Harmondsworth, 1972).
Sadowski, B. (1974). Negativism to food during self-stimulation in the anterior part of the basal forebrain in dogs. *Physiology and Behavior,* **13**, 645-651.
Sales, S. M. (1971). Need for stimulation as a factor in social behavior. *Journal of Personality and Social Psychology,* **19**, 124-134.
Sandler, J., Holder, A. and Dare, C. (1970). Basic psychoanalytic concepts: VII. The negative therapeutic reaction. *British Journal of Psychiatry,* **117**, 431-35.
Sarbin, T. R. (1952). A preface to a psychological analysis of the self. *Psychological Review,* **59**, 11-22.
Sargant, W. (1957). "Battle for the Mind". Heinemann, London.
Sartre, J.-P. (1946). L'Existentialisme est un Humanisme". Nagel, Paris.
Saussure, F. de (1916). "Cours de Linguistique Générale", 5th edition, 1955, Paris, Payot. (English translation by W. Baskin, "Course in General Linguistics", Peter Owen, London, 1960).
Schachter, S. (1964). The interaction of cognitive and physiological determinants of emotional state. *In* "Psychobiological Approaches to Social Behavior". (P. H. Leiderman and D. Shapiro, eds). Stanford University Press, Stanford, California.
Schachter, S. (1970). The assumption of identity and peripheralist-centralist controversies in motivation and emotion. *In* "Feelings and Emotion: The Loyola Symposium". (M. B. Arnold, ed.). Academic Press, New York and London.
Schachter, S. (1971). "Emotion, Obesity and Crime". Academic Press, New York and London.
Schachter, S. (1973). Nesbitt's paradox. *In* "Smoking behavior: motives and incentives". (W. I. Dunn, ed.). Winston, New York, pp.147-155.
Schachter, S. and Singer, J. (1962). Cognitive, social and physiological determinants of emotional state. *Psychological Review,* **69**, 378-99.
Schachter, S. and Wheeler, L. (1962). Epinephrine, chlorpromazine, and amusement. *Journal of Abnormal and Social Psychology,* **65**, 2, 121-128.
Schaeffer, G. H. and Patterson, M. L. (1980). Intimacy, arousal and small group crowding. *Journal of Personality and Social Psychology,* **38**, 2, 283-290.
Schopenhauer, A. (1819). "Die Welt als Wille und Vorstellung". Brockhaus, Leipzig. (Translated by Payne, E. F. J. as "The World as Will and Representation", 2 vols. Dover, New York, 1966).

Schultz, D. D. (1965). "Sensory Restriction: Effects on Behavior". Academic Press, New York and London.

Schultz, J. H. (1932). "Das Autogene Training". Leipzig.

Seligman, M. E. P. (1975). "Helplessness: On Depression, Development and Death". Freeman, San Francisco.

Selye, H. (1956). "The Stress of Life". McGraw-Hill, New York.

Selye, H. (1975). "Stress without Distress". Hodder and Stoughton, London.

Sharpless, S. and Jasper, H. H. (1956). Habituation of the arousal reaction. *Brain*, **79**, 655-680.

Shaw, W. A. (1956). Facilitating effects of induced tension upon the perception span for digits. *Journal of Experimental Psychology*, **51**, 113-117.

Sherrington, C. S. (1966). "The Integrative Action of the Nervous System". Yale University Press, New Haven, Connecticut, (Originally pub. 1906).

Shevrin, H. and Dickman, S. (1980). The psychological unconscious: a necessary assumption for all psychological theory? *American Psychologist*, **35**, 5, 421-434.

Shotter, J. (1975). "Images of Man in Psychological Research". Methuen, London.

Shultz, T. R. (1976). A cognitive-developmental analysis of humour. *In* "Humour and Laughter: Theory, Research and Applications". (A. J. Chapman and H. C. Foot, eds). Wiley, London, pp.11-36.

Shurcliff, A. (1968). Judged humor, arousal, and the relief theory. *Journal of Personality and Social Psychology*, **8**, 4, 360-363.

Shwayder, D. S. (1965). "The Stratification of Behaviour". Routledge and Kegan Paul, London.

Singer, J. L. (1976). "Daydreaming and Fantasy". Allen and Unwin, London.

Simondon, G. (1958). "Du Mode d'Existence des Objects Techniques". Aubier, Éditions Montaigne, Paris.

Smith, C. E. (1971). An atypical session: resistance and the negativistic patient. *Psychotherapy: Theory, Research and Practice*, **8**, 4, 276-279.

Smith, K. C. P. and Apter, M. J. (1975). "A Theory of Psychological Reversals". Picton Publishing, Chippenham (U.K.) 17pp.

Smith, K. C. P. and Apter, M. J. (1977). Collecting antiques: a psychological interpretation. *Antique Collector*, **48**, 7, 64-66.

Snygg, D. (1941). The need for a phenomenological system of psychology. *Psychological Review*, **48**, 404-424.

Snygg, D. and Combs, A. W. (1949). "Individual Behavior: A New Frame of Reference for Psychology". Harper and Row, New York.

Sokolov, E. N. (1960). Neuronal models and the orienting reflex. *In* "The Central Nervous System and Behaviour" (M. A. B. Brazier, ed.). Josiah Macy, Jr. Foundation, New York.

Spiegelberg, H. (1976). "The Phenomenological Movement, Vol. I and Vol. II". Martinus Nijhoff, the Hague (2nd edition).

Spitz, R. A. and Wolf, K. W. (1946). The smiling response: a contribution to the ontogenesis of social relations. *Genetic Psychology Monographs*, **34**, 57-125.

Stampfl, T. G. (1970). Implosive therapy: an emphasis on covert stimulation. *In* "Learning Approaches to Therapeutic Behavior Change". (D. J. Levis, ed.). Aldine, Chicago.

Steiner, G. (1978). "Heidegger". Fontana Modern Masters, Collins, Glasgow.

Stennett, R. G. (1957). The relationship of performance level to level of arousal. *Journal of Experimental Psychology*, **54**, 54-61.

Sternbach, R. A. (1960). Correlates of differences in time to recover from startle. *Psychosomatic Medicine*, **22**, 204-210.

Storr, A. (1970). "Human Aggression". Bantam Books, New York.

Stout, G. F. (1898). "A Manual of Psychology". University Tutorial Press, London.

Suls, J. M. (1972). A two-stage model for the appreciation of jokes and cartoons: an information-processing analysis. *In* "The Psychology of Humor". (J. H. Goldstein and P. E. McGhee, eds). Academic Press, New York and London, pp.81-100.

Sutton-Smith, B. (1972). Games of order and disorder. Paper presented to the Symposium on Forms of Symbolic Inversion, American Anthropological Association, Toronto.

Syme, G. J. and Syme, L. A. (1977). Spontaneous alternation in mice: a test of the mere-exposure hypothesis. *American Journal of Psychology*, **90**, 4, 621-633.

Taylor, C. (1964). "The Explanation of Behaviour". Routledge and Kegan Paul, London.

Taylor, R. (1966). "Action and Purpose". Prentice-Hall, New Jersey.

Thayer, R. E. (1978). Toward a psychological theory of multidimensional activation (arousal). *Motivation and Emotion*, **2**, 1, 1-34.

Thom, R. (1975). "Structural Stability and Morphogenesis". (English translation by D. Fowler). Benjamin, Reading, Massachusetts.

Thoresen, C. E. and Mahoney, M. J. (1974). "Behavioral Self-Control". Holt, Rinehart and Winston, New York.

Thorndike, E. L. (1913). "Educational Psychology". Columbia University Teachers' College, New York.

Titchener, E. B. (1902). "An Outline of Psychology". Macmillan, London.

Tolman, E. C. (1925). Purpose and cognition: the determiners of animal learning. *Psychological Review*, **32**, 285-297.

Tolman, E. C. (1951). A psychological model. *In* "Toward a General Theory of Action". (T. Parsons and E. A. Shils, eds). Harvard University Press, Massachusetts, pp.279-361.

Tosi, D. J. and Hoffman, S. (1972). A factor analysis of the personal orientation inventory. *Journal of Humanistic Psychology*, **12**, 1, 86-93.

Turner, V. (1969). "The Ritual Process". Aldine, Chicago. (Republished by Penguin Books, Harmondsworth, 1974).

Turner, V. (1974). "Dramas, Fields and Metaphors: Symbolic Action in Human Society". Cornell University Press, Ithaca.

Turner, V. (1978). Comments and Conclusions. *In* "The Reversible World: Symbolic Inversion in Art and Society". (B. A. Babcock, ed.). Cornell University Press, Ithaca, pp.276-296.

Valentine, C. W. (1930). The innate bases of fear. *The Pedagogical Seminary and Journal of Genetic Psychology*, **37**, 394-419.

Valentine, C. W. (1956). "The Normal Child and Some of His Abnormalities". Penguin Books, Harmondsworth.

Vansina, J. (1973). "Oral Tradition". Penguin Books, Harmondsworth.

Venturi, R. (1966). "Complexity and Contradiction in Architecture". The Museum of Modern Art, New York, in conjunction with the Graham Foundation for Advanced Studies in the Fine Arts, Chicago.

Vernon, M. D. (1952). "A Further Study of Visual Perception". Cambridge University Press, Cambridge.

Vinnai, G. (1973). "Football Mania, The Players and the Fans: The Mass Psychology of Football". Ocean Books, London. (Originally published in German in 1970).

Wallas, G. (1926). "The Art of Thought". Harcourt Brace, New York.

Wallon, H. (1959). Psychologie et éducation de l'enfance. *Enfance*, 3-4, 195-449.

Wallon, H. (1963). Buts et méthodes de la psychologie. *Enfance*, 1-2, 5-171.

Wallon, H. (1976). "Lecture d'Henri Wallon: Choix de Textes". Editions Sociales, Paris.

Walter, J. A. (1978a). "Sent Away: A Study of Young Offenders in Care". Saxon House, Farnborough, Hants.

Walter, J. A. (1978b). Talking about trouble. *The British Journal of Criminology*, 18, 4, 365-380.

Watson, J. B. (1913). Psychology as the behaviorist views it. *Psychological Review*, 20, 158-177.

Watson, J. B. (1914). "Behavior: An Introduction to Comparative Psychology". Holt, New York.

Watson, J. B. (1919). "Psychology from the Standpoint of a Behaviorist". Lippincott, Philadelphia, Pennsylvania.

Watts, A. W. (1963). "The Two Hands of God: The Myths of Polarity". George Braziller, New York.

Watzlawick, P., Beavin, J. H. and Jackson, D. D. (1967). "Pragmatics of Human Communication: A Study of Interactional Patterns, Pathologies and Paradoxes". Norton, New York.

Watzlawick, P., Weakland, J. and Fisch, R. (1974). "Change: Principles of Problem Formation and Problem Resolution". Norton, New York.

Wauchope, O. S. (1948). "Deviation into Sense: The Nature of Explanation". Faber and Faber, London.

Weber, M. (1922). "Wirtschaft und Gesellschaft, Grundriss der verstehenden Soziologie". (Published in English as "Economy and Society", 3 vols, translated by G. Roth and C. Wittich. Bedminster Press, New York, 1968).

Wertheimer, M. (1961). "Productive Thinking". Tavistock Publications, London.

Wetzel, R. (1966). Use of behavioural techniques in a case of compulsive stealing. *Journal of Consulting Psychology*, 30, 367-374.

Whorf, B. L. (1940). Science and linguistics. *Technology Review*, XLIV, 229ff. Reprinted in Whorf, B. L., "Language, Thought and Reality: Selected Writings of Benjamin Lee Whorf" (J. B. Carroll, ed.), M.I.T. Press, Cambridge, Massachusetts, 1956.

Whiting, J. W. M. and Mowrer, O. H. (1943). Habit progression and regression — a laboratory study of some factors relevant to human socialization. *Journal of Comparative Psychology*, 36, 3, 229-253.

Wiener, N. (1948). "Cybernetics". Wiley, New York.

Wilson, C. P. (1979). "Jokes: Form, Content, Use and Function". Academic Press, London and New York.

Wolpe, J. (1958). "Psychotherapy by Reciprocal Inhibition". Stanford University Press, Stanford, California.

Wood, C. G. and Hokanson, J. E. (1965). Effects of induced muscular tension on performance and the inverted U function. *Journal of Personality and Social Psychology*, **1**, 506-510.

Woodworth, R. S. (1918). "Dynamic Psychology". Columbia University Press, New York.

Worchel, S. and Teddlie, C. (1976). The experience of crowding: a two-factor theory. *Journal of Personality and Social Psychology*, **34**, 30-40.

Wundt, W. M. (1874). "Grundzüge der Physiologishen Psychologie". Engelmann, Leipzig.

Yerkes, R. M. and Dodson, J. D. (1908). The relation of strength of stimulus to rapidity of habit-formation. *Journal of Comparative Neurological Psychology*, **18**, 459-482.

Zajonc, R. B. (1960). Balance, congruity and dissonance. *Public Opinion Quarterly*, **24**, 280-296. Reprinted in: "Attitudes: Selected Readings". (M. Jahoda and N. Warren, eds.). Penguin Books, Harmondsworth, 1966, pp.261-278.

Zajonc, R. B. (1965). Social facilitation. *Science*, **149**, 269-274.

Zillmann, D. (1971). Excitation transfer in communication-mediated aggressive behavior. *Journal of Experimental Social Psychology*, **7**, 419-434.

Zillmann, D. (1972). The role of excitation in aggressive behavior. "Proceedings of the Seventeenth International Congress of Applied Psychology, 1971". Editest, Brussels.

Zillmann, D., Katcher, A. H. and Milavsky, B. (1972). Excitation transfer from physical exercise to subsequent aggressive behavior. *Journal of Experimental Social Psychology*, **8**, 247-259.

Zillmann, D., Mody, B. and Cantor, J. R. (1974). Empathetic perception of emotional displays in films as a function of hedonic and excitatory state prior to exposure. *Journal of Research in Personality*, **8**, 335-349.

Zubek, J. P. (ed.). (1969). "Sensory Deprivation: Fifteen Years of Research". Appleton-Century-Crofts, New York.

Zuckerman, M. (1964). Toward isolating the sources of stress in perceptual isolation. *In* "Sensory deprivation research: Where do we go from here?" (A. M. Rossi, Chairman). Symposium presented at the American Psychological Association, Los Angeles, September, 1964.

Zuckerman, M. (1969). Theoretical formulations: I. *In* "Sensory Deprivation: Fifteen Years of Research". (J. P. Zubeck, ed.). Appleton-Century-Crofts, New York, pp.407-432.

Zuckerman, M. (1971). Dimensions of sensation seeking. *Journal of Consulting and Clinical Psychology*, **36**, 45-52.

Zuckerman, M. (1974). The sensation seeking motive. *In* "Progress in Experimental Personality Research, Vol. 7". (B. A. Maher, ed.) Academic Press, New York and London.

Zuckerman, M. (1978). Sensation seeking and psychopathy. *In* "Psychopathic Behavior: Approaches to Research". (R. D. Hare and D. Schalling, eds). Wiley, New York.

Zuckerman, M., Kolin, E. A., Price, L. and Zoob, I. (1964). Development of a sensation-seeking scale. *Journal of Consulting and Clinical Psychology*, **28**, 477-482.

Zuckerman, M. and Link, K. (1968). Construct validity for the sensation-seeking scale. *Journal of Consulting and Clinical Psychology*, **32**, 4, 420-426.

Zuckerman, M. and Neeb, M. (1979). Sensation seeking and psychopathology. *Psychiatry Research*, **1**, 255-264.

Zuk, G. H. (1971). "Family Therapy: A Triadic-Based Approach". Behavioral Publications, New York.

Appendixes

Appendix A: The Meaning of an Identity

Identities are identified in two different ways. They are either recognized as particular *identities*: Carolyn, London, my car; or they are recognized as members of a particular *class*: a ship, a typewriter, a schoolboy, and so on. In strictly logical terms, a particular identity is also a class, but one which has only one member. Psychologically, however, there is clearly a major difference between identities and classes, and they will therefore continue to be differentiated here. Identities and classes are, of course, closely related. A member of a particular class is often recognized as a unique member of that class: e.g. one might recognize a chair in a concert hall as being a particular chair one has sat on before. And a particular identity is always seen as being a member of a class: one recognizes that a friend is a member of such classes as the class 'human being', 'male', and 'teacher'. Typically, a given identity will be seen to be a member of many different classes at the same time: thus Ivy is a member of the classes 'women', 'wives', 'mothers', 'antique dealers', 'smokers', 'amateur golfers', and so on.

Both classes and identities can be defined in terms of *attributes*. The following brief discussion of the relationship between identities, classes and attributes will be essentially along the lines suggested by Bruner *et al.* (1967), who define an attribute as "any discriminable feature of an event" (p.26). In this they follow Boring (1942):

"A stone is shape, colour, weight, and kind of substance in complicated relation. When such descriptive ultimates are general properties which can vary continuously or discretely, when they are, in short, parameters, they may, if one chooses, be called attributes of the object described" (p.19).

A particular identity is identified by a set of values of attributes which, taken together, are sufficient to specify that particular identity and no other. Thus a particular dog may have the value 'small' for the attribute size, 'brown' for the attribute colour of hair, and so on. Of course only some particular attributes will be relevant to a given type of identity: thus the attribute

358

intelligence, or colour of eyes would not be relevant to any kind of ball, although attributes like size, colour, and material would be. In terms of the relevant attributes, a particular ball may be round, big, red, light, slippery, plastic, and so on.

As far as 'classes' are concerned, particular attributes will, for a given class, determine class membership or exclusion. (The term 'classes' as used here is synonymous with 'categories' or 'sets', and is equated by Bruner et al. with concepts.) So for an identity to be a member of a given class, the requirements may be specified in terms of a value, or range of values, of a certain specified attribute or attributes. Thus, for a particular flower to be identified as a member of a given species, certain attributes have to have certain values: a given number of petals in the corolla, the gynaecium inferior of superior, etc. For an object to be identified as a ball, it has to be round, within certain 'limits of tolerance'. These essential features may be referred to as 'defining attributes'. Knowledge of the value of other attributes adds further information about the identity but does not define it; e.g. a ball can be of any colour and still remain a ball, a dog remains a dog with or without a tail. This difference between defining and non-defining values of attributes is the same as the traditional logical distinction between essential and accidental qualities.

A class may be defined in terms of a single attribute, e.g. the class of objects that are red. But more usually classes are defined in terms of combinations of values of attributes. In general, as Bruner et al. point out, there are three kinds of combinations. Firstly, there are conjunctive classes which are defined in terms of the joint presence of the appropriate value of several attributes, as in determining the species of a flower. Secondly, there are disjunctive classes in which an identity is a member of a class if the values of one attribute are appropriate or if the values of another attribute are appropriate; in general these classes are defined in terms of the presence of any one of a set of appropriate values of attributes. For example, a particular psychiatric condition may be diagnosed if any one kind of specified disturbance is present from a list of disturbances. Thirdly, there are relational classes, which are defined by a specifiable relationship between defining attributes. For example, the concept of 'winning' a game implies doing something better than one's opponent. A class, then, consists of a set of identities which, although individually relatively complex, have certain configurations of attributes, and values of these attributes, in common. These attributes may be objectively specifiable and measurable, or they may be subjective evaluations or feelings, e.g. beautiful, terrifying.

In brief, a given stimulus, which can be characterized in terms of the values of a set of attributes, acquires further meaning through being assigned to a class and also, possibly, through the recognition that it is a particular member of that class, i.e. a particular identity. So one may understand from the clothes that someone wears, e.g. from such values of attributes as the colour blue, that he is a policeman. One may also recognize from other values of attributes, e.g. size of nose, colour of eyes, etc., that he is a particular policeman whom one knows. Meaning in this sense, then, inheres in the values of the attributes, the classes recognized from them and the identities specified by them.

The work of Bruner *et al.* was directed to the question of the way in which concepts are attained or formed. The present analysis, in the context of reversal theory, leads in a different direction, and concerns the way in which mutually-exclusive meanings may be attached to the same identity. It can now be seen that this can in principle occur in three ways. (1) A particular attribute may be seen to have mutually-exclusive values; (2) a particular identity may be seen to belong to mutually-exclusive classes; or (3) a particular identity may be seen as two different identities. Often a contradiction of the first type will lead to a contradiction of one of the other two types, since, for the reasons which have now been given, the latter depend on the former.

Appendix B: Synergy

The use of the term 'synergy' can be traced back to the seventeenth century, where it was used in theology to describe the unorthodox belief that man's will and God's grace could work together to produce salvation. In the nineteenth century it passed into physiology and medicine to describe the way in which different substances, or parts of the body, work together to produce effects which could not be produced by the components separately. This has been the main use of the word in the greater part of the twentieth century to date. For example, barbituric acid derivatives and alcohol have a greater depressant effect than either acting alone, and are said to be synergic. To take another example: although the two divisions of the autonomic nervous system generally function antagonistically, they can function synergistically, such as in intestinal peristalsis and in uterine contractions in labour, where each of the divisions acts alternately to bring about the movement required. In embryology the term is used to refer to an interaction between two tissues in a developing organism such that each causes the other to develop in a way that it would not have done without the interaction. The term has also been used to refer to the union of individual motor processes in global movements. In relation to this, a synergic theory in psychology at the turn of the century held that mental synthesis was due to the union of motor processes (Baldwin, 1902, entry on 'synergy').

Latterly the term has come to be used in a variety of fields of study. Simondon (1958), for example, has used it to refer to the manner in which the properties of different parts of engineering systems act in such a way as to help each other to realize specified effects. 'Synergy' has also become studied as a systems phenomenon in cybernetics and systems theory, and in operational research (viz. Haken, 1974, 1977, 1978, who has described this field of study as 'Synergetics'). Synergy is defined in one book on systems theory (Beishon and Peters, 1972, p.311) as special correlated action or co-operation resulting in unusual or unexpected results.

Maslow (1973) (pp.207-219) refers to some unpublished work by the anthropologist Ruth Benedict, in which she used the term 'high social synergy' to refer to societies in which their institutions ensure mutual advantage for members of the society for their undertakings, and 'low social synergy' for societies which operate in such a way that the advantage of one individual becomes a victory over another. Maslow applied this concept of synergy to those types of interpersonal relationship in which what is to one person's advantage is automatically to the advantage of the other too, as in 'love'. He also applied it to the individual, seeing an integrated person as having high synergy, and a person in conflict with himself as having low synergy. Further, he saw 'self-actualizing' people as those who were able in some way to transcend dichotomies and who could from this point of view be said to display high synergy. The Personal Orientation Inventory (as investigated by Tosi and Hoffman, 1972) based on Maslow's concept of self-actualization, contains a synergy subscale. More recently, Selye (1975) has, in a way similar to Benedict, used the word 'synergy' to refer to the effects of co-operation and teamwork in animal and human societies.

The use of the term in reversal theory is phenomenological, in that it refers to the way in which different meanings in relation to some entity in the phenomenal field interact with each other, to produce special phenomenological effects that could not be achieved by either meaning alone. Thus the different meanings may, through contrast, mutually enhance each other and make each other more vivid—especially where the meanings are strongly opposite in some way. This particular type of synergy therefore may be thought of as a form of 'phenomenological synergy' or 'cognitive synergy'.

Appendix C: The Telic Dominance Scale

Note: (S) = serious-mindedness; (P) = planning orientation; (A) = arousal avoidance; an asterisk (*) denotes the telic choice in each item.

1. (P) Compile a short dictionary for financial reward*
   Write a short story for fun
   Not sure

2. (P) Going to evening class to improve your qualifications*
   Going to evening class for fun
   Not sure

3.(A) Leisure activities which are just exciting
Leisure activities which have a purpose*
Not sure

4.(P) Improving a sporting skill by playing a game
Improving it through systematic practice*
Not sure

5.(A) Spending one's life in many different places
Spending most of one's life in one place*
Not sure

6.(P) Work that earns promotion*
Work that you enjoy doing
Not sure

7.(P) Planning your leisure*
Doing things on the spur of the moment
Not sure

8.(P) Going to formal evening meetings*
Watching television for entertainment
Not sure

9.(A) Having your tasks set for you*
Choosing your own activities
Not sure

10.(P) Investing money in a long term insurance/pension scheme*
Buying an expensive car
Not sure

11.(A) Staying in one job*
Having many changes of job
Not sure

12.(A) Seldom doing things 'for kicks'*
Often doing things 'for kicks'
Not sure

13.(S) Going to a party
Going to a meeting*
Not sure

14.(S) Leisure activities
Work activities*
Not sure

15.(A) Taking holidays in many different places
Taking holidays always in the same place*
Not sure

16.(S) Going away on holiday for two weeks
Given two weeks of free time finishing a needed improvement at home*
Not sure

17.(S) Taking life seriously*
Treating life light-heartedly
Not sure

18.(A) Frequently trying strange foods
Always eating familiar foods*
Not sure

19.(A) Recounting an incident accurately*
Exaggerating for effect
Not sure

20.(P) Spending £100 having an en-
       joyable weekend
       Spending £100 on repaying a
       loan*
       Not sure

21.(A) Having continuity in the place
       where you live*
       Having frequent moves of house
       Not sure

22.(S) Going to an art gallery to enjoy
       exhibits
       To learn about the exhibits*
       Not sure

23.(S) Watching a game
       Refereeing a game*
       Not sure

24.(S) Eating special things because
       you enjoy them
       Eating special things because
       they are good for your health*
       Not sure

25.(P) Fixing long-term life ambitions*
       Living life as it comes
       Not sure

26.(P) Always trying to finish your
       work before you enjoy yourself*
       Frequently going out for enjoy-
       ment before all your work is
       finished
       Not sure

27.(P) Not needing to explain your
       behaviour
       Having purposes for your be-
       haviour*
       Not sure

28.(S) Climbing a mountain to try to
       save someone*
       Climbing a mountain for pleas-
       ure
       Not sure

29.(S) Happy to waste time
       Always having to be busy*
       Not sure

30.(A) Taking risks
       Going through life safely*
       Not sure

31.(S) Watching a crucial match be-
       tween two ordinary sides*
       Watching an exhibition game
       with star performers
       Not sure

32.(P) Playing a game
       Organizing a game*
       Not sure

33.(S) Glancing at pictures in a book
       Reading a biography*
       Not sure

34.(A) Winning a game easily*
       Playing a game with the scores
       very close
       Not sure

35.(A) Steady routine in life*
       Continual unexpectedness or
       surprise
       Not sure

36. (A) Working in the garden*
Picking wild fruit
Not sure

37. (S) Reading for information*
Reading for fun
Not sure

38. (S) Arguing for fun
Arguing with others seriously
to change their opinions*
Not sure

39. (S) Winning a game*
Playing a game for fun
Not sure

40. (A) Travelling a great deal in one's
job
Working in one office or workshop*
Not sure

41. (P) Planning ahead*
Taking each day as it comes
Not sure

42. (P) Planning a holiday*
Being on holiday
Not sure

(Courtesy of the 'Psychological Reversals Study Group')

Appendix D: A Glossary of Terms Used in Reversal Theory

Anxiety
A form of high felt arousal experienced in the arousal-avoidance metamotivational state (qv).

Anxiety-avoidance state
Another name for the arousal-avoidance state (qv).

Arousal (felt)
The degree to which an individual feels himself to be 'worked up' at a given
time, and in this sense the degree of intensity of his feelings of motivation. The
felt arousal dimension defined in this way is different from the sleep–wakefulness
dimension. Felt arousal should also be distinguished from tension (qv).

Arousal-avoidance state
A metamotivational state in which the preferred level of felt arousal is low on the
felt arousal dimension. It forms a pair with the arousal-seeking state (qv), and is
characterized by an avoidance of anxiety.

Arousal-seeking state
A metamotivational state in which the preferred level of felt arousal is high on

the felt arousal dimension. It forms a pair with the arousal-avoidance state (qv), and is characterized by a search for excitement.

Bistability

A system exhibits bistability if it tends to maintain a specified variable, despite external disturbance, within one or another of *two* ranges of values of the variable concerned. This contrasts with homeostasis in which only *one* range of values is involved.

Boredom

A form of low felt arousal experienced in the arousal-seeking metamotivational state (qv).

Cognitive synergy

See synergy

Conformist state

A metamotivational state in which the individual wants, or feels compelled to comply with, some requirement (qv). It forms a pair with the negativistic state (qv).

Displacement

In reversal theory terms this process occurs when the content of a metamotivational state changes without a reversal (qv) occurring, e.g. in the negativistic state, when one salient requirement is substituted for another as the focus of the individual's desire or compulsion to act negativistically.

Dominance

A metamotivational state is said to be dominant if the individual is predisposed to spend longer periods in this state than in the other member of the pair which they together constitute. It implies that there is an innate bias in the individual in favour of one state rather than its opposite, although this may be obscured by environmental influences. (Cf. Operative).

Excitement

A form of high felt arousal experienced in the arousal-seeking metamotivational state (qv).

Excitement-seeking state

Another name for the arousal-seeking state (qv).

Externally-controlled bistability

A bistable situation in which factors external to the value of the variable concerned determine which of the two ranges of values is the preferred range at the moment, and do so irrespective of the value which the variable concerned happens to have at that moment. (Cf. value-determined bistability).

Gratuitous behaviour
Behaviour which is unnecessary, at least in any relatively immediate sense, from the point of view of the survival of the individual or his family or social group. That is, from a biological, or functional, perspective it at least appears to be superfluous.

Identity
A particular object, person, place, situation, or group of people, which can usually be identified by some relatively simple verbal formulation. An identity tends to be particular rather than general, concrete rather than abstract.

Identity synergy
A form of synergy (qv) in which two parallel levels of interpretation of some identity are involved, so that mutually exclusive meanings are assigned simultaneously, but on different levels of interpretation, to that identity. (Cf. Reversal synergy.)

Inconsistency, principle of
This says that some aspects of the way an individual interprets his own experience, and therefore some aspects of his personality, are inherently inconsistent in the sense that opposite interpretations even of the same contents of experience are likely to occur from time to time, and to do so even in the absence of changing external circumstances.

Metamotivational state
A phenomenological state which is characterized by a certain way of interpreting some aspect(s) of one's own motivation. Such metamotivational states as have been identified in reversal theory go in pairs of opposites, only one member of each pair being operative at a given time, but reversal always being possible between members of a pair.

Metamotivational system
A system, presumed to be physiological, which underlies a given metamotivational state (qv), and which generates behaviour performed in that state.

Multistability
A system exhibits multistability if it tends to maintain a specified variable, despite external disturbance, within one or another of a specifiable *set* of ranges

of values of the variable concerned. The simplest case is that of bistability (qv).

Negativism, felt
The degree to which one sees oneself to be acting against a salient requirement (qv). This should not be confused with the negativistic state (qv).

Negativistic state
A metamotivational state in which the individual wants, or feels compelled to act against some requirement (qv). It forms a pair with the conformist state (qv).

Operative
A metamotivational state is said to be operative if it is the state which is prevailing at a given moment, and which therefore determines how the individual interprets some aspect(s) of his motivation at that moment. (Cf. Dominance).

Paradoxical behaviour
Behaviour which is not only unhelpful from the point of view of the survival of the individual or his family or social group, but which tends to militate against it, and which cannot be explained as error or incompetence on the part of the individual concerned. From a biological or functional perspective it is paradoxical because it has the opposite effect to that which behaviour is supposed to have.

Parapathic emotion
Any emotion felt in an 'as if' form. By this is meant that the core of the emotion still has the same feeling quality as its counterpart which goes by the same name; but its meaning to the individual is altered in that it is, as it were, removed one degree from reality and placed in a special phenomenological 'frame'. For example, the emotions felt while reading a work of fiction.

Paratelic state
A metamotivational state in which the individual is oriented towards, or feels the need to be oriented towards, some aspect of his continuing behaviour and its related sensations. It forms a pair with the telic state (qv). It tends to be associated with an interest in activity for its own sake, playfulness, spontaneity, and a preference for high intensity experiences and low felt significance (qv).

Relaxation
A form of low felt arousal experienced in the arousal-avoidance metamotivational state (qv).

Requirement

Some pressure experienced by the individual (e.g. an expectation, convention, law, suggestion, prohibition, command, threat) which he may choose to comply with or act against.

Reversal

In its strictest sense in reversal theory, a reversal is a switch from one meta-motivational state being operative to the other member of the pair of states which they together constitute being operative. (Cf. Shift). The term is also used to refer to other kinds of sudden switches between opposites, such as switches between opposite meanings of a given identity (qv). In general, reversal implies bistability, although bistability does not necessarily imply reversal, since the two preferred ranges of values involved need not be opposite.

Reversal-of-effect

Any type of communication which has an effect that is opposite to that intended by the communicator.

Reversal synergy

A form of synergy (qv) in which only one level of interpretation is involved, reversal occurring between mutually exclusive meanings of the identity at that level of interpretation. (Cf. Identity synergy).

Self-negativism

A form of negativism which occurs when the negativistic state (qv) expresses itself through a desire or compulsion to act against some requirement of the self, rather than against some requirement of an external agency.

Shift

A change which occurs at a given moment in some characteristic of a meta-motivational state, other than its content. For example, a change in the values of a variable, regulated by the underlying metamotivational system, which are experienced as pleasant. (Cf. Reversal; Displacement).

Significance, felt

The degree to which one sees a goal one is pursuing as serving purposes beyond itself. That is, the degree to which one sees one's action at a given time in a context which extends beyond the immediate effects of these actions.

Structural phenomenology

The study of the structure of experience, and the way in which the nature of this structure changes over time. That is, it primarily concerns the structure *of* experience itself, rather than particular structures which occur *within* experience.

Synergy

In the reversal theory sense, this occurs in experience when a given identity (qv) is seen to have opposite or mutually exclusive characteristics, either successively or simultaneously.

Telic state

A metamotivational state in which the individual is oriented towards, or feels the need to be oriented towards, some essential goal or goals. It forms a pair with the paratelic state (qv). It tends to be associated with serious-mindedness, planning ahead, and a preference for low intensity experiences and high felt significance (qv).

Tension

In reversal theory, a feeling that accompanies, and is proportional to, any discrepancy between a preferred and actual level of some variable, the preferred level of which characterizes a metamotivational state. Unlike arousal, tension is always felt as unpleasant. (Cf. Arousal, felt).

Value-determined bistability

A bistable situation in which the value of the variable concerned determines which of the two ranges of values is the preferred range at that moment, external factors being able to determine the preferred range only indirectly through changing the value of the variable. (Cf. Externally-controlled bistability).

Index

A

Abreaction, 262
Action,
 concept of, 2-3, 310
 meaning of, 3
Action specific energy, 130
Action theory, 2-3, 13, 14, 15, 228, 310
Activation, 80
Adaptation-level theory, 176n, 228
Aggression, 99, 100, 112-117, 133n, 198,
 202, 210, 211, 212, 219, 229, 254, 256,
 258, 314
Alienation, 62-63
Alliesthesia, 79n
Ambiguity,
 anthropological theories of, 148-151, 152
 art and, 147-148, 151
 bistability and, 153n
 intolerance of, 146
 reactions to, 145-153, 173-176, 332
 reversal synergy and, 141-145
 types of, 143-145
Ambiguous sentences, 36, 45n, 145
Anger, 99, 101, 108, 109, 111, 112-117,
 119, 122, 128, 198, 211, 212, 217, 259,
 274n, 324
Antique collecting, 128, 155, 166
Antithesis, principle of, 139
Anxiety-avoidance,
 arousal-avoidance and, 107, 133n
 characteristics of, 82-94
 definition, 84, 364
 examples of, 91-92

telic state, relation to, 56-57, 90-91,
 106n, 107-108
Anxiety neurosis, 93, 246-247, 250, 251,
 253, 261, 262, 274n
Apathy, 101, 102, 104, 246, 248, 249, 250,
 251
Architecture, 110, 125, 147, 175, 278, 288,
 289
Arousal-avoidance, see Anxiety-avoidance
Arousal boost, 106n, 134n, 195n
Arousal cycles, 94-101
Arousal, felt,
 character of, 319-320
 definition, 81, 364
 hedonic tone and, 55-57, 83-85, 86, 89,
  90-91, 101-105, 106n, 107, 127,
  152, 174, 239-240, 246-252, 257,
  295, 320
 incompatibility of preferred level of,
  265-269
 physiological arousal and, 55-56, 81, 99,
  107, 123, 199
 relation to telic/paratelic states, 55-57,
  318
Arousal jag, 106n, 134n, 191
Arousal-seeking, see Excitement-seeking
Arousal system, 56, 84-85, 245n, 274n,
 325, 326, 329
Art,
 ambiguity and, 147-148, 151
 contrast effects and, 175-176
 gratuitous, as, 10, 11
 identity synergy and, 159-162
 models and, 176n

paratelic state and, 277, 302
unexpectedness and, 124, 156
Attitude change theories, 146, 229
Attribution theory, 65-66, 74
Autogenic training, 262
Autonomic nervous system, 30, 58, 80, 360
Autonomous events, 65
Autonomy, functional, 77
Autotelic motivation, 65

B

Balance model of bistability, 31-34, 43, 45n, 71, 72-73, 79n, 232
Bateson's theory, see also Meta-communication, 68, 109, 119, 170-171, 182, 275n, 311
Behaviour, see also Gratuitous behaviour, Paradoxical behaviour, Sexual behaviour
abnormal, 5
animal, 307-315
appetitive, 63-64, 94-97
consummatory, 63-64, 94-97, 106n
irrational, 11, 17n
maladaptive, 93, 94
meaning of, 2-5
mental states, relation to, 5-8
minimal, 3-4, 5-6
'testing out', 267
Behaviour modification, 7, 261
Behavioural switches, 38
Behaviourism, 2, 3, 5, 13, 18n, 105, 159, 330
Berlyne's theorizing, 83, 106, 118, 125, 131, 134n, 176n, 191, 195n
Biofeedback, 262, 332n
Bistability, see also Balance model of bistability, Externally-controlled bistability, Value-determined bistability 22-34, 38, 39, 42, 56, 104, 144, 229, 293
definition of, 365
two levels of, 29, 30, 85-86, 320-321
Body-mind relationship, 293-297
Brainstorming, 77-78, 79n, 301

C

Catastrophe theory, 45-46n
Church services, 8, 287, 288

Classical conditioning, see Pavlovian conditioning
Cognitive dissonance theory, 146-147, 210
Cognitive evaluation theory, 74
Cognitive irreversibility, 282
Cognitive synergy, see Synergy
Comic personalities, 180-181, 190
Compliance, 225n
Computer analogy, 3, 9, 13, 158
Computer technology, 23, 31
Conformist state,
definition, 198, 365
depression and, 252
dominance of, 206, 236
excitement-seeking and, 217
experimental subjects and, 224
obedience and, 216-217
requirements and, 201
telic/paratelic relations to, 209, 215, 216-217
Conformist system, see also Conformist state
animals in, 308
biological function of, 299
Contingent factors, in inducing reversals, 41, 68-69, 71, 85, 92, 98, 208-209, 216, 229, 231, 232-233, 237-238, 242, 280, 294, 317, 325, 327
Contrast effects, 60, 152, 174-176, 176n, 288, 292n, 361
Control, cybernetic meaning of, 27, 91
Co-opposition, 189
Counteraction, 225n
Creative thinking, 77-78, 79n, 286, 301 305, 316n
Crowds, 121, 127, 134n, 209, 217, 225n
Crying, 172-173, 176n
Curiosity, 93, 131, 311-313
Cybernetics, 2, 10, 13-15, 16, 18n, 20-21, 23, 245n, 275n, 293, 294, 306, 324, 328, 332, 361
Cycles,
arousal, 94-101
paratelic, 95-96
telic, 95-96

D

Darwin, Charles, 139
Daydreaming, 54, 69, 126, 168-169

Death, problem of, 278, 279, 280, 281, 283
Defence mechanisms, 43-44, 126, 329
Defence reaction, 123
Delinquency, 259
Depression, 101, 225n, 249-252, 257, 261, 274n
Deviance, *see also* Delinquency, Hooliganism, Sexual perversion, 201-204, 205, 225n, 299
Displacement, 75, 208, 210, 211, 212, 214, 215, 220, 243, 272, 321, 327, 365
Dominance, *see also* Telic Dominance Scale,
  bistable system, in a, 27-28, 29, 33, 39, 58
  metamotivational, 58, 206, 230-236, 242, 365
  psychopathology, relation to, 247-248, 252, 266-267, 268, 270, 272
Double-bind, 170-171, 182
Dreaming, 43, 70, 81, 126, 191
Drive, concept of, 80, 131-132
Drive reduction theory, 131-132, 310

E

Equilibrium, 19-20, 44n, 45n, 130
Embarrassment, 189, 254, 324
Emotions, *see also* Arousal, felt, Parapathic emotions,
  arousal and, 107
  bipolar, 41
  metamotivation and, 324
  synergy and, 324
Empathy, 110, 119-121, 123, 126, 128, 189, 256
Encapsulation, 52, 56, 320
Encounter groups, 263-264
Endogenous attributes, 65-66
Ends pleasure, 65
Ethology, 311, 315
Excitation-transfer theory, 99
Excitement-seeking,
  animals, in, 311-313
  arousal-seeking and, 107, 133n
  characteristics of, 82-94
  definition, 84, 365
  examples of, 7, 91-92
  negativism and, 118-119, 127, 128, 219, 256, 258-259, 267, 279

paratelic state, relation to, 56-57, 90-91, 106n, 107-108
  pathological, 256-259, 267
  techniques used in, 117-128, 278-279, 301
Existentialism, 14, 222
exogenous attributes, 65-66
Experiential states, *see* Mental states
Experientialism, 13
Experimental method, reversal theory implications for, 58, 134n, 223-224, 226n, 230, 315
Exploration, 93, 124, 131, 311-313
Externally-controlled bistability, 24-27, 29, 33, 42, 84, 153n, 332n, 365
Eysenck's theorizing, 105, 228, 235, 257, 274n

F

Fabulation, 292n
Facilitation, social, 121
Family,
  double-bind in the, 170-171
  rows in the, 101, 112, 114, 119, 265, 268, 269, 272
  therapy and the, 264-273
  well-being of, 49, 68, 242
Family therapy, 270-273, 298
Fantasy, 69, 122, 126, 169, 176n, 211, 212, 245, 255, 277, 278, 290, 292n, 301, 329
Fear, 87, 108, 110-111, 115, 116, 124, 125, 133n, 274n, 287
Feedback, negative, 20-22, 29, 31, 32, 85
Fiction, 118, 120, 121, 128, 301
  functional, 219
Figure-ground reversals,
  perceptual, 35-37, 144
  phenomenal field, in, 67, 164-165, 171, 178-179, 205, 214-215, 322-323
Flow state, 65
Football, 68, 109, 120, 121, 124, 155, 164, 219, 229, 259, 287-288, 322
Frame, paratelic, 109, 110, 112
Freudian theory, *see also* Psychoanalysis 42, 46n, 126, 128-130, 133, 134n, 191, 224, 225n, 226n, 233, 255, 260, 270, 286, 294
Frustration, 41, 46n, 68-69, 85, 121-122, 127, 128, 198, 209-212, 216, 220, 231, 232, 237, 242, 244, 259, 280, 317, 325, 327

depression and, 251-252
two types of, 210, 251-252
Frustration-aggression, 122, 198, 212
Functional fiction, 219
Functionalism, 16-17, 226n

G

Ganser syndrome, 225n
Gestalt psychology, 16, 144, 153n
Gestalt therapy, 220, 263, 298
Goal,
  anticipation, 54, 59, 76, 126, 238, 329
  essential and inessential, 47, 48-49, 50,
    53, 58, 60-61, 66-67, 78-79, 93
Gratuitous act, 221-222
Gratuitous behaviour, 9-12, 14, 60, 299,
  307, 309, 366
Grief, 111, 120, 172
Guilt, 108, 111, 172, 203, 224, 254, 287

H

Helplessness, learned, 250
Hermeneutic theory, 331-332
Heteronomous events, 65
Homeostasis, 19-23, 28, 29-31, 32, 56,
  128-133, 226, 231, 245n, 321, 365
Homesickness, 155, 169
Hooliganism, 114, 117, 202, 204, 307,
  322-323
Homospatial thinking, 316n
Hull's theory, 105n, 128, 131, 133
Humour, see also Laughter,
  arousal and, 184-189, 194-195n
  awareness of opposites and, 316n
  identity synergy and, 177-184, 290-291,
    316n
  parapathic emotions and, 111, 189
  paratelic state and, 184-189, 324
  self-referential, 181-182
  social aspects of, 187, 188-189
  transition vs. non-transition, 178-179
  theories of, 190-194
Husserl's phenomenology, 12, 16, 18n, 72,
  79n, 86n, 159, 332

I

'I' and 'me', 220-223
Identity,
  definition, 137, 366
  meaning of, 137, 358-360
  personal, 303-305
Identity synergy, see also Synergy
  definition, 154, 366
  emotion and, 324
  humour and, 177-184, 290-291, 316n
  religion, in, 289-291
  reversal synergy and, 142, 154, 164-165
Illumination, 286
Imaginative variation, method of, 86
Implosive therapy, 262
Impulsiveness Scale of Eysenck, 235
Incongruity,
  attitudes and, 146
  theories of humour, 192-194
Inconsistency, 14, 17n, 41, 44, 133
  cognitive, 146-147
  personality, in, 8-9, 227-230, 332
  Principle of, 8-9, 366
Insight, 309
Institutionalization, 114, 282, 302
Intentionality, 45n, 72, 206, 213

J

Janusian thinking, 306
Jazz, 156, 164
Jokes, 181, 184, 189, 191, 193
  innocent vs. tendentious, 191
Jung's theory, 19

L

Lability,
  bistable system in, 28
  metamotivational, 69, 236-238, 260
Laughter, see also Humour, 68, 178, 187,
  188, 194n, 195n, 291
Lefthandedness, 245n
Lévi-Strauss's theory, 15, 64, 138-139,
  153n
Lewin's theory, 19-20, 51, 128, 130-131,
  133
Linguistics,
  Chomskian, 7, 145, 148
  psycho-, 45n
  structural, 15, 138
  Whorfian, 137
Logotherapy, 263
Lorenz's motivational theory, 128, 130, 133
Love, 108, 312, 361
Lying, 169-170

M

Make-believe synergy, 55, 60, 119, 157-162, 163, 174, 177, 179, 185, 186, 194n, 277, 300, 306, 316n
Mania, 101, 250
Manic-depression, 38, 250
Marxist theory, 62-63
Masks, function of, 162, 176n
Maslow's theory, 45n, 135n, 361
Mauvaise foi, 222
Maze-running, 309, 310, 312, 313, 314
Meaning,
　effort after, 146, 173
　meaning of, 136-137, 153n, 350-360
　measurement of, 139-140
　opposites and, 137-141, 175
Means pleasure, 65
Mechanistic explanations, see Cybernetics
Mental states, 4, 7, 14-15, 35, 39-40, 227, 261
　animals, in, 315
　behaviour, relationship to, 5-8, 231
Meta-communication, 68, 119, 170-171, 187, 188-189, 272, 273, 311
Metamotivational lability, 236-238, 260
Metamotivational reversal, 30, 33, 40-42, 85, 317-321
　factors inducing, 41, 42, 44, 68-75, 85, 208-213, 231-233, 236-238, 280, 317, 324-325
　three steps in, 33, 42-43, 71-73, 206-207, 208, 236, 317-318, 325
　voluntary control of, 70, 93-94, 213, 216, 237-238, 325-330
Metamotivational states, see also Conformist state, Negativistic state, Paratelic state, Telic state,
　definition, 39-43, 366
　indicators of, 298
　metamotivational systems, relation to, 30, 35, 40, 295, 298, 315, 366
　theoretical status of, 34-35
Metamotivational systems, see also Metamotivational states
　animals, in, 307-315
　definition, 366
　evolution and, 298-307
　physiology and, 40-41, 297-298
　reversals between, 30, 317-321
Metaphor, 151, 168, 280

visual, 176n
humour and, 184
Minimal behaviour, 3-4, 5-6
Models, see also Computer analogy,
　art and, 176n
　synergy and, 158
Moods, 41
Motivation,
　autotelic, 65
　extrinsic/intrinsic, 64-65, 74, 79n
　hydraulic models of, 130
　theories of, 128-133
Multistability, 21-22, 30-31, 33-34, 153n, 366
Mysticism, 290-291
Mythologic, 291

N

Nasal cycle, 79n
Necker cube, 31, 35, 36, 67, 144, 164
Negative feedback, 20-22, 29, 31, 32, 85
Negative therapeutic reaction, 224
Negativism,
　adolescence, in, 304-305
　barriers and, 211, 212, 218, 259
　deviance and, 201-204
　schizophrenia, in, 197, 200
　testing and, 196-197, 224, 226n
Negativism, felt, see also Negativism, Negativistic state, Self-negativism
　character of, 319-320
　definition, 198-199, 367
　hedonic tone and, 206-207, 241, 320
　negativistic state, difference from, 198-199
Negativistic period in development, 196-197, 221, 236, 303-304
Negativistic state, see also Negativism, Negativism, felt, Self-negativism
　anger and, 134n, 198, 211, 212, 217
　definition, 198
　depression and, 252
　deviance and, 201-204
　dominance of, 206, 236
　excitement-seeking and, 118-119, 127, 128, 219, 256, 258-259, 267, 279
　telic/paratelic states, relation to, 209, 215, 218-219, 279, 305-306
Negativistic system, see also Negativistic state

animals, in, 313-315
evolutionary advantage of, 303-307, 316n
Nemesism, 226n
Neoteny, 300, 305
Nesbitt's paradox, 89
Neurophysiology, 293, 294, 295-297, 332n
Non-transition humour, 178-179, 185
Nostalgia, 155
Novelty, 123-124, 127

O

Obedience, 113, 216-217
Obsessionality, 44, 46n, 71, 260, 263
Oedipus complex, 226n, 270
Offence mechanisms, 126, 262, 329
Operant conditioning, 204, 225n, 308, 309-310, 312, 314, 316n
Operative state, 27-28, 29, 33, 53, 230-231, 244, 367
Opposition, cognitive, 137-141, 182, 291, 361
Optimal arousal theory, 82-83, 84, 86, 87, 93, 102, 104, 105, 128, 129, 132-133, 191, 195n, 311
Orgasm, 86, 95, 96, 118, 254
Orienting reaction, 123
Over-excitement, 101, 102, 104, 246, 248, 249, 250, 251

P

Paintings, 10, 11, 159, 160, 162
Paradoxical behaviour, 9-12, 60, 220, 223, 299, 307, 331, 367
Parapathic emotions, 108-112, 114, 119, 124, 127, 128, 186, 189, 198, 211, 217, 243, 264, 277, 301, 367
Paratelic cycle, 95-96
Paratelic state,
   alternation with telic, 75-78
   arousal and, 55-57, 184-189, 284, 318
   characteristics of, 50-58, 238-239
   conformist/negativistic states, relation to, 209, 215-220, 277, 279, 305, 306
   definition, 47, 367
   depression and, 251-252
   etymology, 48
   examples, 49-50, 59-60
   excitement-seeking, relation to, 56-57, 90, 91, 106n, 107-108

humour and, 184-189, 324
thinking styles and, 277, 278, 284, 300-301
Paratelic system, see also Paratelic state
   animals in, 308-313
   evolutionary advantage of, 299-303
Pavlovian conditioning, 38, 45n, 94, 314
Perceptual reversals, 35-37
Performance anxiety, 253
Phenomenal field, 47, 54, 78n, 165, 172, 295
   figure-ground structure in, 47, 57, 67, 164-165, 171, 172, 178-179, 205, 214-215, 216-217, 223, 300-301, 321-322, 326, 328
   negativism in, 198, 199, 297
   synergy and, 164-165, 172, 178, 323-325
   unconscious processes and, 297, 325
Phenomenological psychology, 1, 12-15, 18n, 295
Phenomenological states, see Mental states
Phenomenological synergy, see Synergy
Phenomenology, 12-15
   structural, 15-17, 18n, 79n, 331, 368
Phobia, 93, 125, 253, 262, 263
Physiological processes, reversal theory, in, 293-298
Placing need, 146
Play, 10, 61-62, 74, 79n, 185-186, 264, 299-300, 302-303, 306, 311
Poetry, 60, 108, 148, 159, 168, 281
Pollution, 149-150
Pornography, 175, 219
Pre-intentionality, 71-72, 205-206, 213, 317, 318
Primal therapy, 262
Principle of Inconsistency, 8-9, 366
Progressive relaxation, 262
Projective tests, 153n, 235
Prophecy, disconfirmed, 283
Psychoanalysis, 17n, 43-44, 46n, 130, 180, 191, 224-225, 226n, 270
Psychodrama, 264
Psychology
   behaviourist, 2, 3, 5, 13, 18n, 105, 159, 330
   clinical, 5, 7, 224, 246
   cognitive, 5, 138
   experimental method in, 58, 134n, 223-224, 226n, 230, 315
   Gestalt, 16, 144, 153n

Psychology *(cont.)*
  phenomenological, 1, 12-15, 18n, 295
  specialization in, 1
Psychopathy, 256-260, 261, 267, 274n
  inadequate/ aggressive distinction in,
    258-259

R

Rational-emotive therapy, 263
Reactance, 201, 218
Reaction-formation, 43-44, 226n, 260
Real/imaginary synergy, *see also* Make-
  believe synergy, 157-162, 163, 169
Reflexes,
  conditioned, 38
  unconditioned, 37-38
Regulation, cybernetic meaning of, 27
Reinforcement, 58, 93, 131-132, 204, 261,
  273, 308, 309, 310, 312, 314, 316n
Relief,
  relaxation, as, 87, 90
  release, as, 173, 192, 324
  theories of humour, 191-192
Religious materials,
  examples of, 276-277, 278
  individual production of, 285-286
  synergies in, 288-291
  three steps in development of, 278-286,
    292n
  use of by church, 287-288
Repertory grid technique, 140
Repression, 43
Requirement, definition of, 198, 368
Requisite Variety, Law of, 306
'Resistance to satiation', 310, 311
Reticular activating system, 80, 123
Retroflection, 220
Reversal, *see also* Figure-ground reversals,
  Metamotivational reversal, Reversal
  synergy,
  anthropology, in, 153n
  bistable system, in, 28, 30, 33
  chronological, 46n
  definition, 28, 368
  lability, 236-238, 260
  means-ends, 50
  psychoanalytic theory, in, 43-44, 46n
  psychology, in, 34-39
  psychopathological, 38, 252-255, 260
  reflex, of, 37-38

sexual response patterns, of, 39
  therapeutic, 262, 263-264, 272-273
Reversal-of-effect, 268-269, 272, 273, 368
Reversal synergy, *see also* Ambiguity,
  Synergy
  ambiguity and, 141-145
  definition, 136, 368
  emotion and, 172-173, 324
  identity synergy and, 142, 154, 164-165
  religious narrative, in, 289
Risk-taking, 10, 124, 125, 127, 128, 229,
  245, 256, 301, 302, 329
Rites de passage, 149, 164
Roles, 229
  discrepant, 224
Rorschach test, 153n

S

Sacredness synergy, 156, 157, 290-291,
  292n
Safety, *see* Security, effects of
Satiation, metamotivational, 41, 46n, 69-
  70, 71, 85, 98-99, 100, 105, 106n, 112,
  212-213, 225n, 229, 231, 232, 237,
  242, 243, 280, 317, 325, 330
Schachter's two-factor theory, 92-93
Scheme theory, 79n
Schizophrenia, 171, 197, 200, 222-223
Security,
  effects of, 68, 88-89, 103-105, 108, 121,
    124, 127, 155-156, 164, 169, 176n,
    217, 269, 271, 275n, 280, 287, 300,
    312, 313
  humour, and, 134n, 192
Self, concept of, 220, 226n
Self-actualization, 45, 361
Self-concept, *see* Self-image
Self-dramatization, 111, 120, 133n, 169,
  263, 264
Self-esteem, 48-49, 68, 77, 98, 221, 236,
  251, 253, 322
Self-image, 49, 142, 162-163, 220-221,
  303, 307, 316n
Self-negativism, 200, 220-223, 226n, 243,
  251, 305, 307, 327, 368
Self-perception theory, 74
Self-persuasion, 286
Sensate focusing, 255
Sensation-seeking, 132-133, 235, 259,
  274n, 311

Sensoristasis, 82
Sensory deprivation, 132
Set, 282, 301, 315
Sexual behaviour, 12, 39, 95, 96, 97, 99,
    106n, 111, 118, 119, 121, 122, 126,
    127, 128, 129, 237, 253-255, 256, 311
Sexual dysfunction, 253-255, 281
Sexual excitement, 99, 100, 118, 125, 127,
    243, 253, 255, 270, 274n
Sexual perversion, 125, 126
Shift, 75, 102-105, 127, 134n, 239-240,
    242, 262, 295, 321, 368
Significance, felt, 52-54, 56, 59, 71, 72-73,
    78n, 91, 124-125, 127, 134n, 212, 238,
    244, 247, 252, 317, 318, 319, 320, 321,
    330, 368
Simile, 168, 184
Skinnerian conditioning, see Operant
    conditioning
Slapstick, 182-183, 184
Soccer, see Football
Sorrow, 172, 324
Spontaneous alternation, 312, 313
Startle reaction, 123
States, see also Mental states, Metamotiva-
    tional states
    cybernetic, 4, 17n, 45n,
    dominant, in a bistable system, 27-28,
        29, 33, 39, 58
    flow, 65
    preferred, definition of, 22, 40
    sleep/waking, 70, 81
    transitional, 149, 164-165, 166, 304
Stimuli,
    collative properties of, 125-126
    different functions of, 104-105
    ecological properties of, 125, 127
    psychological properties of, 125
Stress, 38, 273n-274n, 314
Structural anthropology, 15, 138-139
    ambiguity and, 148-151, 152
Structural phenomenology, 15-17, 18n,
    79n, 331, 368
Structural-functionalism, 16
Structuralism, 15-17
    phenomenological, 18n
Superiority theories of humour, 192, 195n
Synergy, see also Identity synergy, Make-
    believe synergy, Reversal synergy
    acceptable/unacceptable, 171-173, 324

ambiguity and, 141-145, 154, 173-174
arousal and, 134n, 173, 174, 184-189,
    245, 280, 292n, 324
definition, 55, 136, 153n, 360-361, 369
etymology, 141
make-doubt, 159
make-real, 163, 169
mechanism of, 173-176
multiple, 189-190, 289, 290, 291
negativism and, 306
obtainable/unobtainable, 169
phenomenal field in, 164-165, 172, 178,
    323-325
real/apparent, 177-194, 209, 290, 324
real/imaginary, 157-162, 163, 169
religious, 288-291
sacredness, 156, 157, 290-291, 292n
security/risk, 156, 169
single and dual identities, of, 165-169,
    184
systems concept, as, 361
telic and paratelic states, and, 112, 122,
    136, 151-153, 154, 218, 279, 281
Symptom prescription, 274n
Systems theory, see Cybernetics

T

Telic cycle, 95-96
Telic Dominance Scale, 233-236, 245,
    361-363
Telic state,
    alternation with paratelic, 75-78
    anxiety-avoidance, relation to, 56-57,
        90-91, 106n, 107-108
    arousal, and, 55-57, 318
    characteristics of, 50-58, 238-239
    conformist-negativistic states, relation to,
        209, 215-220
    definition, 47, 369
    depression and, 251-252
    etymology, 48
    example, 58-59
    goals in, 48-49
    thinking styles and, 277, 300-301
Telic system, see also Telic state
    animals, in, 308
    biological function of, 299
Tension, 40, 42, 73, 89, 90, 102, 105n,
    244, 320, 332n, 369

Tension (*cont.*)
  anxiety and, 89, 207, 274n
  frustration and, 210
Testing, psychological, 196-197, 224, 226n
Theatre,
  comedy and, 183-184, 186
  paratelic state and, 68, 70, 110, 112, 119, 188, 243
  synergies in, 158, 160-162, 167
Theology, 281-282
Therapy, 7, 38, 94, 120, 126, 255, 261-264, 298, 331, 332n
  eclectic approach to, 264
  resistance to, 218, 224
Tiredness, effects of, 103-104, 105, 213, 238, 239
Toys, psychology of, 154, 157, 158, 161, 162, 167, 176n, 178-179, 323
Traits,
  concept of, 228
  dominance and, 230, 233
  personality inconsistency and, 228-230
Trance, 103
Transcendental meditation, 262
Transition humour, 178-179, 185

Triangles, pathological, 269-270
Trinities, religious, 288
Two-factor theory of emotion, 92-93

U

U-curve, inverted, 82, 83, 84, 86, 106n

V

Vacuum reaction, 130
Value-determined bistability, 24-27, 29, 33, 84, 153n, 332n, 369

W

"War of the Worlds", 133n, 281
Word association, 138
Work, 61-62, 74

Y

Yerkes-Dodson law, 83

Z

Zillmann's theory, 85, 99